THE SCARECROW AUTHOR BIBLIOGRAPHIES

1. John Steinbeck (Tetsumaro Hayashi). 1973.
   See also no. 64.
2. Joseph Conrad (Theodore G. Ehrsam). 1969.
3. Arthur Miller (Tetsumaro Hayashi). 2nd ed., 1976.
4. Katherine Anne Porter (Waldrip & Bauer). 1969.
5. Philip Freneau (Philip M. Marsh). 1970.
6. Robert Greene (Tetsumaro Hayashi). 1971.
7. Benjamin Disraeli (R.W. Stewart). 1972.
8. John Berryman (Richard W. Kelly). 1972.
9. William Dean Howells (Vito J. Brenni). 1973.
10. Jean Anouilh (Kathleen W. Kelly). 1973.
11. E.M. Forster (Alfred Borrello). 1973.
12. The Marquis de Sade (E. Pierre Chanover). 1973.
13. Alain Robbe-Grillet (Dale W. Frazier). 1973.
14. Northrop Frye (Robert D. Denham). 1974.
15. Federico Garcia Lorca (Laurenti & Siracusa). 1974.
16. Ben Jonson (Brock & Welsh). 1974.
17. Four French Dramatists: Eugène Brieux, François de Curel, Emile Fabre, Paul Hervieu (Edmund F. Santa Vicca). 1974.
18. Ralph Waldo Ellison (Jacqueline Covo). 1974.
19. Philip Roth (Bernard F. Rodgers, Jr.). 2nd ed., 1984.
20. Norman Mailer (Laura Adams). 1974.
21. Sir John Betjeman (Margaret Stapleton). 1974.
22. Elie Wiesel (Molly Abramowitz). 1974.
23. Paul Laurence Dunbar (Eugene W. Metcalf, Jr.). 1975.
24. Henry James (Beatrice Ricks). 1975.
25. Robert Frost (Lentricchia & Lentricchia). 1976.
26. Sherwood Anderson (Douglas G. Rogers). 1976.
27. Iris Murdoch and Muriel Spark (Tominaga & Schneidermeyer). 1976.
28. John Ruskin (Kirk H. Beetz). 1976.
29. Georges Simenon (Trudee Young). 1976.
30. George Gordon, Lord Byron (Oscar José Santucho). 1976.
31. John Barth (Richard Vine). 1977.
32. John Hawkes (Carol A. Hryciw). 1977.
33. William Everson (Bartlett & Campo). 1977.
34. May Sarton (Lenora Blouin). 1978.
35. Wilkie Collins (Kirk H. Beetz). 1978.
36. Sylvia Plath (Lane & Stevens). 1978.

THEODORE DREISER AND THE CRITICS, 1911 - 1982:

a bibliography with selective annotations

by
JEANETTA BOSWELL

Scarecrow Author Bibliographies,
No. 73

The Scarecrow Press, Inc.
Metuchen, N.J., & London
1986

Library of Congress Cataloging-in-Publication Data

Boswell, Jeanetta, 1922–
    Theodore Dreiser and the critics, 1911-1982.

    (Scarecrow author bibliographies ; no. 73)
    Includes indexes.
    1. Dreiser, Theodore, 1871-1945--Bibliography.
I. Title. II. Series.
Z8241.7.B67 1986   [PS3507.R55] 016.813'52   85-14405
ISBN 0-8108-1837-X

Dedicated to

the memory of my sister,
WYNELLE TARBUTTON,
whom Dreiser would have understood;

and

to the memory of my husband,
FRED BOSWELL,
who understood Dreiser.

CONTENTS

INTRODUCTORY REMARKS

Although he was given a long life, 1871-1945, Theodore Dreiser was never without his problems. As a child he was haunted by the constant spectre of poverty and hunger, and although he would become wealthy enough by the time he died in Hollywood, he apparently was never able to leave the early years of his life in the past. He also became a famous American novelist in the half century of his endeavors, but apparently he never felt that his work was adequately honored; he did not receive the Nobel laureate for literature in 1930 when this prestigious award was bestowed on Sinclair Lewis. This was a bitter pill for Dreiser to swallow, and he did not do so with grace and magnanimity toward the other writer.

In the end, however (that is, forty years since his death), he seems to have come out fairly well: his critical reputation is rather plentiful, he is studied by scholars and undergraduate students alike--witness the number of doctoral dissertations which are turned out annually and the number of his books now available in paperback. Furthermore, Dreiser's works are now being published in a scholarly, uniform edition, and this was one honor he did not enjoy during his lifetime. One critic raised the question of whether so much writing had not turned into a "Dreiser industry." As with the critical literature on any great writer, some of it clearly serves no purpose other than to secure tenure for the professor who wrote it. But I believe this variety of scholarship is in a vast minority and is hardly worth raising a serious question. There are many hundreds of knowledgeable and dedicated scholars and critics of Dreiser, and it is from them that the author's reputation will be ultimately debated.

It is not surprising that Dreiser was never among the most popular of America's great authors. His vision of life was entirely too dark, too bitterly pessimistic for the average American to tolerate, even educated Americans, who would accept the tragic view provided it was created in some kind of historical British or Greek context, or at best in a highly symbolic mode of nineteenth-century American literature. However, Dreiser was not merely tragic; in fact, it can be argued that he was not tragic at all. Certainly his characters were not men and women of "extraordinary stature." Look for no Agamemnons, Hamlets, Macbeths, or Captain Ahabs in his directory of assorted miserable human beings. Yet his men and women are painfully real and suffer as painfully as the mother across the street who watches her child die, or the wino derelict who dies on the street in a bitterly cold winter, or the confused teenager who points a gun at his head and pulls the trigger, or the old man whose wife died thirty years ago and who has since lived a dirty, lonely meaningless existence. Dreiser perhaps did not rise to tragic heights, but he certainly heard the "eternal note of sadness," the "turbid ebb and flow of human misery," and in spite of certain rhetorical shortcomings he certainly managed to convey this sad vision in work after work. It is not difficult to find passages that illustrate this generalization, but nothing could do so more accurately than the concluding lines from Twelve Men (1919):

> My feeling at the time was as if I had been looking at a beautiful lamp, lighted, warm, and irradiating a charming scene, and then suddenly that it had been puffed out before my eyes, as if a hundred bubbles of iridescent hues had been shattered by a breath. We toil so much, we dream so richly, we hasten so fast, and lo! the green door is opened. We are through it, and its grassy surface has sealed us forever from all which apparently we so much crave--even as, breathlessly, we are still running.

In compiling this bibliography I have tried to be as objective and comprehensive as possible. The items listed here are basically contained within the 1911-1982 time period, although there are a few pieces which antedate 1911. For the most part I have dealt with English criticism published in America, but again there are some exceptions in cases of well-known European critics whose work has been translated into English or who have sometimes written in the English language. For the most part I have not listed reviews of Dreiser's works which were written for magazines and newspapers when the books were first published. These reviews have been listed in an admirable work edited by Jack Salzman, The Critical Reception (1972). I have listed reviews when the authors had other important essays or when the reviewer has an otherwise well-established reputation. I learned a long time ago that a "foolish consistency" has no value, except perhaps to reviewers of bibliographies.

In compiling the annotations, I have tried to use the words of the authors whenever possible. For the most part I have quoted a passage which seems to be the heart of the author's message, and which therefore illuminates the surrounding material. In some cases the writing is so diffuse that such a passage is impossible to come by, in which instance I have given a brief summary/commentary or discarded the idea of annotation altogether. Mine is not the first bibliography on Dreiser, and I have drawn heavily on my predecessors, to whom I am deeply grateful. These previous works are all listed

in my compilation and are itemized in the index. As to the format
of my work, I have found it generally preferable to cast all items
(biography, criticism, etc.) into one alphabetical listing of authors
and to maintain a chronological listing under each author. The bibliography is followed by a detailed subject index.

In conclusion, it is always a pleasure to acknowledge the many
helping hands which were extended my way: my brother, who kept
life moving easily and smoothly; my assistants, Bill and Kathy Abra-
hamson, who checked out books, copied articles, and found information that seemed utterly lost; the library of UTA and particularly the
Interlibrary Loan staff, who saw me to the end of another book.
And finally, as Allen Tate said in one of his incomparable sonnets,
"I must think a little of the past." I must remember the young graduate student who first studied Dreiser when she wrote her Master's
thesis in 1953, the husband who read all of Dreiser's works, and the
sister who resembled so much one of life's pitiful failures for whom
Dreiser held so much compassion.

Jeanetta Boswell
Arlington, Texas
February 14, 1985

THE BIBLIOGRAPHY

1 ANONYMOUS (listed chronologically). "With the Novelists." New-
   ark Evening News, June 8, 1907. P. 12, part 2. Reprinted
   in Pizer (1981), pp. 160-161.
       "It is essentially a serious study ... so serious that the
   author cannot forbear more or less moralizing as his narrative
   unfolds. It is a sordid enough drama, but in its disagreeable
   features Mr. Dreiser seeks to appeal to the thoughtful rather
   than to those persons greedily desirous of the sensation in
   fiction."

2 "Arriving Giant in American Fiction." Current Literature, 53 (December, 1912), 696-697.

3 "Fiction Built on Fact." Minneapolis Sunday Journal, December 1,
   1912. P. 4, part 2. Editorial.

4 "Recent Reflections of a Novel-Reader." Atlantic Monthly, 111
   (May, 1913), 689-691.
       "The Financier is an imposing book, both in intention and
   execution. If it resembles a biography more than a work of
   art, that, doubtless, is an aspect of the matter with which the
   author deliberately reckoned before he began." This work presents an intimate picture of the development of a man of financial genius whose kind is only too common in America. Should
   the type become extinct and the novel survive, our descendents
   will have in it the means of reconstructing for themselves the
   business life and immorality of a whole period.

5 Theodore Dreiser: America's Foremost Novelist. New York: John
   Lane, 1916-1917.
       Contains items by Edgar Lee Masters, Merton Lyon, John
   Cowper Powys, etc.

6 "Dreiser's Novels as a Revelation of the American Soul." Current
   Opinion, 62 (May, 1917), 191.

7 "Dreiser's Arraignment of Our Intellectual Aridity." Current
   Opinion, 62 (May, 1917), 344-345.

8   "Theodore Dreiser Looking Backward." New York Times Book
    Review, December 24, 1922. P. 14.
        Dreiser is justified in writing an autobiography, but not 500
    pages up to the point where he begins as a novelist. This
    volume is not sentimental; it is highly realistic. The style is
    that of a scientist-reporter. He had no idea how to write, only
    an obsession that he was born to write. His real feelings are
    often concealed under the reportorial manner of his writing,
    but the reader never fails to feel Dreiser's reactions to his
    experiences. The pages live.

9   "Literary Lunch." Literary Review, 4 (August 2, 1924), 936-937.

10 A Book About Theodore Dreiser and His Work. New York: Boni
    and Liveright, c. 1925.

11 "Freer Verse Than Usual." New York Times, September 10, 1926.
    P. 4.

12 "Enemies of Society." New Republic, 63 (May 8, 1929), 318-320.

13 "Dark Blue Dreiser." Literary Digest, 106 (July 26, 1930), 17.
        Review of Tragic America (1930). "Mr. Dreiser has power
    to probe the mysteries and describe the weary inevitabilities
    of the human soul. He has a deep and sympathetic understand-
    ing of the somber banalities that lie beneath the surface of hu-
    man lives. He paints them ruthlessly and realistically, yet with
    curious affection quite alien to the sterile mood of his more
    rebel-minded imitators."

14 "Shall It Be Dreiser? Possible Winner of This Year's Nobel Prize
    in Literature." Commonweal, 12 (October 22, 1930), 622.

15 "Slap! Slap!" Literary Digest, 109 (April 11, 1931), 15-16.
        At a recent dinner given to honor a visiting Russian novel-
    ist, Dreiser slapped Sinclair Lewis for accusing him of stealing
    three thousand words from a book on Russia by Mrs. Lewis
    (Dorothy Thompson). The story broke widely into newspapers,
    and one reporter regrets it was stopped. The episode should
    have been big enough to silence them both for awhile.

16 "Dreiser on the Sins of Hollywood." Literary Digest, 109 (May
    2, 1931), 21.

17 "Dreiser's Feud with Kentucky." Literary Digest, 111 (November
    28, 1931), 9.

18 "Dreiser on the Real Sins of Hollywood." Liberty, June 11, 1932,
    pp. 6-11. Reprinted in Authors on Film, edited by Harry M.
    Geduld. Bloomington: Indiana University Press, 1972.

19 "Poor Dreiser." Bookman, 75 (November, 1932), 682-684.

20 "The Liberation of American Literature." London Times Literary
    Supplement, June 15, 1933. Pp. 401-402.

21 "American Writers Look Left." London Times Literary Supplement,
    February 22, 1936. Pp. 145-146.

22 "Theodore Dreiser Dies at the Age of 74." New York Times,
    December 30, 1945.
        Gives details of his death followed by a review of his life.
    Dreiser had appeared in the news in recent years chiefly in
    connection with two things--his attacks on the English upper
    classes and his complete conversion to Communism.

23 "Vale." Saturday Review of Literature, 29 (January 5, 1946), 16.

24 "Dreiser the Great." Newsweek, 27 (March 25, 1946), 102.
        Review of The Bulwark, in which he says: "Whatever his
    faults, his virtues were overwhelming. At his best he stood
    head and shoulders over contemporaries. He was a powerful,
    complex individual who groped his way through life and through
    pages of millions of words. His life was a quest, always trying
    to find out the whys and where-fores of life. The Bulwark
    stands with the best that ever came from his labored pen....
    It is beautiful and profound and written with grace of style
    too often absent from Dreiser's powerful and awkward prose."

25 "Valedictory." Time, 47 (March 25, 1946), 102.
        Review of The Bulwark. Points up the irony that "for years
    Puritans attacked most of his novels for their frankness and
    coarseness. This novel is a tender tribute to all that was good
    in the forces which bitterly attacked him ... it is a timeless
    story of family life, the story of five children and what hap-
    pens to each. The story has been told many times, but seldom
    with more balanced compassion or gentle insight. The closing
    chapters are of a searching, level melancholy beauty which can-
    not be expected of any living American author."

26 "The Theodore Dreiser Collection." Library Chronicle (University
    of Pennsylvania), 14 (October, 1947), 34.

27 "Production Notes on George Stevens' 'A Place in the Sun.'" A
    Paramount Picture, January, 1950.
        "George Stevens' 'A Place in the Sun' is his first production
    for Paramount and easily is one of that studio's most important
    pictures." It has a topflight producer and director in Stevens;
    a stellar cast headed by three stars who possess terrific box-
    office following and histrionic integrity; a modern story based
    on a Theodore Dreiser best-seller, An American Tragedy, first
    published in 1925.

28 "Production Notes on William Wyler's 'Carrie.'" A Paramount
    Picture, November, 1950.
        William Wyler's "Carrie" promises to be one of the most Pro-
    vocative and powerful pictures ever made at Paramount. Pro-
    duced and directed by Wyler, it co-stars Laurence Olivier in
    his first Hollywood film in a decade, and Jennifer Jones. "Car-
    rie" is based on Theodore Dreiser's classic best-seller Sister
    Carrie, with the screen script by Ruth and Augustus Goetz.
    It is a big-budgeted, quality production, reflecting the pains-
    taking care and entertainment excellence of Wyler's many past
    successes.

29 "A Re-Examination of Dreiser." Times Literary Supplement, 21
    (December, 1951), p. 12.

30 "Dreiser on the Communists." Masses and Mainstream, 8 (Decem-
    ber, 1955), 23-25.

31 "Background for An American Tragedy." Esquire, 50 (October,
    1958), 155-157.

32 "Centennial Report." Dreiser Newsletter, 2 (Fall, 1971), 1-2.

33 "Reappraising Theodore Dreiser." Times Literary Supplement,
    January 1, 1971. P. 13.

34 The American Novel and the Nineteen-Twenties. Stratford-on
    Avon Studies, No. 13. London: Edward Arnold, 1971.

35 "Apostle of Naturalism." M.D. (Medical Newsmagazine), 15 (July,
    1971), 111-117.

36 "Dreiser on An American Tragedy in Prague." Dreiser Newslet-
    ter, 4 (Spring, 1973), 21-22. Discussion with a Mr. Kohl,
    February 8, 1927.

37 Dramatic Highlights from "Free" by Theodore Dreiser. Audio
    Tape. Hollywood, Calif.: Center for Cassette Studies, 1973.

38 "How He Climbed Fame's Ladder." Success, 1 (April, 1898).
    Reprinted in American Literary Realism, 6 (Fall, 1973), 339-
    344.

39 "The Real Howells." Ainslee's, 5 (March, 1900). Reprinted in
    American Literary Realism, 6 (Fall, 1973), 347-351.

40 "Myself and the Movies." Esquire, 20 (July, 1943). Reprinted
    in Esquire, 80 (October, 1973), 156, 382.

41 "An Unpublished Chapter from An American Tragedy.: Pros-
    pects, 1 (1975), 1-8.

42 Literary Writings in America: A Bibliography. Millwood, N.Y.:
    KTO Press, 1977. Vol. 3, pp. 2954-2978.

43 AARON, Daniel. Writers on the Left: Episodes in American
    Literary Communism. New York: Harcourt, Brace, and World,
    1961. "Investigations and Reports: Dreiser," pp. 177-180 et
    passim.
        After his Russian trip, Dreiser became more vocal in his
    criticism of American capitalism, and by 1931 he could say quite
    flatly that any solution for the difficulties of the world, and
    particularly those of America, was Communism. Trips to the
    Pittsburgh mining area in June of that year ... only confirmed
    what he had been saying and would say again: "American work-
    ers everywhere were the economic victims of those giant cor-
    porations."

44 ADAMIC, Louis. "Theodore Dreiser: An Appreciation."
    Haldeman-Julius Monthly, 1 (January-March, 1927, 93-97.

45 _____. My America: 1928-1938. New York: Harper's, 1938.
    Dreiser, pp. 109-110.
        From 1931 Diary in New York: "Theodore Dreiser called a
    meeting of writers, artists, and generally 'intellectuals' in his
    apartment at the Ansonia. He sent me an invitation and I went
    not knowing what it would be about.... There were about
    fifty people present when Dreiser called the meeting to order
    and announced that things were in a terrible state! What are
    we, what is America, going to do about it? ... There was
    misery. There were breadlines in America. Nobody knew how
    many people were unemployed, starving, hiding in their holes.
    Perhaps millions. Dreiser spoke for twenty minutes, folding,
    unfolding his handkerchief.... Nothing definite came out of
    this. Dreiser's own great honesty and bewilderment had en-
    gulfed everybody. By-and-by the meeting closed and people
    began to leave...."

46 ADAMS, James Donald. "Speaking of Books: Dreiser." New
    York Times Book Review, July 18, 1943. P. 2.

47 _____. "Heavy Hand of Dreiser," in The Shape of Books to
    Come. New York: Viking, 1944. Pp. 54-83. Reprinted as
    The Writer's Responsibility. London, Secker and Warburg,
    1946. Pp. 62-88.
        His part in American fiction is historical, but better writers
    followed in the trail he cleared. He brought depth and scope
    to writing but not elevation. His touch was heavy and earth
    bound. Young writers did not copy his style, but did turn
    to the idea that matter was everything and manner nothing.
    One cannot say that Dreiser "can afford the luxury of clumsi-
    ness." No writer can afford that. Not only in craftsmanship
    but in thinking, and lack of clarity and logic he failed. Of
    the three great clarities--purpose, thought, expression--

Dreiser had only the first. His thinking is as heavy and confused as his prose.

48 _____. "Speaking of Books: <u>New York Times Book Review</u>, <u>Book Review</u>, February, 16, 1958. P. 2.

49 _____. "Speaking of Books: Dreiser." <u>New York Times Book Review</u>, April 6, 1958. P. 2.

50 ADAMS, Richard P. "Permutations of American Romanticism." <u>Studies in Romanticism</u>, 9 (Fall, 1970), 249-268.
   The fundamental impulse of romanticism was the shift from staticism to dynamism. For Dreiser, "underlying and motivating all these inconsistent articles of conscious faith was a deep, brooding, and abiding conviction of life, change, and movement in the world and in human experience, which made the static moral codes he rejected irrelevant or relatively harmless." He had no direct way of expressing this abiding conviction, but he did not let fear of self-contradiction keep him from trying to express it as best he could.

51 ADCOCK, Arthur St. John. "Theodore Dreiser," in <u>The Glory Was Grub Street</u>. London: Sampson Law and Marston, 1928. Pp. 43-52. Reprinted, Freeport, N.Y.: Books for Libraries Press, 1969.
   As a realist Dreiser has affinities with Defoe and with Dostoevsky--he has the same direct narrative method, the same undecorated style and, as they do, relies for his effectiveness, not on selecting salient incidents, events, characteristics, but on conscientiously piling up every little detail of circumstance affecting his people or their history. Except that he is never grotesque or extravagant in his humor, he has curious affinities with Hogarth--he is a frankly, unreservedly realistic, and has the same severe, practical moral tendency.

52 ADLER, Betty. "Unmasked." <u>Menckeniana</u>, No. 25 (Spring, 1968), 16.

53 ADLER, Elmer. <u>Breaking into Print</u>. New York: Simon and Schuster, 1937. Dreiser, pp. 67-71. Reprinted, Freeport, N.Y.: Books for Libraries Press, 1968.
   Reprints "The Early Adventures of 'Sister Carrie' " which first appeared in <u>Colophon</u>, Part V, February, 1931. Dreiser tells the story "of the trials and tribulations attendant upon the publication of his first novel, his search for a publisher, finding an enthusiastic Frank Norris, and his subsequent disappointment."

54 AGAR, Herbert. "Cynicism and Sentimentality in America." <u>New Statesman</u>, 4 (June 28, 1931), 28.

55 AHNEBRINK, Lars. <u>The Beginnings of Naturalism in American</u>

Fiction. Uppsala: Lundequistska Bokhandeln, 1950. Also
published by Cambridge: Harvard University Press, 1950.
Reprinted, New York: Russell and Russell, 1961. Dreiser,
p. 7 et passim.
Does not study Dreiser significantly but emphasizes Garland,
Crane, and Norris. Contains good European background and
good analysis of theory of naturalism, pp. 166-232.

56 _____. "Dreiser's Sister Carrie and Balzac." Symposium, 7
(November, 1953), 306-322.
Article is based on the premise that "although the linkages
between the two writers seem obvious even to the casual reader,
few critics have gone into any detailed comparisons." Concludes that "Dreiser's attention to detail is similar to Balzac's.
The emphasis on contemporary life, the stress laid on setting,
the excessive attention paid to things, objects, and facts, all
this Dreiser saw in Balzac's writings. It was perhaps Balzac
more than any other writer who helped Dreiser visualize the
color of existence and confirmed him in his belief that what
he saw and felt was stuff out of which could come great creative art."

57 _____. "Garland and Dreiser: An Abortive Friendship."
Midwest Journal, 7 (Winter, 1955-1956), 285-292.
When Garland read Sister Carrie in 1902, he was most enthusiastic with its realistic qualities and faithful representa-
tions. However, when Dreiser asked Garland to come to his
defense in 1915 and write a denunciation of those who would
suppress The "Genius," Garland refused to do so, and Dreiser
never spoke to him again.

58 ALDEN, John. "Theodore Dreiser." Library Chronicle, 15 (Summer, 1949), 68-69.
Concerns a manuscript added to the Dreiser Collection at
the University of Pennsylvania.

59 ALGREN, Nelson. "Dreiser's Despair Re-Affirmed in The Stoic."
Philadelphia Inquirer, November 23, 1947. P. 12.

60 ALLEN, Frederick Lewis. "Best Sellers: 1900-1935." Saturday
Review of Literature, 13 (December 7, 1935), 3-4, 20-26.
Interesting analysis of public tastes during these years,
showing that they abound in clues to the changes in the public mind. Dreiser is not considered, although An American
Tragedy, published in 1925, did sell quite well. This article
is based on something like the "ten best-sellers" list.

61 ALLEN, Walter. The Modern Novel in Britain and the United
States. New York: Dutton, 1964. Dreiser, pp. 66, 81-86.
Dreiser faced the facts of American life more squarely and
grappled with their implications more resolutely than any other
novelist of the first two decades of the century. This is why

he reamins a founding father of the modern American novel,
one of its permanent points of reference and, in the first two
decades of the century, a period during which little of significance was happening in the American novel, a heroic figure,
a solitary giant.

62 _____. The Urgent West: The American Dream and Modern
Man. New York: Dutton, 1969. Dreiser, pp. 193-195.
Dreiser shows us the American dream unrealized and turned
sour. He was one of the first American novelists to do so,
and certainly none before him had done so with anything like
his power. After Dreiser's worm's-eye view of the American
dream and the American struggle, it was impossible for writers to fall in with Howells' optimism; and Dreiser becomes the
central figure of a miscellaneous group of poets and novelists
who from many points of view question the assumptions beneath Howells' optimism.

63 ALMAN, David. "Review of F. O. Matthiessen's Theodore Dreiser."
Book Find Club Brochure, 1951.

64 ALPERT, Hollis. "Double Bounty from Hollywood." Saturday
Review of Literature, 34 (September 1, 1951), 28-30.
Review article of "A Place in the Sun" (based on Dreiser's
An American Tragedy) and Tennessee Williams' "A Streetcar
Named Desire." Of the two films, Alpert says, "Coming together they are rather an embarrassment of riches ... amd some
proof that Hollywood can cast aside all those restrictive pressures which prevent the American screen from acknowledging
the facts of life." In the end, the feeling one has is that the
screen has been illumined by a hand altogether accomplished.

65 ANDERSON, Carl R. The Swedish Acceptance of American Literature. Philadelphia: University of Pennsylvania Press, 1957.
Dreiser, pp. 77-81 et passim.
Reviews several critical opinions of Dreiser in Sweden, most
of which describe his style as "heavy, melancholy, formless,
and colorless." His philosophy fared even worse, raising ob-
jections with his determinism and denial of free will. Contains
an extensive listing in Swedish of American authors translated
into Swedish 1916-1945. Also a list of library holdings in Sweden, of which Dreiser is not greatly impressive.

66 ANDERSON, David D. "Chicago as Metaphor." Great Lakes Review, 1 (Summer, 1974), 3-15.

67 ANDERSON, Margaret. My Thirty Years' War. New York: Covici
and Friede, 1930. Pp. 3-34 et passim.
Discusses the outrage her favorable review of Sister Carrie
produced.

68 ANDERSON, Sherwood. "Dreiser." Little Review, 3 (April,
     1916), 54. Reprinted in Pizer (1981), pp. 13-14.
         "Theodore Dreiser is old--he is very, very old. I do not
     know how many years he has lived, perhaps thirty, perhaps
     fifty, but he is very old. Something gray and bleak and hurt-
     ful that has been in the world almost forever is personified in
     him.... The tears run down his cheeks and he shook his
     head. That is a good picture of Dreiser. He is old and he does
     not know what to do with life, so he just tells about it as he
     sees it, simply and honestly. The tears run down his cheeks
     and he shakes his head.... Heavy, heavy the feet of Theodore.
     How easy to pick his books to pieces, to laugh at him. Thump,
     thump, thump, here he comes, Dreiser, heavy and old."

69 _____. "An Apology for Crudity." The Dial, 63 (November
     8, 1917), 437-438. Reprinted in Kazin and Shapiro (1955),
     pp. 81-83.
         Sees no incongruity in the fact that American literature is a
     "crude" affair. Life in America is "for the most part an ugly
     affair." A man like Dreiser is true to something in the life
     about him. There is no other road. If one would avoid neat,
     slick writing, he must at least attempt to be brother to his
     brothers and live as the men of his time live. He must share
     with them the crude expression of their lives.

70 _____. Horses and Men. New York: B. W. Heubsch, 1923.
     Introduction contains remarks about Dreiser, same as 1916 ar-
     ticle first printed in Little Review. Reprinted in A Book About
     Theodore Dreiser and His Work (c. 1925).

71 _____. "An American Tragedy: A Review." Saturday Review
     of Literature, 2 (January 9, 1926), 475. Reprinted in Wayne
     Gard, ed., Book Reviewing (1927), pp. 88-92.
         "America has many men of note just now, walking about,
     doing their work, helping to mold our minds. How clearly
     Dreiser stands out among them all. There will not be another
     like him here. He is to my mind the biggest, most important
     American of our times. As a writer the man is often crude,
     dull sometimes with unbelievable dulness, honest, tender. His
     tenderness is the finest thing of all. How can anyone--a writer
     like myself--help being sorry his tenderness does not run out
     more directly toward words? Surely the man does not love
     words. He is so often unbelievably brutal with them. I pick
     up this new, big novel of his, An American Tragedy, and on
     every page there are sentences that make me cringe, words
     that make me cringe...."

72 _____. "Sherwood Anderson to Theodore Dreiser." American
     Spectator, 1 (June, 1933), 1.

73 _____. "The Dreiser," in No Swank. Philadelphia: Centaur,
     1934. Pp. 13-16.

Book is a collection of short, impressionistic pieces, in which Anderson strives to capture the essence of the subject. In his sketch of Dreiser he says: "The Dreiser is a big man. There is something burly, impulsive, crude and tender. When he comes into a room where you are sitting with others it is like a freight engine making its way slowly and majestically through railroad yards...."

74 _____. Sherwood Anderson's Memoirs. New York, Harcourt, Brace, 1942. Dreiser, pp. 333-340 et passim. Reprinted as Sherwood Anderson's Memoirs: A Critical Edition, edited by Ray Lewis White. Chapel Hill: University of North Carolina Press, 1969.

"Dreiser's Party," an account of Anderson's first meeting with Dreiser; valuable for its detailed portrait.

75 _____. The Portable Sherwood Anderson, edited by Horace Gregory. New York: Viking, 1949. Contains an essay-article titled "Dreiser," pp. 557-562; and a letter to Dreiser from Anderson, pp. 606-612.

Article much the same as 1916 publication (see above). Additional remarks are interesting: "The feet of Theodore are making a path, the heavy brutal feet. They are tramping through the wilderness of lies, making a path. Presently the path will be a street, with great arches overhead and delicately carved spires piercing the sky. Along the street will run children, shouting 'Look at me. See what I and my fellows of the new day have done'--forgetting the heavy feet of Dreiser...."

In the letter, dated January 2, 1936, Anderson says: "Dear Teddy: In your play American Tragedy, the play ends by the pronouncement that we can forgive a murderer but that society cannot be forgiven. To tell the truth, Ted, I think it nonsense to talk this way about society. I doubt if there is any such thing. If there has been a betrayal in America I think it is our betrayal of each other...."

76 _____, ed. with Introduction. Free and Other Stories by Dreiser. New York: Boni and Liveright, 1918. Modern Library edition. Reprinted 1925. Also reprinted, St. Clair Shores, Mich.: Scholarly Press, 1971. Introduction reprinted in Sherwood Anderson: The Writer at His Craft, edited by Jack Salzman et al. Mamaroneck, N.Y.: Paul P. Appel, 1979. Pp. 3-7.

77 ANDREWS, Clarence A., ed. with Introduction. Sister Carrie. New York: Airmont, 1967.

78 ANGOFF, Allan, ed. American Writing Today. New York: New York University Press, 1957.

This book, a printing of a special edition of Times Literary Supplement, contains many references to Dreiser and his influence; also contains a contemporary (1925) review of An American Tragedy.

79 ANGOFF, Charles. H. L. Mencken: A Portrait from Memory. New York: Yoseloff, 1956. Dreiser, pp. 99-101 et passim.

80 ANISIMOV, Ivan. "The Path Laid by Dreiser." Inostrannaja Literature, 11 (November, 1958), 219-232. Author and publication Russian; article is in English.

81 ANTUSH, John V. "Money in the Novels of James, Wharton, and Dreiser." Ph.D. diss., Stanford University, 1968. DA, 29 (1968), 558A.
    Dreiser's novels reflect the vision of life which money represents to the poor, to the middle class, and to the wealthy. The financier trilogy exposes some of the illusions generated by money in the American metaphysic; and in the final analysis, Cowperwood, who entered the business world a knight in search of a grail, passes out of that world little more than a charlatan with a dream turned nightmare.

82 ANZILOTTI, Rolando. "Introduzione." Racconti, translated by Diana Bonaccossa. Bari, Italy: De Donato, 1971.
    Italian translation of 1956 text Best Short Stories of Theodore Dreiser, edited by James T. Farrell. Contains bibliography of works by and about Dreiser in English and Italian.

83 APPEL, Paul P., ed. Homage to Sherwood Anderson, 1876-1941. Mamaroneck, N.Y., P. P. Appel, 1970. Introduction, "Sherwood Anderson," was first printed in Story, 19 (September-October, 1941), pp. 1-2.

84 ARAGON, Louis   "When We Met Dreiser." New Masses, 58 (January 29, 1946), 6-7.

85 ARENS, Egmont. "The Right to Love." New York Call, March 30, 1918. Call Magazine, pp. 6, 16.

86 ARMS, George. "The Bulwark: A Chronology." Dreiser Newsletter, 11 (Fall, 1980), 10-14.
    Calls attention to the anachronisms which evoked a good deal of comment from reviewers and critics when the novel was published. Feels that this could be overlooked if the novel itself did not make so much of time. Despite the fact that three editors finished the work after Dreiser's death, one might expect a reasonable internal consistency in the matter of dates. Continues by supplying a complete chronology with pages, although several unresolved inconsistencies still remain.

87 ARNAVON, Cyrille. "Theodore Dreiser and Painting." American Literature, 17 (May, 1945), 113-126.

"Scattered references to painting would be desultory and
irrelevant if Dreiser had not devoted a full length novel to the
career of a painter. In a universe which is unaccountable because it is merely an occasion for bewilderment and dismay,
a welter of forces, and an interplay of chemical reactions, because art heightens the consciousness of a privileged moment
and conditions a more intense experience of things though it
it remains a mystery--it is yet an unquestionable datum in so
far as it is a vital force and urge...."

88   _____. Theodore Dreiser: Romancier American. Paris: Uni-
      versité de Lille, Centre de Documentation Universitaire, 1956.
      In French; has not been translated.

89   ARNOLD, Ann J. "Naturalism in Dreiser's Female Characters."
      MA thesis, University of Mississippi, 1969.

90   ARVIN, Newton. "An American Case History." New Republic
      (August 6, 1931), 318-320.
      Review of Dawn. It would have profited, like any of his
      novels, by being far more simplified, stylized, and hence "dis-
      torted" than it is. It has all the defects and most of the
      merits of his novels, and it throws additional light on the heavy
      limitations that have kept Dreiser from true distinction as a
      writer of prose fiction. Like the novels, it is a document
      rather than an imaginative performance; and its documentary
      value--its picture of small-town life in Indiana and of Chicago
      life in the eighties.

91   _____. "Fiction Mirrors America." Current History, 42 (Sep-
      tember, 1934), 610-616.

92   ASKEW, Melvin W. "The Pseudonymic American Hero." Bucknell
      Review, 10 (March, 1962), 224-231.

93   ASSELINEAU, Roger. "Theodore Dreiser's Transcendentalism."
      English Studies Today, Second Series, 11 (1961), 233-243.
      Edited by G. A. Bonnard, Bern: Francke Verlag, 1961. Re-
      printed in Pizer (1981), pp. 92-103. Also reprinted in Asse-
      lineau, The Transcendentalist Constant in American Literature.
      New York: New York University Press, 1980. Pp. 99-114.
      Based largely on Dreiser's 1926 book of poetry, Moods.
      Supports argument with many comparisons of Dreiser with pas-
      sages from Emerson and Whitman. Points up that Dreiser is
      a naturalist to all appearances, and also a transcendentalist
      which is largely hidden from view and has been observed by
      only a few bold critics. Dreiser saw no conflict involved; be-
      lieved (as did Emerson) that life was made up of opposites.
      However, with Dreiser "this keen perception of an underlying
      mystery in all things is spoilt ... by a disquieting sense of
      the purposelessness and meaninglessness of the world."

94 ATHERTON, Gertrude. "The Alpine School of Fiction." Book-
      man, 55 (March, 1922), 26-33.
          Article is based on Madison Grant's The Passing of the Great
      Race, a book of anthropology, regarded by the author as "re-
      markable with its warning of tremendous import to civilization."
      Using this anthropological frame of reference, she divides fiction
      into two schools: the Alpine and the Nordic and says the Al-
      pine school is perishing from too much in-breeding, gentility,
      and other degenerative factors. The Nordic school applauds
      new adventure, new life, new infusions of blood; Dreiser clearly
      relates to this latter.

95 ATKINSON, Hugh C. Merrill Checklist of Theodore Dreiser.
      Columbus, Ohio: Charles E. Merrill Co., 1969.
          Forty-three pages of bibliography, with no annotation or
      index. Covers criticism through 1966 and excludes that which
      author considers obsolete.

96 _____. Theodore Dreiser: A Checklist. Canton, Ohio: Kent
      State University Press, 1971.
          Is called a guide, rather than a definitive listing. Consists
      of 104 pages, covering Dreiser's major works (listed alphabeti-
      cally with major publications of the work). Selected Introduc-
      tions, Prefaces, and Miscelleneous Works by Dreiser; published
      letters (5 items); biographies; bibliographies (10 items); pp.
      19-47 contain a good listing of Dreiser's work as a newspaper-
      man in St. Louis, Chicago, and Pittsburgh. Unsigned articles
      not listed.
          Books and dissertations about Dreiser, pp. 49-53. Articles
      about Dreiser, pp. 55-95, especially good. Concludes with a
      selected list of reviews of Dreiser's major works, pp. 97-104.
      Not many, but carefully chosen and representative.

97 AUCHINCLOSS, Louis, ed. with Introduction. Sister Carrie.
      Cleveland: Charles E. Merrill, 1969. Facsimile of 1900 edition.
      Introduction reprinted in Auchincloss, Life, Law, and Letters.
      Boston: Houghton Mifflin, 1979. Pp. 111-119.
          Asserts that the greatness of Sister Carrie lies in the amoral
      enthusiasm for life; objects, however, to the ending of the
      novel in which a woman who has pursued nothing but creature
      comforts suddenly turns into a "restless artist."

98 AUERBACH, J. S. "Authorship and Liberty." North American
      Review, 207 (June, 1918), 902-917. Reprinted as "Oral Argu-
      ment Against the Suppression of 'The Genius'," in Essays and
      Miscellanies, Vol. 3. New York: Harpers, 1922. Pp. 130-
      148.
          "In the controversy are involved questions of more import-
      ance than are usually submitted to a court of justice. For if
      the circulation of a book of its achievement can be forbidden,
      this officious and grotesque Society will have been given a

roving commission for further mischief, and freedom of thought
and expression dealt a staggering blow from which it will not
soon recover. If, on the other hand, your decision be as we
think it should be, it will undo a great injustice not only to
a distinguished author and to the community at large, but will
be a kind of charter right for author and publisher and even
the participant in public debate."

99   AUSTIN, Mary. "Sex in American Literature." Bookman, 57
     (June, 1923), 385-393.
         " ... All Dreiser's people love like the peasants in a novel
     by Bojer or Knut Hamsun. His women have a cowlike com-
     plaisance such as can be found only in peoples who have lived
     for generations close to the soil; his men in their amours re-
     semble those savages who can count five only, on the fingers
     of one hand. Having used up one set of digits they begin all
     over on the other hand and count five again. So 'the Genius'
     and 'the Financier' pass from Susan to Jane and from Jane to
     Maria and so to Edith and Emily, by nearly identical progres-
     sions learning nothing at all and teaching their author very
     little."

100 AVARY, Myrta Lockett. "Success and Dreiser." Colophon,
     n.s., 3 (Autumn, 1938), 598-604.
         Success was a magazine which Dreiser edited. "For impor-
     tant as our work on Success seemed to all of us at the time,
     none of us, surely, every dreamed that it would be Theodore
     Dreiser who, almost alone would make the magazine remem-
     bered, or that the issues we saw rushed out would become
     'collectors' items,' our crowded pages counted, numbered and
     analyzed in a quarterly for bookmen."

101 BABBITT, Irving, et al. Criticism in America: Its Function
     and Status. New York: Harcourt, Brace, 1924. Dreiser,
     pp. 261-286 in Mencken, "Footnote on Criticism," 1922.

102 _____. "The Critic and American Life." Forum, 79 (Febru-
     ary, 1928), 161-176.

103 BAIRD, James Lee. "The Movie in Our Heads: An Analysis of
     Three Film Versions of Theodore Dreiser's An American Trag-
     edy." Ph.D. diss., University of Washington, 1967. DA,
     28 (1967), 557A.
         One detailed scenario by Eisenstein (1930) and two completed
     films, by Sternberg (1931) and Stevens (1951), have been made
     from Dreiser's novel. The purpose of this dissertation is to
     examine first Dreiser, then each of the three film versions,
     to find the main sources of power in Dreiser's work and to

determine whether any of the three filmmakers had been successful in transferring the essence of Dreiser to the screen.

104 BAKER, Monty R. "Theodore Dreiser: A Checklist of Dissertations and Theses." Dreiser Newsletter, 5 (Spring, 1974), 12-21.
     Lists 68 dissertations and 61 MA theses, all without annotation. This compilation is based primarily on Dissertation Abstracts and Dorothy Black's Guide to Lists of Master's Theses (Urbana: University of Illinois, 1973). Introductory note says, "If this list serves its purpose, which is to show without further elaboration what has been written on Dreiser's career, the areas remaining for thesis and dissertation topics will reveal themselves more clearly."

105 BALDWIN, Charles S. "Theodore Dreiser," in The Men Who Make Our Novels. New York: Moffat, Yard, 1919. Pp. 58-63. Revised edition, New York: Dodd, Mead, 1924. Pp. 141-153.
     Says that Dreiser "echoes Fielding's mature convictions concerning life, and descends directly through Fielding from the Shakespeare of King Henry IV." Sometimes Dreiser interprets life as a blur of nothingness, to which only Joseph Conrad may be compared. In America Dreiser is unique.

106 BALLOU, Robert O., ed. with Introduction. Twelve Men. New York: Random House, 1928. Modern library edition.

107 BANNING, Margaret Culkin. "Changing Moral Standards in Fiction." Saturday Review of Literature, 20 (July 1, 1939), 3-4.
     Shows that the morals of fiction, as in life, revolve to a great extent around the chastity of women and the general attitude toward it. In story and fact it is accepted that the safety of the race depends upon its women. Discusses a number of fallen women in literature, including Sister Carrie at the turn of the century, who created something of a scandal, but shows that by 1939 standards were far more flexible, tolerant and considerate of the "Scarlet Woman."

108 BANTA, Richard E. "Theodore Dreiser: 1871-1945," in Indiana Authors and Their Books, 1816-1916. Scranton, Pa.: Haddon Craftsman, 1949. Pp. 90-92.

109 BARBAROW, G. "Dreiser's Place on the Screen." Hudson Review, 5 (Summer, 1952), 290-295.
     Discusses "A Place in the Sun" as a serious film, which has been selected as one of the best in several categories. Regrets that the movie version of Dreiser's novel has been oversimplified and that a great many of the omissions were unnecessary. Concludes that the movie reduces a great novel to pulp.

110 BARRETT, E. Boyd. "Modern Writers and Religion." Thinker,
     3 (May, 1931), 32-38.

111 BARRETT, Phyllis Whiteside. "More American Adams: Women
     Heroes in American Fiction." Ph.D. diss., Rhode Island,
     1979. DA, 40 (1979), 847A-848A.
     Bringing together the critically neglected portraits of such
     important women protagonists as Hawthorne's Hester, Dreiser's
     Carrie, etc., one sees that they are not what we might be
     tempted to label "American Eves," all part of a separate though
     perhaps equal American literary tradition. On the contrary,
     they are American Adams--like Huck, Natty, Jake Barnes,
     Jay Gatsby, and all the rest.

112 BARTELL, James Edward. "The Ritual of Failure: Pattern and
     Rhythm in the Novels of Theodore Dreiser." Ph.D. diss.,
     University of Washington, 1971. DA, 32 (1972), 5174A.
     This dissertation demonstrates that each of Theodore Drei-
     ser's eight novels is structured by essentially the same com-
     plex narrative pattern and that the repetition of this pattern
     produces a strong subliminal rhythm that gives the novels
     their direction, unity, and that sense of life's relentless, on-
     ward movement that has so impressed his readers.

113 BAUER, L. "Revival of Dreiser." Theatre Arts, 35 (August,
     1951), 16-17.

114 BAUSKA, Barry. "The Land of Oz and the American Dream."
     Markham Review, 5, (1973), 21-24.

115 BAYER, Roberta M. "Voyage into Creativity: The Modern
     Kunstlerroman: A Comparative Study of the Development of
     the Artist in the Works of Hermann Hesse, D. H. Lawrence,
     James Joyce, and Theodore Dreiser." Ph.D. diss., New
     York University, 1974. DA, 35 (1975), 7245A.
     Studies The "Genius" as an esample of the novel in which
     the artist develops and expresses himself in terms of his art.
     Narration is chronological, depicting important stages in the
     protagonist's development as an artist. Structure is dominated
     by the voyage archetype, which functions on several levels:
     psychological, social, and creative. The psychological voyage
     centers around the young artist's quest to develop a sense of
     identity and personal worth.

116 BEACH, Joseph Warren. "English Speech and American Writers."
     New Republic, 29 (December 28, 1921), 123-125.
     An anxious problem confronts the lover of the English lan-
     guage these days in the shape of many of our most interesting
     novels. Can we admit among reputable works of literary art
     stories so badly written? It is possible to tolerate much of
     this bad writing, as in Thomas Hardy, but with Dreiser the

"slovenliness" goes too far. Charges that half of Dreiser's
problem is affectation, half the vulgar errors come from his
pretentiousness, the way he tries to decorate his page with
odds and ends suitable, if rightly used, to Indiana oratory
of the eighties.

117 _____. "The Naive Style." American Speech, 1 (August,
1926), 576-583. Reprinted in Beach, The Outlook for American Prose. Chicago: University of Chicago Press, 1926.
Pp. 177-196.
     As a novelist and a writer of autobiography he attracts us
by the solidity of his information and the unparalleled honesty
and candor with which he goes about to enlighten us. In A
Book About Myself, Dreiser has given us an illuminating account of newspaper work and the life of newspaper men in
the West. He has drawn a picture of himself and his early
milieu in Chicago, which is a social document of the highest
order ... yet the book remains a discouraging sample of the
naive style, and the reader is irritated on every page with
sentences so crudely put together that he is sure to be re-
pelled by the incoherence of the rhetoric.

118 _____. "The Realist Reaction: Dreiser," in The Twentieth
Century Novel. New York: Century, 1932. Pp. 320-331.
     His books are solidly built around a central idea. They
are documented in a manner worthy of his admired Balzac and
even suggestive of the more colossal structures of Zola. His
style is all of a piece with his general want of concern for
imaginative writing as such. As a whole, his books are of
extreme interest because of the large spirit, the passionate
intelligence which informs them. His writing does not bear
too close inspection in detail, because he has not approached
it with an esthetic intention.

119 BECHHOFFER, Carl Eric. The Literary Renaissance in America.
London: Heinemann, 1923. Dreiser, pp. 92-99.
     Calls Dreiser one of the most interesting figures in con-
temporary American prose writing, and says The Titan is the
best of his novels: "the figure of Cowperwood, the financier,
reckless, daring, mediaeval in his ruthlessness, love of luxury, and lust for women, is a marvellous piece of work."
Dreiser's erratic, prolix, and yet monumental style is so American, so completely typical of the vast country from which he
comes, that he is as much a cultural figure as a literary figure. He is essentiallly the voice of revolt against the English
tradition in America, the representative of the vast, bewildered, latently powerful immigrant races that do not understand or do more than pretend to appreciate the current standards of American civilization.

120 BECKER, George J. "Realism: An Essay in Definition." Modern Language Quarterly, 10 (June, 1949), 184-197.

The third phase of realism may be called philosophical and seems to rest on a contradiction. While the basic ideal of the movement was and is absolute objectivity, it is almost impossible not to pass at least implicit judgment on man and his fate. Dreiser often mentioned blind biological forces which he called "chemisms," but the significant element in his pattern of causality seems to be societal conditioning. Stated in the mildest possible terms, Naturalism insists on the existence of limitations to the efficacy of human personality and endeavor, and it places the boundaries of those limitations rather close at hand.

121   . "Theodore Dreiser: The Realist as Social Critic." Twentieth Century Literature, 1 (October, 1955), 117-127.
Even though Dreiser tried in his last years to assert that his art had always been an instrument of social action, the record is against him, for as artist he held consistently to the belief that his sole duty was to present life "in the round." He examined the human situation as he encountered it, probing for causes to such depth that he undermined current glib explanations and forced a more profound understanding of the forces that make character in our time.

122   , ed. Documents of Modern Literary Realism. Princeton, N.J.: Princeton University Press, 1963.
Reprints several valuable documents concerning realism and/or naturalism:
Theodore Dreiser, "True Art Speaks Plainly" (1903), pp. 154-156.
Malcolm Cowley, "A Natural History of American Naturalism" (1947), pp. 429-451.
Stuart P. Sherman, "The Naturalism of Mr. Dreiser" (1915), pp. 452-464.
Roger Sherman Loomis, "A Defense of Naturalism" (1919), pp. 535-548.
Philip Rahv, "Notes on the Decline of Naturalism" (1942), pp. 579-590.

123 BEDFORD, Richard C. "Place Reference in Chapter Headings of Sister Carrie." Annual Reports of Studies, 26 (1975), 51-63. Kyoto, Japan: Doshisha Women's College of Liberal Arts. Article in English; Japanese publication.

124   . "Dreiser's Uncomic Non-realism." Annual Reports of Studies, 27 (1976), 75-101. Article in English; Japanese publication.

125 BELLOW, Saul. "Dreiser and the Triumph of Art." Commentary, 11 (May, 1951), 502-503. Reprinted in Kazin and Shapiro (1955), pp. 146-148. Review of Matthiessen's Theodore Dreiser (1951).

It is true that the biography was left unfinished, but there
is no indication that Matthiessen's position would have changed.
Matthiessen defends Dreiser against the usual charges, but
throughout one senses confusion and pain. This biography
will do nothing for Dreiser's popularity.

126 BENARDETE, Jane, ed., with Introductions. "Theodore Dreiser:
Native American Naturalist," in American Realism. New York"
Putnam's, 1972. pp. 313-317. Reprints selections from Dreiser's autobiographical works, and some other selections and
letters about him, pp. 318-383.
   Always serious and thoughtful, Dreiser never acquired artistic polish, yet he captained the battle for free expression
in the novel and courageously refused to bow to social pressure or to echo conventional idealistic formulas. For Dreiser
man's tragedy lies in his sense of forces that govern the universe and his pathetic awareness of his inability to control
them. There is no room in this dark vision for the essentially
sentimental assurance that "the ideal is a light that cannot
fail" for this light may never dawn.

127 BENCHLEY, Robert. "Mr. Benchley Interviews Theodore Drei-
ser." Life, 87 (April 15, 1926), 10. Reprinted in Benchley,
The Early Worm. New York: Holt, 1927. Pp. 78-79, as "An
Interview with Theodore Dreiser." Parody.
   "I found the author of An American Tragedy reading a large
volume of law reports. 'Working on a new book?' I asked.
'It's a new book to me,' replied Dreiser. 'I don't know about
you.' ... 'Oh, I'm all right,' I retorted. 'A little dizzy when
I stand up--but then, one doesn't have to stand up much,
does one?' ... 'Does two, does three, does four,' sallied the
author, up to one hundred.
   "I could see that we were treading on dangerous ground and,
fearful lest the interview be ruined, I continued, wetting my
thumb."

128 _____. Compiling An American Tragedy," in The Early Worm
(1927), pp. 246-250. Reprinted in The Benchley Roundup,
edited by Nathaniel Benchley. New York: Harpers, 1954.
Parody.
   Suggestions as to how Theodore Dreiser might write his next
Human Document and save five years' work. For example:
"Note to Printer: Attached find copy of Thurston's Street
Guide. Print names of every street listed therein, beginning
with East Division and up to, and including Dawson. Reprint
the above paragraph twenty-five times."

129 BENDER, Eileen T. "On Lexical Playfields: Further Speculation on 'Chemisms.' " Dreiser Newsletter, 6 (Spring, 1975),
12-13.
   Karl, Baron von Reichenbach, is credited with the first use

of the word "chemism" by the OED. First appears in 1851.
Clearly, however, "chemism" was Dreiser's deliberate choice
rather than an unfortunate slip. Dreiser, in his use of the
language of science and pseudoscience, reveals that same mixture of heterodoxy and credulity--offering another key to the
mind of his age.

130 BENET, William Rose. "Theodore Dreiser," in Encyclopaedia
     Britannica, 14th edition. London, New York, and Chicago:
     Encyclopaedia Britannica, 1929. Vol. 6, pp. 645-646.
     Biographical sketch with brief commentary on principal works
     through An American Tragedy. Concludes with a basic bib-
     liography of works and biographical studies.

131 _____. "Contemporary Poetry." Saturday Review of Litera-
     ture, 12 (June 29, 1935), 18.
     Reviews Dreiser's "weighty volume," Moods, Cadenced and
     Declaimed, a collection of 250 prose poems. Compares this
     work with Stephen Crane, who did this sort of thing much
     better, and more briefly. Says in conclusion, "there is much
     of the obvious presented in an entirely uninspired manner;
     and the occasional curses at an anthropomorphic God seem
     rather sophomoric." Concedes that there are occasional pas-
     sages good to find for their thoughtfulness, but they are
     hard to find.

132 BENNETT, Arnold. "The Future of the American Novel." North
     American Review, 195 (January, 1912), 76-83. Written for the
     North American Review in 1903 and published here for the
     first time.
     Remarks directed to Sister Carrie: "I am told that this fine
     and somber work was ignored in America until England began
     to discuss it, and that even then its reception in the country
     of its birth was on the zero side of tepid.... Sister Carrie
     was one of a special series of American novels issued by an
     English publisher noted for the fine quality of his fiction. "

133 _____. "Books of the Year," in The Savour of Life: Essays
     in Gusto. Garden City, N.Y.: Doubleday, Doran, 1928.
     Pp. 293-313; Dreiser, pp. 303-305.
     Refers to An American Tragedy. Remarks similar to those
     in Journal (see below).

134 _____. The Journal of Arnold Bennett. New York: Viking,
     1932. Vol. 3, pp. 153-158 et passim.
     Sunday, May 23, 1926. "Dreiser's An Ameriacan Tragedy.
     I have already read 150 pages of this novel. The mere writ-
     ing is simply bloody--careless, clumsy, terrible. But there
     is power, and he holds you, because his big construction is
     good. The book quite woke me up last night, just as I was
     going off to sleep...."

Saturday, May 29, 1926. "I have now finished the 1st vol.
of Dreiser's An American Tragedy, and it is certainly in its
main features exceedingly good, and true. The psychology
again and again strikes you by its fineness and also by its
originality...."
Wednesday, June 2nd, 1926. "After lunch I finished An
American Tragedy by Dreiser. This book must be 250 or
300,000 words long. Taken as a whole it is very fine and impressive. He has held it together everywhere magnificently.
It has no humour, and lots and lots of original, true psychological observations. This must be one of the very finest
American novels."

135 BENNETT, Jesse Lee. "The Incomplete Sceptic." New Repub-
     lic, 20 (October 8, 1919), 297-298.
     Review of "The Hand of the Potter." It is a tragedy. An
     abnormal boy has been in prison for injuring one little girl.
     He assaults and kills another upon release. His parents are
     caught up in the maelstrom of New York, and cannot control
     the situation. The title is from Omar Khayyam: "What, did
     the Hand then of the Potter shake?" and implies that the boy
     was a mistake of God. All this is naive. Can it be that Drei-
     ser does not know that the great literatures of the world are
     filled with tragedies all the more human and tragic because
     they start with no thought of a fatherly divinity?

136 BERCOVICI, Konrad. "Romantic Realist." Mentor, 18 (May,
     1930), 38-41.

137 BERG, Ruben G. "Theodore Dreiser--Sherwood Anderson,"
     in Moderne Amerikaner. Stockholm: H. Geber, 1925. Pp.
     100-125.

138 BERKEY, John C., and Alice M. Winters. "The Heinemann Edi-
     tion of Sister Carrie." Library Chronicle, 44 (1979), 43-70.

139 _____, et al., eds. (Alice Winters, James L. W. West, Neda
     Westlake). Sister Carrie. Philadelphia: University of Pen-
     nsylvania Press, 1981. Pennsylvania edition, 679 pp. with
     historical and textual commentary, pp. 501-678. Review-
     analysis by Richard W. Dowell, Dreiser Newsletter (Spring,
     1981), pp. 1-8.

140 BERNARD, Kenneth O. "Theodore Dreiser's Determinism: A
     Detour of Faith." MA thesis, Columbia University, 1956.

141 _____. "The Flight of Theodore Dreiser." University of Kan-
     sas City Review, 26 (June, 1960), 251-259.
     Argues that Dreiser took flight from life, around 1900, and
     only with difficulty found his way back. He finally reconciled
     into a harmonious whole the element of his mother's mysticism
     and his father's bitter view of fate.

142 BERRY, Thomas Elliott. The Newspaper in the American Novel,
     1900-1969. Metuchen, N.J.: Scarecrow, 1970. Dreiser, pp.
     40, 47-50 et passim.
     "Although Dreiser attacks the moral code, the social system
     and the business world, he never singles out the newspaper
     for a prolonged analysis and consideration.... Dreiser's fail-
     ure to consider the institution of the newspaper more fully
     is surprising because of his close association with the news-
     paper and magazine world.... [I]n An American Tragedy he
     condemns the practice of obtaining news at any cost and pass-
     ing final judgments without concern for truth. This novel
     stands, in essence, as an indictment of the newspaper as a
     co-partner with a prejudiced jury, organized religion, and
     society in general in condemning unjustly, and exacting a
     cruel vengeance on one of its members."

143 BERRYMAN, John. "Through Dreiser's Imagination the Tides
     of Real Life Billowed." New York Times Book Review, March
     4, 1951. Reprinted in Highlights of Modern Literature, edited
     by Francis Brown. New York: New American Libarary, 1954.
     Pp. 118-123. Also reprinted in Kazin and Shapiro (1955),
     pp. 149-153. Also reprinted in Berryman, The Freedom of the
     Poet. New York: Farrar, Straus & Giroux, 1976. Pp. 185-
     189.
     Review of Matthiessen's Theodore Dreiser (1951). "Matthies-
     sen is nearly always right. He attributes Dreiser's formidable
     descriptive power to a freshness of eye and obstinate memory
     fused with a deep sense of changingness which made it seem
     historically important to preserve appearance. He analyzes
     handsomely the debts to Balzac and Spencer and the devices
     used by the novelist to organize his materials."

144 _____, ed. with Introduction. The Titan. New York: New
     American Library, 1965. Reprinted in Berryman, The Free-
     dom of the Poet (1976), pp. 190-197.

145 BERTHOFF, Warner. "Lives of the Americans: Theodore Drei-
     ser," in The Ferment of Realism: American Literature, 1884-
     1919. New York: Free Press, 1965. Pp. 235-244.
     "There remains, with Dreiser, the problem of style; the
     stumbling block it presents has not been exaggerated. In
     many respects Dreiser's working style is a remarkably effec-
     tive instrument of exposition--inclusive, adaptable, open to
     intensifying accents, capable of strong concentration and com-
     plex emphasis, distinctly novelistic. But there is no denying
     that the idiom he writes in is often labored and toneless. So-
     lecisms, blunders of diction, grotesque lapses into 'fine' writ-
     ing abound; and they rather increase in frequency as his
     career advances."

146 _____. "Dreiser Revisited." Modern Occasions, 2 (Winter,
     1972), 133-136.

147 BIDDLE, Edmund R. "The Plays of Theodore Dreiser." Ph.D.
     diss., University of Pennsylvania, 1965. DA, 26 (1965), 3325A-
     3326A.
        Since 1893 Dreiser had thought of play writing as a natural
     medium for him, one to which he had wanted, some day, to
     return. Dreiser wrote a number of one-act dramas, Plays of
     the Natural and Supernatural (1916), and one full-length play,
     The Hand of the Potter (1917). Dreiser's play-writing talent
     needed proper encouragement. Torn between his admirers
     and detractors, he was unable to recognize intelligent criti-
     cism when it came his way. Had he swallowed his sensitivity
     and tried to become a better playwright, he might have made
     a substantial contribution to the drama.

148 BIGELOW, Blair Ferguson. "The Collected Newspaper Articles,
     1892-1894, of Theodore Dreiser," 2 vols. Ph.D. diss., Bran-
     deis University, 1972. DA, 34 (1973), 305A.
        The articles included in this work are those Dreiser wrote
     as a full-time newspaper reporter between June 1892 and No-
     vember 1894. The articles included are those that Dreiser
     attributed to himself in several sources. Several articles
     named by Dreiser could not be located. The articles collected
     here were originally published in the Chicago Daily Globe, the
     St. Louis Republic, and the Pittsburgh Dispatch.

149 BIRD, Carol. "Theodore Dreiser Speaks." Writers' Monthly,
     2 (May, 1929), 25-28.

150 BIRSS, John H. "Records of Theodore Dreiser" A Bibliograph-
     ical Note." Notes and Queries, 165 (September 30, 1933),
     229.

151 BISHOFF, Robert E., Jr. "Changing Perspectives" An Ameri-
     can Tragedy from Literature to Film." Ph.D. diss., Univer-
     sity of Massachusetts, 1974. DA, 35 (1974), 440A.
        This study illustrates that a significant value in the study
     of filmed adaptations rests in the fact that, simply in their
     nature as adaptations, they illustrate in a profound and ob-
     vious way the subjective and individual perspectives that
     exist concerning any given situation or event. This study
     also illustrates that these individual perspectives need not
     be regarded as hostile, but can instead be seen as providing
     complementary angles of vision that will expand our collective
     awareness and understanding.

152 BISHOP, Bert O. "A Study of the Correlation of Theodore
     Dreiser's Journalistic Experience to His Work as a Creative
     Artist." MA thesis, Southern Illinois University, 1960.

153 BIZAM, Lenke. Theodore Dreiser. Budapest: Gondolat, 1963.

154 BLACKMUR, Richard P. "The Economy of the American Writer."
     Sewanee Review, 53 (Spring, 1945), 175-185.
       This is an analysis of the publishing market for American
     authors. Concludes that there is no market for great writ-
     ers, only popular, simple-minded publications such as The
     Saturday Evening Post. The ever-increasing reading public
     nearly assures publication of nearly anything that comes along,
     but quality magazines are very scarce.

155 BLACKSIN, Ida. "Theodore Dreiser and the Law." MA thesis,
     New York University, 1948.

156 _____. "Law and Literature: Dreiser and the Courts."
     Ph.D. diss., Michigan State University, 1969. DA, 31 (1970),
     1261A.
       This dissertation presents an analysis of the legal case study
     found in Dreiser's An American Tragedy. It demonstrates
     how Dreiser gave meaning to the dry facts gathered from the
     "Gillette case" by showing all of the social forces leading up
     to the tragedy that are special to the American scene in such
     a way as to make it a plea for Clyde Griffiths and an indict-
     ment of American society. In conclusion this dissertation pre-
     sents a special bibliography of articles and studies on Crim-
     inology and Law, Capital Punishment and Fenology, and a
     Table of Cases of all the cases cited in the study.

157 BLACKSTOCK, Walter. "Theodore Dreiser--The Aspirant: A
     Study of His Early Literary Career." Ph.D. diss., Yale Uni-
     versity, 1952. DA, 31 (1971), 6592A.
       This study covers more than three hundred of Dreiser's
     early contributions to newspapers and magazines, from 1892 to
     1911, and includes the period of his newspaper reporting for
     the Chicago Daily-Globe, the St. Louis Globe-Democrat, etc.
     Dreiser's early writings have been examined not only in terms
     of the development of his prose style and narrative technique,
     but especially in terms of their themes. Their analysis shows
     them to fall into three major classifications: Success, Art (the
     Artist and the Beautiful), and American Progress.

158 _____. "Theodore Dreiser's Literary Style." Florida State
     University Studies, 11 (1953), 95-116. Edited by Weymouth
     T. Jordon. Tallahassee: Florida State University, 1953.

159 _____. "Dreiser's Dramatizations of American Success."
     Florida State University Studies, 14 (1954), 107-130.

160 _____. "Dreiser's Dramatizations of Art, the Artist, and the
     Beautiful in American Life." Southern Quarterly, 1 (October,
     1962), 63-86.
       Says that Dreiser was not a naturalist in the manner of Zola,
     but a monist. Many of his characters are in truth in search

of the spiritual, not the material. Some actually achieve a
kind of ideal beauty, but most of them fail miserably in their
quest. Carrie is perhaps the best example of a Dreiser character who dreams such happiness as she may never feel.

161 _____. "The Fall and Rise of Eugene Witla: Dramatic Vision
of Artistic Integrity in The 'Genius'." Language Quarterly,
5 (1967), 15-18.

162 BLAIR, Walter; Theodore Hornberger; and Randall Stewart; eds.
The Literature of the United States: An Anthology and a
History. 2 vols. New York: Scott, Foresman, 1953. Dreiser,
pp. 767-780, Vol. 2.
Mainly a biographical sketch and review of published works.
It is easy to point out weaknesses in Dreiser's novels; he
lacks a sense of humor; his prose is pedestrian; the piling up
of detail makes for dull reading. But his work is important, both
historically and intrinsically. No other American novelist has
documented his stories quite so carefully or has written a social record of American life so convincingly authentic.
Reprints "The Second Choice," from Free and Other Stories
(1918). Although Dreiser can be best appreciated in toto,
this story illustrates the essential characteristics of his work.

163 BLAKE, Fay Montaug. "The Strike in the American Novel."
Ph.D. diss., University of California (Los Angeles), 1970.
DA, 31 (1970), 3539A.
Published in the following item. Explores many uses of the
strike and points out that Dreiser's Sister Carrie used a strike
to show dramatically the moral degeneration of one of the central characters, Hurstwood. Concludes that between 1930 and
1945 the Depression loomed large in novels portraying strikes.
The number of novels using strikes increased dramatically,
and in a great many extreme disenchantment with capitalism
was evident.

164 _____. The Strike in the American Novel. Metuchen, N.J.:
Scarecrow Press, 1972. Based on 1970 dissertation above.
Dreiser, pp. 83-85.
The most successful use of the strike in this period (1895-
1910) is in Sister Carrie. Here it becomes a powerful artistic
device through which a man's gradual breakdown is detailed.
Against the backdrop of the strike Hurstwood plays out his
last desperate effort to regain his manhood. Dreiser's own
sympathies with the working class are evident in the novel,
but he has not set out to convert us to any sort of sociological or economic theory. He uses the strike entirely for artistic purposes, and he does so responsibly and superbly well.

165 BLAKELEY, Carolyn F. "Naturalism in the Novels of Theodore
Dreiser." MA thesis, Atlanta University, 1964.

166 BLANKENSHIP, Russell. "Theodore Dreiser," in American Literature as an Expression of the National Mind. New York: Holt, 1931. Pp. 532-541.

Mainly biographical details which conclude with the observation that Dreiser is by far the most significant writer now working in the American field. He is certainly not the cleverest, or the most electric, or the most cheering, but he is the most powerful, and from the standpoint of literary development he is the most significant.

167 BLOCK, Haskell M. "Dreiser's An American Tragedy," in Naturalistic Triptych: The Fictive and the Real in Zola, Mann, and Dreiser. New York: Random House, 1970. Pp. 54-77.

An American Tragedy is not a reproduction of literal reality, but, drawn from real life experience, it heightens and intensifies our understanding of reality. Dreiser's art comes closer than that of perhaps any other major novelist of our time to breaking down the anthithesis between life and art. His illumination of the human condition is through an art that on occasion is so close to reality as to threaten to blur the separation of the fictive and the real. To the extent that Dreiser is an artist, An American Tragedy transcends the documentary and the purely historical; without its documentary foundations, however, the novel could not have exercised its hold on Dreiser's imagination.

168 BLOOM, Robert. "Past Indefinite: The Sherman-Mencken Debate on an American Tradition." Western Humanities Review, 15 (Winter, 1961), 73-81.

Reviews the public argument which began in December 1915 and lasted beyond 1925 with the publication of An American Tragedy. Essentially Sherman maintained that regardless of Dreiser's pretensions to veracity and to an objective, photographic transcription of life, the novelist was actually committed to a simple naturalistic philosophy which ordered and determined his books. Mencken, champion of the new literature at large and of Dreiser in particular, took up the challenge with characteristic vigor. By 1926 Sherman had somewhat modified his position in his review of An American Tragedy, which he hails as "exhaustive and veracious."

169 BLUEFARB, Sam. "The Middle-Aged Man in Contemporary Literature: Bloom to Herzog." College Language Association Journal, 20 (September, 1976), 1-13.

Examines six middle-aged characters in contemporary literature to see if some sort of prototypal pattern exists. Begins with Joyce's Leopold Bloom, continues with James' Lambert Strether, Dreiser's George Hurstwood, Eliot's J. Alfred Prufrock, Hemingway's Colonel Richard Cantwell, and Saul Bellow's Herzog. Concludes that perhaps the best we can expect is that these characters maintain their sanity in the face of

pressures which have stripped them of a sense of adventure.
Remarks that Hurstwood shows us the tragedy of the middle-
aged man who tries desperately to have the best of both worlds.

170 BOAK, Arthur E. R. World History. Boston: Houghton Mif-
     flin, 1947. "The Common Man Demands a Place in the Sun,"
     pp. 390-403.

171 BOAS, George. Courbet and the Naturalistic Movement. Balti-
     more: Johns Hopkins University Press, 1938.
        Refers to Gustave Courbet, French painter, 1819-1877, a
     leader of realism in painting. Naturalism was as much a way
     of thinking about the world as of representing it. If the Na-
     turalistic movement stood for one thing preeminently it was
     perhaps the transfer of the scientific point of view into ar-
     tistry.

172 BOCKSTAHLER, Oscar L. "Contributions to American Litera-
     ture by Hoosiers of German Ancestry." Indiana Magazine of
     History, 38 (September, 1942), 231-250.

173 BODE, Carl. Mencken. Carbondale: Southern Illinois Univer-
     sity Press, 1969. "Dreiser and the Fruits of Dissidence,"
     pp. 103-130.
        Mencken held Sister Carrie to be a "novel of magnitude"
     and had been one of the rare readers to see it when it came
     out in 1900. Dreiser found Mencken impressive as well as at-
     tractive, responding to Mencken's youthful assurance, learn-
     ing in the process to respect the cast of his mind. Dreiser
     also could not help being affected by Mencken's admiration of
     his work and the cogency of his reasons. As time went along
     Dreiser asked Mencken's opinion about manuscripts. They
     met at intervals and corresponded constantly, Mencken writing
     with his usual drive and wit, Dreiser with an elephantine im-
     itation.

174 BODENHEIM, Maxwell. "On Writing." Saturday Review of Liter-
     ature, 2 (February 13, 1926), 562. Letter attacking Sherwood
     Anderson's art; Dreiser briefly referred to.

175 BOLCH, Dorothy H. "Hardy's Jude and Dreiser's Clyde: The
     Spiritual and the Materialistic Approach to Naturalism." MA
     thesis, University of North Carolina, 1969.

176 BORGES, Jorge Luis. An Introduction to American Literature,
     edited and translated by L. Clark Keating and Robert O.
     Evans. Lexington: University of Kentucky Press, 1971.
     First published in Spanish, 1967. Dreiser, p. 34.
        Refers to influence of Stephen Crane on Dreiser. Comments
     briefly on life and names publications. Considers An Ameri-
     can Tragedy the greatest.

177 BOSHA, Francis J. "The Restored Text of Dreiser's Sister
     Carrie: A Consideration of the Pennsylvania Edition." Thought
     Currents in English Literature, 54 (1981), 37-46.

178 BOSWELL, Charles, and Lewis Thompson. Surrender to Love:
     The Carlyle Harris Case. New York: Privately printed, 1955.
     Refers to a murder case in 1893 by Carlyle Harris who sent
     a girl poisoned powders.

179 BOURNE, Randolph. "Desire as Hero: A Review of The 'Gen-
     ius'." New Republic, 5 (November 20, 1915), fall literary
     supplement, 5-6. Reprinted in Pizer (1981), pp. 243-246.
       For all its dull and rather cheap texture, the book is set
     in a light of youthful idealism. Nobody but Dreiser could
     manage this fusion, but it is there. For the Genius the golden
     glow shines from everything. Always there is a sense of the
     miraculous beauty of girls, the soft clinging of charming at-
     mospheres. Of sordid realists Dreiser is certainly the most
     idealistic. He still believes in, and still gives, a sense of
     the invincible virginality of the world.

180 _____. "The Novels of Theodore Dreiser." New Republic,
     2 (April 17, 1915), 7-8.

181 _____. "The Art of Theodore Dreiser." Dial, 62 (June 14,
     1917), 507-509. Reprinted in Bourne, History of a Literary
     Radical and Other Essays. New York: B. W. Huebsch, 1920.
     Reprinted New York: Viking Press, 1948. Pp. 195-204.
     Article reprinted in Kazin and Shapiro (1955), pp. 92-95.
     Also reprinted in Lydenberg (1971), pp. 81-85 and in Pizer
     (1981), pp. 15-18.
       There stirs in Dreiser's books a new American quality. It
     is not at all German. It is an authentic attempt to make some-
     thing artistic out of the chaotic materials that lie around us
     in American life. Dreiser interests us because we can watch
     him grope and feel his clumsiness. He has the artist's vision
     without the sureness of the artist's technique. That is one
     of the tragedies of America. But his faults are those of his
     material and of uncouth bulk, and not of shoddiness. He ex-
     presses an America that is in process of forming. The inter-
     est he evokes is part of the eager interest we feel in that
     growth.

182 BOWER, Marie Hadley. "Theodore Dreiser: The Man and His
     Times: His Work and Its Reception." Ph.D. diss., Ohio State
     University, 1940.

183 BOWERS, Claude. "Memories of Theodore Dreiser," in My Life:
     The Memories of Claude Bowers. New York: Simon & Schus-
     ter, 1962. Pp. 153-172.
       Reviews his acquaintance with Dreiser until his death in

1945. Was one of admiration and respect, although towards
the end he had lost much of his contact. Twenty years went
by, and Dreiser published nothing. He wondered if financial
success had "chilled his creative power." Comments on the
two novels published after Dreiser's death, The Bulwark and
The Stoic. Feels that perhaps The Bulwark "more than most
of his other books reveals the man, his tenderness, his sympathy with the weaknesses of human nature, his deep undercurrent of religious feelings." Concludes that Dreiser is one
"of the most heroic and significant figures in our literary history."

184 BOWRON, Bernard. "The Making of an American Scholar."
    Monthly Review, 2 (October, 1950), 212-222.

185 BOYD, Ernest. Portraits: Real and Imaginary. New York:
    George H. Doran, 1924. Reprinted New York: AMS, 1970.
    Dreiser, pp. 168-170.
       Describes a visit-interview with Dreiser. Dreiser talked
    about his own work, the mystery of how he was able to write,
    etc. In conclusion, Boyd says, "It was dawn before I stood
    once more on the doorsteps shaking hands with him, this in-
    teresting personality without a single personal idea. What
    had fascinated me was precisely that quality which gives his
    work its peculiar flavor, the phenomenon of a wholly natural,
    native genius.... Out of all these laborious platitudes on
    wealth and art and sex and economics, those proofs of tech-
    nical helplessness in the art of writing, of selection, there
    emerged a picture of a man of unspoiled sensitiveness to the
    storm and stress of nature, of an elemental energy and pas-
    sionate desire to understand. Theodore Dreiser is a primi-
    tive, and his art must be measured in corresponding terms."

186 BOYNTON, H. W. "Varieties of Realism." The Nation, 110
    (May 1, 1920), 595-600.

187 BOYNTON, Percy H. "American Authors of Today: Theodore
    Dreiser." English Journal, 12 (March, 1923), 180-188. Re-
    printed in Boynton, Some Contemporary Americans. Chicago:
    University of Chicago Press, 1924. Pp. 126-144.
       His desire to explain is harnessed with his inability to sug-
    gest. Perhaps it is just as well that Dreiser does not attempt
    to work through suggestion, "he is a Flemish artist, capable
    of spending two weeks on a broom handle." Dreiser's philos-
    ophy is a balance between Emerson's and Mark Twain's. He
    has no philosophical formula, but is a continual asker of ques-
    tions.

188 _____. Literature and American Life. Boston: Ginn, 1936.
    Dreiser, pp. 789-792.
       Anyone who has had Dreiser held up to him as a morbid

anatomist of souls might well begin a direct acquaintance with him by reading Twelve Men. Almost every subject of these dozen portraits, to use Dreiser's own formula, "deliberately and of choice holds fast to many, many simple and human things, and rounds out life, or would, in a natural, normal, courageous, healthy way."

189 _____. "Theodore Dreiser," in America in Contemporary Fiction. Chicago: University of Chicago Press, 1940. Reprinted New York: Russell & Russell, 1963. Pp. 131-144.

Biographical detail with special comment on An American Tragedy. Of this work Boynton says it was "written out of the depths from reading Herbert Spencer. Clyde is a chemical atom in a whirl of unknown forces. Some responses are inborn, some the result of experience. Clyde is never an agent, always an instrument. Not presented as either weak or wicked, simply as the son of his father and the product of his upbringing. Drifts from one set of accidental conditions to another. Dreiser surrounds this story with a shadowy background."

190 BRADBURY, Malcolm, and David Corker. "The American Risorgimento: The Coming of the New Arts," in American Literature Since 1900, edited by Marcus Cunliffe. London: Barrie & Jenkins, 1975. Pp. 17-47.

191 BRADFORD, Gamaliel. The Journal of Gamaliel Bradford, edited by Van Wyck Brooks. Boston: Houghton Mifflin, 1933. Dreiser, p. 423.

"July 2, 1926: Trying to read Dreiser's An American Tragedy, a solid piece of realism.... Sincere, vigorous, straightforward stuff. There is merely the surface of things ... and in this Dreiser there does not seem to me to be the faintest suggestion of the power of genius in style. It is all dead, uninspired, utterly ... and not the faintest gleam of humor."

192 BRAZILLER, George. "How Will Dreiser Be Honored?" Book Find News, 2 (April, 1946), 10.

193 BRENNAN, Stephen Christopher. "Dreiser and Balzac: A Literary Source for Hurstwood and Carrie." American Notes and Queries, 17 (1978), 21-24.

194 _____. "The Composition of Sister Carrie: A Reconsideration." Dreiser Newsletter, 9 (Fall, 1978), 17-23.

The strong influence of Arthur Henry on the writing of Sister Carrie has long been acknowledged--and for good reason. In the well-known letter Dreiser wrote to Mencken in 1916, he gives full credit to his friend for nagging him, first to write short stories, then a novel. In the same letter Dreiser says that it was Henry's pressuring that drove him to fin-

ish the book when he dropped it twice in disgust and that
the cutting of the book was based primarily on Henry's suggestions.

195 _____. "Sister Carrie and the Tolstoyan Artist." Research
Studies, 47 (1979), 1-16.

196 _____. "The Making of Sister Carrie." Ph.D. diss., Tulane, 1978. DA, 40 (1979), 1466A.
As the legend goes, Dreiser sat down one day in the fall
of 1897 and, mystically inspired and writing out of the heart
of his own experience, produced one of the most significant
novels in American literature--Sister Carrie. Convinced of
the truth of his work, Dreiser forced Doubleday, Page to
honor their agreement to publish the book. Because of his
courageous fight against the "suppression" of Sister Carrie,
he became a great hero in the naturalists' struggle against
the legends, however, this one does not bear close scrutiny.

197 BRIDGEWATER, Patrick. "Fictional Superman" Jack London
and Theodore Dreiser," in Nietzsche in Anglo-Saxony. Leicester, England: Leicester University Press, 1972. Pp. 163-
172.

198 BRINSLEY, Henry. "The Genius of Mr. Theodore Dreiser and
Some Other Geniuses." Vanity Fair, 5 (December, 1915),
41, 112.

199 BRITTON, Joe S. "Dreiser's Views of Women." MA thesis,
Southern Illinois University, 1957.

200 BRODERICK, John C. Theodore Dreiser's "Sister Carrie": A
Study Guide. Bound Brook, N.J.: Shelley Publishing Co.,
1963.

201 BRODMERKEL, Alexander H. "A Comparison of the Novels of
Thomas Hardy and Theodore Dreiser." MA thesis, Columbia,
1932.

202 BROER, Barbara J. "A Study of Theodore Dreiser's Technique
in The Financier, The Titan, and The Stoic." MA thesis,
Sacramento State College, 1969.

203 BROGUNIER, Joseph. "Dreiser in Paperback: Riches and
Rags." Dreiser Newsletter, 4 (Spring, 1973), 1-4.
Interest in Dreiser has not ebbed in these ten years, nor
has it merely maintained its level. It has rather grown; and
thus one is confronted with the paradox that Dreiser is at-
tracting more readers at a time when the number of his texts
in paperback has declined. The Dreiser revival waxes strong:
only Sister Carrie is in quality paperback; and quality paper-

backs of his other novels are clearly needed and would find
an eager market.

204 BROOKS, Cleanth; R. W. B. Lewis; and Robert Penn Warren;
eds. American Literature: The Makers and the Making, 2
vols. New York: St. Martin's Press, 1973. Dreiser, Vol. 2,
pp. 1877-1922.
Consists of 20-page introduction, principally biographical,
with excerpt from An American Tragedy. Introduction also
emphasizes the composition and thematic development of this
work. Concludes that Dreiser was the first American writer
not of the old American tradition. Though born in America,
he was definitely the outsider, the yearner, and that fact determines the basic emotion of his work.

205 BROOKS, Obed. "The Problem of the Social Novel." Modern
Quarterly, 6 (Autumn, 1932), 77-82.

206 BROOKS, Van Wyck. Letters and Leadership. New York:
Heubsch, 1918. Dreiser, pp. 15 et passim.

207 _____. "According to Dreiser." The Nation, 110 (May 1,
1920), 595-596.
Review of Hey-Rub-a-Dub-Dub. The Dreiser who emerges
in these essays is anything but the pachydermatous animal
that has caused so much alarm in respectable circles. He is
very like a perplexed and weary child, dazzled by a kaleido-
scope in which he is able to discern no thread of meaning.
One receives the impression of an essentially passive, diffi-
dent, and highly sensitive spirit that has been hurt by life
and is yet perpetually charmed anew by its "active, dancing,
changeful" beauty.

208 _____. "The Literary Life in America," in Emerson and
Others. New York: Dutton, 1927. Pp. 221-250.
How much one would like to assume that the American writer
is a sort of Samson bound with the brass fetters of the Phi-
listines and requiring only to have those fetters cast off in
order to be able to conquer the world! That, as I understand
it, is the position of Mr. Dreiser, who recently remarked of
certain of our novelists: "They succeed in writing but one
book before the iron hand of convention takes hold of them!"
In this sense the American environment is answerable for the
literature it has produced. But what is significant is that the
American writer does show less resistance.

209 _____. "Theodore Dreiser." University of Kansas City Review, 16 (Spring, 1950), 187-197.

210 _____. "Theodore Dreiser," in The Confident Years: 1885-
1915. New York: Dutton, 1952. Pp. 301-320.

Mainly a biographical account. Says in conclusion, "he
was tortured by a sense of the tragedy of living. As a reporter in St. Louis he was obsessed with the 'lightning of
chance' that was always striking blindly, leaving in its wake
for some good fortune, for others destruction and death--an
obsession that led him to say later, 'I acknowledge the Furies.
I believe in them. I have heard the disastrous beating of
their wings.' He was tormented by the contradictions of life,
and felt he must explore the mysteries."

211 _____. John Sloan: A Painter's Life. New York: Dutton,
     1955.
     Refers to the American painter, 1871-1951. Dreiser, pas-
sim; several references to The "Genius."

212 _____. Howells, His Life, and World. New York: Dutton,
     1959. Dreiser, passim.
     Discusses the interest which Howells expressed in the early
work of Crane and Norris but did not support or encourage
Dreiser in his early efforts. Dreiser, however, found Howells "truly generous and humane, one of the noblemen of literature" with a genuinely honest outlook on life and a fresh approach to writing.

213 _____, and Otto L. Bettman. Our Literary Heritage: A Pic-
     torial History of the Writer in America. New York: Dutton,
     1956.
     This work is an abridgment with illustrations of the five
volumes in Brooks's history of American literature. Dreiser
is reprinted from The Confident Years (1952), pp. 201-205.

214 BROUN, Heywood. "Theodore Dreiser at His Best in His New
     Book, Twelve Men." New York Tribune, April 26, 1919. P.
     10.
     "Whatever faults may be found here and there, it seems to
me that Twelve Men is an interesting and readable book, and
an exceptionally fine piece of work as well...."

215 _____. "It Seems to Me." New York World, February 20,
     1926. P. 15.
     Quotes much from John Macy, who regards An American
Tragedy as one of the greatest American novels.

216 _____. "Tragedy in No Man's Land." Stage, 13 (April,
     1936), 35.

217 BROWN, Carroll T. "Dreiser's The Bulwark and Philadelphia
     Quakerism." Bulletin of the Friends Historical Association,
     35 (Autumn, 1946), 52-61.

218 BROWN, Deming. "Sinclair Lewis and Theodore Dreiser," in

Soviet Attitudes Toward American Writing. Princeton, N.J.:
Princeton University Press, 1962. Pp. 239-271.
Scholarly, well-documented study. Discusses the reasons
Russians drawn to Dreiser and concludes that Dreiser's novels
"attracted the critics mainly because they probed the economic
and social weaknesses and sore spots in America." Dreiser
has become the most popular twentieth-century American writer
in Russia, and at the same time the favorite subject of literary studies. More dissertations for advanced degrees were
devoted to Dreiser than to all other American writers combined.

219 BRYER, Jackson R., ed. Fifteen Modern American Authors:
A Survey of Research and Criticism. Durham, N.C.: Duke
University Press, 1969. "Theodore Dreiser," by Robert H.
Elias, pp. 101-138. Republished in 1973, with some revision
as Sixteen Modern American Authors.

220 BRYSON, Norman. "Universe and 'Multi-universe': John Cowper Powys as a Critic of Dreiser's Fiction." Powys Review,
2 (Winter-Spring, 1979-1980), 24-32. Followed by Powys'
"Four Essays on Dreiser," pp. 33-49.

221 BUCCO, Martin. "The East-West Theme in Dreiser's An American Tragedy." Western American Literature, 12 (Fall, 1977),
177-183.
Often in serious fiction the travelers finally realize that a
higher value adheres to the journey rather than to the journey's end. To make this outcome tenable the writer develops
his plot and selects his details in the light of process instead
of progress. But such is not the case in Dreiser's pessimistic An American Tragedy (1925). Clyde's family will continue
in stages further west, while Clyde's destiny lies not in that
direction, but further and further East. For Clyde the moment of lost hope is "as when night at last falls upon the faintest remaining gleam of dusk in the west." The mythic directions are as devoid of value as the journey's mysterious end.

222 BUCHESKY, Charles Stanley. "The Background of American
Literary Naturalism." Ph.D. diss., Wayne State University,
1971. DA, 32 (1972), 6368A.
In this presentation the author has used primary texts, literary histories, monographs, critical articles, and historical
and philosophical writings. Also included are important works
of five major figures of American naturalistic fiction: Norris,
Crane, Dreiser, Steinbeck, and Hemingway. Materialistic naturalism as found in these writers, was a view of nature, in-
dependent of a deity, as the embodiment of the laws and processes of the physical universe.

223 BUCHHOLZ, John Lee. "An American Tragedy: The Iconography
of a Myth." Ph.D. diss., Texas Christian University, 1972.
DA, 33 (1973), 4399-4400A.

This study proposes that the root of Dreiser's power is embodied in his selection and organization of his fictional materials; in short, in his art. Dreiser's narrative power is remarkably analogous in effect to the motion picture: the reader
shares the immediate perceptions of Dreiser's protagonist as
he confronts the material facts of his life--cities, buildings,
clothes, vehicles, and social rituals. This immediate and personal attachment to the facts of American experience generates
the powerful emotion and the sense of individual destiny proper
to tragic vision.

224 BUCKINGHAM, Willis J. and Barnett Shepherd. "Unquiet An-
     chorage: Dreiser's Revisions of 'When the Sails Are Furled.'"
     Research Studies, 48 (June, 1980), 105-115.
        In 1898 Dreiser visited a famous home for aged sailors, hop-
     ing to find material for an illustrated sketch. A rather rou-
     tine article quickly resulted, but in the years that followed,
     he republished the article twice, thoroughly reworking it for
     each occasion. When compared with each other, and with two
     articles from which Dreiser copied parts of his original essay,
     these five documents allow us a rare work-bench perspective
     on Dreiser, and suggest that what he saw at the sailors' home
     touched some of his deepest and most characteristic feelings
     about the pathos of the human condition.

225 BUDENZ, Louis Francis. Men Without Faces: The Communist
     Conspiracy in the U. S. A. New York: Harper, 1950. Drei-
     ser, pp. 242-245.
        Dreiser permitted the Communist party to announce his mem-
     bership in 1945, when some big move became necessary to off-
     set the demoralization resulting from the spotlight thrown on
     "Browderism." To my knowledge, however, he had been a
     party member since the early thirties; and as far back as
     1933 had publicly lent his name to the Red cause, thereby se-
     curing for the party the allegiance of many lesser writers.

226 BULLARD, F. Lauriston. "Boston's Book Ban Likely to Live
     Long." New York Times, April 28, 1929. Part 3, pp. 1, 7.

227 BULLOCK, Shan F. "London Letter." Chicago Evening Post,
     Friday Literary Review, January 3, 1913. P. 4.

228 BUNGE, Nancy. "Women as Social Critics in Sister Carrie, Wines-
     burg, Ohio, and Main Street." Midamerica, 3 (1976), 46-55.

229 BURBANK, Rex. Anderson. New York: Twayne, 1964. Drei-
     ser, pp. 49-51.

230 BURGAN, Mary E. "Sister Carrie and the Pathos of Naturalism."
     Criticism, 15 (Fall, 1973), 336-349.
        Article seeks to investigate the kinds of pathos in Sister

Carrie in order to define their aesthetic dimension in Dreiser's art. There are indeed different kinds of pity in the early novels of Dreiser, and although a survey of their types will not justify them all, it may help to explain a peculiar kind of rhetorical appeal which is characteristic not only of Dreiser's art but of naturalistic writing generally.

231 BURGUM, Edwin Berry. "Theodore Dreiser, 1871-1945." New Masses, 58 (January 15, 1946), 6.

232 _____. "Dreiser and His America." New Masses, 58 (January 29, 1946), 7-9, 22. Reprinted as "Theodore Dreiser and the Ethics of American Life," in The Novel and the World's Dilemma. New York: Oxford University Press, 1947. Pp. 292-301.
Dreiser's novels are the most accurate in our literature of life as it was actually lived during the period of capitalist expansion and its apparent stabilization in monopoly. And since his understanding of American life was thus accurate, he was able the more soundly and profoundly to fathom its baffling effect upon the American character.

233 _____. "The America of Theodore Dreiser." Book Find News, 2 (March, 1946), 10-11, 21-22.

234 BURKE, Harry Rosecrans. "Dreiser and the Riddle of the Sphinx," in From the Day's Journey: A Book of By-Paths and Eddies About Saint Louis. St. Louis: Miner Publishing, 1924. Pp. 165-171. Illustrated by Sheila Burlingame.
Recollections of Dreiser when he was a reporter in St. Louis, with a final comment: "A hundred fascinating stories lie within the covers of A Book About Myself, but here is no place to tell them. Dreiser has puzzled out the riddle of existence. Rub-a-dub-dub! It measures the same in the end. The coral insect is as great as man, and perhaps in its perspective not less futile. 'What do you make of life, Dreiser?' Rub-a-dub-dub. Thus Dreiser has answered the riddle of the Sphinx. Noise and nothing."

235 BURKE, John Michael. "A Bibliography of Soviet Russian Translations of American Literature." Ph.D. diss., Brown University, 1972. DA, 33 (1973), 3576A.
The number of Soviet translations of American literature in the period since the end of World War II has varied considerably. In the initial postwar period, the number of authors reached an all-time low. The number increased slowly during the fifties, the works of older classic American authors leading the way. Jack London and Mark Twain were far ahead in the number of copies printed. Also high in the listings were the works of Dreiser, Howard Fast, etc. From 1948 to 1968 Dreiser proved to be the most popular with editions totaling over ten million copies.

236 BURKE, Kenneth. "A Decade of American Fiction." Bookman,
     69 (August, 1929), 561-567.
        Considers principally the so-called "artistic" writers of the
     1920's. Regards such writers as Dos Passos and Dreiser as
     affording "no new enlightenment. The dishes-in-the-sink tra-
     dition is carried to fulfillment."

237 BURKE, Thomas. "America's Villified [sic] Author." T. P's
     and Cassell's Weekly (London), 8 (June 4, 1927), 178.

238 BUTLER, Gerald J. "The Quality of Emotional Greatness."
     Paunch, No. 25 (February, 1966), 5-17.
        Points out numerous passages in which Dreiser depicts Car-
     rie as one who lives on the basis of her feelings, directs
     her life on this basis. She never really "thinks" about any-
     thing, but simply proceeds with the flow of life according to
     her feelings.

239 BUTLER, Robert James. "Movement in Dreiser's Sister Carrie."
     Dreiser Newsletter, 11 (Spring, 1980), 1-12.
        American literature is densely populated with heroes and
     heroines who try "to find in motion what was lost in space,"
     people on the move who are in quest of settings which are
     fluid enough to accommodate their passion for a radical inde-
     pendence and completely open possibilities. Sister Carrie
     epitomizes this American tradition, for it is in many ways a
     novel about the possibilities and limitations of motion.

240 BYERS, John R., Jr. "Dreiser's Hurstwood and Jefferson's
     Rip Van Winkle." PMLA, 87 (May, 1972), 514-516.
        Points up the possibility that the most suggestive influence
     on Dreiser's character is a play with the "most famous stage
     tramp of the nineteenth century, the Joseph Jefferson ver-
     sion of 'Rip Van Winkle.' " Examples are convincing as Byers
     draws a parallel between Van Winkle and Hurstwood, both men
     of some little position who fall from prominence to beggary.

241 BYRNE, Donn. "Twelve Men." New York Times Review of
     Books, May 11, 1919. P. 276.
        Letter to editor.

242 CABELL, James Branch. "Protégés of the Censor," in Some
     of Us. New York: McBride, 1930. Pp. 77-88.
        In the novels of Anderson and Dreiser is "realism" reason-
     ably naked and unabashed; and my lack of love for realism
     has been expressed in several thousand pages. Yet here also
     is honesty, here is frankness; here is human tolerance. When
     a helping hand toward public applause is proffered to these
     three by the prude's dishonesty and by that wincing intoler-

ance of all frankness which the censor embodies, then the considerate cannot but be delighted.

243 CAIRNS, William B. A History of American Literature. New York: Oxford University Press, 1912. Does not discuss Dreiser specifically; is interesting for an early study of the literary scene when Dreiser first published Sister Carrie.

244 CALLOW, James T., and Robert J. Reilly. Guide to American Literature from Emily Dickinson to the Present. New York: Barnes and Noble, 1977. Dreiser, pp. 51-53.

245 CALVERT, Beverlee. "A Structural Analysis of Jennie Gerhardt." Dreiser Newsletter, 5 (Fall, 1974), 9-11.
Interesting, but somewhat strained, analysis of the novel as revolving around the numbers 62, 52, and seven-chapter units. Concludes that Dreiser deliberately did not write a Chapter 63, thus leaving Lester dead and Jennie alone, her future undecided. Dreiser closes out the story with a dash --indicating there was more to follow--a question mark, and an unwritten chapter.

246 CALVERTON, Victor F. "The Decade of Convictions." Bookman, 71 (March-August, 1930), 489.
Theodore Dreiser, who has come closer than any other American writer to describing certain of the more obvious but formidable aspects of our industrial civilization, became H. L. Mencken's great inspiration. What Mencken saw in Dreiser and that which made Dreiser an important figure in American literature for many other critics of that period was that futilitarian philosophy which became a mood of the age in the decade following the war. The disillusionment of those days found its most vivid expressions in cynicism rather than despair. Even gaiety began to revolve around the sneer.

247 _____. "The Radical Approach." Modern Quarterly, 6 (Winter, 1931), 16-27.
Article is a reply to Hazlitt's article "Art and Social Change" (1931). Hazlitt believes that the critic should, or at least can, express a judgment regarding the value of a work of art which has nothing to do with class objectives. Calverton believes this is an expression of the leisure class philosophy and does not apply to the literature produced by the rise of another social class, the proletariat, which has already developed an ideology of its own.

248 _____. "Left-Wing Literature in America." English Journal, 20 (December, 1931), 789-798.
Left-wing literature signifies difference in content rather than form. Left-wing writers in America have employed practically the same type of form that right-wing writers have used.

They have differed from them in their choice of content and
expression of conclusions. Left-wing writers as a group are
more than literary rebels. Literary rebels believe in revolt
in literature; left-wing writers believe in revolt in life. As
a group they are convinced that present-day industrial society
is based upon exploitation and injustice. Theodore Dreiser
above all has surprised his reading public by his sudden and
complete swing toward the left. Although his novels are not
left in spirit, his recent advocacy of a left-wing political pro-
gram and his more recent interest in the miners' strike have
revealed the development of a new philosophy on his part.

249 _____. "Pathology in Contemporary Literature." Thinker,
      (December, 1931), n.p.

250 _____. Liberation of American Literature. New York: Scrib-
      ner's, 1932. Reprinted New York: Octagon Books, 1973.
      Dreiser, pp. 406-412.
      It was not until the twentieth century, as the conditions
      of life all over the country conspired against the perpetuation
      of the romantic outlook, broke the spinal tie of the colonial
      complex and made America face the spectacle of a civilization
      which was rapidly destroying every tradition which it had
      cherished, that the realistic movement could become the dom-
      inant movement of the day. It was Theodore Dreiser, seeing
      and sensing that change which had come over the nation, who
      came to stand as the great exponent of that movement. He
      can be called the father of "candid realism" and yet Dreiser's
      candor never went any further than the individual. He never
      ventured into the field of social candor.

251 _____. "Marxism and American Literature." Books Abroad,
      7 (April, 1933), 131-134.

252 _____. "Proletarianitis." Saturday Review of Literature,
      15 (January 9, 1937), 3-4, 14-15.

253 CAMPBELL, Charles L. "An American Tragedy: or Death in
      the Woods." Modern Fiction Studies, 15 (Summer, 1969),
      251-259.
      Reviews the trend of studies on American Tragedy, but points
      up that no critic has sufficiently examined the significance
      of the novel as a major expression of the American imagina-
      tion. Considered as such it becomes a complex symbolic
      achievement comparable to The Great Gatsby. The symbolism
      of Dreiser's novel is defined largely by its affinities with Tho-
      reau's Walden; by deliberate allusion to that work, Dreiser
      united the nineteenth- and twentieth-century versions of the
      American myth in a comprehensive symbolic vision and pro-
      ceeds from this to a major statement about American life.

254 CAMPBELL, Ernestine B. "Dreiser as a Critic of American Po-
     litical and Economic Life." MA thesis, Atlanta University,
     1948.

255 CAMPBELL, Hilbert H. "Dreiser in New York: A Diary Source."
     Dreiser Newsletter, 13 (Fall, 1982), 1-7.
     Comments on relation between Dreiser and Sherwood Ander-
     son. Their correspondence is extensive; however, personal
     contact between the two men was quite limited. This article
     is based on a diary kept by Mrs. Sherwood Anderson in 1933-
     1934, in which she provides "some interesting accounts and
     impressions of Dreiser." A number of excerpts are quoted.

256 CAMPBELL, Louise. "New Books; Speaking of Dreiser." Phila-
     delphia Evening Public Ledger, July 18, 1934. P. 18.

257 _____, ed. with Commentary. Letters to Louise. Philadel-
     phia: University of Pennsylvania Press, 1959.
     A valuable series of Dreiser letters to Louise Campbell from
     1917 to 1945, with a running commentary by Campbell, his
     typist-editor.

258 CANDELA, Joseph L., Jr. "The Domestic Orientation of Ameri-
     can Novels, 1893-1913." American Literary Realism, 13 (1980),
     1-18.
     Detailed, thorough discussion presented in several divisions:
     1) Alcoholism and the Home, in which Crane's Maggie is dis-
     cussed; 2) Individualism and Society, in which Kate Chopin's
     The Awakening is principally the example; and 3) Woman and
     the City, in which Sister Carrie is discussed. Perhaps more
     than any other novelist of this category, Dreiser saw the
     tinsel attraction and felt the raw terror of the city.

259 CARGILL, Oscar. "The Naturalists," in Intellectual America:
     Ideas on the March. New York: Macmillan, 1941. Reprinted
     1948 and 1959. Pp. 107-128.
     Contains good background on realism and naturalism, French,
     English, etc. Of Dreiser Cargill says: "Over all forerunners
     towers Dreiser. In him rather than in Hardy or Zola is found
     the very quintessence of naturalism. Hardy believed in a Fate
     which might capriciously become good again; Zola worked for
     a better moral order; but Dreiser believes in nothing and works
     for nothing."

260 CARLSON, Constance Hedin. "Heroines in Certain American
     Novels." Ph.D. diss., Brown University, 1971. DA, 32
     (1972), 5175A.
     Dreiser not one of primary novelists discussed: Edith Whar-
     ton, F. Scott Fitzgerald, and John Updike. Other authors
     are discussed in relation to these three, the heroine of one
     held in balance with the heroine of another to enhance or clar-

ify an observation. The space given a novelist does not parallel his traditional position in the hierarchy of the American
novel.

261 CARNEGIE, Dale. "God's Mercy and Three Gin Rickeys Brought
a Titan to American Literature," in Five-Minute Biographies.
New York: Greenberg, 1937. Pp. 235-238.

262 CARRINGER, Robert, and Scott Bennett. "Dreiser to Sandburg:
Three Unpublished Letters." Library Chronicle, 40 (1976),
252-256.

263 CARROLL, Lawrence. "Sister Carrie." Reedy's Mirror, 21
(April 25, 1912), 6-7.

264 CARTER, John "Dreiser Reduced Literature to Its Own Level."
New York Times Book Review, August 9, 1925.

265 CASTLE, John F. "The Making of An American Tragedy."
Ph.D. diss., University of Michigan, 1953. DA, 14 (1954),
388.
The purpose of this study is to lessen some of the existing
uncertainty concerning Dreiser's use of the factual method usually associated with naturalistic fiction. Based largely on
An American Tragedy, the dissertation tries to show the nature and amount of Dreiser's dependence upon the court records and newspaper accounts of the Gillette case in 1906. Also
discussed is the method he used to transform the documents
into a work of art.

266 CAWELTI, John G. "Dream or Rat Race: The Failure of Success," in Apostles of the Self-Made Man. Chicago: University of Chicago Press, 1965. Pp. 227-236.
The novels of Theodore Dreiser show how one writer, who
began as a devotee of success, became increasingly critical
of the dream ... his early novels are marked by a considerable ambivalence about the ideal of success. On one hand,
he was a great admirer of successful men and an ardent ex-
ponent of the success philosophy promulgated by Orison Swett
Marden. On the other, as a reader of Spencer and a convinced, if somewhat naive, social and biological determinist,
Dreiser thought that extreme voluntarism and its emphasis on
morality were nonsense.

267 CERF, Bennett, ed. The Bedside Book of Famous Short Stories. New York: Random House, 1940. Dreiser, p. 1330.
Reprints "The Lost Phoebe" and comments that "with its
ease and grace and beauty, is sifficient evidence that Dreiser
can, and often does, write beautifully."

268 _____. At Random. New York: Random House, 1977. Dreiser, pp. 14, 27, et passim.

269 CESTRE, Charles. "Theodore Dreiser." Revue Anglo-Ameri-
     caine (August, 1926), n.p. In French.

270 _____, and B. Gagnot. "Theodore Dreiser." Anthologie de
     la Littérature Americaine. Paris: Delagrave, 1926. Pp. 143-
     148. French translation of Chapter 26 of The "Genius."

271 CHAMBERLAIN, John "Minority Report of the Novelists," in
     Farewell to Reform: The Rise, Life, and Decay of the Pro-
     gressive Mind in America. 2nd edition New York: John
     Day, 1933. Reprinted Chicago: Quadrangle Books, 1965.
     Pp. 86-118.
        Dreiser was not clever enough to fake, and where he ob-
     viously fails, as in the erotic passages which he is unable to
     expand in terms of inner truth, we can easily assume that he
     is guessing and eliding. He cannot fool us. He could never
     have entered the society of the Dinosaur Age by the methods
     of Ivy Lee; he simply had to tell the truth in terms of raw
     gobs of visual fact because he was too clumsy, too insensitive
     to subtlety to get by with the methods of flattery and cozen-
     ing. Because of this congenital inability to lie, Dreiser, even
     though he may have once desired to create fictional trade goods
     in order to become rich, has turned out figures that are re-
     alistically true to the imagination of emerging plutocratic Amer-
     ica.

272 _____. "Theodore Dreiser Remembered." New Republic, 89
     (December 23, 1936), 236-238. Reprinted in Malcolm Cowley,
     ed., After the Genteel Tradition. New York: W. W. Norton,
     1936. Pp. 21-27. Reprinted in Kazin and Shapiro (1955),
     pp. 127-131.
        "The five minutes spent driving through Warsaw (Indiana)
     suddenly explained to me Dreiser's whole relation to the liter-
     ature of his times and to the movement of ideas that killed the
     rule of the genteel tradition in America. This was not the re-
     sult of an attempt at mystical penetration on my part ... catch-
     ing an idea from a cross-wind merely because my car had
     slowed down to fifteen miles an hour.... Dreiser had not con-
     sciously attacked the sway of the genteel tradition when he
     wrote Sister Carrie. That book had been a natural; it was a
     yea-saying to what he had learned in Warsaw, not a nay-
     saying to the conventional New England schoolmarm. Indeed,
     his own school teachers had been both sympathetic and help-
     ful.

273 CHANDA, Asoke Kumar. "From the Picaro to the Young Man
     from the Provinces: The Theme of Social Climbing in European
     and American Fiction." Ph.D. diss., University of Illinois,
     1977. DA, 39 (1978), 207A.
        Sister Carrie is used as an example of the idealistic Young
     Man from the Provinces in quest of the rich possibilities of

life embodied in the highest civilization, who succeeds and then falls back to his provincial origins, and whose failure is redeemed by his discovery of self.... The literary characteristics of the four "ideal types" are not defined in a vacuum but in their problematical relationships to the attitudes to, and possibilities of, social climbing prevailing during the four respective periods.

274 CHANDLER, Raymond. "Writers in Hollywood." Atlantic Monthly, 88 (December, 1945), 50-54. Reprinted in 119 Years of the Atlantic, edited by Louise Desaulniers, with an Introduction by Robert Manning. New York: Atlantic Monthly Company, 1977. Pp. 408-414.
Does not deal directly with Dreiser, but does depict a shabby worthless atmosphere in which nothing flourishes but phoniness and affectation. This atmosphere attracted Dreiser in his later years and he died in Hollywood where he was buried amid the gloss and tinsel.

275 CHANG, Wang-Rok. "The Bulwark: Dreiser's Last Stand." English Language and Literature, 8 (June, 1960), 36-42. Published in Korea.

276 CHAPMAN, Arnold. "Theodore Dreiser: Triumph of the Trivial," in The Spanish-American Reception of United States Fiction, 1920-1940. Los Angeles: University of California Press, 1966. Pp. 112-117. University of California Publications in Modern Philology, Vol. 77.
Dreiser's foreign reputation came neither quickly nor uniformly. In France he has been little known; there, the first translation was of Twelve Men in 1923, and no other was made during the twenties. An American Tragedy led off with German and Swedish translations in 1927, and Danish the next year; and for the next three or four years he was at the peak of his popularity. One Berlin publisher brought out translations of all Dreiser's major fiction by 1929, with somewhat unexpected consequences in Spanish America. The thirties passed Dreiser by, and he had to wait his turn for the general war-effort quickening even to take a humble place among the hosts of North American authors. Dreiser has evoked little comment from Spanish Americans. Out of his times and no longer a pioneer, he is received coolly, as something the northern neighbors are proud of, but a bit of a museum piece all the same.

277 CHASE, Stuart. "Review of Tragic America: or Mr. Dreiser in a China Shop." New York Herald Tribune Books, January 24, 1932. Pp. 1-2.
Calls the book a "four hundred and thirty-five page indictment of the American system.... The general approach is that of the trust busters of the Nineties. We are bedeviled

by great corporations, growing ever more huge, profitable, greedy and devouring. The corporations in turn are ridden by a handful of caesars, growing ever more wealthy, grasping and domineering.... If he had given us tragic America in terms of the emotion of a great poet, the book would have been a fine and permanent work.... But one cannot fail to salute the spirit behind it; the spirit of one, who, having fame, success, money, is uncompromisingly pledged to the cause of the common man."

278 CHASE, Richard. The American Novel and Its Tradition. New York: Doubleday, 1957. Dreiser, pp. 203-204, et passim.
Many later writers, the two greatest being Dreiser and Faulkner, have shown that naturalism remains a useable technique. Dreiser performed the considerable service of adapting the colorful poetry of Norris to the more exacting tasks imposed upon the social novelist. Faulkner, a more universal genius than Dreiser and less specifically deriving from Norris, allies the naturalistic procedures with certain of the classic motives of fiction. But it is in Norris that we see the glories and perils of naturalism in their sheerest form.

279 CHATTERJEE, Raj. "Genius Bright and Base." Times of India, January 19, 1971. P. 8.

280 CHESTERTON, G. K. "The Skeptic as Critic." Forum, 81 (February, 1929), 65-69.

281 CHEVALIER, H. M. "Farewell to Purity." Modern Monthly, 6 (March, 1934), 11-13.

282 CHURCH, Richard. "The American Balzac." Spectator, 10 (July 25, 1931), 133-134.

283 CHURCHILL, Allen. The Literary Decade. Englewood Cliffs, N.J.: Prentice-Hall, 1971. "Those Dreiserian Waves: Theodore Dreiser ... Horace Liveright," pp. 201-217.
Book deals with the commercial publishing scene of the Twenties, centered in mid-Manhattan. The huge success of An American Tragedy also focused the literary spotlight on publisher Horace Liveright, who had so long coddled Dreiser, advancing him at least twenty-five thousand dollars against hoped-for royalties, while simultaneously displaying remarkable tolerance for the titan's aberrations, procrastinations, and prevarications. In return Dreiser gave his devoted publisher only contempt. Ever since the unhappy experience with Nelson Doubleday in 1900, Dreiser had loathed publishers ... accusing them of betraying his genius. This accumulated resentment had been dumped on Liveright's head.

284 CHURCHILL, Douglas W. "Pointing at Hollywood." New York Times, March 12, 1939. Sec. 11, pp. 5-6.

285   CLARK, Edwin. "Self-Revelations." Yale Review, n.s., 20
       (June, 1931), 856-859.

286   CLAYTON, Charles C. Little Mack: Joseph B. McCullagh of
       the St. Louis Globe-Democrat. Carbondale: Southern Illinois
       University Press, 1969. Dreiser, passim.

287   CLEATON, Irene and Allen. Books and Battles: American
       Literature, 1920-1930. Boston: Houghton Mifflin, 1937.
       "Dreiser Lumbers On," pp. 251-254.
           Dreiser produced most of his best work before the decade
       began, but was considered a major literary figure of the twen-
       ties. In the twenties he produced A Gallery of Women, and
       Dreiser Looks at Russia. An American Tragedy, a massive
       double-decker, was his principal work of the decade, and this,
       too, was barred by certain libraries. This novel exhibits all
       of Dreiser's virtues and defects. He never wrote well for more
       than a few sentences at a time, but in this he sunk to depths
       that are almost inconceivable in a literate man. As he ap-
       proached the end of a life of struggle, disappointment, antag-
       onism and achievement in the face of every handicap, there
       is something majestic about him--lonely, honest, understanding,
       pitying, disillusioned, and yet hopeful as a child is hopeful
       that on some distant tomorrow life will be more nearly toler-
       able for sensitive men.

288   COATES, John Horner. "Sister Carrie." North American Re-
       view, 186 (October, 1907), 288-291. Reprinted in Pizer (1981),
       pp. 166-168.
           Sees Dreiser's novel as a "promise for the future," and
       says that rarely has a new novelist shown so singular a power
       of virile earnestness and serious purpose with unusual faculty
       of keenly analytic characterization and realistic painting of
       pictures. His people are real people; he compels you to know
       them as he knows them, to see the scenes amid which they
       move as he sees them. He shows absolute sincerity, he plays
       you no tricks; he is rigidly uncompromising, he scorns to tam-
       per with the truth as he knows it, refuses any subterfuges
       or weak dallying with what, to him at least, are the crucial
       facts of life.

289   COBLENTZ, Stanton.A. The Literary Revolution. New York:
       Frank Maurice, 1927. Reprinted New York: Johnson Reprint
       Corp., 1969. Dreiser, pp. 151-152.
           Quotes a particularly bad sentence from An American Trag-
       edy, then comments: " ... this sentence was not culled from
       the class exercise of a High School Sophomore; it represents
       the work of one of America's most eminent and most exper-
       ienced literary craftsmen ... the fact that he has done so
       poorly is all that counts." Dreiser seems to demonstrate that
       lucidity of style is "retreating along with truth and appropri-
       ateness to the limbo of the outworn and the neglected."

290 COCHRANE, R. H. "Correcting Mr. Dreiser." New York Times, April 15, 1932. P. 20. Letter to editor.

291 COHEN, Keith. "Eisenstein's Subversive Adaptation," in The Classic American Novel and the Movies, edited by Gerald Peary and Roger Shatzkin. New York: Ungar, 1977. Pp. 239-256.
Refers to An American Tragedy.

292 COHEN, Lester H. "Theodore Dreiser: A Personal Memoir." Discovery, No. 4 (September, 1954), 99-126.

293 _____. " ... And the Sinner--Horace Liveright." Esquire, 54 (December, 1960), 107-108.

294 _____. "Locating One's Self: The Problematics of Dreiser's Social World." Modern Fiction Studies, 23 (Autumn, 1977), 355-368.
Article is based largely on an essay which Dreiser wrote in 1920, "A Counsel to Perfection," in which he is concerned with the location of man in the universe, and "concentrates on a fundamental dualism of human experience." The essay is not so much about freedom and determinism as it is about the notion that one's understanding of the world depends upon one's stance or perspective. Continues with a review of some of Dreiser's principal characters, and concludes with the observation that those who are able to "deal with the mass and to locate themselves and relocate themselves" with respect to it are those who survive.

295 COHN, Ruby. Dialogue in American Drama. Bloomington: Indiana University Press, 1971. Dreiser, pp. 172-176.
Dreiser's interest in drama was not primarily commercial. With earnest industry, Dreiser produced plays as he did poems, short stories, articles, autobiography, along with the novels for which he is remembered. He wrote his plays between 1911 and 1916 during which he published little, but conceived most of his major works. And yet his plays are poor stuff. Dreiser tended toward dreariness or fantasy. He went on to write only one full-length--very full-length--drama. The Hand of the Potter, which Mencken compared to a jelly-fish, for lack of structure.

296 COLLINS, Norman. The Facts of Fiction. London: Victor Gollancz Ltd., 1932.
Written from British perspective. Does not treat Dreiser directly, but makes interesting observations in chapter "The New Battle of the Books," pp. 276-284, with regard to realism and naturalism.

297 COLUM, M. M. "Marxism and Literature." Forum (March, 1934), n.p.

298 COMBS, George Hamilton. "Theodore Dreiser and James Branch
     Cabell, the Unheavenly Twins," in These Amazing Moderns.
     St. Louis: Bethany Publishers, 1933. Pp. 75-85.
         As artists, Dreiser and Cabell commit suicide in their obses-
     sion with sex problems, and in their failures to see anything
     but physical urges in the unfoldings of the dramas of human
     life. We go with them when they assert that man is part ani-
     mal; we bid them good-bye when they declare that man is all
     animal. We agree with them in that we live close by the jungle
     and that at times its hot breath touches every forehead; we
     deny that we live in the jungle, toil in the jungle, and that
     in the jungle we die.

299 COMBS, Richard E. "Theodore Dreiser," in Authors: Critical
     and Biographical References. Metuchen, N.J.: Scarecrow
     Press, 1971. P. 48.
         Brief, but highly selective items.

300 COMMAGER, Henry Steele. "Determinism in Literature," in The
     American Mind. New Haven: Yale University Press, 1950.
     Pp. 108-122.
         In Dreiser determinism is less violent. His emphasis was
     rather on the remorselessness of Fate than on its malevolence,
     on the helplessness of man than on his brutality. His volumes
     assert more of a mechanical and less of an animalistic interpre-
     tation of life--more of Haeckel and Loeb and less of Nietzsche.
     Man is not a wild animal, but a poor fool, and pity is the
     dominant quality. Dreiser was obsessed with power, but not
     so much sheer animal power as the more complicated and less
     amenable power of social and economic machinery. The city
     rather than the wilderness provided his background, and his
     characters pit their strength against their fellow beings.

301 COMMINS, Dorothy. What Is an Editor: Saxe Commins at Work.
     Chicago: University of Chicago Press, 1978. Dreiser, pp.
     20-24, et passim.
         Reminiscences by Commins' widow, letters and memoirs. Was
     one of the editors at Random House from 1933 to 1957, during
     which time Dreiser, and many other noted authors, was under
     contract to the publishing firm. Dreiser did not publish ex-
     tensively with Random House.

302 CONRAD, Lawrence Henry. "Theodore Dreiser." Landmark
     (London), 12 (January, 1930), 29-32.

303 CONROY, Jack. "Theodore Dreiser." Inland: The Magazine
     of the Middle West, No. 40 (Autumn, 1963), 9, 13-15. Re-
     printed in The American Book Collector, 15 (February, 1965),
     11-16.

304 CONSTANTINE, J. Robert. "Debs and Dreiser: A Note."
     Dreiser Newsletter, 5 (Spring, 1974), 1-5.

Article is based on three documents recently released by the Eugene V. Debs Foundation in Terre Haute: an essay by Upton Sinclair in which he describes a large speaking engagement of Debs in Hollywood, attended by Dreiser; and two letters from Dreiser to Debs in which he expresses admiration and praise for the work for labor unions which Debs devoted himself to.

305   COOK, George. "The Rocking Chair in Dreiser's Sister Carrie." Texas A & I University Studies, 1 (1968), 65-66.

306   COSGROVE, William Emmett. "Marriage and the Family in Some Nineteenth-Century American Novels." Ph.D. diss., University of Iowa, 1972. DA, 32 (1972), 6967A.
       The image of the family is found in nearly all literature. The conventional family in fiction is an independent unit consisting of parents and children united by love and controlled by authority, living together in a common home, and offering its members identity, importance, and protection. The traditional restrictions of family often clash with the individual's desire for freedom. The naturalists, including Dreiser, portray families broken down or distorted by environment. For the naturalist the family has become a prison of poverty and hate.

307   COULOMBE, Michael Joseph. "The Trilogy as Form in Modern American Fiction. " Ph.D. diss., Purdue University, 1970. DA, 31 (1970), 1792A.
       Much of the potential in the form, which seems to be highly adaptable to pervasive modern American themes and subject matter, is exploited by several of America's serious twentieth-century writers. Included in this study are Dreiser's "Trilogy of Desire," John Dos Passos' U.S.A, William Carlos Williams' "Stecher Trilogy," Richter's "The Awakening Land," Faulkner's Snopes trilogy. The trilogy provides the scope and breadth for the account of a man's entire lifetime. It provides a large canvas for the treatment of historical forces and significant social or economic changes. Each novel within the trilogy can depict a stage in a man's lifetime or career or isolate a step in a historical process.

308   COURSEN, Herbert R., Jr. "Clyde Griffiths and the American Dream." New Republic, 145 (September 4, 1961), 21-22.
       Questions are raised by this novel, not answered. The questions are ominously relevant today in a society which continues to promote the star-spangled dream with media far more pervasive than those which captured Clyde Griffiths. The tragedy which Dreiser would have us consider is not the murder and subsequent execution; it is that no one learns anything from Clyde's example; nothing is decided. Those in authority are perplexed in the extreme, yet must act out

their parts within a framework which somehow doesn't fit the
exigencies of Clyde's plight.

309 COURTNEY, W. L. Old Saws and Modern Instances. London:
Chapman and Hall, 1919. Dreiser passim.
     Realism means above all else a devotion to the bare and
explicit truth of human life and human character, and the
avoidance of all romantic or poetic devices for obscuring the
main issues.

310 COWIE, Alexander. "The New Heroine's Code for Virtue."
American Scholar, 4 (Spring, 1935), 190-202.
     The heroine of the American novel, like her sister in actual
life, has changed in many ways in the past ten or twelve
years. The accomplishments of women have been promptly reflected in fiction. Yet the establishment of a new code for
virtue remains one of the more notable achievements of the
epoch. Cites Sister Carrie (1900), which tried to show that
a heroine need not be wholly condemned if under stress of
economic pressure she feels impelled to part with her chastity.
At the time of its publication, Dreiser's novel had very little
influence on the formula whereby a heroine kept her chastity
or suffered the wages of sin.

311 _____. The Rise of the American Novel. New York: American Book, 1938. Reprinted 1948. Dreiser passim.
     After reviewing the modern period, he concludes: "All told
there were hundreds of novels (not to be discussed in this
survey) which in one way or another bore the plaint of the
economically depressed. Loosely they may be grouped as of
two main types: the labor novel of city life exemplified by
Dreiser, and the land novel or the sage of the soil...."

312 COWLEY, Malcolm. "Nobel Prize Oration." New Republic, 88
(August 19, 1936), 36-38.

313 _____. "Naturalism's Terrible McTeague." New Republic,
116 (May 5, 1947), 31-33. This article, expanded and revised, was published as "Not Men: A Natural History of
American Naturalism." Kenyon Review, 9 (Summer, 1947),
414-435. Reprinted in Evolutionary Thought in America, edited
by Stow Persons. New Haven: Yale University Press, 1950.
Pp. 300-333, as "Naturalism in American Literature." Also
reprinted in Cowley, A Many-Windowed House (1970), pp. 116-
152, as "A Natural History of American Naturalism."
     Includes much that is not Dreiser. Reviews the entire Na-
turalistic movement from its origins in Europe to America in
the works of Crane and Norris. Concludes that Naturalists
"as a group are men of defective hearing, but almost all have
keen eyes for new materials," as did Dreiser who said of Chicago: "It is given to some cities, as to some lands, to suggest romance, and to me Chicago did that hourly...."

314 _____. "Sister Carrie's Brother." New Republic, 116 (May
      26, 1947), 23-25. Reprinted in Kazin and Shapiro (1955),
      pp. 171-181, combined with "The Slow Triumph of Sister Car-
      rie," as "Sister Carrie: Her Fall and Rise." Also reprinted
      in Lydenberg (1971), pp. 52-62; and in Cowley, A Many-
      Windowed House (1970), pp. 153-165, as "Sister Carrie's
      Brother."
         Contains biographical detail and some critical comment. Of
      his abilities to write, Cowley says: "Dreiser could describe
      anything, from the stupid to the sublime, because in a sense
      he could describe nothing; he never learned to look for the
      exact phrase.... There are moments when Dreiser's awkward-
      ness in handling words contributes to the force of his novels,
      since he seems to be groping in them for something on a
      deeper livel than language; there are crises when he stutters
      in trite phrases that are like incoherent cries."

315 _____. "The Slow Triumph of Sister Carrie." New Republic,
      116 (June 23, 1947), 24-27. Reprinted in The American Novel:
      Criticism and Background Readings, edited by Christof Wege-
      lin. New York: Free Press, 1972. Pp. 310-314. Also re-
      printed in Kazin and Shapiro (1955), pp. 171-181 as part of
      "Sister Carrie: Her Fall and Rise." Also reprinted in Lyden-
      berg (1971) and in Cowley (1970).
         History of the novel, Sister Carrie, when and how it was
      written. Encompasses the story of its publication, failure,
      and later success. Dreiser wrote his second novel, Jennie
      Gerhardt, in 1911 and Carrie was re-issued. By then the
      standards of the American public had changed, and by 1920
      Dreiser and the younger novelists had "ceased to be rebels;
      instead they were the dominant faction. It was a long and
      finally a triumphant chapter in the history of American letters
      that began with the lost battle over Sister Carrie."

316 _____. "The Last Flight from Main Street." New York Times
      Book Review, March 25, 1951. P. 1. Reprinted in Highlights
      of Modern Literature, edited by Francis Brown. New York:
      New American Library, 1954. Also reprinted in Sinclair Lewis:
      A Collection of Critical Essays, edited by Mark Schorer. Engle-
      wood Cliffs, N.J.: Prentice-Hall, 1962. Pp. 143-146.
         Even Dreiser, who never learned to write better than he did
      in his first book, and whose later novels, except An Ameri-
      can Tragedy, were all of them massive disappointments--even
      the Old Unteachable showed a sort of growth at the end and
      wrote the last chapter of his last novel, The Bulwark, on what
      was for him a completely new emotional level. He made his
      peace with the fathers and rounded out his story. On the
      other hand, Sherwood Anderson--and after him Thomas Wolfe--
      stood frantically still. They burst on our vision and amazed
      us, but then they simply kept bursting like Roman candles,
      with no surprises after the first pink star.

317 _____. The Literary Situation. New York: Viking, 1954.
    "Naturalism: No Teacup Tragedies," pp. 74-95.
    Reviews briefly the naturalistic philosophy in terms of early
    century writers, and then comments in greater length on Amer-
    ican writers since the 1930's. Many writers, including Drei-
    ser, tried to find epical, modern, distinctly American sub-
    jects--no teacup tragedies here--and most of them planned
    trilogies or whole interrelated series of novels that would be
    realistic in treatment but would be based on an essentially
    romantic emotion.

318 _____. A Many-Windowed House: Collected Essays on Amer-
    can Writers and American Writing, edited with an Introduction
    by Henry Dan Piper. Carbondale: Southern Illinois Univer-
    sity Press, 1970. Reprints "A Natural History of American
    Naturalism," pp. 116-152; and "Sister Carrie's Brother," two
    articles combined, pp. 153-165.

319 _____. "An Evening at Theodore Dreiser's." Michigan Quar-
    terly Review, 18 (Summer, 1979), 491-494. Reprinted in Cow-
    ley, The Dream of Golden Mountains: Remembering the 1930's.
    New York: Viking, 1980. Pp. 51-62.
    The "evening" was the same one recalled by Louis Adamic
    in his book My America (1938) with many of the same details.
    However, Cowley continues with other details following the
    meeting, saying: "Many of the writers present agreed with
    Dreiser that it was their duty to do something about the de-
    pression, since the politicians and financiers had done nothing
    whatever." At the time the Communist Party was all too eager
    to take advantage and to make use of their enthusiasm. A
    new organization took shape called the National Committee for
    the Defense of Political Prisoners. The committee consisted
    mostly of literary men, with Dreiser as its first chairman and
    Lincoln Steffens its treasurer.

320 _____, ed. After the Genteel Tradition: American Literature
    Since 1910. New York: W. W. Norton, 1936. Reprinted New
    York: Peter Smith, 1959. "Theodore Dreiser Remembered,"
    by John Chamberlain, pp. 21-27.

321 CRAWFORD, Bruce. "Theodore Dreiser: Letter-Writing Citi-
    zen." South Atlantic Quarterly, 53 (April, 1954), 231-237.
    Article is a review of Crawford's correspondence with Drei-
    ser. At the outset he says: "In his latter years Theodore
    Dreiser cultivated a fairly regular correspondence with a proud
    circle of fellow citizens; I happened to be one of them. Most
    of the correspondence, now being collected, shows the pas-
    sionate interest he took in a wide variety of public matters.
    He wrote heatedly about industrial despotism, mis-treatment
    of the little man, democracy, political gangsterism, technoc-
    racy, Soviet Russia, Britain's titled snobs, World War II,

and the Pullman Company's policy of fostering a superior class, based on money. The author of <u>An American Tragedy</u> toward the end was an indignant, letter-writing citizen, more than the brooding novelist."

322 CRIMMINGS, Constance Deave. "Some Women in Dreiser's Life and Their Portraits in His Novels." MA Thesis, North Texas State University, 1974.

323 CROY, Homer. <u>Country Cured</u>. New York: Harper, 1943. Dreiser, pp. 142-145.

Remembers when he worked for Dreiser as a "cub" during the time Dreiser was editor of three Butterick women's magazines. Recalls the incident of a story in which a woman smokes a cigarette at the end: Dreiser refused to edit it out. Croy says: "The matter of the cigarette made an impression on me, and what Dreiser said made an impression, and I decided I would try to meet life squarely and to deal, as much as I could, with its fundamentals."

324 CRUNCHER, Jerry. "Epitaphs for Living Lions." <u>Forum</u>, 80 (July, 1928), 78-81.

325 CUNLIFFE, Marcus. "Realism in American Prose: From Howells to Dreiser." <u>The Literature of the United States</u>. Baltimore: Penguin, 1954. Pp. 185-212.

There is considerable disagreement about Dreiser's stature as a novelist. Perhaps we can agree that Dreiser had a particular significance for Americans, whether or not they like him. Only Americans fully share his intimation that it is all, so to speak, in the family. He gives them a relief from good manners. Dreiser knows the pattern: it is <u>there</u>, in his writing, complex, a maze of streets, buildings, fields, rivers, etc. ... things understood. Dreiser's is the truth of feeling, and of incident. His novels are often as formless as life itself, but they are not lifeless.

326 _____, ed. <u>American Literature since 1900</u>. London: Barrie and Jenkins, 1975. "The American 'Risorgimento': The Coming of the New Arts," by Malcolm Bradbury and David Corker, pp. 17-47.

Allusion is to the period of or the movement for the liberation and political unification of Italy, beginning about 1750 and lasting until 1870.

327 CURRY, Martha Mulroy. "The 'Writer's Book' by Sherwood Anderson: A Critical Edition." Ph.D. diss., Loyola University (Chicago), 1972. <u>DA</u>, 32 (1972), 6968A.

An introduction describes the editorial procedures, comments on the condition of the manuscript, and analyzes the "Writers' Book" in the light of Anderson's biography, his other works, and his critical theories. Especially interesting are Anderson's views and opinions on Theodore Dreiser's American Tragedy and Sister Carrie and on Sinclair Lewis' Main Street.

328 _____. The "Writer's Book" by Sherwood Anderson: A Critical Edition. Metuchen, N.J.: Scarecrow Press, 1975.
Based on dissertation item above.

329 CURTI, Merle Eugene. The Growth of American Thought. New York: Harpers, 1943 and 1951. Dreiser, pp. 555-560.
The impact of science and above all of the new biology of Darwin and his disciples profoundly altered ideas of mind and society in the last of the nineteenth century. It would be too much to say that the basic conceptions of life were transformed by the influence of natural science; the vast intellectual shifts were at first of course merely suggested by pioneer scholars. Theodore Dreiser in An American Tragedy attributed the disintegration of human character to a competitive, ruthless, materialistic urban environment.

330 DAHLBERG, Edward. Alms for Oblivion. Minnesota: University of Minnesota Press, 1964. "My Friends Stieglitz, Anderson, and Dreiser," pp. 3-16.
Dreiser is the greatest dollar genius of the American novel. The best interpretation of any of his books is the Mount Kisco mansion he had, which resembled a Log Cabin syrup can. He had a luxurious writing table made out of an airplane wing, and in his heyday he went to parties with a pair of autocratic Russian hounds. Everybody in a Dreiser novel wants dollars. Sister Carrie sacrifices Hurstwood for money ... and so do all other characters in the novels.

331 _____. "Dahlberg on Dreiser, Anderson, and Dahlberg." New York Times Book Review, January 31, 1971. Pp. 2, 30-31.
Based on the premise than an author needs an older man of letters to guide him and that Dreiser and Anderson were his teachers. Dahlberg recounts what he learned from Dreiser during his meetings with the novelist.

332 DAILLY, C. "Jennie: A Daughter of Nature." Annales de l'Université d'Abidjan, 5 (1972), 145-150.
Also published in Spanish, South America.

333 DANA, Harry. "Russia Looks at Dreiser." New Masses, 3 (February, 1929), 18-20.

334 DANCE, Daryl. "Sentimentalism in Dreiser's Heroines: Carrie and Jennie." College Language Association Journal, 14 (December, 1970), 127-142.

Dreiser is usually hailed as a pioneer of American realism
who freed American literature from Victorian restraints, from
nineteenth-century idealism and optimism, and from the ever-
present moralizing of domestic sentimentalism. It is interesting to note that Dreiser is a mixture of both the new realism
and naturalism and the old sentimentalism that had dominated
American literature from its inception. In Carrie and Jennie
we have two heroines whom Dreiser places within a sentimental
framework, but who are essentially modern, realistic, American heroines, whose fall is the result of the society in which
they live.

335 DARROW, Clarence. "Touching a Terrible Tragedy." New York
     Evening Post Literary Review, January 16, 1926. Pp. 1-2.
     Reprinted in Salzman (1971), pp. 5-9.
     "I finished Theodore Dreiser's latest story just before going
     to bed last night. The haunted face of a helpless boy, strapped
     to an iron chair at Sing Sing, and the wan form of a dead
     girl floating on a lonely black lake surrounded by tall pine
     trees in Northern New York were still haunting me when I
     awoke. I hardly can think of the 800 pages of An American
     Tragedy as a book. It does not leave the impression that
     goes with reading a story; the feeling is rather that of a
     series of terrible physical impacts that have relentlessly shocked
     every sensitive nerve in the body."

336 DASH, Irene. "The Literature of Birth and Abortion." Re-
     gionalism and the Female Imagination, 3 (1977), 8-13.
     Includes An American Tragedy.

337 DAVIDSON, Cathy N. and Arnold E. "Carrie's Sisters: The
     Popular Prototypes for Dreiser's Heroine." Modern Fiction
     Studies, 23 (Fall, 1977), 395-407.
     Sister Carrie mirrors the conventional fiction of its time,
     for Theodore Dreiser employed well-established plot devices
     to examine the same manners and mores prescribed by his
     now forgotten contemporaries. But the moral image reflected
     in various widely read turn-of-the century novels is, in Drei-
     ser's work, refracted and distorted, inverted and reversed.
     At times, Sister Carrie even seems to parody the formulae im-
     plicit in late nineteenth-century popular literature. Dreiser
     will tantalize the reader with an almost archetypal situation
     only to turn the scene to a purpose that would have appalled
     earlier advocates of unassailable virginity and transcendent
     purity.

338 DAVIS, David Brion. "A Reappraisal of Early Naturalism in
     America." Unpublished paper, Harvard University, 1953.
     See article following.

339 _____. "Dreiser and Naturalism Revisited," in Kazin and

Shapiro (1955), pp. 225-236.   Based on the paper listed
above.
   Dreiser was unquestionably the central figure of the early
naturalistic movement in America; and while his philosophical
speculations were often vague, his work exemplified the stages
in mood which began in awe and wonder and ended in a compassionate acceptance of the forces of nature. But since Dreiser lacked formal training and artistic discipline, his emotions
often shot ahead of his ability to express himself. When he
identified himself too closely with a character trapped by circumstance, he tended to rely on the most adolescent cliches
and forced speculations. This has provoked and tired many
sensitive readers and has led them to overlook some of Dreiser's basic assumptions. It is too easy to ignore what he actually wrote and classify him as a Zola-type materialist who
occasionally showed inconsistent emotional lapses of pity and
sympathy.

340   DAVIS, Elmer. "The Red Peril."   Saturday Review of Litera-
      ture, 8 (April 16, 1932), 661-662.
         Comments on Dreiser's Tragic America. Remarks that he
      does not know "how sound Dreiser's communism may be in the
      eye of the orthodox, but it has evidently bitten deeply enough
      into him to rid him of the taint of bourgeois virtues." He
      used to be a good newspaperman, but this book is full of mis-
      statements. In his novels he has analyzed character and moti-
      vated behavior as well as any man now writing, but his treat-
      ment of the character and motives of real people in Tragic
      America is often simply childish. Dreiser the artist knew a
      great deal about human beings; Dreiser the convert and mis-
      sionary casts away the "filthy rags of profane knowledge, and
      glories in the all-sufficient garment of faith."

341   DAVIS, Joe. "The Mind of Theodore Dreiser: A Study in De-
      velopment." Ph.D. diss., Emory University, 1960. DA, 22
      (1961), 255-256.
         The dominant characteristic of the life and works of Dreiser
      was always a search for value, especially those moral and
      ethical values which usually emanate from strong religious be-
      liefs. Dreiser was always a humanitarian and a moralist. His
      basic sympathies were with those hapless individuals whose
      resources were pitifully inadequate for the demands of life.

342   DAVIS, Nancy Hightower. "The Women in Theodore Dreiser's
      Novels." Ph.D. diss., Northwestern University, 1969. DA,
      30 (1970), 3003A.
         Two of the major influences upon Dreiser's depiction of his
      heroines were his concern with the condition and fate of the
      individual in America's exploitive capitalistic society and his
      revulsion against what he considered the irrationality of con-
      ventional morality. The first chapter of this dissertation is

devoted to the women in Dreiser's life who help to account
for his outlook, and in the next six chapters Dreiser's fictional heroines are analyzed.

343   DEAL, Borden. The Tobacco Men, with Introduction by Hy
      Kraft. New York: Holt, Rinehart, and Winston, 1965.
      See Kraft (1965).

344   DEBOUZY Marianne. "Theodore Dreiser." Les Langues Mo-
      dernes, 60 (March-April, 1966), 157-162.

345   DEEGAN, Dorothy Yost. The Stereotype of the Single Woman
      in American Novels. New York: Columbia University Press,
      Dreiser, pp. 49-56.
      Though more than half a century intervenes between Hep-
      zibah Pyncheon and Jennie Gerhardt, the theme of economic
      necessity among women still persists. Jennie was driven by
      poverty, and had been scarcely more trained to earn her liv-
      ing than the older woman. Hepzibah would have been horri-
      fied at Jennie's solution of her problem; but Jennie would like-
      wise have looked with disapproval upon Hepzibah's gross in-
      efficiency in the kitchen and her bigoted sense of her own im-
      portance. Vocationally, both women were domestics; both lives
      were hemmed in by the daily round of living, but Jennie,
      through a combination of personal endowment and circumstance
      --Fate, Dreiser would call it--was able to use her domestic
      ability as an asset in her extra-legal relationships.

346   DE FABREQUES, Jean, ed. with Introduction. Jenny Gerhardt.
      Paris: Catalogne, 1933. Pp. v-xii. In French.

347   DE JOVINE, F. Anthony. The Young Hero in American Fiction.
      New York: Appleton, 1971. Discusses An American Tragedy,
      pp. 33-35, et passim.
      Clyde Griffiths of An American Tragedy is another example
      of an other-directed person in an agonized search for his
      identity. There is little in him that can be admired; at best
      he must be pitied. He lies, fakes, and pretends in an effort
      to acquire comfort, security, and social status. He even plans
      to murder a helpless girl ... and although the circumstances
      which lead up to the culmination of the act are clouded with
      uncertainty as to his actual guilt, he is guilty by virtue of
      his intentions and deliberations. Under the influence of the
      young minister while he is on death row, Clyde gives evidence
      of some qualities of character that could lead to his rehabilita-
      tion, but societal mores are stacked too heavily against him,
      and he is finally executed.

348   DEKLE, Bernard. "Theodore Dreiser: A Tortured Life," in
      Profiles of Modern American Authors. Rutland, Vt.: Tuttle,
      1969. Pp. 38-43.

No other author of his stature has survived so much hostile
criticism or displayed so much paradoxical thinking. Yet despite his inconsistencies and blunders, Dreiser's place in modern American literature seems firmly established. Whether
Dreiser was actually a great artist has been much debated,
but his historical importance is undeniable. He looked on life
as none of his predecessors had done, and he was not afraid
to tell what he saw. Dreiser led a tortured life, but he made
something out of his torments.

349 DELL, Floyd. "A Great Novel." Chicago Evening Post Literary
Review, November 3, 1911. P. 1-2. Review of Jennie Gerhardt.
Here is a story, a rather unusual story, told in an extra-
ordinarily lucid and sympathetic manner. There are no sur-
prises, no shocks, no bits of splendid writing--just the tale
of a woman from girlhood to middle age, in her relations with
her mother, her father, her lovers, her child. Each one lives.
We know them intimately. The story moves on, without any
straining for effects, without a sign of effort. There is page
after page of utterly simple narrative.

350 _____. "Theodore Dreiser's Chicago." Chicago Evening Post,
Friday Literary Review, February 23, 1912. P. 1.

351 _____. "Chicago in Fiction," Parts I and II. Bookman, 38
(November, 1913), 270-277; and 38 (December, 1913), 375-
379.

352 _____. "Mr. Dreiser and the Dodo." Masses, 5 (February,
1914), 17. Comments on A Traveler at Forty.
Mr. Dreiser is impressive in all his books, and not least of
all in his new one. It is an account of a trip through Europe,
and it shows, even more clearly than his novels, the philosophy of--what shall I call it? ... It is a philosophy which has
been apparent in all his writings. In his novels he has given
a broad and impartial account of life as he has seen it lived.
He has described the just and the unjust with a calm and even
balance. He has looked on our dreams and our lusts, as might
some cynical and compassionate god: and we have been prop-
erly awed.

353 _____. "The 'Genius' and Mr. Dreiser." New Review, 3
(December 15, 1915), 362-363.
Nothing would satisfy his pride but he must tell it all, from
beginning to end, not neglecting a single economic fact nor a
single scrap of background, nor a single incident, nor a single
thought of any of his characters which would serve to illuminate his theme or contribute to its solid reality. Dreiser tried
to put in everything and make it part and parcel of a gigantic
and moving story, which should break the heart with pity and
terror.

354 _____. "Talks with Life Authors." Masses, 8 (August, 1916),
        36.

355 _____. "American Fiction." Liberator, 2 (September, 1919),
        46-47.

356 _____. Homecoming: An Autobiography. New York: Farrar
      and Rinehart, 1933. Reprinted Port Washington, N.Y.: Ken-
      nikat Press, 1969. Dreiser, pp. 268-270.
      "Theodore Dreiser, who had been living uptown, moved
      down into the Village, and I saw a good deal of him--a large,
      cumbrous, awkward, thoughtful, friendly person, with no
      small talk except a few favorite joshing sillinesses, but with a
      great zest for serious conversation. A Teutonic sentimental-
      ist at heart, I thought him.... And equally at heart, a brave
      lover of the truth, and a rugged, stubborn and gallant fighter
      for it. I respected him deeply, and laughed at him--a combin-
      ation which he found it hard to understand; I admired the
      things he could do in writing which nobody else could do--
      the simple and poignant truths of life; and I thought his phil-
      osophic notions bosh and his historical ideas mere uneducated
      ignorance."

357 DEMARKOWSKI, Carl John. "Theodore Dreiser's Novels: Ca-
      veats of a Maturing Transcendentalism." Ph.D. diss., Toledo
      University, 1981. DA, 41 (1981), 4712A.
      Dreiser has been called a mechanist, a pessimist, a deter-
      minist, the antithesis of a transcendentalist. Such criticism
      is based largely on Dreiser's first six novels with the last
      two regarded as mystical works written by a senile Dreiser.
      This dissertation proposes, however, that the last two novels
      are the outgrowth of a transcendental philosophy that was
      merely less evident in the first six novels.

358 DE MILLE, George E. "American Criticism Today." Sewanee
      Review, 35 (July, 1927), 355-358.

359 _____. Literary Criticism in America. New York: Harcourt,
      1931. Reprinted New York: Russell and Russell, 1967. Drei-
      ser in "Sherman," pp. 245-276.
      The great exponent of naturalism in modern literature Sher-
      man found to be Dreiser; Dreiser, therefore, was Sherman's
      particular aversion, in whom he could see no literary excel-
      lence whatever. He is "the vulgarest voice yet heard in Amer-
      ican literature." He "colors the news." His method is the
      "certification of the unreal by the irrelevant."

360 DE MUTH, James David. "Small Town Chicago: The Comic Per-
      spective of Finley Peter Dunne, George Ade, and Ring Lardner
      (1890-1920)," Ph.D. diss., University of Minnesota, 1974.
      DA, 36 (1975), 3711A.

American humorists of the late nineteenth-century were confronted by a society which differed from the communities which
they had traditionally portrayed and endorsed. For such
novelists as Henry Blake Fuller, Frank Norris, and Theodore
Dreiser, Chicago was a compelling symbol of social evil; alienation, corruption and loss are the essential themes of their
Chicago novels. Dissertation argues that the popular art of
Dunne, Ade, and Lardner could not be sustained in the urban
setting.

361 DENNY, Margaret, and William H. Gilman, eds. The American
    Writer and the European Tradition. Minneapolis: University
    of Minnesota Press, 1950. "American Naturalism: Reflections
    from Another Era," by Alfred Kazin, pp. 121-131.
    See Kazin (1950).

362 DESAI, Rupin. "Delusion and Reality in Sister Carrie." PMLA,
    87 (May, 1972), 309-310.
       Article is a response to Hugh Witemeyer (PMLA, March,
    1971). Objects to the premise that "love and the theater both
    beckon toward fairyland" for Carrie. This may be true of the
    Chicago episodes, but once Carrie and Hurstwood go to New
    York, she "becomes in many ways wiser, more practical, and
    levelheaded." In New York, the theater becomes for Carrie
    the one way to avoid starvation. She may still be fascinated
    with the bright lights and glitter, but she is primarily moti-
    vated by the need to survive.

363 DEW, Marjorie. "Realistic Innocence: Cady's Footnote to a
    Definition of American Literary Realism." American Literary
    Realism, 5 (Fall, 1972), 487-489.
       Bases article on Edwin H. Cady's definition, found in The
    Light of Common Day, in which he says that one essential of
    realism is an "active disbelief in the health or safety of ro-
    mantic individualism," or a belief in solidarity and social vi-
    sion. This may have been true of the so-called "genteel"
    realists, but fails to include such obvious realists as Crane,
    Norris, and especially Dreiser, whose characters always go
    against the "healthy and safe" mores of society.

364 DICKSON, Lovat. "The American Novel in England." Publish-
    ers' Weekly, 134 (October 29, 1938), 1586-1590.

365 DICKSTEIN, Felice Witztum. "The Role of the City in the Works
    of Theodore Dreiser, Thomas Wolfe, James T. Farrell, and
    Saul Bellow." Ph.D. diss., City University of New York,
    1973. DA, 33 (1973), 6350A-6351A.
       This dissertation focuses on the works of four novelists in
    an effort to determine how these authors use the city as a
    tool in the artistic creation of their novels. Begins with Drei-
    ser, who is a seminal figure in the tradition of the urban novel.

Many of the themes and problems which recur in later city
novels find early expression in Dreiser's novels, and his wide-
ranging treatment of various aspects of urban life opened the
door for later writers. Dreiser uses the city in different ways
in each of his novels in relation to character, plot, and thematic development.

366 DIGBY, Kenelm. "The Literary Lobby." New York Evening
Post Literary Review, April 3, 1926, p. 12; April 10, 1926,
p. 20; and April 24, 1926, p. 12.

367 DINAMOV (also DYNAMOV), Sergei. "Theodore Dreiser Is Coming Our Way." Literature of the World Revolution (Moscow),
No. 5 (1931), 126-132.

368 _____. "Theodore Dreiser Continues the Struggle." International Literature, Nos. 2 and 3 (1932), 112-115.

369 DONALDSON, Norman and Betty. How Did They Die? New
York: St. Martin's Press, 1980. Dreiser, pp. 101-102.

370 DONALDSON, Scott, and Ann Massa. American Literature:
Nineteenth and Early Twentieth Centuries. New York: Barnes
and Noble, 1978. Dreiser, pp. 74-80.

371 DOODY, Terrence. Confession and Community in the Novel.
Baton Rouge: Louisiana State University Press, 1980. Pp.
101-132.
    Draws a comparison between Clyde of An American Tragedy
and Jay Gatsby of The Great Gatsby, both published in 1925,
an era of official national optimism. Both novels rise from the
same great clichés to tell the story of a young man who changes
his name as he leaves home and heads East, not West, to escape his history and fashion a destiny for himself. Clyde and
Gatsby are both naive, self-centered, and not very sensitive
young men on the make in a society where "making it" is an
idiom of both sex and commerce. However, crime does not
pay in either novel, and both young men die proving that the
American dream does not always come true.

372 DOS PASSOS, John. "Harlan: Working Under the Gun." New
Republic, 69 (December 2, 1931), 62-67.
    Article is an analysis of the coal mining industry in Harlan
County in eastern Kentucky, which was "brought into the
spotlight this summer by the violence with which the Coal
Operators' Association" carried on its attack against the owner
of the mines. This matter relates to Dreiser in that he attempted to organize a Writers Committee to investigate the conditions of this and other mining communities and to add their
voices to the protest of the exploited workers in the coal mines.

373 _____. The Theme Is Freedom. New York: Dodd, Mead,
     1956. Dreiser, pp. 73-88.
          Discusses "The Revolution of 1932," following the stockmar-
     ket collapse of 1929 and the partial breakdown of the free en-
     terprise system of which it was a symptom. This provided
     the Marxists with a great deal of ammunition. Discusses Drei-
     ser's involvment with the Communist Party that was trying to
     organize its own trade unions. "Equity" was the word Dreiser
     used continually. He wanted equity. Like so many of his
     words it was a hard one to corner. It led him, strangely,
     into a communist camp in later years. This equity meant tak-
     ing away everything the rich had.

374 DOUGLAS, George H. "Dreiser's Enduring Genius." Nation,
     212 (June 28, 1971), 826-828.
          Is a tribute to Dreiser on the 100th anniversary of his birth,
     and thinks the event will be little noted. For the most part
     Dreiser has become associated with the 1920's, but this is a
     mistake. Dreiser survives because we still live in the world
     he so richly revealed. Perhaps the cruel edge of Dreiser's
     world has been blunted somewhat, perhaps the rawest mani-
     festations of the old capitalist order have passed away, but
     the world he gave us is still very much our own, and to get
     at the heart of it we can scarcely do better than return to
     his work.

375 _____. "Ludwig Lewisohn on Theodore Dreiser." Dreiser
     Newsletter, 4 (Fall, 1973), 1-6.
          Reviews the Lewisohn criticism of 1932, which "seems to be
     the bedrock of modern thinking about Dreiser." Lewisohn
     seems to be behind the tradition which leads to most of the
     later Dreiser critics such as Kazin, Elias, Matthiessen, and
     Moers--if not in actual paternity, at least in temporal priority.
     What came later was largely an expansion of the ideas which
     originally appeared in nuclear form in Expression in America.

376 DOWELL, Richard Walker. "Three Stages of Dreiser's Deter-
     minism." MA thesis, University of Colorado, 1960.

377 _____. "Theodore Dreiser and Success: A Shifting Alle-
     giance." Ph.D. diss., Indiana University, 1967. DA, 28
     (1968), 4595A-4596A.
          Throughout his career Dreiser shifted between such positions
     as Social Darwinism and Communism. Just as frequently his
     personal fortunes shifted. Dissertation argues that there is
     a high correlation between Dreiser's personal success and his
     philosophical positions. Enjoying prosperity, he espoused
     philosophies of strength; experiencing defeat, he identified
     with the underdog and pled his cause. When shifts occurred
     during the composition of a novel, the result was philosophical
     and artistic inconsistency.

378 _____. "Sister Carrie: An Attack on the Gospel of Wealth."
Indiana English Journal, 3 (Spring, 1969), 3-10.

379 _____. " 'On the Banks of the Wabash': A Musical Whodunit."
Indiana Magazine of History, 6 (June, 1970), 95-109.
Reviews various inconsistencies surrounding the composition
of this song, and concludes that Paul Dresser probably had
more to do with the writing than did Theodore Dreiser.

380 _____. "Dreiser Holdings at the Lilly Library." Dreiser
Newsletter, 1 (Spring, 1970), 13-15.

381 _____. "Checklist: Dreiser Studies in 1969." Dreiser Newsletter, 1 (Fall, 1970), 14-18. Subsequent Checklists in each
Fall issue, principally by Frederic E. Rusch.

382 _____. " 'You Will Not Like Me, I'm Sure': Dreiser to Miss
Emma Rector, November 28, 1893 to April 4, 1894." American
Literary Realism, 3 (Summer, 1970), 259-270.
Letters of the same period to Miss Sara Osborne White, who
became Dreiser's first wife, are not accessible to scholars;
however, these letters to Miss Rector may very well be similar
and therefore offer an insight to Dreiser's early romantic period. Article includes text of five letters.

383 _____. "Dreiser's Contribution to 'On the Banks of the Wabash': A Fiction Writer's Fiction!" Indiana English Journal,
6 (Fall, 1971), 7-13.

384 _____. "Medical Diary Reveals First Dreiser Visit to the University of Pennsylvania." Library Chronicle (University of
Pennsylvania), 38 (Winter, 1972), 92-96.

385 _____. "Dreiser's Address to the Future." Dreiser Newsletter, 4 (Fall, 1973), 10-11.
Includes text of 1936 Dreiser statement placed in a time cap-
sule, to be opened in 2936 A. D. This venture, sponsored
by Max Schuster, of Simon and Schuster, was terminated in
1968 when Schuster opened the box and revealed its contents.
The statement by Dreiser reveals his generally pessimistic
tone toward the future: "Considering the vast and changing
stream of life, what could be important? My answer is no thing."

386 _____. "Ask Mr. Markle?" Dreiser Newsletter, 8 (Spring,
1977), 9-14.
Refers to Augustus Robert Markle, a neighbor of the Dreiser
family for at least a year of their residence in Terre Haute,
Indiana. Has earlier been held to be a real authority on early
Dreiserana, but now appears to be largely based on a personal dislike and antipathy for Dreiser. Markle papers are
on file at the Fairbanks Memorial Library, Terre Haute, Indiana.

387 _____. "Dreiser and Kathleen Mavourneen." Dreiser Newsletter, 8 (Fall, 1977), 2-4.
     Includes complete copy of the letter-poem which Dreiser
wrote in 1939. In 1965 W. A. Swanberg preserved the lady's
anonymity by calling her "Estelle Manning." Has now been
established that the poem was written to Elizabeth Kearney
Gore, sister of Patrick Kearney who adapted An American
Tragedy for the stage in 1926. Elizabeth and Dreiser were
long-term friends and were together for the last time four
days before his death in 1945.

388 _____. "Sister Carrie Restored." Dreiser Newsletter, 12
(Spring, 1981), 1-8.
     Reviews changes that were made in the 1900 published text
and in the original manuscript which forms the basis for the
Pennsylvania edition of Sister Carrie. Differences consist
mostly of deletions, or editings, which have been returned to
the published novel. In the final analysis, the Pennsylvania
edition is certainly a different Sister Carrie. Whether or not
it is a better novel will depend on the preferences of the individual. Some readers may still prefer the shorter version,
arguing that Dreiser's writing always needed editing, and that
nothing valuable was lost in the process.

389 _____. "Critical Essays on Theodore Dreiser." Dreiser Newsletter, 12 (Spring, 1981), 18-20.
     Review-essay of Donald Pizer's collection, Critical Essays
on Theodore Dreiser (1981). Comments on the principles of
selection, and says, "Pizer has produced a volume of thirty-
seven significant essays which are placed in a meaningful
historical context and bring Dreiser up to date. Critical Essays will supersede The Stature of Theodore Dreiser (1955)
as a mainstay of Dreiser scholarship."

390 _____. "Dreiser's Debt to His Contemporaries." Dreiser
Newsletter, 13 (Spring, 1982), 1-9.
     Dreiser was never receptive to the idea that his work had
been influenced by any other author, and uniformly discour-
aged speculation about possible literary influence. This article
does not challenge his view, but examines certain passages in
Dreiser's American Diaries, 1902-1926, in which he clearly records his dependence on the writings of others during a very
traumatic period of his life and occasionally records his immediate reaction to those works. He sought out the current
literature to occupy him during a time of pain and frustration
and to prepare him for the literary career he hoped someday
to resume.

391 _____. "Dreiser's Diaries." Dreiser Newsletter, 13 (Spring,
1982), 17-20.
     Review article on American Diaries, 1902-1926, edited by

Thomas Riggio et al. (1982). Says the editors are to be commended. Riggio has provided an informative introduction which focuses on the intellectual, psychological and sexual needs reflected in the diaries and demonstrates how these same needs ultimately inspired and/or shaped Dreiser's other literary projects. The editors made the decision to leave all misspellings and grammatical errors uncorrected. Says in conclusion, "the product of this decision is a quite readable text that reflects Dreiser's casual approach to the diaries and many of his literary idiosyncrasies."

392 _____. "Will the Real Mike Burke Stand Up, Please!" Dreiser Newsletter, 14 (Spring, 1983), 1-9.
Refers to Mike Burke, a masonry foreman for the railroad for which Dreiser worked following his six-week hospitalization for the nervous breakdown which he suffered in the years after 1900 publication of Sister Carrie. The character appeared in numerous Dreiser compositions, including Twelve Men (1919), as "The Mighty Rourke."

393 _____. "Dreiser's Courtship Letters: Portents of a Doomed Marriage." Dreiser Newsletter, 15 (Spring, 1984), 14-20.
Based on an examination of the courtship letters which are contained in a collection of Dreiserana at the Lilly Library of Indiana University. Except for the work by Dr. Vera Dreiser, My Uncle Theodore (1976), this collection has been closed to research until 1983. The sixty-nine letters have been heavily edited, with whole pages removed and lines blacked out, but what remains is a "rich biographical source for the study of Dreiser's early years in New York," and his courtship of Sara who became his first wife.

394 _____, and Robert P. Saalbach, eds. The Dreiser Newsletter, Vol. 1, Number 1, Spring 1970. English Department, Indiana State University, 217 North 6th Street, Terre Haute, Indiana, 47809. Continuous publication, Spring and Fall Issues, to present date.

395 _____; James L. W. West, III; and Neda Westlake; eds. An Amateur Laborer. Philadelphia: University of Pennsylvania Press, 1983.
Consists of 207 pages with text preceded by 30-page Introduction by Dowell, "careful and scholarly." This work by Dreiser is a manuscript, hitherto unpublished, of his earlier days. Most of the events are familiar, by way of biographies. It is a fragment, and yet some of the writing is far more vivid and realistic than anything else which has been written about these earlier events in the novelist's life.

396 DOYLE, Susan F. "Dreiser's An American Tragedy: A Structural Analysis." MA thesis, University of Florida, 1969.

397 DRAKE, William A., ed. Criticism in America. New York: Har-
     court, Brace, 1926. "Dreiser," by Robert L. Duffus, pp. 46-
     61.
         See Duffus (1926).

398 DREIDEN, Simon. "Theodore Dreiser in the Soviet Union."
     New Masses, 58 (January 29, 1946), 9.

399 DREISER, Edward. "My Brother Theodore." Book Find News,
     2 (March, 1946), 14-15.

400 DREISER, Helen. My Life with Dreiser. Cleveland: World,
     1951.
         Personal memoir by Dreiser's second wife. Author regards
     her book as a "small contribution to his biography ... and
     that the story of Dreiser would otherwise be incomplete."
     Says she will endeavor to be truthful, even as Dreiser tried
     to tell the truth. Concludes with death and funeral, revealing
     that "just before the casket was closed, I placed the poem I
     had written beside him."
         The poem, a fourteen-line sonnet, praises the light which
     Dreiser shed on the windows of the mind, and concludes with
     the thought that his song is "now afloat/In that one crystal
     clear immortal note."

401 _____. "Talk by Mrs. Theodore Dreiser given at the presen-
     tation program at the Los Angeles Public Library." Mrs. Drei-
     ser presents a manuscript of "Nigger Jeff" and "The Blue
     Sphere" to the library and read correspondence from Farrell,
     Mencken, and Masters. No date available.

402 DREISER, Theodore. Published works listed below. The fol-
     lowing notes are taken from Philip Gerber, Theodore Dreiser
     (1964). Other works, based on uncollected manuscripts, etc.,
     are listed throughout this bibliography; also various editions,
     particularly those with significant editorial Introductions and
     Notes are also listed throughout, under the principal editor's
     name. The following list serves as a guide to Dreiser's pri-
     mary publications.

     a) Original Manuscripts:

         The majority of Dreiser's manuscripts reside in the Dreiser
     Collection of the University of Pennsylvania Library, Phila-
     delphia. Dreiser personally deposited many of his papers
     there, and they were added to after his death by Helen
     Dreiser. Included are manuscripts of the majority of his
     books; galley and page proof; first, subsequent, and for-
     eign editions of the novels; correspondence; notes and work-
     sheets; clippings files; portraits and busts by various art-
     ists. The manuscript of Sister Carrie, presented to H. L.

Mencken, resides in the New York Public Library. The
manuscript of <u>Dawn</u> resides in the Library of Indiana University, Bloomington.

b) Novels (arranged in order of publication):

<u>Sister Carrie</u>. New York: Doubleday, Page, 1900.
<u>Jennie Gerhardt</u>. New York: Harper, 1911.
<u>The Financier</u>. New York: Harper, 1912. Completely re-
vised edition, New York: Boni & Liveright, 1927.
<u>The Titan</u>. New York: John Lane, 1914.
<u>The "Genius."</u> New York: John Lane, 1915.
<u>An American Tragedy</u>. New York: Boni & Liveright, 1925.
<u>The Bulwark</u>. Garden City: Doubleday, 1946.
<u>The Stoic</u>. Garden City: Doubleday, 1947.

c) Stories and Collections (arranged in order of publication):

<u>Free and Other Stories</u>. New York: Boni & Liveright, 1918.
<u>Chains</u>. New York: Boni & Liveright, 1927.
<u>Fine Furniture</u>. New York: Random House, 1930.
<u>The Best Short Stories of Theodore Dreiser</u>, ed. by Howard
Fast. Cleveland: World, 1947.
<u>The Best Short Stories of Theodore Dreiser</u>, ed by James
T. Farrell. Cleveland: World, 1956.

d) Drama (arranged in order of publication):

<u>Plays of the Natural and the Supernatural</u>. New York:
John Lane, 1916.
<u>The Hand of the Potter</u>. New York: Boni & Liveright,
1918.

e) Poetry (arranged in order of publication):

<u>Moods, Cadenced and Declaimed</u>. New York: Boni & Live-
right, 1928. Revised edition, New York: Simon and
Schuster, 1935.
<u>The Aspirant</u>. New York: Random House, 1929.
<u>Epitaph: A Poem</u>. New York: Heron Press, 1929.

f) Autobiography (arranged to provide the best chronological
sequence of Dreiser's life):

<u>Dawn</u>. New York: Liveright, 1931.
<u>A Book About Myself</u>. New York: Boni & Liveright, 1922.
Editions beyond the 7th appear as <u>Newspaper Days</u>.
<u>A Traveler at Forty</u>. New York: Century, 1913.
<u>A Hoosier Holiday</u>. New York: John Lane, 1916.

g) Letters:

> Letters of Theodore Dreiser, 3 vols., ed. by Robert H.
> Bliss. Philadelphia: University of Pennsylvania Press,
> 1959.

h) Non-Fiction (arranged in order of publication):

> "Life, Art, and America," reprinted from The Seven Arts,
> February, 1917.
> Twelve Men. New York: Boni & Liveright, 1919.
> Hey, Rub-a-Dub-Dub! New York: Boni & Liveright, 1920.
> The Color of a Great City. New York: Boni & Liveright,
> 1923.
> Dreiser Looks at Russia. New York: Liveright, 1928.
> A Gallery of Women. New York: Liveright, 1929.
> My City. New York: Liveright, 1929.
> "What I Believe," Forum, November 1929. Pp. 279-281.
> Dreiser's own statement of his mechanistic philosophy. As
> he puts it, "My intention is solely to present my reactions
> to a world that is as yet completely immersed in mystery."
> Tragic America. New York: Liveright, 1931.
> "Presenting Thoreau," Introduction to The Living Thoughts
> of Thoreau. New York: Longmans, Green, 1939. Pp.
> 1-32.
> America Is Worth Saving. New York: Modern Age Books,
> 1941.
> To the Writer's League of America. Hollywood, May 13,
> 1941.

403 DREISER, Vera, with Brett Howard. My Uncle Theodore: An
Intimate Portrait of Theodore Dreiser. New York: Nash, 1976.
Author is a consulting and clinical psychologist. Book is
based on what she saw and heard over the years from within
the family circle, including the stories her father told her,
family records and correspondence, and her personal contacts
since childhood with the entire Dreiser family, especially "Uncle
Theo." Consists of some 238 pages with a number of family
photographs. Does not presume to be scholarly, but is written
in an easy, readable style, without being silly or chatty. Of
Dreiser she says in the Prologue: "No one who knew Theodore
Dreiser or his work is able to discuss him dispassionately.
He is either adored or thoroughly disliked. His books are
among the best, or not even worth mentioning. No one who
reads, however, seems to be indifferent. This is greatness.
A man who arouses such controversy is a man who didn't go
unnoticed through life. Right or wrong he tried to find answers for himself and indirectly for others. A man who goes
through life looking for answers, disagreeing with things as
they are, saying so, and challenging the status quo, pays a
high price."

404 DREW, Elizabeth A. A Modern Novel: Some Aspects of Contemporary Fiction. New York: Harcourt, 1926. Dreiser, pp.
146-147.
   He will use extravagantly unreal and stilted dialogue, bathos
   and cliché are always at his pen's point; we are told that
   women are witty, but we never hear any wit; we are assured
   that they are charming, but we never feel a particle of their
   charm; he has no picturesque quality, no humor, no subtlety,
   no elegance--nothing but this ugly solidity of craftsmanship
   and a terrific determination to express somehow the forms of
   life and the forces of life which he has seen and felt with such
   intensity.

405 DRUMMOND, Edward J., S.J. "Theodore Dreiser: Shifting
Naturalism," in Fifty Years of the American Novel, ed. by
Harold C. Gardiner. New York: Scribner's, 1951. Pp. 33-
47.
   Although he was a professed agnostic, there was in most of
   his work an implied frame of reference and a norm of values.
   He was a determinist, but one who worked hard to find success and recognition, and who urged reform through socialism
   and communism. He was a materialist who not only was sincerely sympathetic, but who had a streak of soft idealistic
   monism in his make-up that was eventually to lead him to a
   position which Emerson could have understood. He struggled
   with censorship for over two decades, yet it was censorship
   which focused light upon his work and, indirectly at least,
   assisted much in having his real importance assayed and recognized.

406 DUDDING, Griffith. "A Note Concerning Theodore Dreiser's
Philosophy." Library Chronicle, 30 (Summer, 1964), 36-37.

407 DUDLEY, Dorothy. Forgotten Frontiers: Dreiser and the Land
of the Free. New York: Harrison Smith and Robert Haas,
1932. Reprinted as Dreiser and the Land of the Free. New
York: Beechhurst Press, 1946.
   First biography of Dreiser and is often inaccurate. Is called
   a "novel of facts." Is a chronological narrative of Dreiser's
   life and writings, with a good deal that seems "made up"--
   conversations, for instance. Has many quotations from Dreiser,
   but is not a scholarly work. It does read easily and enter-
   tainingly. One critic refers to the work as "impressionistic
   rather than analytic, declarative rather than systematic--a
   drawer full of likely treasures." She must bear credit for
   having shown the wealth and complexity of material available,
   and for having pointed to what would have to be done by
   future scholars.

408 DUFFEY, Bernard I. The Chicago Renaissance in American
Letters. East Lansing: Michigan State University Press,
1954. Dreiser, pp. 135-136, et passim.

Comments in a chapter devoted to Floyd Dell, which includes
remarks on Dreiser, who was in Chicago at the time gathering
material for his novel on Frank Cowperwood, the prototype of
whom was Frank C. Yerkes. From Dreiser, Floyd Dell learned
of Edgar Lee Masters but failed to follow up the lead because
he found the pre-Spoon River verses uninteresting. In turn,
he introduced Dreiser to the Chicago group, and as a result
Dreiser wrote to Mencken calling his attention to the Chicago
writers and urging him to do something about them "right
away." Here lay the basis for Mencken's later and famous
salutes to Chicago.

409 DUFFUS, Robert L. "The Wherefore of Literary Anarchism."
New York Globe and Commercial Advertiser, April 28, 1923.
P. 10.

410   . "Dreiser's Undisciplined Power." New York Times
Book Review, January 10, 1926. Pp. 1, 6.
Review of An American Tragedy. Says he has achieved
what may be described as an ironic pity. He has approached
a little nearer to the mind of Thomas Hardy ... is not to be
recommended as fireside reading for the tired business man;
yet, as a portrayal of one of the darker phases of the American character, it demands attention.

411   . "Dreiser." American Mercury, 7 (January, 1926),
71-76. Reprinted in American Criticism, ed by William A.
Drake. New York: Harcourt, Brace, 1926. Pp. 46-61.
Dreiser has been the recipient of countless uppercuts, solar
plexus jabs, rabbit punches, and left hooks to the jaw. No
other American writer, except maybe Whitman, has received
so many thumps upon his obstinate head, so many kicks upon
his stubborn shins. He has been impaled upon the Comstock's
grotesque lance; he has even been apologized for by his friends,
who have complained sadly about his style. Yet his head is
not only unbowed--it is not even bloody.

412   . "Theodore Dreiser Mounts the Soapbox." New York
Times Book Review, February 9, 1941. P. 22.
Review-article on America Is Worth Saving (1941). The intended effect of Mr. Dreiser's words in this volume is obvious.
It is to create a sentiment adverse to aid to England or sympathy for England in her struggle against Hitler. It is Dreiser's privilege to make this effort ... it is his privilege to be
wrong-headed. Let us hope that the time will never come when
the spirit of Hitlerism will gain sufficient ground in America
to deny him or any one else that privilege.

413 DUFFY, Richard. "When They Were Twenty-One, II--A New
York Group of Literary Bohemians." Bookman, 38 (January,
1914), 521-531.

Discusses Dreiser during the time he was writing Sister
Carrie. The gathering place was "Maria's" in West Twelfth
Street, where writers and artists congregated to talk to each
other, and to hear themselves talk. Describes Dreiser as he
always sat in a rocking chair "if he could find one," and he
sat in it to rock. If he was not talking he would be humming
a tune, of which he had hundreds in his head. Every few
days when Dreiser made an appearance, he would announce
that he had writen ten thousand words, or twenty as the case
might be. By the time he finished Sister Carrie he had written twice as much as would be published.

414 DUGGAN, Margaret. "An Interpretive Study of The 'Genius.' "
     Ph.D. diss., Boston College, 1966.

415 DUNLOP, C. R. B. "Law and Justice in Dreiser's An American
     Tragedy." University of British Columbia Law Review, 6
     (Fall, 1971), 379-403.

416 _____. "Human Law and Natural Law in the Novels of The-
     odore Dreiser." American Journal of Jurisprudence, 19 (1974),
     61-86.
     Focuses on The Financier and The Titan to show that Dreiser
     is torn between a view of the world as disordered and amoral,
     and a yearning for a fundamental law which can be used to
     measure and judge modern society and human law.

417 DUNN, Jacob P. Indiana and Indianians. Chicago: American
     Historical Society, 1919. Dreiser, pp. 1185-1189.

418 DURGIN, Chester. "The Band Wagon: The Story Behind the
     Story." Long Island Daily Press, May 22, 1926. Pp. 1, 2.

419 DURHAM, Frank. "Mencken as Missionary." American Litera-
     ture, 29 (January, 1958), 478-483.
     Discussion based on letters to Henry Sydnor Harrison from
     H. L. Mencken on the occasion of trying to suppress Dreiser's
     The "Genius." Quotes a long 425-word letter from Mencken,
     to which Harrison did not make a reply.

420 DUSTMAN, Marjory P. "Theodore Dreiser's An American Trag-
     edy: A Study." Ph.D. Diss., University of Southern Cali-
     fornia, 1965. DA, 26 (1965), 367.
     Begins with the premise that Dreiser's novel has been read
     and discussed more than studied. This dissertation "studies"
     An American Tragedy in relation to the original murder case
     which was Dreiser's model, in regard to structure and thematic
     development, and with reference to the naturalistic technique
     and philosophy. Finally the matter of Clyde's status as a
     tragic protagonist is established: he is a modern tragic fig-
     ure.

421 EARNEST, Ernest. "The American Ariel." South Atlantic Quar-
     terly, 65 (Spring, 1966), 192-200.
     Uses the term "ariel" to describe an archetype which was
     poet and singer with a longing to be free and a lack of lasting
     human affections. Names Dreiser's Eugene Witla of The "Gen-
     ius" as an example of this type: "Driven by what Dreiser
     calls Eugene's idea of perfection, Witla tirelessly pursues
     women. He leaves a dull middle-class home and heads first
     for Chicago and then New York. He has one affair after the
     other, abandoning a string of women, not for the sake of his
     art, but motivated by simple exploitation."

422 _____. The Single Vision: The Alienation of American Intel-
     lectuals, 1910-1930. New York: New York University Press,
     1970. Dreiser, pp. 40-42, et passim.
     Dreiser was cast in the role of martyr for the cause of liter-
     ary freedom. Even his champions spoke of the inescapable
     dullness and "the general stupidity and stodginess" of some of
     his novels. In fact all of the admirers of Dreiser deplored his
     heavy-handed style and his bad word-sense. There was, of
     course, the undeniable force of the man, and he created some
     memorable characters. Much of the enthusiasm for Dreiser, it
     would appear, grew out of the anti-Puritan crusade of the era.
     Instead of being evaluated as a novelist he becomes a cause.
     Critical attacks on Dreiser were largely moralistic.

423 EASTMAN, Max. "Is the Novel at a Dead End?" in The Literary
     Mind: Its Place in an Age of Science. New York: Scrib-
     ner's, 1931. Pp. 225-237.
     It is important to remember that Dreiser with all his talk
     about "chemisms" has a passionate antagonism toward any push-
     ing to extremes of a genuinely scientific attitude. Dreiser got
     rid of his religion, or tried to, but he did not accept, or enter
     into, the scientific conception of what it is to understand. He
     did not join the march of science. And so he stands there,
     just as all serious-hearted literature in this era stands, unable
     to "imagine any explanation ... that would be either true--or
     important if true."

424 EATON, Walter Prichard. "Revolt from Realism." Virginia Quar-
     terly Review, (October, 1934), 515-528.
     Article is principally concerned with drama, an art form
     which could not pay very strict homage to the tenets of real-
     ism or naturalism as practised by William Dean Howells or The-
     odore Dreiser after him. Of realism, Eaton says: "realism in
     art is a method, a technique, and its purpose is to express
     human truths and to rouse the emotions of an audience. Some
     truths can best be expressed that way; others cannot be ex-
     pressed that way at all.... We glorified the method, the tech-
     nique, to an extent which blinded us to its shortcomings...."

425 ECKLEY, Grace. "Griffin's Irish Tragedy, The Collegians and
    Dreiser's American Tragedy." Eire-Ireland (St. Paul, Minne-
    sota), 19 (1977), 39-45.
        Refers to the novel by Gerald Griffin (1803-1840), The Col-
    legians (1828), a tragic tale of peasantry and gentlefolk. From
    the novel Dion Boucicault made a famous melodrama, The Col-
    leen Bawn.

426 EDELSTEIN, Arthur. "Realism and Beyond: Essays in Twentieth-
    Century Fiction." Ph.D. diss., Stanford, 1976. DA, 38
    (1977), 1377A-1378A.
        Dissertation consists of 14 essays on writers of the twentieth
    century, with an introduction and epilogue. The governing
    concern is the transformation of the American literary sensi-
    bility between 1890 and the present, beginning with Stephen
    Crane and Dreiser--"realists on all fours"--and concluding with
    an essay on the "madness" novel.

427 _____, ed. with Introduction. Sister Carrie. New York:
    Harper and Row, 1965.

428 EDGAR, Pelham. "American Realism, Sex, and Theodore Drei-
    ser," in The Art of the Novel. New York: Macmillan, 1933.
    Pp. 244-254.
        Dreiser represents an entirely new American fiction, inde-
    pendent of British. Darwin and Herbert Spencer were his in-
    tellectual parents. He saw nothing in the realism of Howells
    to emulate. Crane and Norris were to his liking, but Balzac
    and Zola were his real literary parents.

429 EDGETT, E. F. "Dreiser and His Titan." Boston Evening
    Transcript, May 23, 1914. P. 8. Reprinted in Pizer (1981),
    pp. 235-236.
        In spite of its tremendous shortcomings, The Titan never-
    theless commands admiration and respect. Dreiser's knowledge
    of affairs in the world of business and society is remarkable.
    He is never at a loss for a scheme wherewith to explain Cow-
    perwood's methods, or with his explanation of them. His pic-
    tures of the time and place are vigorous and graphic.

430 EDMINSTON, Susan, and Linda D. Cirino. Literary New York:
    A History and Guide. Boston: Houghton Mifflin, 1976. Drei-
    ser, passim.

431 EDWARDS, Oliver. "Moby Theo." London Times, January 19,
    1956. P. 11.

432 _____. "A Compelling Novel." London Times, August 5,
    1965. P. 13.

433 EHRLICH, Carol. "Evolutionism and the Female in Selected

American Novels, 1885-1900." Ph.D. diss., University of
Iowa, 1973. DA, 35 (1974), 399A.
   This study encompasses twelve novels which contain a variety
of comments about women in the context of evolutionism. Four
basic themes emerge: social mobility and class stratification,
mental health and illness, atavism, and strict determinism.
Although the authors differ in their use of evolutionist ideas,
their overall tendency is to follow conventional beliefs about
the female's true nature and proper behavior. Among authors
studied are Howells, Crane, Dreiser, Oliver Wendell Holmes,
and Ellen Glasgow.

434 EHRMANN, Bertha K. Max Ehrmann: A Poet's Life. Boston:
     Humphries, 1951. Dreiser, pp. 37-39.
        Was aware of Dreiser's growing importance during the 1930's
     and there was some correspondance between Max Ehrmann and
     Dreiser. Throughout his Journal, Ehrmann makes many re-
     marks about Dreiser, as in June 1932: "His great virtue is
     devotion to truth about external facts. The facts of the inner
     life: the whole background of aspirations, exaltations, exper-
     ience and scholarship unified into a knowing, reposeful per-
     sonality--to these he is a stranger."

435 EICHELBERGER, Clayton. A Guide to Critical Reviews of United
     States Fiction, 1870-1910. Metuchen, N.J.: Scarecrow Press,
     1971.
        Reviews of Sister Carrie that appeared in the Athenaeum
     (London), The Bookman, The North American Review, and
     the New Orleans Daily Picayune.

436 EISENSTEIN, Sergei M. Film Form: Essays In Film Theory,
     edited and translated by Jay Leyda. New York: Harcourt,
     Brace, 1949. Dreiser, pp. 96-103.
        Essay originally printed in a Moscow magazine, 1932. Has
     been previously translated and printed in Close Up, March
     1933 and in June 1933 (London). Discusses the early filming
     of An American Tragedy. The question of Clyde's guilt or in-
     nocence is crucial to the production of this film. "Not Guilty"
     is the verdict in this film and that, of course, determines the
     entire production slant.

437 ELIAS, Robert H. "The Romantic Stoicism of Theodore Dreiser:
     A Study of His Attitude Toward Industrialism and Social Re-
     form." MA thesis, Columbia University, 1938.

438 _____. "Theodore Dreiser: Or, the World Well Lost." Book
     Find News, 2 (March, 1946), 12-13, 22.

439 _____. "Theodore Dreiser: Apostle of Nature." Ph.D. diss.,
     University of Pennsylvania, 1948.
        Published in the following item.

440   . Theodore Dreiser: Apostle of Nature. New York: Knopf, 1949. Revised edition, Ithaca, N.Y.: Cornell University Press, 1970. Excerpt reprinted in Kazin and Shapiro (1955), pp. 188-203, Chapter 9, "The Survival of the Fittest." In 354 pages, fifteen chapters, with good index and notes to the chapters. Chapter titles indicate scope of work:

1. Boyhood Dreams
2. Facts versus Fancies
3. Go East, Young Man ...
4. First Principles
5. Spectator
6. Sister Carrie
7. To Live
8. Editorial Days
9. "The Survival of the Fittest ... "
10. The Significance of the Unfit
11. "Nature's Way Is Correct ... "
12. Society and Science
13. For the Underdog
14. The Red Dawn
15. The Creative Force

Is called a "definitive" biography, and is based upon an acquaintance with Dreiser, interviews with him, a prolonged examination of his correspondence and manuscripts, and conversations with many of his surviving friends and relatives. Has interpreted Dreiser's life and work critically in terms of the moral, financial, religious, and philosophical problems that confronted him from his childhood to his last days. Work is both readable and thoroughly documented. Remains the best biographical work on Dreiser.

441   . "The Library's Dreiser Collection." Library Chronicle, 17 (Fall, 1950), 78-80. Dreiser at the University of Pennsylvania.

442   . "Theodore Dreiser," in Fifteen Modern American Authors, edited by Jackson R. Bryer. Durham: Duke University Press, 1969. Pp. 101-138. Reprinted with a 19-page supplement in Sixteen Modern American Authors, edited by Jackson R. Bryer. New York: Norton, 1973. Pp. 123-179.
Bibliographical essay in five parts: Bibliography, Editions, Manuscripts and Letters, Biography, and Criticism, which is arranged according to General, Individual works, and Foreign. Composition has good organization and comment, but items do not contain complete bibliographical information, lacking magazine volumes, page numbers, etc.

443   . "Bibliography and the Biographer." Library Chronicle, 38 (Winter, 1972), 25-44.

444 _____. "Theodore Dreiser and the Tragedy of the Twenties."
    Prospects: An Annual of American Cultural Studies, 1 (1975),
    9-16.
    Sees the novel as inseparable from the historical moment.
    Clyde's death in 1925 pre-figured the self-defeating consequen-
    ces of the self-insulting society of the twenties: the retribu-
    tion that was the Crash. This was the tragedy of the twen-
    ties.

445 _____, ed. Letters of Theodore Dreiser, 3 vols. Philadel-
    phia: University of Pennsylvania Press, 1959.
    Three volumes contain over 1,000 pages and cover the years
    1897 to 1945. Vol. I, 1897-1921, Vol. II, 1922-1935, and Vol.
    III, 1936-1945, the year of Dreiser's death. The work is ¬
    called a "selection," although it contains nearly 600 letters.
    Editor confirms that Dreiser was not "among the great letter
    writers," but that he was capable of writing a good letter.
    All the letters, from first to last suggest the extent to which
    Dreiser's sense of his own limitations was counterbalanced by
    the sense of how only he must save himself.
    Volume I contains a complete Table of Contents, in which
    dates and recipient of letter are listed for all three volumes.
    This is a particularly good feature of the work.

446 ELLINGSON, H. K. "A Review of Chains." Colorado Springs
    Telegraph, May 22, 1927.
    Regards this collection of 15 of Dreiser's shorter stories as
    one of his best works and says: "considered singly many of
    these stories are nothing short of powerful in their dramatic
    effect; but considered collectively, they are virtually over-
    whelming in their power to render the reader aware of the
    utter cruelty of mankind."

447 _____. "Theodore Dreiser." Colorado Sunday Gazette &
    Telegraph, June 14, 1931.
    Remarks on Dawn, the recently published autobiography.
    Is an avowed admirer of Dreiser and says, "it isn't often that
    we are confronted by unvarnished truth in this country, every-
    body being more or less dedicated to the task of concealing the
    truth.... No wonder there is a concerted move on foot to be-
    little Dreiser. A lot of people now think it is smart to join
    this move."

448 ELLISTON, H. B. "Mr Dreiser and Russia." New York Times,
    March 3, 1928. P. 16.
    Letter to editor.

449 ELVEBACK, Helen B. "The Novels of Theodore Dreiser with an
    Analysis of His Other Writings." Ph.D. diss., University of
    Minnesota, 1946.

450 ENGLAND, D. Gene. "A Further Note on the 'Dreiser' Annotations." Dreiser Newsletter, 4 (Fall, 1973), 9-10.
Refers to a copy of Nicholas Blood, Candidate, a novel by Arthur Henry, published in 1890. The copy in question is housed at the University of Texas at Austin, and has been thought to be annotated by Dreiser. This now appears to be in error, and it is not known who annotated the edition. See other articles by Ellen Moers.

451 ENSOR, Allison R. " 'All of Us Fail': Theodore Dreiser Writes A Creator of Nick Carter." Dreiser Newsletter, 8 (Fall, 1977), 19-20.
Based on a letter which Dreiser wrote to a Mr. Eugene T. Sawyer, one of the original creators of the famed Nick Carter series of detective stories. Sawyer praised Dreiser as "having arrived," and Dreiser replied: "To me all of us fail ... then we see clearly how minute we are and what tools and scrub brushes we are for higher--inscrutable and to me at least-- merciless things."

452 EPSTEIN, Joseph. Ambition: The Secret Passion. New York: Dutton, 1980. "The Lobster and the Squid," pp. 69-96, Dreiser passim.
Dreiser took on the subject of ambition in America with a directness and complex understanding of all that it involved, and surpassed all other writers of our time. Whatever was closed to him in the way of elegance and grace and subtlety, Dreiser knew all about ambition: about its excitement, about its heartbreak, and above all, about the desire behind it. In one way or another all of Dreiser's novels are about ambition and success in America. The episode of the lobster and the squid appeared in The Financier, the first of the trilogy of "desire" and is a classic metaphor for success and ambition: one eats or is eaten, the ten-year-old Frank Cowperwood decides, and "that's the way it has to be, I guess," he commented to himself. That squid wasn't quick enough. At the end of The Stoic, Frank Cowperwood is dead, and all that he worked and strove for is quickly dissipated by his heirs.

453 ERNST, Morris, and William Seagle. To the Pure ... A Study of Obscenity and the Censor. New York: Viking, 1928. Pp. 44 et passim.
Reviews case against The "Genius" and the lesser case against An American Tragedy. Concludes that there must be a necessity for a re-valuation of obscenity.

454 ERSKINE, John. "American Business in the American Novel." Bookman, 73 (July, 1931), 449-457.
Is principally a discussion of Sinclair Lewis and his winning the Nobel prize "for his general excellence as a novelist, but in particular for his portrait of Babbitt," the small-time bus-

iness man of America. Raises the question of why the Swedish academy preferred Lewis' book to say that of Booth Tark-
ington's The Plutocrat. The simple truth is that Lewis created a truer portrait, not of the business man as America
sees him, but as Europe sees him. Dreiser's Cowperwood
trilogy, perhaps the truest of all novels, on American business was not considered.

455 FADIMAN, Clifton. "Dreiser and the American Dream." The
     Nation, 135 (October 19, 1932), 364-365.
     Dreiser's defects are eloquent of struggle. To hack a path
     through the jungle of American life was no easy task at the
     beginning of the century--no task for a thin-skinned or cul-
     tivated writer. Dreiser is a realist. He deals descriptively
     with material directly before him, but he is also a romanti-
     cist whose attitude is one of horror and joy and wonder.

456 _____, ed. with Comment. "Dramatic Highlights from An Amer-
     ican Tragedy." Audio-tape. Hollywood, Calif.: Center for
     Cassette Studies, 1971.

457 FARGION, Louisa. " 'Sister Carrie' e 'Nana.' " Acme (Italy),
     31 (1978), 429-442. In Italian.

458 FARRAG, Aida Ahmed. "Functions of Settings in Certain Nat-
     uralistic Novels." Ph.D. diss., Toronto University, 1978.
     DA, 40 (1979), 836A.
     Asserts that the description of places and things is "half
     the battle" in the naturalistic novel whose concern is to give
     an accurate documentation of man's condition and position
     within his enviroment. Dissertation is based on a study of
     Zola's Une Page d'amour, Crane's Maggie, and Dreiser's
     Sister Carrie. In his work Dreiser relies heavily on meta-
     phor to dramatize the impact that large cities have upon the
     individual.

459 FARRELL, James T. "James T. Farrell Revalues Dreiser's
     Sister Carrie." New York Times Book Review, July 4, 1943.
     P. 3. Reprinted in The League of Frightened Philistines.
     New York: Vanguard, 1945. Pp. 12-19 as "Dreiser's Sister
     Carrie." Also reprinted in Kazin and Shapiro (1955), pp.
     182-187 as "Dreiser's Sister Carrie."
     Dreiser won his battle, and today he is a living American
     literary tradition. He helped to raise American life, its con-
     trasts of grandeur and misery, its streets and cities, its trag-
     edies, and its vulgarities, to the level of world literature.
     But how does his first novel read today? Is it merely a novel
     of historic significance, or does it retain its value now, so
     many years after it was written? It truly re-creates a sense

of an epoch: it is like a door which permits us entry into
the consciousness of an America that is no more. But it is
no mere document. It is a powerful and tragic story, created
with an unrelenting logic; his novel is just as fresh and alive
today as when it was written.

460   . "An American Tragedy." New York Times Book Review, March 6, 1945. Pp. 6, 16.

461   . "Some Aspects of Dreiser's Fiction." New York Times
Book Review, April 29, 1945. P. 7; also May 6, 1945, P. 6.

462   . "Social Themes in American Realism." English Journal,
35 (June, 1946), 309-314. Reprinted in Farrell, Selected Essays, edited by Luna Wolf. New York: McGraw-Hill, 1964.
Pp. 3-13.
Since the 1890's American writers of the realistic tradition
have been trying to tell the story of the human consequences
of the advance of American civilization ... a pioneer in this
tradition was Theodore Dreiser. With Dreiser, the conditions
of life and the ideals of success in America are thematic: the
motif of development or awareness, when treated by him, is
secondary to these. His characters usually take on the color
of their environment. Failure and tragedy in his novels are
to be interpreted as consequences of the pitiless force of circumstances. His heroes and heroines are seeking to rise socially, to change their class status.

463   . "Theodore Dreiser: In Memoriam." Saturday Review
of Literature, 29 (January 12, 1946), 15-17, 27-28. Reprinted
in Farrell, Literature and Morality. New York: Vanguard,
1947. Pp. 26-34.
His great books are not only works which convey awesome
depth of feeling for the condition of man, they also try to
tell the truth. He shows pity and compassion for the tragic
web of life, but is pitiless in delineation. Continued to show
that circumstances, biological impulses are stronger than the
will.

464   . "Theodore Dreiser." Chicago Review, 1 (Summer,
1946), 127-144. Reprinted in Farrell, Selected Essays, edited
by Luna Wolf (1964), pp. 150-168.
Dreiser laid down a broad description of patterns of American experience; his successors have been more intensive in
their treatment, more detailed. Following him, the major scene
of American realism has become the city. If regarded socially,
Dreiser's influence is equally profound. We can generalize the
statement about his influence by declaring that he oriented
twentieth-century realistic fiction in America. In addition he
served as the living example of a writer who had stubbornly
struggled to express himself sincerely; he did not surrender

to the censors or to the prudes; he became a living literary tradition during his own lifetime.

465 _____. "Dreiser's Posthumous Novel: A Major American Work." Call, 13 (July 1, 1946), 5.
Review of The Bulwark, in which Farrell says, "What is most important about this novel is that it is a full and serious story which tells us of the complete life experience of a man. At the same time, it deals with the quality of ideals in modern America.... The Bulwark adds another massive panel to Dreiser's fictional re-creation of the story of American ideals."

466 _____. "Greatness of Dreiser Is Attested in Final Novel." Philadelphia Sunday Bulletin Book Review, November 9, 1947. P. 2.
Review of The Stoic.

467 _____. "Dreiser's The Stoic Powerful." Chicago News, December 3, 1947.
The Stoic is, if anything, more moving and more powerful than its two predecessors. Cowperwood is now presented both as an individual and as a force. The social and the biological tragedy of man, so pitilessly and yet so compassionately described in his books, in reality is an expression of this life force. This is universal creativity, whether it be for good or for evil.

468 _____. "Some Correspondence with Theodore Dreiser." General Magazine and Historical Chronicle (University of Pennsylvania), 53 (Summer, 1951), 237-252. Reprinted in Farrell, Reflections at Fifty and Other Essays. New York: Vanguard Press, 1954. Pp. 124-141. Also reprinted in Kazin and Shapiro (1955), pp. 36-50.
Correspondence of the period 1943-1945. Letters to the end of Dreiser's life indicate that he was preoccupied with concluding the last volume of his trilogy, The Stoic. Farrell was preparing to write Dreiser about the novel when he heard news of his death.

469 _____. "Dreiser." New York Times Book Review, January 8, 1956. P. 22.
Letter to editor.

470 _____. "James T. Farrell Recalls H. L. Mencken." Toledo Blade, November 26, 1961. Section 2, p. 7.
Letter to editor.

471 _____. "Dreiser's Tragedy: The Distortion of American Values." Prospects, 1 (1975), 19-28.
At the end of a Dreiser novel my feeling is often one of wonder about the irreconcilable, irrefragable aspects and

characteristics of different destinies; rich and poor, strong and weak, the contrast of grandeur and misery, failure and success. There have been many youths in American life like Clyde Griffiths. They may have been a little more or less sophisticated. They may not have ended in the electric chair. They possibly lived out their lives in what Thoreau called quiet desperation. But they lived for false values. They lived for aspirations similar to Clyde Griffiths', and their lives were more or less marked by the same emptiness.

472 _____, ed. with Introduction. Sister Carrie. New York: Sagamore Press, 1957.

473 _____, ed. with Introduction. Best Short Stories of Theodore Dreiser. Cleveland: World, 1956. Reprinted Greenwich, Conn.: Fawcett, 1961. Also reprinted New York: Thomas Y. Crowell, 1974.

474 _____, ed. with Introduction, "A Dreiser Revival." Theodore Dreiser. New York: Dell, 1962. Pp. 7-15. Laurel-Dell Reader series. Introduction reprinted in James T. Farrell Literary Essays, 1954-1974, edited by Jack Allan Robbins. Port Washington, N.Y.: Kennikat Press, 1976. Pp. 26-33.

475 FARRELLY, John. "Finis." New Republic, 117 (December 22, 1947), 28.
Brief comment on The Stoic, Dreiser's last novel which was not finished when he died. It is not an ingratiating book as it stands, but should not be read apart from The Financier and The Titan. For students of Dreiser's work it has its interests, and for readers curious about the trilogy, it at least lands Frank Cowperwood in the grave, though it cannot be said to lay his ghost.

476 FAST, Howard. "He Knew the People." Sunday Worker, December 30, 1945. P. 3.

477 _____. "Dreiser's Short Stories." New Masses, 60 (September 3, 1946), 11-12.

478 _____, ed. with Introduction. The Best Short Stories of Theodore Dreiser. Cleveland: World, 1947. Pp. 7-11.

479 FECHER, Charles A. Mencken: A Study of His Thought. New York: Knopf, 1978. Dreiser, passim.

480 FELD, Rose C. "Interview with Dreiser." New York Times Book Review, December 23, 1923. Pp. 6-7.

481 FICKE, Arthur Davison. "Portrait of Theodore Dreiser." Little Review, 2 (November, 1915), 6-7.
Poem about Dreiser.

482 _____. "Dreiser as Artist." Saturday Review of Literature,
    2 (April 17, 1926), 724.
        Letter to editor in which he agrees with Sherwood Anderson's
    "laudatory" review of An American Tragedy and refutes a reader
    who disagrees with Anderson's assessment of the novel.

483 FIEDLER, Leslie A. Love and Death in the American Novel.
    New York: Criterion Books, 1960. Revised edition, New
    York: Stein and Day, 1966. Dreiser, pp. 247-255. Excerpt
    reprinted in Lydenberg (1971), pp. 45-51, as "Dreiser and
    the Sentimental Novel."
        It is only Dreiser who proves capable of reviving that theme
    of seduction for serious literature, for he takes it seriously,
    finding in the impregnation and abandonment of helpless women
    no mere occasions for melodrama (as in Twain) or for exer-
    cises in irony and contrasting style (as in Crane). Dreiser
    is qualified first of all by his essentially sentimental response
    to the plight of the oppressed, by what he himself calls "an
    uncritical upswelling of grief for the weak and helpless."
    There is in him none of the detachment and cynicism of Crane,
    none of the utter blackness and pessimism of Twain; he is as
    "positive" through his tears as any female scribbler.

484 FIELD, Louise Maunsell. "American Novelists Vs. the Nation."
    North American Review, 235 (June, 1933), 552-560.
        Does not discuss Dreiser directly, but undertakes to show
    that America will not permit its novelists to function truthfully
    and tell the facts about any particular section of the country.
    America wants romance, and anyone--of whom Dreiser is a
    member--who tells the truth is called "a damned liar."

485 FIENBERG, Lorne Michael. "Changing Perspectives on the
    Businessman in the American Novel, 1865-1914." Ph.D. diss.,
    University of California (Berkeley), 1977. DA, 38 (1978),
    4825A.
        This dissertation deals with the variety of world views of
    different social groups towards the businessman and the Amer-
    ican business system during the period of intense economic
    growth of 1865 to 1914. Concludes the study with Dreiser's
    The Financier and The Titan, which are seen as the culmina-
    tion of the process of change in American novelists' views of
    society, and the world view of the entrepreneurial system in
    America.

486 FIGG, Robert M., III. "The Effect of Naturalism upon Form in
    the American Novel from 1893 to 1925." Ph.D. diss., Univer-
    sity of North Carolina, 1965. DA, 26 (1966), 3951A.
        Based upon the belief that Naturalism is not simply an ex-
    treme form of realism, identical in kind though differing in
    degree. Maintains that the difference results from the dif-
    ferent conceptions of reality held by realist and naturalist:

for the realist, the actual empirical world is reality; for the
naturalist, reality consists in the amoral laws of nature which
undergird the empirical world rather than the world itself.
These definitions are explored in terms of eleven novels by
Stephen Crane, Frank Norris, and Dreiser.

487 FILLER, Louis. "Dreamers, and the American Dream." South-
     west Review, 40 (Autumn, 1955), 359-363.
     Principally a review of Kenneth Lynn's The Dream of Suc-
     cess in which the fallacy of confusing authors with the char-
     acters they create is discussed. One notable example is Drei-
     ser, who recorded the dreams of persons whom he had known,
     but was not always in touch with what has been called the
     "American dream." Dreiser did not betray America by pre-
     senting its sordid, ugly aspects.

488 _____. "Sense, Sentimentality, and Theodore Dreiser."
     Salamagundi, 1 (1966), 90-97.

489 _____. "A Tale of Two Authors: Theodore Dreiser and
     David Graham Phillips," in New Voices in American Studies,
     edited by Ray B. Browne, Donald M. Winkleman, and Allen
     Hayman. Lafayette, Ind.: Purdue University Press, 1966.
     Pp. 35-48.
     It was natural to compare Dreiser's version of American
     life with that which he was apparently opposing. Dreiser was
     held to be telling the truth, in contrast to authors of what
     was called the "sweetness and light" school. Dreiser was not
     contrasted with the muckrakers and Dreiser was not a muck-
     raker. Nor, could he be associated with his fellow-Hoosier,
     David Graham Phillips. Their methods and goals seemed so
     different as to scarcely warrant explication. Both authors
     were actors in a drama of intellectual effort which can enlighten
     our present cultural circumstances.

490 FINKELSTEIN, Sidney. "Six Ways of Looking at Reality."
     Mainstream, 13 (December, 1960), 31-42.

491 FISCHER, Louis. "Russia Adopts Dreiser." New York Herald
     Tribune Books, October 4, 1931. P. 9.

492 FISHBEIN, Leslie. Rebels in Bohemia: The Radicals of "The
     Masses," 1911-1917. Chapel Hill: University of North Caro-
     lina Press, 1982. Dreiser, pp. 34-35 et passim. Revised by
     Daniel Aaron.
     Includes Dreiser in comments concerning Puritanical views
     held with regard to sex. Dreiser complained that in his youth
     he had been taught to sham piety and to shun most human
     experience. The cult of purity by repressing sexual energy
     distorted its final expression: "If ever a people has refined
     eroticism to a greater degree than the American, I am not
     aware of it," commented Theodore Dreiser.

493 FISHER, Philip. "Looking Around to See Who I Am: Dreiser's
     Territory of the Self." English Literary History, 44 (1977),
     728-748.
        Long analysis of Clyde Griffiths in An American Tragedy.
     Argues that Dreiser's presentation is not merely the reflection
     of methods inherent in Naturalism, but is an actual represen-
     tation of one method of knowing oneself. Traces Clyde from
     the opening scene in which he appears with his family as
     street preachers to the final scene in which he is prepared
     for his execution. Clyde never looks inward, is never intro-
     spective. The question of identity is always in relation to
     where he is, the time and the place.

494 FISHKIN, Shelley Fisher. "Documentary Impulses in American
     Literature: The Vicissitudes of a Creative Problem." Ph.D.
     diss., Yale, 1977. DA, 39 (1978), 1565A-1566A.
        Dissertation focuses on five American poets and novelists
     who served apprenticeships in their youths as "documentors
     of fact," journalists: Walt Whitman, Mark Twain, Dreiser,
     Hemingway, and Dos Passos. They have all been preoccupied
     with the impulse to record and communicate the physical, so-
     cial, psychological, and political facts of American life that
     they have witnessed. Each writer had to grapple with the
     problem of converting fact into fiction, and each one approached
     the problem in his own way. Amazingly enough, they each
     arrived, independently, at the same solution.

495 FITZGERALD, George L. "Dreiser's Credo." Forum, 83 (Jan-
     uary, 1930), p. xxxviii.

496 FITZPATRICK, Vincent de Paul, III. "Mencken, Dreiser, and
     the Baltimore Evening Sun." Menckeniana, No. 60 (Winter,
     1976), 1-5.
        Traces Mencken's comments on Dreiser in the Evening Sun
     from 1911-1925.

497 _____. "Dreiser, Mencken, and the American Mercury Years."
     Dreiser Newsletter, 10 (Fall, 1979), 13-16.
        In December 1923, Mencken left the editorship of Smart Set,
     ending his 15-year career as book reviewer. In looking back,
     Mencken found he had referred to Dreiser more than seventy
     times, although he still did not know that it was Dreiser who
     had gotten him the job. In January 1924, Mencken and George
     Jean Nathan founded the American Mercury, a broader based
     forum from which to discuss American culture and politics.
     In his book review column called "The Library" in the "Clini-
     cal Notes" column, and in his "Editorial" essays, Mencken dis-
     cussed Dreiser several times.
        Article lists 15 items in which Mencken comments on Dreiser.
     The friendship, however, finally ended when Mencken wrote
     an unfavorable review of An American Tragedy in March 1926.

498   _____. "Two Beasts in the Parlor: The Dreiser-Mencken
Relationship." Ph.D. diss., SUNY (at Stony Brook), 1979.
DA, 40 (1979), 850A.
    The Dreiser-Mencken relationship has been explored in part
by a number of critics. This dissertation, however, offers
the first full-length study of the alliance and draws upon a
sizable amount of new material, principally letters and materials in Mencken's journals and notes. The careers of the
two men were intertwined and, to a degree, interdependent.
Each man's friendship with the other proved to be the most
significant literary relationship in his career.

499   _____. "Gratitude and Grievances: Dreiser's Inscriptions
to Mencken." Dreiser Newsletter, 12 (Fall, 1981), 1-16.
    Reviews the various phases of the Dreiser-Mencken relation-
ship in terms of the various books and manuscripts which
Dreiser gave to Mencken. The friendship was long, tumul-
tuous and, to say the very least, mutually beneficial. For
more than thirty years, these robust individuals--men who
were highly opinionated and stubborn, writers whose reach
sometimes exceeded their grasp--laughed and played and
drank together and sometimes fought bitterly.

500 FLANAGAN, John T. "Dreiser's Powerful Posthumous Novel."
Chicago Sun Book Week, March 24, 1946.
    In The Bulwark there is evidence of the old conviction that
life is a confusion of opposing motives and ideals, and that
man is pretty much the pawn of fickle and perverse gods.
There is also the fine old Dreiser pity and compassion for
the suffering victims of the gods. In this novel, however,
there is a new note: There is a strong positive statement
of belief that man can achieve not only peace but happiness
in this troublous world. And he can achieve it in one way--
by a love which transcends the material and the personal.

501   _____. "Theodore Dreiser in Retrospect." Southwest Review, 31 (Autumn, 1946), 408-411.
    Throughout his life he assailed a society which stacked the
cards against the frail and the weak and the poor. We are
still too close to Dreiser to evaluate his achievements justly.
Was a shaggy genius with obvious faults and striking merits.
His name is now written in large letters. May be reduced
aesthetically, but his influence will not be denied. One thing
is certain: American fiction would not have flowered when
and as it did if Dreiser had never lived.

502   _____. "Dreiser's Style in An American Tragedy." Texas
Studies in Language and Literature, 7 (Autumn, 1965), 285-
294.
    Readers have generally been impressed by Dreiser's narra-
tive power, his ability to build up and sustain a long, de-

tailed story, as in An American Tragedy. Dreiser's characters
also linger in the memory, they retain life in retrospect. On
the other hand, from beginning to end, the quality in his
fiction which most annoyed reader and critic was his style.
Dreiser's stylistic faults are of two kinds, verbal and syntac-
tical: The first category includes inaccuracies, pretentiousness, archaisms, faulty idiom, triteness, inappropriate use of
foreign terms, and unfortunate coinages. The second category includes faulty reference, dangling modifiers, failures in
agreement, and a curious substitution of participial construc-
tions for finite verbs.

503 _____. "Theodore Dreiser's Chicago." Revue des Langues
Vivantes, 32 (1966), 131-144.
    Four of Dreiser's novels, Sister Carrie (1900), The Finan-
cier (1912), The Titan (1914), and The "Genius" (1915), are
located partly or wholly in Chicago, and An American Tragedy
(1925) includes Chicago scenes. Dreiser's use of background
is highly authentic, and studied as a group these novels record a vivid period in the history of Chicago.

504 FLEISSNER, R. F. "The Macomber Case: A Sherlockian Analysis." Baker Street Journal, 20 (September, 1970), 154-
156, 169.
    Looks at "The Short Happy Life of Francis Macomber,"
(1938), by Hemingway, and wonders if Mrs. Macomber's slay-
ing of her husband is not the same ambiguous affair that
Dreiser created in An American Tragedy (1925), in Clyde's
murder of Roberta.

505 FLINT, R. W. "Dreiser: The Press of Life." Nation, 184
(April 27, 1957), 371-373.
    Article is principally a review of F. O. Matthiessen's Theo-
dore Dreiser, the book he was working on when he died.
Disagrees with most critics who did not find Matthiessen's
book satisfactory, aside from its state of incompleteness. Comments specifically on Matthiessen's grasp of Twelve Men, "one
of Dreiser's best and least-known" works. Contends that
Dreiser, although utterly lacking in sophistication, was able
to do what he had to do.

506 FLIPPEN, Charlie C., Jr. "The Influence of Journalistic Experience on Three American Novelists: Theodore Dreiser, Sinclair Lewis, and Ernest Hemingway." MA thesis, University
of North Carolina, 1966.

507 FLYNN, Dennis, and Jack Salzman. "An Interview with James
T. Farrell." Twentieth Century Literature, 22 (February,
1976, 1-10.

508 FOERSTER, Norman. American Criticism. Boston and New

York: Houghton Mifflin, 1928. Reprinted New York: Russell and Russell, 1962. Dreiser, p. 223, et passim.
No significant comment on Dreiser; see Chapter 5, "The Twentieth Century," for good background material.

509 FOLLETT, Helen and Wilson. "The Younger Generation," in Some Modern Novelists: Appreciations and Estimates. New York: Holt, 1918; London: Allen and Unwin, 1919. Pp. 350-352.
Dreiser likes to remind us that man at his best is only a beast: we like to answer that man at his worst is still man--and the women in Dreiser's books have not the spiritual possibilities which could turn their material failure into tragedy. In ignoring the importance of the ideal faculty, Dreiser cuts off the half of life which gives all the meanings to the half he treats; which is perhaps why all the passions of his books seem so perfunctory. It is enough to point out that he belongs to nothing in the present; not that he is in advance of his age, but that he has stood still while his age was going somewhere.

510 FORD, Corey (pseudo. for John Riddell). "Blue-print for Another American Tragedy," in Meaning No Offense. New York: John Day, 1927. Pp. 65-72.
Satire and parody of Dreiser's novel as the following passage clearly indicates:
"Dusk--of a summer night.
And the tall walls of an American novel of perhaps 250,000 words, such walls as in time may linger as a mere fable.
And in the center of this tall edifice, or building, a solitary man working alone very patiently by himself--a man of about fifty years, tall, with blue overalls, heavily built, yet not stout, perhaps five feet ten inches or five feet eleven inches in height, wearing a khaki shirt, with grey hair, open at the neck, black shoes, white socks, with a slight stoop, also suspenders...."

511 _____. "A Gallery of Dreiser." Vanity Fair, 3 (February, 1930), 58-59, 82.
Parody.

512 _____. "Dawn Jawn," in In the Worst Possible Taste. New York: Scribner's, 1932. Pp. 17-27.
Another satire and parody composed as a letter from "John Riddell" on the subject of writing his own autobiography. In conclusion, Ford says: "In this letter to Theodore Dreiser, stylistically ponderous like all the novels of our Great American Glacier, the impressionable Riddell has evidently attempted to produce an autobiography of his own youth in the manner of Mr. Dreiser's recent bit of alluvial deposit, entitled Dawn. Unfortunately, owing to the natural exigencies of space as

well as one or two lamentable lapses into correct English which
crept into this letter unawares, biographers feel that Riddell
failed lamentably in his effort to capture the full soporific and
blundering effect of Mr. Dreiser's style...."

513 FORD, Edwin H. "Theodore Dreiser," in A Bibliography of
     Literary Journalism in America. Minneapolis: Burgess, 1937.
     P. 22.
         Lists six books by Dreiser--The Color of a Great City (1923),
     A Book About Myself (1922), Dreiser Looks at Russia (1928),
     Hey, Rub-a-Dub-Dub (1920), A Traveller at Forty (1920),
     and Dawn (1931)--which give information of Dreiser's back-
     ground in journalism. Also lists nine books and five articles
     which deal with the subject. In the Foreword, the author
     says: "More than ever today is there a need for the liter-
     ary journalist; for the writer who is sufficiently journalistic
     to sense the swiftly changing aspects of this dynamic era,
     and sufficiently literary to gather and shape his material with
     the eye and the hand of the artist."

514 FORD, Ford Madox. "Dreiser." American Mercury, 40 (April,
     1937), 488-496. Reprinted in Ford, Portraits from Life. Bos-
     ton: Houghton Mifflin, 1937. Pp. 164-182. Also reprinted in
     Kazin and Shapiro (1955), pp. 21-35 as "Portrait of Dreiser."
         It is because he renders for us this world of fantastic in-
     certitude that Dreiser's work is of such importance, the note
     above all being that of incertitude. And most important of
     all, neither Mr. Dreiser, the private gentleman, nor Dreiser,
     the personality that emerges from his books, has any settled
     panacea for world improvement or even for world enlighten-
     ment. They have between them one settled passion--but
     neither has any more pattern than has a chart of the Milky
     Way. They will, passionately, like you and me, see one as-
     pect of life one day and another the next.

515 FORGUE, Guy Jean, ed. with Introduction and Notes. Letters
     of H. L. Mencken. New York: Knopf, 1961. Reprinted Bos-
     ton: Northeastern University Press, 1981.
         Contains 84 letters to Dreiser, from March 7, 1909, to March
     19, 1943, near the end. Later there are three letters to Helen
     Dreiser after Dreiser's death. Mencken died in 1956.

516 FORREY, Robert James. "Theodore Dreiser: The Flesh and
     the Spirit." Ph.D. diss., Yale University, 1971. DA, 33
     (1972), 309A.
         This is a study of the conflict between religion and natural-
     ism in the life and work of Dreiser. Throughout his career,
     and not just at the end, as is sometimes assumed, Dreiser was
     torn between the spirit of the Sermon on the Mount and the
     Survival of the Fittest, between compassion and selfishness,
     asceticism and sensualism, between the weak and the strong,

the poor and the rich, the failures and the successes. Too
much emphasis is generally given to Dreiser's naturalistic
thought, and not enough to his spiritual nature.

517 _____. "Theodore Dreiser." Dreiser Newsletter, 4 (Spring,
1973), 23-24.
  A poem about Dreiser, perhaps better than usual for this
kind of poem. The imagery is violent and brutal, the setting
of Dreiser and his early home near the slaughterhouse. Over
all the image of his mother prevails, "singing, hanging clean
sheets/ To dry in the sun." In conclusion, we get to the
point: "his dear dead mutt, Snap, tagging at his heels, wag-
ging his tail/ United in one last vision of light."

518 _____. "Dreiser and the Prophetic Tradition." American
Studies, 15 (Fall, 1974), 21-35.
  The idea that there is a strong religious element in Dreiser's
fiction is not new. Many critics and writers have already suggested this in different ways. What they have rarely empha-
sized, however, is that Dreiser was religious not only at the
end but also at the beginning of his career. I think, furthermore, that one can characterize the religious spirit in which
he began and ended his career as prophetic. It is possible
to distinguish four types of religious responses: the ritualis-
tic, the mystical, and apocalyptic and the prophetic. The
prophetic differs from the others in being more concerned
with the now than the hereafter; with social justice, rather
than salvation; and with the spirit, rather than the letter of
religious law.

519 _____. "Theodore Dreiser: Oedipus Redivivus." Modern
Fiction Studies, 23 (1977), 341-354.
  Article is based largely on a Freudian analysis of Dreiser's
works, principally An American Tragedy, which he sees as a
demonstration of the father-son relationship; in conclusion,
he sees The Bulwark as Dreiser's testament of acceptance of
the father. In final chapters we enter into the peaceable
kingdom in which the father speaks to the Father, and father
and daughter are reconciled in spiritual love.

520 FOSTER, Charles H. "The 'Theonomous Analysis' in American
Culture," in Studies in American Culture: Dominant Ideas
and Images, edited by Joseph J. Kwiat and Mary C. Turpie.
Minneapolis: University of Minnesota Press, 1960. Pp. 189-
206.
  Thinks we have made too much of Dreiser's own statements
that he found life confused and meaningless, and cites a number of examples which point this up. Examples are drawn
from his early fiction, some short stories, and in his poetry.
Also finds it significant that Dreiser edited a book of selections by Thoreau. His was a lifelong struggle in the midst

of autonomy toward theonomous values. Perhaps more than
any other writer of the early twentieth century Dreiser marks
the transition from autonomy to the theonomic concerns, if
not certainties, expressed finally by Anderson, Eliot, Faulkner, and Warren.

521 FOSTER, William Z. "Communist Party's Tribute to Dreiser."
     Sunday Worker, December 30, 1945. P. 2.

522 FOWLER, Gene. Beau James: The Life and Times of Jimmy
     Walker. New York: Viking, 1949. Dreiser, pp. 36-38 et
     passim.
     Mostly relates Jimmy Walker to Paul Dresser who tried to
     encourage Walker's musical hopes. Draws a contrast between
     Paul and Theodore: Paul having too much natural gaiety to
     become a brooding realist. Also refers to Sarah White, "Aunt
     Jug" to the Walker children, who at the time was separated
     from Theodore but not divorced.

523 FRANK, Waldo. "Emerging Greatness." Seven Arts, 1 (Novem-
     ber, 1916), 73-78. Reprinted in The Achievement of Sher-
     wood Anderson, edited by Ray Lewis White. Chapel Hill:
     University of North Carolina Press, 1966. Pp. 20-24.
     Remarks directed primarily to Anderson's first novel, Windy
     McPherson's Son. "I was not certain that Dreiser was a
     classic until I had read this novel of Mr. Anderson. Its first
     half is a portal from which emerges an American soul. This
     portal is the immediate past, and in the works of Mr. Dreiser
     we find its definite expression. Beside their magnificent mass-
     rhythms, the opening chapters of Anderson are paltry. One
     feels that the uneasy spirit of Sam McPherson has come forth
     from the choking structures of Mr. Dreiser ... who has caught
     the crass life of the American, armoring himself with luxury
     and wealth that he misunderstands, with power whose heritage
     of uses he ignores. His books are a dull, hard mosaic of ma-
     terials beneath which one senses vaguely a grandiose move-
     ment: this is Dreiser, and this enough. But with Anderson
     the elemental movement begins to have form and direction; the
     force that causes it is being borne into the air."

524 _____. "Chicago," in Our America. New York: Boni and
     Liveright, 1919. Pp. 117-146. Good review of Our America
     by Jacob Zeitlin. Nation, 110 (May 1, 1920), 595.
     With reference to Masters, the author says: "It does not
     create in three dimensioned form the multiple life of our Amer-
     ican town ... that theme is the Despair of all his middle-
     generation, the cry, part anguished and part wistful, of those
     who have lost old gods and found no new ones. Perhaps the
     most majestic monument of this transition by which America
     needed to journey upward into birth is in the novels of The-
     odore Dreiser.... He has professionally followed writing all

his life, and has come East to New York; yet deeply he expresses a muffled music of which Chicago is the tonal key."

525 _____. "Theodore Dreiser: The Colossus of Children," in Time Exposures (by Search-light, pseudo.). New York: Boni and Liveright, 1926. Pp. 159-164.

He has no power of analysis, no eye for characterization. He is cultureless, formless, uncontrolled. And yet he has the grace of one who has truly lived, he has the light and the mysterious mark of genius. If there be any writer in our midst worthy of our homage, worthy to be called our master, it is this neolithic Dreiser. For such a child as he, courageous, enthusiastic, spiritually pure, must be father to the American Man--if ever there is to be one.

526 _____. "Our Arts: The Rediscovery of America: XII." New Republic, 54 (May 9, 1928), 343-347.

Begins by pointing out that every work of art has two aspects which may be considered separetely: esthetically it is an organism endowed with its own life; and culturally it is a sum of elements, psychological and social. The aim of this article is strictly cultural, to show the portrait of American life which certain art forms contribute to creating. Of Dreiser, he says: "In the books of Dreiser, the reflection of our jungle is more deep, more profound, and more engaging. His tune is plaintively self-suffering ... his richer temperament makes darker the reflected chaos of our world."

527 FRANKLIN, Pauline M. "American and English Criticism of Theodore Dreiser." MA thesis, University of Iowa, 1926.

528 FRANZ, Eleanor Waterbury. "The Tragedy of the 'North Woods.' " New York Folklore Quarterly, 4 (Summer, 1948), 85-96.

529 FRAZIER, Alexander S. "The Influence of Darwinism on Theodore Dreiser's Concept of the American Businessman." MA thesis, Bowling Green State University, 1966.

530 FREEDMAN, William A. "A Look at Dreiser as Artist: The Motif of Circularity in Sister Carrie." Modern Fiction Studies, 8 (Winter, 1962-1963), 384-392.

Maintains that there is a good deal to be learned from Dreiser's prose, and that perhaps too much has been said about Dreiser's shortcomings. An important measure of literary success is artistic depth, the degree to which a writer can suffuse his work with a subsurface atmosphere of suggestion and undertone complementary to the surface action and significance. This article examines the motif of circularity, in the recurrence of events and repetitiousness of Carrie's striving, and also in the unavoidable futility of that striving.

531 FREEMAN, John. "An American Tragedy." London Mercury, 16 (October, 1927), 607-614.

532 FREEMAN, Joseph. An American Testament: A Narrative of Rebels and Romantics. New York: Farrar, Rinehart, 1936; London: Victor Gollancz Ltd., 1938. Dreiser, passim. Author was one of the editors of New Masses, a left-wing magazine published from 1926 to 1940. The history of this publication began/ in 1911 with the organization of a weekly journal The Masses, which became consistently more Socialistic in its policy until it was suppressed by the government in 1918. Three months later the editors founded The Liberator, a weekly journal of social criticism with an increasingly radical point of view. In 1922 it became affiliated with the Communist party and was suspended in 1924. It was revived in 1926 as The New Masses. Among the authors who interested the editors of this publication was Dreiser.

533 FRENCH, Warren. The Social Novel at the End of an Era. Carbondale: Southern Illinois University Press, 1966. Dreiser, pp. 173-174. The novel with which early reviewers most frequently compared Native Son was An American Tragedy which also dealt with a poor and irresponsible young man who is executed for his part in a girl's death. The parallel, however, is not really close, despite the superficial similarity of the incidents. Even though Clyde was not technically responsible for the death of his sweetheart, he had carefully plotted to murder her. He wanted her out of the way, when he calculated that he might have a chance to marry an heiress. Society was responsible for his criminal intentions because it inspired him with meretricious ideals.

534 _____, ed. The Twenties: Fiction, Poetry, Drama. Deland, Fla.: Everett-Edwards, 1975. "Strange Bedfellows: The Waste-Land and An American Tragedy," by Carol Clancy Harter, pp. 51-64.

535 FRIEDE, Donald. The Mechanical Angel: His Adventures and Enterprises in the Glittering 1920's. New York: Knopf, 1948. Dreiser, p. 22 et passim. Recalls a number of episodes in which Dreiser figured. One of the better examples: "I sat next to him, watching his reactions as the story he had created was unfolded on the stage before him. He sat there massively, intensely, as completely absorbed by the play as if all of it were something he was seeing and hearing for the first time.... He would not get up in the intermission. He would not talk. He just sat there. And when the curtain went down on the death-cell scene he turned to me, and I could see that there were tears in his eyes. 'The poor boy!' he said. 'The poor bastard! What a shame!' " Refers to Clyde Griffiths.

536 FRIEDRICH, Gerhard. "Theodore Dreiser's Debt to Woolman's
    Journal." American Quarterly, 7 (Winter, 1955), 385-392.
    It is curious that Dreiser should have come under the spell
    of John Woolman's pen. There is still a tendency to stereo-
    type Dreiser as a verbose and ponderous exponent of natural-
    ism, of biological drives and economic pressures, who was
    first intrigued by the success of unscrupulous business mag-
    nates, then fascinated and moved by the tragic purposeless-
    ness of life. Such an estimate passes over too lightly some
    traits which were involved in Dreiser's discovery of Woolman's
    Journal. How did he happen to become acquainted with it,
    and what did he find? This article traces in detail and logi-
    cally the major steps in an answer to this question.

537 _____. "A Major Influence on Theodore Dreiser's The Bul-
    wark." American Literature, 29 (May, 1957), 180-193.
    Quotes from Rufus M. Jones' A Boy's Religion from Memory,
    in which is said that Quakerism is still a living force. Whether
    Dreiser who lived in Philadelphia in 1902-1903 and who had
    published Sister Carrie with its curious Quaker intrusion,
    happened to read the passage quoted above is an open ques-
    tion. We have, however, thirty-six years later in his own
    work that he read with great interest the revised and enlarged
    edition of Jones' book. He owned a copy of the book, reis-
    sued under the title Finding the Trail of Life, and underlined
    in it the introductory passage.

538 _____, ed. with Introduction. "The Dreiser--(Rufus M.)
    Jones Correspondence." Bulletin of the Friends Historical
    Association, 50 (Spring, 1957), 23-24. Correspondence with
    Rufus Jones, 1938-1945.

539 FROHOCK, Wilbur M. "Lionel Trilling and the American Reality,"
    in Strangers to This Ground. Dallas: SMU Press, 1961.
    Pp. 31-34.
    Trilling shows that Dreiser's diction is no better than his
    thought, which is muddled, undisciplined, uneducated, un-
    original, and vulgar. Trilling would probably agree that
    Dreiser was also a victim of imprecision in feeling, that he
    does not know the nature of an emotion, and so never can
    find the word to define it. I suspect the real difficulty is
    that Dreiser does not properly know what his own feelings
    are and is taking refuge from his own vagueness in the in-
    appropriate adjective and the false tone.

540 _____. Theodore Dreiser. Minneapolis: University of Min-
    nesota Press, 1972. 48-page pamphlet. Reprinted in Seven
    Novelists in the American Naturalist Tradition: An Introduc-
    tion, edited by Charles Child Walcutt. Minneapolis: Univer-
    sity of Minnesota Press, 1974. Pp. 92-130. Also reprinted
    in American Writers: A Collection of Literary Biographers,

2 vols., edited by Leonard Ungar. New York: Scribner's, 1974. Vol. I, pp. 497-520.
Brief, overall review of life and works. Concludes with selective bibliography and list of Dreiser's works. He did not solve such dilemmas as good and bad, strength and weakness, morality, free will, etc., but he did refuse to sweep them away. Europeans have long been trying to tell us that this kind of novelist should command more than perfunctory respect.

541 _____. "The State of Dreiser Criticism on His Centenary," in Geschichte und Gesellschaft in der Amerikanischen Literatur, edited by Karl Schubert and Ursula Muller-Richter. Heidelberg: Quelle & Meyer, 1975. Article in English in German publication.

542 FUESSLE, Newton A. "An Admirer of Dreiser." Reedy's Mirror, 25 (September 8, 1916), 576.
Letter to the editor.

543 FULLER, Henry B. "Chicago Novelists." Literary Review, 3 (March 18, 1922), 501-502.

544 FURMANCZYK, Wieslaw. "Theodore Dreiser's Worldview in the Light of Unpublished Materials." Ph.D. diss., University of Warsaw, 1966.

545 _____. "The Conception of External Forces in Theodore Dreiser's Philosophical Notes." Acta Philologica, 1 (1968), 23-42.
Based largely on dissertation listed above.

546 _____. "Theodore Dreiser's Philosophy in Notes on Life." Dreiser Newsletter, 3 (Spring, 1972), 9-12.
One of the basic feataures of Dreiser's philosophy in his Notes on Life is determinism, which arises from his deep conviction that man's life is mechanistically conditioned. Other ideas grow out of this basic assumption: man has no free will, there are no absolute moral laws, man and nature are subject to the same laws, etc. Dreiser's ideas reflect the influence of many thinkers, such as Darwin, Spencer, Haeckel, and Loeb, yet he accepted only those views which confirmed his own observations. His Notes on Life show that he was an inquiring writer.

547 FURST, Lilian R. "A Question of Choice in the Naturalistic Novel: Zola's Thérèse Raquin and Dreiser's An American Tragedy," in Modern American Fiction: Insights and Foreign Lights, edited by Wolodymyr T. Zyla and Wendell M. Aycock. Proceedings of the Comparative Literature Symposium, Vol. 5. Lubbock: Texas Tech Press, Interdepartmental Committee on Comparative Literature, 1972. Pp. 39-55.

Scientific determinism applied to human conduct means that man is reduced to the level of a mere instrument: the instrument of heredity, environment, and the pressure of the moment. Man is robbed of choice. But what is questionable is the actual operation, within particular novels, of scientific determinism, especially the implication that determinism negates freedom of choice. Are the characters in practice really as devoid of choice of action as the theory of scientific determinism would suggest? This is the question raised by an examination of Zola's Thérèse Requin and Dreiser's An American Tragedy.

548 _____. "Innocent or Guilty? Problems in Filming Dreiser's An American Tragedy." Connecticut Review, 9 (1976), 33-40.

549 GABRIEL, Ralph Henry. The Course of American Democratic Thought. New York: Ronald Press, 1940. Dreiser, pp. 373-375.
Is man free? Is he master of his destiny? The scientist replies that he can only find determinism in nature, a law of cause and effect. An anthropologist pictures the individual as the product of cultural determinism. We are in the stream, thought William Graham Sumner, and are swept along by its current. We shall certainly not change its course. Such remarks are appropriate to Dreiser.

550 GALE, Zona. "Period Realism." Yale Review, n.s., 17 (Autumn, 1933), 111-124.

551 GARD, Wayne, ed. Book Reviewing. New York and London: Alfred A. Knopf, 1927. Reprints "An American Tragedy: A Review," by Sherwood Anderson (1926), pp. 88-92.

552 GARDNER, Paul. "Dreiser, Pirandothello, War and Waltzes." Canadian Forum, 12 (August, 1932), 437-438.

553 GARNER, Stanton. "Dreiser and the New York Times Illustrated Magazine: A Bibliographical Supplement." Papers of the Bibliographical Society of America, 69 (1975), 118-119.

554 GARNETT, Edward. "American Criticism and Fiction," in Friday Nights. New York: Knopf, 1922. Pp. 297-303.
Remarks concerning The Titan: in this novel Dreiser rarely introduces a character without giving a comprehensive sketch of his past and his social position, and we soon grow bored by the multiplicity of explanations and conversations, all of equal significance. There is no play of light and shade in the novel, but everything is exhibited in the hard, level glare of

an enormous chamber lit from the ceiling. Crowds of people come and go, and one remembers little more of them than of a file of faces passing in an interminable procession.

555 GARRATY, John A. Interpreting American History: Conversations with Historians, 2 vols. New York: Macmillan, 1970. "A Century of Realism in American Literature," Vol. 2, pp. 289-311. Reprinted in American Heritage, 21 (June, 1970), 12-15, 86-90 as "A Century of American Realism." See under Kazin, Alfred (1970), "An Interview with Alfred Kazin."

556 GASSER, Larry Winston. "Social Reform in the Late Nineteenth-Century American Strike Novel." Ph.D. diss., University of Denver, 1974. DA, 36 (1975), 887A-888A.
Strike novels of the late nineteenth century in America provide an excellent way to examine how social reform affects the writing of fiction. Novels of this period fall into three categories: those against strikes, those for strikes, and those which do not actually take sides. Many authors used the strike but few of them did so effectively. One of the best examples is that of Dreiser's use of the strike to illuminate the final stage of his protagonist's long decline in Sister Carrie.

557 GEDULD, Carolyn. "Wyler's Suburban Sister: Carrie, 1952," in The Classic American Novel and the Movies, edited by Gerald Peary and Roger Shatzkin. New York: Ungar, 1977. Pp. 152-164.

558 GEISMAR, Maxwell. The Novel in America: Writers in Crises. New York: Houghton Mifflin, 1942. Dreiser passim.

559 _____. "Dreiser and the Dark Texture of Life." American Scholar, 22 (Spring, 1952), 215-221.
This article is derived from Geismar's work Rebels and Ancestors (1953). Reviews selected aspects of Dreiser's life to indicate that his was a search for a way to express the passions and appetites he had felt in American society. The established literary code of the 1900's was the happy, roseate description of life. For Dreiser life had its darker phases, the coarse and the vulgar and the cruel and the terrible. This was the beginning of his own literary career--the dark texture of life as he had himself felt it.

560 _____. "Jezebel on the Loop." Saturday Review of Literature, 36 (July 4, 1953), 12.
Adopts the tone of a turn-of-the-century literary critic and reviews the Modern Library publication of Sister Carrie in 1953. Among other derogatory remarks, he says: "the new century dawns in social turmoil and philosophical anarchy.... The publishers were undoubtedly correct in returning it to

their deepest cellars--safely away from the light of reason
and common sense, and from the riots it might well provoke
on the part of an outraged American citizenry."

561   _____. "Theodore Dreiser: The Double Soul," in Rebels
and Ancestors: The American Novel, 1890-1915. Boston:
Houghton Mifflin, 1953. Pp. 287-379.
    Long, detailed account of Dreiser and his publications. In
six parts: The Last Victorian, Fairy Tales of the Nineties,
The Animal Kingdom, Poet of Desire, Receding Arctic Shores
of Mind, and The Ultimate Dark. In conclusion, Geismar says:
"So in four decades of literary pioneering, he could hardly
be denied the final moment of surrender and peace which was
described in The Bulwark.... It was a love, Dreiser said,
that went beyond human passion and its selfish desires and
ambitions. It was a unity with all nature in which there was
nothing fitful or changing or disappointing, nothing that
glowed one minute and was gone the next. Perhaps the 'good
intent' which Solon Barnes established as the method of his
salvation on earth, was indeed a universal language, and the
only one which could express the imperfect circumstances of
human destiny."

562   _____. "A Novelist True to Himself in a Shifting World."
New York Times Book Review, November 20, 1955. P. 4.

563   _____. American Moderns: From Rebellion to Conformity.
New York: Hill and Wang, 1958. Dreiser, pp. 49-53.
    There is little question that Dreiser is the most distinguished
member of the whole group of modern American novelists. His
novels have been obscured by a fog of errors and misconcep-
tions. The terms used to establish his literary position (ele-
phantine, doltish, coarse, dismal, flatulent) are still used by
the New Critics to describe him today. What gave his work
its remarkable texture, its glamour, was simply his sense of
the variety of life on all its levels.

564   _____. "Society and the Novel," in A Time of Harvest:
American Literature, 1910-1960, edited by Robert E. Spiller.
New York: Hill and Wang, 1962. Pp. 33-41.
    Discusses the question of "Who is to blame, indeed, in the
whole panorama of Dreiser's fiction, where poor, helpless human beings are always jostled and buffeted by the winds and
tides of their own temperaments and passions." Dreiser's view
of the universe was that of a turbulent dark whirlpool which
sucked down the individual into its abysmal depths. Yet
there was often a kind of lyrical pagan admiration for all the
beauties of existence, even in their violence, despite all their
cruelty. Like Hawthorne, he had the tragic sense only high
artists have.

565 _____. "The Shifting Illusion: Dream and Fact," in American Dreams, American Nightmares, edited by David Madden.
Carbondale: Southern Illinois University Press, 1970. Pp.
45-57.
   Repeats some of the ideas expressed in other writings, but
adds: "It was Dreiser, the greatest modern American realist,
just as Melville was the greatest novelist of the 19th-Century,
whose work most clearly showed the twisting and turnings of
the American Dream concept. In the beginning of his career
he envisioned the 'American Century' in which he foresaw
another blooming of our native culture and art. By 1925 An
American Tragedy described his whole society as a monstrous
trap, which corrupted such average souls as Clyde Griffiths
through its visions of instant cash and hot culture."

566 _____, ed. with Introduction. Sister Carrie. New York:
Pocket Books, 1949. Abridged version. Introduction reprinted as "Theodore Dreiser," in American Moderns (1958).

567 GELFANT, Blanche H. "The American City Novel, 1900-1940:
A Study of the Literary Treatment of the City in Dreiser,
Dos Passos, and Farrell." Ph.D. diss., University of Wis-
consin, 1951.
   Published 1954 in the following item.

568 _____. "Theodore Dreiser: The Portrait Novel," in The
American City Novel. Norman: University of Oklahoma Press,
1954. Pp. 42-94.
   Dreiser's interpretation of the city, growing as it did out
of a typical social experience of the times, has a broad historical relevancy, as well as significant implications for the
development of American fiction. His personal discovery summarizes and comprehends a social experience of the times; in
coming to the city, observing it, responding to it, and evalu-
ating and finally rejecting it, Dreiser went through a typical
pattern of hope and disillusionment.

569 GELLERT, Hugo. "The Titan." New Masses, 7 (September,
1931), 6-7.

570 GENT, George. "Two Subjects for Centennial: Dreiser and
Johnson." New York Times, October 12, 1971. P. 48.

571 GERBER, Philip L. Theodore Dreiser. New York: Twayne,
1964. T. U. S. A. series, #52. Bibliography, pp. 201-211.
   Consists of some 200 pages with good selective bibliography
and index. Contains a complete listing of Dreiser's published
works. Presents a well-ordered review and discussion of
Dreiser's life and works, in the following chapters:
   1. The Well of Memory: Dreiser's Youth
   2. A Waif Amid Forces: Sister Carrie

3. The Washerwoman's Daughter: Jennie Gerhardt
4. Financier, Titan, and Stoic: A Trilogy of Desire
5. Self-Portrait of the Artist: The "Genius"
6. "Society Should Ask Forgiveness": An American Tragedy
7. God and Mammon: The Bulwark
8. "The World's Worst Great Writer": Dreiser's Artistry

More authors than not are sent to the junkheaps by the indifference of generations immediately following them. But in Dreiser's case the passage of time has resulted only in a steady accretion of reputation and in a niche in American literature which seems ever more clearly defined, more permanent, more secure.

572 _____. "Two Dreisers Plus One." Dreiser Newsletter, 1 (Spring, 1970), 6-10.

Review-article of Two Dreisers by Ellen Moers (1969), and Theodore Dreiser: His World and His Novels by Richard Lehan (1969). Mostly complimentary of the two volumes, saying Ellen Moers "has produced a volume that can hold its own with any Dreiser study thus far published." Of Lehan's study, Gerber says it is "sparkling with details gleaned from intensive work on the Dreiser papers," but that it is full of errors, typographical slips and otherwise. "Facts take a bad mauling."

573 _____. "A Tragedy Ballad." Dreiser Newsletter, 2 (Spring, 1971), 5-6.

Concerns firsthand interviews and documents based on the Grace Brown-Chester Gillette crime and trial on which Dreiser based his American Tragedy. Reprints the ballad which some unknown person composed on the sensational crime.

574 _____. "The Alabaster Protégé: Dreiser and Berenice Fleming." American Literature, 43 (May, 1971), 217-230.

Article traces the life and character of Emilie Grigsby, the real-life prototype of Berenice Fleming who enters Dreiser's novel The Titan as Cowperwood's beautiful young mistress and finally concludes the trilogy after Cowperwood's death in The Stoic. The real-life Emilie is a close parallel to Dreiser's fictional creation.

575 _____. "Dreiser's Financier: A Genesis." Journal of Modern Literature, 1 (1971), 354-374.

Traces the life and career of financier Charles T. Yerkes, Chicago streetcar magnate until he died in 1905. Dreiser was very much interested in this story, beginning with his youthful interest in streetcars, and finally incorporated most of the details into his trilogy of Frank Cowperwood. Article concludes with an editorial from the New York World, dated February 4, 1906, which fell into Dreiser's hands. It is possible to speculate that this editorial, outlining in skeleton the life and career of Yerkes, was the spark which began Dreiser's composition. Six years later a bulky manuscript, The Financier, went to press at Harper's. "An American writer and his subject had found each other."

576   . "Dreiser Meets Balzac at the 'Allegheny Carnegie.'" Carnegie Magazine, 46 (April, 1972), 137-139.

577   . "Dreiser's Debt to Jay Cooke." Library Chronicle (University of Pennsylvania), 38 (Winter, 1972), 67-77.
Refers to Jay Cooke: Financier of the Civil War by Ellis Paxton Oberholtzer. Shows how Dreiser borrowed and made use of some of the details and incidents for The Financier.

578   . "The Financier Himself: Dreiser and C. T. Yerkes." PMLA, 88 (January, 1973), 112-121.
Article addresses the question of why did Dreiser select Charles T. Yerkes as the model for Cowperwood. Yerkes, represented a Dreiser ideal--the Machiavellian prince, crafty, unillusioned, endowed with the ability to drive the human flock into a corner, to organize its chaos and manipulate its indecision, to extract from it the maximum personal gain. On the other hand, the great vacuum in Dreiser's portrait of Yerkes was his omission of that sense of humor which powered Yerkes, a fountain of inner laughter. This quality Dreiser could not use in creating his grim figure.

579   . "Frank Cowperwood: Boy Financier." Studies in American Fiction, 2 (August, 1974), 165-174.
Article examines the composition of Chapters I, II, and III of The Financier and shows how Dreiser had to use some initiative in creating the first ten years in the life of Frank Cowperwood. Based as it was on the life of Charles Yerkes, a rich documentation was accessible, but not much material from his birth to the time he left school to go to work. For this part of his novel Dreiser drew principally from five sources: facts from Yerkes' biography, public offices and directories, Dreiser's own boyhood, influences from reading, and details from the life of Jay Cooke.

580   . "Dreiser's Stoic: A Study in Literary Frustration." Literary Monographs, 7 (1975), 85-144. Edited by Eric Rothstein and Joseph Wittreich, Jr. Madison: University of Wisconsin Press, 1975.
Examines the history of Dreiser's third book of the trilogy, and accounts for the extraordinary delay in its composition. Dreiser's notes end with the death of Cowperwood, and all that follows was essentially the work of Helen Dreiser after Theodore died in 1945.

581 _____. "Hyde's Tabbs and Dreiser's Butlers." Dreiser Newsletter, 6 (Spring, 1975), 9-11.
Is a discussion of The Buccaneers, a novel by Henry M.
Hyde, published in 1904. It is thought that Dreiser modeled
the characters of Aileen and Edward Butler of The Financier
from Hyde's characters, the Tabbs. Hyde's book may also
have suggested a basic situation--antipathy between a powerful father and a dynamic lover, with the girl in the middle.

582 _____. "Dreiser: 'Extreme and Bloody Individualism,' " in
American Literary Naturalism: A Reassessment, edited by
Yoshinobu Hakutani and Lewis Fried. Heidelberg: Carl Winter, 1975. Pp. 107-121.
Were Dreiser even one-half as crude, blundering, blind,
addle-pated, heavy-handed and generally inept as his detrac-
tors would make him out to be, then he should have served
his immediate purpose and perished with his times. As mainly
a trailblazer though the jungle of Victorian prudery, he would
rate probably no more than a sentence in any standard literary history. To admire his compassion for the human atom
tossed in a storm of forces called Life does little to explain
his importance as the dominant novelist of the first quarter
of the twentieth-century.

583 _____. Plots and Characters in the Fiction of Theodore Dreiser. Hamden, Conn.: Archon Books of Shoe String Press,
1977.
Contains 153 pages, consisting of a Chronology, 85 pages
of summaries of Fiction, arranged alphabetically, novels and
short stories. Summaries of plots are readable, although quite
naturally overly simplistic. Remainder of book is alphabetical
listing of characters, even minor ones, with identifying tags.
Characters are also named at the end of each summary. Work
is excellent for what it purports to do--a handy and useful
reference to what for most readers is a gargantuan proposition: keeping all of Dreiser's characters and plot movements
somewhat straight.

584 _____. "The Financier Orders His Tomb." Dreiser Newsletter, 10 (Spring, 1979), 8-13.
Article concerns the tomb which Charles Yerkes had built
for himself at Greenwood cemetery in Brooklyn, and Frank
Cowperwood's tomb which is described in the closing pages
of The Stoic. Dreiser, typically so careful to be faithful to
his real-life prototypes, did not know the Yerkes tomb.

585 _____. "Dating a 'Letter to Louise.' " Dreiser Newsletter,
12 (Spring, 1981), 12-17.
Comments on a letter which Mrs. Louise Compbell seems to
have misdated, giving it as August 1, 1926. Article shows
how this date could not be correct, and finally comes to rest
on August 1, 1932, a date in which it "finds its logical home."

586 _____. "Theodore Dreiser," in Dictionary of Literary Biography, Vol. 9, Part 1, ed. by James J. Martine. Detroit:
Gale Research, 1981. Pp. 236-257.

587 _____. "Cowperwood Treads the Boards." Dreiser Newsletter, 13 (Fall, 1982), 8-17.
Discusses the efforts of an ambitious, lifetime friend and
admirer of Dreiser's to create a stage version of The Financier
and The Titan. Dreiser was never impressed with the scenario, which would have been a play breaking all records in
length of production. Nothing ever came of the script, either
as a play or motion picture.

588 _____. "Dreiser's Internal Tug-of-War." Dreiser Newsletter, 14 (Fall, 1983), 16-19.
A review of Lawrence E. Hussman's Dreiser and His Fiction
(1983). Says inb conclusion: "Whether or not one is willing
finally to go all the way with Hussman's hypothesis, one will
find the individual chapters of his book well argued, well-
written, and valuable always for their insights." As a whole
the book achieves a sense of unity not commonly found in such
studies.

589 _____, ed. with Introduction. The Financier. Cleveland:
World, 1972. Included in A Trilogy of Desire (1974).

590 _____, ed. with Introduction. The Titan. Cleveland: World,
1972. Included in A Trilogy of Desire (1974).

591 _____, ed. with Introduction. The Stoic. Cleveland: World,
1972. Included in A Trilogy of Desire (1974).
Reprinted in three volumes, New York: Thomas Y. Crowell,
1974. Apollo editions.

592 GERSTENBERGER, Donna, and George Hendrick. The American Novel, 1789-1959: A Checklist of Twentieth Century Criticism. Denver: Swallow, 1961. Dreiser, pp. 60-66. Vol.
II, criticism written 1960-1968. Chicago: Swallow, 1970.
Pp. 74-78.
Latest edition lists 55 studies of individual works, 29 general studies, and 5 bibliographical works.

593 GIBBERD, Mabel. "A Study of Dreiser's Major Characters."
MA thesis, University of Chicago, 1931.

594 GIBBS, Donald. "Dreiser the Dull." Forum, 78 (December,
1927), 155-156.

595 GILENSON, Boris. "Dreiser in the Soviet Union." Soviet Life,
No. 8 (August, 1971), 55-57.
Written to commemorate the centennial of Dreiser's birth.

Reviews Dreiser's relation to and comments on the Communist system and Russian novelists, and describes Dreiser's popularity in the Soviet Union.

596 _____. "Our Friend Dreiser (on the Centenary of His Birth)," translated by Monica White. Soviet Literature, No. 4 (1972), 172-175.
Reviews Dreiser's interests in Russian literature and his sympathies with the Soviet system, and shows why Dreiser is still one of the favorite American authors in Russia.

597 GILKES, Martin. "Discovering Dreiser." New Adelphi, 2 (December 2, 1928), 178-181.

598 GILMAN, Lawrence. "The Biography of an Amorist." North American Review, 203 (February, 1916), 290-293.
Review of The "Genius," in which the outline of the story and the character of Eugene Witla are summerized. In conclusion Gilman says: "Dreiser is an emotional historian, a master in his comprehension and delineation of sexual emotion. He has no taste, his tyle is amazingly bad; in details of execution he is naively crude and uncouth, and yet despite all this, it is hard to read him without being engrossed, and persuaded, and deeply moved.... Out of the vast welter and surge, the plethoric irrelevancies of this cyclopean novel, emerges a sense of the infinite sadness and mystery of human life.

599 GILMER, Walker. Horace Liveright: Publisher of the Twenties. New York: David Lewis, 1970. Dreiser pp. 39-59 et passim.
Reviews Liveright's relationship with Dreiser over a period of ten or twelve years. Dreiser was not easy to get along with, and although his publisher was always honest and fair with him, in spite of a good many "rotten reviews," Dreiser was cantankerous and convinced that he was being cheated out of money and publicity which he deserved.

600 GINGRICH, Arnold. "How to Become the Second-Best Authority on Almost Anything." Esquire, 55 (April, 1961), 6.

601 _____. Nothing But People. New York: Crown, 1971. Dreiser, pp. 230-232.
Sub-title is "The Early Days at Esquire: A Personal History, 1928-1958." Recalls a visit with Mencken and Dreiser: "I thought I would at least be in for an intellectual treat, as I had found so much to admire in each man's writings, and I felt sure that I would in any case get in on some memorable conversation, if only in a mouselike role.... I felt like poor little lost Poland, invited to arbitrate the differences between two great and contentious neighbors, and as unable to contend with Mencken's Prussia as with Dreiser's Russia...."

Evening devoted largely to a discussion of Vodka and sau-
sages, subjects on which Gingrich had not imagined there
was so much information.

602 GISSEN, Max. "What Must America Do?" New Republic, 104
     (May 26, 1941), 736-737.
         Reviews four books--by Stuart Cloete, Sir Norman Angell,
     Clarence K. Streit, and Theodore Dreiser--which pose the
     question of whether the United States can exist as a working
     democracy in a Hitler-dominated world. The work by Drei-
     ser is America Is Worth Saving, in which it is argued that
     America could survive as a democracy if Hitler won the war.
     Most of this book is utter nonsense and would indicate that
     Dreiser had nearly lost touch with reality. Has he seen the
     newspapers lately?

603 GLAENZER, Richard Butler. "Snap-Shots of American Novel-
     ists: Dreiser." Bookman, 46 (September, 1917), 28. Poem,
     later reprinted in Literary Snapshots. New York: Brentano's,
     1920.
         Brief, 11 lines of free verse, in which Dreiser is praised
     for "at least" having created "Two women and one man/ Who
     cannot die." How many others "Can preserve their own puny
     souls/ From daily living death?" The deathless characters
     are not specified, but are presumably Sister Carrie and Jen-
     nie Gerhardt, and Clyde Griffiths. The poet possibly has in
     mind the three main characters of An American Tragedy, two
     women and one man.

604 GLICKSBERG, Charles I. "Two Decades of Literary Criticism."
     Dalhousie Review, 16 (July, 1936), 229-242.

605 _____. "Proletarian Fiction in the U.S.A." Dalhousie Re-
     view, 17 (April, 1937), 22-32.

606 _____. "Literature and Science: A Study in Conflict."
     Science Monthly, 59 (December, 1944), 467-472.

607 _____. "Fiction and Philosophy.: Arizona Quarterly, 13
     (Spring, 1947), 5-17.
         The object of the writer of fiction is to communicate all he
     knows and feels about life, to reveal the truth about every
     aspect of experience that falls within his framework. What-
     ever is is "right," in the sense that it is a part of the flux
     and phantasmagoria of life. Throughout his troubled career,
     Dreiser sought to discover a clue to the meaning of the uni-
     verse, a formula that would explain the inscrutable welter of
     life. Life was beautiful, but it was not meaningful. Hence
     there were no final truths, no sustaining purpose, no prin-
     ciple of justice in Nature. He saw that the individual had no
     particular importance in the scheme of things. The individual

is but an infinitesimal cog in a greater machine. The novelist can make no meaningful affirmation about life.

608 _____. "Dreiser and Sexual Freedom," in The Sexual Revolution in Modern American Literature. The Hague: Martinus
Nijhoff, 1971. Pp. 33-46.
   As Dreiser portrays him, man is no longer responsible for
his actions and therefore the question of innocence or guilt,
good or evil, does not arise. The naturalistic writer of fiction aims ambitiously to report the whole truth of life, from
the lowest reaches to the highest. In his efforts to delineate
people as they are, not as they ought to be, he directs attention to those biological passions which in many temperaments are the determinants of fate.

609 GOHDES, Clarence, ed. Russian Studies of American Literature.
Chapel Hill: University of North Carolina Press, 1969. List
of Russian published articles, translations, and dissertations
on Dreiser, 1925-1963. Consists of 126 items compiled by
Valentina A. Libman, and translated by Robert V. Allen.

610 GOIST, Park Dixon. From Main Street to State Street: Town,
City, and Community in America. Port Washington, N.Y.:
Kennikat, 1977. Dreiser, pp. 68-79.
   Dreiser became a novelist of the city, and in his books he
attempted to define the meaning of large cities for American
life. With Sister Carrie he initiated the so-called "urban novel,"
with all of its identifying characteristics: there is no real
community in the city; people live and die alone; the closest
and most intimate relationships are easily abandoned. The
city of Dreiser is the epitome of non-community.

611 GOLD, Michael. "Six Open Letters: Dear Theodore Dreiser."
New Masses, 7 (September, 1931), 5.

612 _____. "The Gun Is Loaded, Dreiser." New Masses, 15
(May, 1935), 14-15.

613 _____. "The Dreiser I Knew," in The Mike Gold Reader,
edited by Samuel Sillen. New York: International Press,
1954. Pp. 159-164.
   Description of Dreiser very striking: "A Titan of the novel,
Dreiser looked like a lop-sided giant in the flesh. Around
his massive head there rested an aura of profound brooding.
This was Dreiser's most obvious feature, and many artists
who sketched or painted him always seized on it. I remember one symbolic portrait that showed Dreiser against the
crowded background of a tenement street. The huge figure
seems brooding over the poverty, observing and understanding like a lonely conscience all the crumbling houses, dirty,
packed streets and swarms of pale kids. Would any artist

sketch one of our literary successes today in such an attitude
of pity and love? No, it is unthinkable."

614 GOLDBERG, Isaac. The Man Mencken: A Biographical and
Critical Survey. New York: Simon and Schuster, 1925. Reprinted New York: AMS Press, 1968. Dreiser, passim.
Reviews early events which led to Mencken's meeting Dreiser, who was impressed with him from the beginning. Then
to Mencken's surprise, came the invitation to be the literary
critic of Smart Set. He assumed the editor or the assistant
editor had got him the post. Not until he left the magazine
did he know that Dreiser had been responsible for the ap-
pointment. By November, 1908, Mencken was in full blast,
practising in the field of letters the same methods and manners that were to make "The Free Lance" a column to be
feared.

615 _____. "In the World of Books: Theodore Dreiser as Poet."
Haldeman Julius Weekly, September 8, 1928.
Begins with an assumption that nothing a great man does
can be utterly without interest. Concludes, however, that
this book, Moods, Cadenced and Declaimed, a collection of
poems is almost totally without merit: "Everywhere is the
sign of a groping, stumbling, clumsy, mumbling intelligence....
He needs the vast background of a novel, against which and
through which he may stumble on his path to beauty. Give
him elbow room, and he'll find it."

616 GOODFELLOW, Donald M. "Theodore Dreiser and the American
Dream." Carnegie Series in English, 5 (1959), 53-66. Reprinted in Six Novelists: Stendhal, Dostoevsky, Tolstoy,
Hardy, Dreiser, and Proust, edited by William M. Schulte et
al. Pittsburgh: Carnegie Institute of Technology Press,
1959. Pp. 145-156. Reprinted Freeport, N. Y.: Books for
Libraries Press, 1972.
Reviews Dreiser's novels through An American Tragedy to
demonstrate what the author's American dream consisted of.
Concludes that Dreiser was nearly hypochondriacal on the subjects of poverty, loneliness, the want of the creature comforts and pleasures of life. Experience had marked him with
a horror of being without work. He would eventually succeed
in becoming well-to-do and successful.

617 GOSSE, Edmund. Father and Son. New York: Scribner's,
1907. Reprinted London: Heinemann, 1922. Dreiser, passim.

618 GRABO, Carl H. The Technique of the Novel. New York:
Scribner's, 1928. Reprinted New York: Gordian, 1964.
Dreiser, pp. 258-263.
Dreiser's defects of method are not necessarily inherent in
the technique of naturalism. Selection is more difficult in so

loose a design than in one employing the old-fashioned plot. The merit of the naturalistic method is that it avoids the rigidities of plot and creates a more convincing picture of the flow of experience and the accidents of destiny.

619 GRAHAM, Bessie. The Bookman's Manual. New York: Bowker, 1941, 1948, 1954, 1958, 1960. 1960 edition by Hester R. Hoffman. Dreiser, passim.

Essentially same material in each issue, with bibliographical material updated. With Mencken he waged a long fight against censorship that changed the public attitude toward the novelist who pictured life as he saw it.

620 GRAHAM, Don B. "Dreiser's Maggie." American Literary Realism, 7 (Spring, 1974), 169-170.

Based on the idea that Dreiser inadvertently refers to Stephen Crane's novel Maggie: A Girl of the Street in Chapter 4 of Sister Carrie. In this scene a young man calls out to her, "Say, Maggie, if you wait, I'll walk with you." The name Maggie was in popular usage of the day, but it does reveal a curious connection in the two novels.

621 _____. " 'The Cruise of the Idlewild': Dreiser's Revisions of a 'Rather Light' Story." American Literary Realism, 8 (Winter, 1975), 1-11.

Gives a background of rejections of story beginning in 1904 until its publication in 1918 in Dreiser's first collection of short fiction, Free and Other Stories. Dreiser had himself published the story in 1909 in his magazine The Bohemian. Main body of article consists of illustrations of changes which Dreiser made in the text over a period of years, eventually creating a new, clearer, more philosophical and psychological work.

622 _____. "Aesthetic Experience in Realism." American Literary Realism, 8 (Winter, 1975), 289-290.

The realistic novel seems preoccupied with a wide variety of aesthetic data, including painting, sculpture, music, theater, architecture, interior decor, and landscapes. Before the novel became "demeublized," as Willa Cather thought it ought to be, the meuble or furniture was vastly important. Uses novels by Frank Norris to illustrate how some of the finest dramatizations of perception occur at those moments when Gilded Age art impinges upon the lives of the characters. What is true of Norris is true of many other realist-naturalists too.

623 _____. "Dreiser and Thoreau: An Early Influence." Dreiser Newsletter, 7 (Spring, 1976), 1-4.

Discusses Dreiser's early short story "The Shining Slave Makers," and attempts to show that the essential elements

of the story are contained in the "Brute Neighbors" chapter
of Walden in the famous passage on ants. Makes a good case
for this influence, since it is a matter of record that Dreiser was familiar with Thoreau at an early age.

624 _____. "Dreiser's Use of the 'English Jefferies' in Jennie
Gerhardt." Dreiser Newsletter, 8 (Spring, 1977), 6-8.
   Jefferies is Richard Jefferies (1848-1887), an English essay-
ist and naturalist of considerable renown in his day. The
essay which Dreiser draws upon is "Beauty in the Country,"
subtitled "The Making of a Beauty." Dreiser quotes and par-
aphrases most of this essay in Jennie Gerhardt in the seduction scene. In later revisions of the novel he omitted most
of this influence, but still associated it with the seduction
scenes.

625 _____. "Dreiser's Ant Tragedy: The Revision of 'The Shining Slave Makers.'" Studies in Short Fiction, 14 (1977),
41-48.
   Outlines the allegory of the story, which was originally
based on Thoreau's famous ant passage in Walden and shows
how Dreiser revised the story from around 1900 to 1918 when
it was published as "McEwen of the Shining Slave Makers,"
in Free and Other Stories.

626 _____. "Psychological Veracity in 'The Lost Phoebe': Dreiser's Revisions." Studies in American Fiction, 6 (Spring,
1978), 100-105.
   Story was first published in 1916 and again in 1918 in Free
and Other Stories. This article examines the revisions which
Dreiser made in his story, and concludes that these changes
serve to validate "the ghost-plot as a credible psychological
drama."

627 GRATTAN, C. Hartley. "Mrs. Wharton and Mr. Dreiser."
Nation, 121 (September 30, 1925), 361.
   Review of a biography of Edith Wharton and Theodore Dreiser. The work on Dreiser, a monograph by Burton Rascoe,
is more favorably received, perhaps because in the long-run
Grattan considers Dreiser to be "potentially the more enduring
because he is more in the main stream of American life."

628 _____. "Upton Sinclair on Current Literature." Bookman,
75 (April, 1932), 61-64.
   A summary of a conversation with Upton Sinclair. He holds
Dreiser in high esteem and considers An American Tragedy
one of the great novels of the world. He is deeply impressed
with Dreiser's courage in going to the Kentucky coal fields
to see for himself how badly American men and women can be
treated and raising his voice, loudly and emphatically, in denunciation of the group that is responsible for these conditions.

629 _____. "Dreiser as Hero." Saturday Review of Literature,
     9 (January 14, 1933), 377.
     Review of Dorothy Dudley's Forgotten Frontiers: Dreiser
     and the Land of the Free. Concludes basically a favorable
     analysis by saying: "Miss Dudley's story of his career is as
     rough and rugged as Dreiser himself and fits the man almost
     perfectly."

630 GRAY, Patrice K. "The Lure of Romance and the Temptation
     of Feminine Sensibility: Literary Heroines in Selected Popular
     and 'Serious' American Novels, 1895-1915." Ph.D. diss.,
     Emory University, 1981. DA, 42 (1981), 2130A.
     This dissertation is a study of the various ways in which
     selected American novelists have relied upon, manipulated,
     or transcended the formula of romance, the prevailing liter-
     ary convention of the time. Includes novels by Edith Wharton
     Willa Cather, Henry James, and Theodore Dreiser's Sister Car-
     rie and Jennie Gerhardt. Concludes that the women who read
     romances derived a good many cultural benefits.

631 GREBSTEIN, Sheldon Norman. "Dreiser's Victorian Vamp."
     Midcontinent American Studies Journal, 4 (1963), 3-12. Re-
     printed in Fizer, ed., Sister Carrie (1970), pp. 541-551. Also
     reprinted in Wegelin, ed. (1972), 325-337.
     In short we find that in Sister Carrie, the novel which be-
     gan the revolution against prudery in America, Dreiser has
     created a Victorian Vamp: a woman who is precisely that
     mixture of strengths and weaknesses which the nineteenth
     century conceived her to be, but who is at the same time in
     her unrequited sexual sins the first modern heroine. Eve-
     like, she yields to the flesh, but in the strongest Victorian
     tradition she does so only out of the confusion and need en-
     gendered by woman's innate helplessness and man's predatory
     lustfulness. In accord with the highest fashion of the time
     she has no animality, no passion, no sexuality of her own.

632 _____. "An American Tragedy: Theme and Structure," in
     The Twenties, Poetry and Prose: Twenty Critical Essays,
     edited by Richard Langford and W. E. Taylor. Deland, Fla.:
     Everett-Edwards Press, 1966. Pp. 62-66. Reprinted in Pizer
     (1981), pp. 313-321.
     Thematically An American Tragedy is a resonant work which,
     like all enduring literary creations, reverberates on multiple
     levels of meaning, at one and the same time bearing individual,
     social, and universal implications. We need look no farther
     than the novel's title for an outline of its theme, each word
     in the title signifying a thematic dimension. Structurally the
     novel is by far the most carefully planned of Dreiser's novels,
     each "Book" deliberately matched to a major aspect of its situ-
     ations and themes. The three Books achieve considerable sym-
     metry, the first two dealing with cause and the third with
     effect.

633 _____. "Theodore Dreiser (1871-1945)," in The Politics of
        Twentieth Century Novelists, edited with Introduction by
        George A. Panichas. New York: Hawthorn Press, 1971.
        Pp. 231-250.
        With so well-examined a subject as Dreiser's politics, what
        remains to be said? Article deals with three phases of the
        problem: Dreiser's portrayal of political events in his novels
        as conspiracies in which the select few prevail over common
        ideals and public welfare; Dreiser's depiction of social opinion
        as a relentless force impinging upon individual conduct; and
        finally his treatment of heredity and environment which pro-
        duced confusion between class and caste in the portrayal of
        his characters and confounded a liberal's hope of individual
        and social progress with a fatalist's sense of futility in the
        face of overwhelming biological forces.

634 _____, reader. Sister Carrie (Audio tape). Twentieth-
        Century American Novel Series. Deland, Fla.: Everett-
        Edwards, 1971.

635 GREEN, Elizabeth and Paul. "Theodore Dreiser," in Contem-
        porary American Literature. Chapel Hill: University of
        North Carolina Press, 1925. Pp. 12-15.
        Dreiser stands as one of the sturdiest, heaviest, and most
        significant figures in contemporary American literature. A
        philosopher of sorts, believing in the ultimate extinction of
        the human race, unable to see any final purpose in existence,
        adhering to a doctrine of ceaseless change, and declaring that
        man at best is but a puny creature set amid mysterious and
        terrifying powers. And yet, as pitiable as he conceived man
        to be, few writers love and sympathize with their subjects
        as Dreiser does.

636 GREEN, William. "Dreiser Says Union Assists Operators; Green
        Makes Denial." Pittsburgh Press, June 26, 1931. P. 2.

637 GREENBERG, Emil. "A Case Study in the Technique of Real-
        ism: Theodore Dreiser's 'An American Tragedy.' " MA the-
        sis, New York University, 1936.

638 GREGORY, Charles. "Dreiser, Herman Theodore," in Makers of
        Modern Culture, edited by Justin Wintle. New York: Facts
        on File, 1981. Pp. 136-137.

639 GREGORY, Horace. "Middle Western Gloom: Theodore Drei-
        ser's Characters in Their Setting." Common Sense, May,
        1934.

640 _____. "In the Large Stream of American Tradition." New
        York Herald Tribune Books, March 24, 1946. Pp. 1-2.
        Review of The Bulwark, in which he says "it lacks the en-
        ergy and force that we associate with the writing of his Cow-

perwood novels and <u>Sister Carrie</u>; but the book carries with
it a lyrical overtone and unexpected charm. Here, as in earlier novels, Dreiser is the great and critical biographer of that
figure which was once called the 'American Business Man.' "

641 GRIFFIN, Ernest G. "Sympathetic Materialism: A Re-reading
of Theodore Dreiser." <u>Humanities Association Bulletin</u>, 20
(1969), 59-68.
    Focuses primarily on the Cowperwood trilogy, and argues
that Dreiser's pity and sympathy for his characters is not
inconsistent with his materialistic view of life. As a matter
of fact, man is all the more pitiable if he is caught in the
meaningless flux of a mechanistic universe.

642 GRIFFIN, Joseph Patrick. "The Short Stories of Theodore
Dreiser: A Critical Study." Ph.D. diss., Notre Dame, 1974.
<u>DA</u>, 35 (1975), 4521A.
    Dissertation consists principally of a history of Dreiser's
publication of his short stories, some 28 between 1896 and
1938, in a selection of magazines that reflected a wide range
in American literary taste. Study also includes a history of
Dreiser's rejections and his dogged pursuits until finally some
of his stories were accepted. Concludes that although some
of his short stories are without much "saving merit" there
are several that deserve the label of excellence.

643 _____. "Dreiser's Short Stories and the Dream of Success."
<u>Etudes Anglaises</u>, 31 (1978), 294-302.

644 _____. "Dreiser's Later Short Stories." <u>Dreiser Newsletter</u>.
9 (Spring, 1978), 5-10.
    Studies the six short stories which Dreiser published in
American periodicals after the publication of <u>Chains</u> in 1927.
These consist of "Fine Furniture," "Townsend," "Solution,"
"Tabloid Tragedy," "A Start in Life," and "The Tithe of the
Lord." Although these later stories are of uneven merit,
they indicate that Dreiser did not stop development in this
genre, and that towards the end he began to erase most of
the lines between sketch and story.

645 _____. " 'When the Old Century Was New': An Early Dreiser Parody." <u>Studies in Short Fiction</u>, 17 (1980), 285-289.
    Refers to Dreiser's first published story of any length,
"When the Old Century Was New," a story which has received
scant attention from the critics. It is his only work of the
historical romance genre, and it begins to appear that this
is not a serious work but a parody of the historical romance,
a satire of the story which was so prevalent in 1901 when
Dreiser was reading a number of popular magazines with the
purpose of trying to begin his own publishing career.

646 _____. "Dreiser Experiments with Form: Five Stories from
      Chains." English Studies in Canada, 8 (June, 1982), 174-
      186.

647 GRIFFIN, Robert J. "Carrie and Music: A Note on Dreiser's
      Technique," in From Irving to Steinbeck: Studies in Honor
      of Harry R. Warfel, edited by Motley Deakin and Peter Lisca.
      Gainesville: University of Florida Press, 1972. Pp. 73-81.
      Article is based on Dreiser's special interest in a belief
      that people often communicate by means other than verbal.
      Throughout the novel, much is made of various sounds and
      the reactions to them. The various sounds are often de-
      picted as having something of a musical effect. The power
      of music constitutes a major motif in the novel, chiefly as a
      language of the heart, expressing those feelings which words
      so inadequately convey, and the power of music to move per-
      sons of a profound nature.

648 GRIFFITH, Clark. "Sister Carrie: Dreiser's Wasteland."
      American Studies, 16 (1975), 41-47.
      Sees the narrator of Sister Carrie as a voice not unlike
      that of Tiresias in The Wasteland, detached and yet infinitely
      pitying. Dreiser perhaps anticipated in 1900 the wasteland-
      theme of modern literature. He might have had his own views
      about how to care, and about what was valuable enough to
      warrant being cared for. By showing the tragic consequences
      of a failure to care deeply and humanly, he joined such other
      "mourners at the graveside of human passion."

649 GROSCH, Anthony Richard. "Chicago Novels: An Introduction
      for Teachers." Ph.D. diss., Northwestern University, 1978.
      DA, 40 (1979), 3300A.
      This study chose thirty-one novels as representative, sug-
      gesting that Chicago novels have been written from the city's
      earliest years to the present, covering almost two hundred
      years of its existence. These novels are grouped into four
      divisions chronologically. Dreiser's Sister Carrie is discussed
      in the section called "The Powerful and often corrupt City."

650 GROSS, Dalton H. "George Sterling's Letters to Theodore
      Dreiser, 1920-1926." Dreiser Newsletter, 4 (Spring, 1973),
      14-20.
      George Sterling occupied a prominent position in California
      literary circles. From the late 1890's until his suicide at the
      Bohemian Club in 1926, Sterling knew and was respected by
      such diverse figures as Jack London, Upton Sinclair, etc.
      Mencken published Sterling's poetry in his Smart Set, and
      Dreiser declared that Sterling was greater than any we had
      thus far produced. These letters reveal that Dreiser found
      in him good companionship, and poetic tastes and philosophic
      attitudes similar to his own.

651 GUIGUET, Jean. _Sister Carrie and Dreiser._ Paris: Lettres
Modernes, 1978. In French; has not been translated.

652 GUILLON, Pierrette. "The Influence of Balzac on the Novels
of Theodore Dreiser." MA thesis, Brown University, 1948.

653 HACKETT, Francis Horizons. "Correctness," in _Horizons: A
Book of Criticism._ New York: B.W. Huebsch, 1919. Pp. 13-20.
Article is primarily concerned with Stuart P. Sherman's
critical approach to literature, and particularly with reference
to Dreiser: "The essence of Mr. Sherman's criticism is American correctness, that bloodless correctness to which New England has given its wintry flavor. He is a man of mind, grave,
responsible and careful.... He thinks Mr. Wells is a dangerous faun and Dreiser a satyr."

654 HAIGHT, Anne (Lyon). _Banned Books: Informal Notes on Some
Books Banned for Various Reasons._ New York: Bowker,
1935. Revised edition, 1955. Dreiser, pp. 81-82 in new edi-
tion.
Lists _Sister Carrie,_ The _"Genius,"_ An American Tragedy,
Dawn (as late as 1953 in Ireland). In 1933 the Nazis burned
The _"Genius"_ and _An American Tragedy_ because they "con-
tained low love affairs."

655 HAILEY, Virginia L. "Religion in the Novels of Theodore Dreiser." MA thesis, Southern Illinois University, 1951.

656 HAKUTANI, Yoshinobu. "Dreiser and French Realism." _Texas
Studies in Languages and Literature,_ 6 (Summer, 1964), 200-
212.
Reviews the evidence that Dreiser was influenced by French
realism and learned much from the manner and temperament
in which Balzac painted his Paris world. Also that it is plaus-
ible to assume that Dreiser knew Zola's _Le Roman experimental_
(1881), which was translated into English by Belle Sherman in
1893. Concludes that for Dreiser the literary influences were
hardly a conscious process. His process of creating fiction
was not slow or cold; it was a passionate, emotional process
in accord with his own concept and his own experience.

657 _____. "Sinclair Lewis and Dreiser: A Study in Continuity
and Development." _Discourse,_ 7 (Summer, 1964), 254-276.

658 _____. "Dreiser Before _Sister Carrie:_ French Realism and
Early Experience." Ph.D. diss., Pennsylvania State Univer-
sity, 1965. _DA,_ 27 (1966), 774A.
Dreiser had read Darwin before he became acquainted with
Zola's works, and as early as 1894 he had discovered Spencer

and other English naturalists at the time that he discovered
Balzac.

659 _____. "Sister Carrie and the Problem of Literary Naturalism." Twentieth Century Literature, 13 (April, 1967), 3-17.
Reviews the evidence that Sister Carrie is constructed according to the principles of naturalism--both as to plot and
characterization--but then argues that "man's striving for
the ideal is the keynote at the heart of Sister Carrie." In
conclusion Hakutani says: "The works of Dreiser's early
phase are not in a true sense naturalistic in their views of
life. While the first novel is colored by the terms of the so-
called Darwinism or Spencerian philosophy, these terms do
not shape the essential voice Dreiser the artist is trying to
convey.

660 _____. "Theodore Dreiser's Editorial and Free-Lance Writing." Library Chronicle (University of Pennsylvania), 37
(Winter, 1971), 70-85.
Based on Dreiser's magazine articles between 1895 and 1899,
and shows how this work, rather than earlier newspaper articles, is the best guide to understanding Dreiser's philosophy
of life and his somewhat uncertain wavering between pessimistic determinism and optimistic idealism.

661 _____. "Dreiser and American Magazines of the 1890's."
Library Chronicle 43 (Spring, 1978), 55-80.

662 _____. "The Making of Dreiser's Early Short Stories: The
Philosopher and the Artist." Studies in American Fiction,
6 (Spring, 1978), 47-63.
Disagrees with the critical view that Dreiser's short stories
"add little to an analysis of the novels and may be compared
to a painter's sketches." Article discusses each story in
terms of its contraditions, within the story, and between the
different stories. Sees this ambivalence as the early stage of
Dreiser's practice of applying the theory of determinism as
well as designing his stories with a historical, and often personal significance.

663 _____. "Theodore Dreiser, Japan, and World War II." Resources for American Literary Study, 8 (Autumn, 1978), 188-
192.
Reviews the attraction Japan has had for earlier writers,
Emerson and Thoreau, for example, and the interest Dreiser
had in the East prior to the War. He was not as opposed to
Hitler as most Americans were, but when the Japanese attacked
Pearl Harbor he called it "the thug tactic--of sneaking up with
a lead pipe." From this point on he supported President
Roosevelt wholeheartedly and urged other American writers
to cooperate with their government, for as he put it, "We
have a war to win."

664 _____. "The Dream of Success in Dreiser's _A Gallery of Women_." _Zeitschrift für Anglistik und Amerikanistik_, 27 (1979), 236-246. Published in Leipzig, Germany; article in English.

665 _____. "_Native Son_ and _An American Tragedy_: Two Different Interpretations of Crime and Guilt." _Centennial Review_, 23 (Spring, 1979), 208-226.
Points out that several early reviewers of _Native Son_ saw the similarities to Dreiser's novel as to theme and technique. This article, however, focuses on the differences in the two novels, saying that "the comparison is of limited value." Concludes that the chief difference lies in the fact that Wright's character "has opted for the identity of a murderer," and that Clyde is presented from beginning to end as a victim of the forces over which he has no control.

666 _____. "Dreiser and Rose White." _Library Chronicle_, 44 (Spring, 1979), 27-31.
Refers to the younger sister of Sarah White, Dreiser's first wife. Some evidence that Dreiser preferred Rose, who seemed more sophisticated.

667 _____. _Young Dreiser: A Critical Study_. Rutherford, N.J.: Fairleigh Dickinson University Press, 1979; London: Associated University Press, 1980.

668 HALDEMAN-JULIUS, Emanuel. "Dreiser into His Own." _Haldeman. Julius Weekly_ (Girard, Kansas), October 10, 1925. Pp. 1-2.

669 _____. "What the Editor Is Thinking About: Theodore Dreiser." _Haldeman-Julius Weekly_, August 7, 1926. P. 4. Reprinted in _The Fun I Get Out of Life_. Big Blue Book, No. B-8. Girard, Kansas: Haldeman-Julius, 1927. Pp. 79-83.

670 _____. _The First Hundred Million_. New York: Simon and Schuster, 1928. Reprinted New York: Arno Press, 1974. No index. Dreiser, p. 270 et passim.
Refers briefly to Dreiser as editor of the _Delineator_, a women's magazine in which Haldeman-Julius advertised his "Little Blue Books" series.

671 _____. _The Big American Parade_. Boston: The Stratford Company, 1929. Dreiser, pp. 287 et passim.
Dreiser, who had neither patriotic nor political motives, who was an unterrified, unmoral realist, felt the full force of Puritanical public opinion. His early novels were betrayed by publishers, censored, and damned. He was considered a menace to all that the older America held dear and true. He was too slightly impressed by conventional moral values, too

unmorally or scientifically interested in the dissection of psychology. But Dreiser has lived to see the vindication of his
theory, if not his style, of fiction and to see himself become
a best seller, with hundreds of thousands of newly emanci-
pated Americans rushing to get his American Tragedy, where
only a few years ago his Sister Carrie was anathema.

672 _____. The Outline of Bunk. Boston: The Stratford Com-
      pany, 1929. Dreiser, pp. 236 et passim.
      What strangely confused ideas of morality some people do
      have! There are solid citizens who are unmoved by a great
      national scandal such as Teapot Dome, yet who seem per-
      sonally to resent in the name of virtue a casual episode of
      illicit love on the part of a neighbor. The well-known tired
      business man reads Elinor Glyn with leering gusto and re-
      fers to Theodore Dreiser as a most immoral writer whose
      novels should be suppressed.

673 _____. The World of Haldeman-Julius, with a Foreword by
      Harry Golden; compiled by Albert Mordell. New York: Twayne
      Publishers, 1960. Dreiser and Mencken, passim.

674 _____, ed. Haldeman-Julius as a Writer on Free Thought.
      Girard, Kansas: Haldeman-Julius, 1951.

675 HALEY, Carmel O'Neill. "The Dreisers." Commonweal, 18
      (July 7, 1933), 265-267.
      Accounts of Paul and Theodore Dreiser and of their father
      by a friend of Mary Frances Dreiser.

676 HALFMANN, Ulrich. "Dreiser and Howells: New Light on Their
      Relationship." Amerikastudien, 20 (1975), 73-85.
      Article has its origin in this author's "Interviews with Wil-
      liam Dean Howells" (American Literary Realism, 6, Fall, 1973).
      In an abstract of "Dreiser and Howells ... (ALR, 8, Autumn,
      1975, p. 375) Halfmann says, "Dreiser's first article on Howells,
      in 1898, is largely a fake. Dreiser probably never personally
      interviewed Howells for Success Magazine, but rather sub-
      mitted a questionnaire which Howells answered. Given Drei-
      ser's plagiarism and his disagreements with Howells, the docu-
      ments of the entire Dreiser-Howells relationship fall into a
      pattern which makes psychological sense."

677 HALLECK, Reuben Post. "The Novel: Theodore Dreiser,
      1871--," in The Romance of American Literature. New York:
      American Book, 1934. Pp. 309-314.
      Newspaper writing was the school in which Dreiser learned
      to write fiction. His training along such lines explains his
      liking for exactness and for detailed facts. His newspaper
      experience also enabled his realistic fiction to cover fields un-
      touched by Howells and James, adding striking materials from

commercial and industrial life. His early experiences brought
him in contact with the seamy side of life, which he stresses
too much. But this objection cannot detract from his good
points, his sympathy and close observation.

678 HALSEY, Van R. "Fiction and the Businessman: Society
Through All Its Literature." American Quarterly, 11 (Fall,
1959), 391-402.
Article is not primarily concerned with novels by such literary figures as Sinclair Lewis, Dreiser, etc., but rather "the
dozens of business novels which are generally much more
favorable in their treatment." Also concerned with the large
body of magazine fiction of mass circulation status, the "interminable stream of sugar-coated, situational and stereotyped"
business stories. Remarks that Dreiser's trilogy on Cowperwood is one of the giants in the field.

679 HANDY, William J. "A Re-examination of Dreiser's Sister Carrie." Texas Studies in Language and Literature, 1 (Autumn,
1959), 380-393. Reprinted in Handy, Modern Fiction: A For-
malist Approach. Carbondale: Southern Illinois University
Press, 1971. Also reprinted in Pizer, ed., Sister Carrie
(1970), pp. 518-527.
Today we can say with some assurance that Dreiser will
survive. Granted that Dreiser's style is awkward, that he
is verbose, and that his diction is faulty. The important
consideration is What are the stylistic devices employed and
what are the particular literary effects achieved by these devices?

680 _____. "Saul Bellow and the Naturlaistic Hero." Texas Studies in Language and Literature, 5 (Winter, 1964), 538-545.
Compares the tradition of naturalism since 1945 in the novels
of James Jones and Norman Mailer. The hero in each work is
much more complex than the heroes of Dreiser's novels, yet
each comes to the same ignominious end as Dreiser's characters. Each struggles to maintain a sense of his integrity
in a world which is not only inimical to individual values but
one which has lost the capacity to comprehend them. For
Salinger, Bellow, and Malamud, there was a new awareness
of what individual existence could mean: the individual's determination to discover, amid a welter of inner as well as outer
determining forces, a self which could be accepted and af-
firmed.

681 HANEY, John Louis. "Dreiser Plan Has Many Faults." New
York Evening Journal, May 15, 1931. P. 38.

682 _____. "Theodore Dreiser," in The Story of Our Literature:
An Interpretation of the American Spirit. New York: Scribner's, 1939. Pp. 264-265.

Regards work of Dreiser as "detailed studies of American
life." Unfortunately Dreiser permits vulgarity and a tiresome
insistence on details to detract from the artistry of even his
best work.

683 HANLEY, Richard Eugene. "Place to Place: A Study of the
Movement Between the City and Country in Selected Twentieth-
Century American Fiction." Ph.D. diss., SUNY at Bingham-
ton, 1981. DA, 42 (1981), 2130A-2131A.
Dissertation investigates two patterns of movement recorded
in twentieth-century American fiction: the move towards the
country and the move to the city. Dreiser is included with
those in the second group, who generally portray their characters in some state of befuddlement, awe, hope, and fascination with the prospects of the city.

684 HANSEN, Erik A. "Theodore Dreiser," in Sven M. Kristensen,
ed., Fremmede Digtere in detao Arbundrede, 2 vols. Copenhagen: G. E. C. Gad, 1967. Vol. 1, pp. 217-228.

685 HANSEN, Harry. "The First Reader: A Review of Chains."
New York World, May 22, 1927. P. 8.
We may even say this book is made up of chips from the
novelist's workbench, yet taken as a whole it gives us a
glimpse of this author's relentless peering into life. He finds
this or that emotion, this tragedy, worth study. He plays
with the skeins of fate--sees where they lead.

686 _____. "The First Reader: Dreiser in Russia." New York
World, November 10, 1928.
Review of Dreiser Looks at Russia.

687 _____. "The First Reader: Moods, Cadenced and Declaimed."
New York World, August 9, 1928.
The whole book is autobiographical, and probably the best
service that it performs is to reveal the author's mind. There
are some fine lines in the collection, and the simplicity and
directness of the moods enhance their value.

688 _____. "The First Reader: Dreiserian Women." New York
World, November 30, 1929. P. 13.
Review of A Gallery of Women.

689 _____. "The First Reader: Review of Dawn." New York
Evening World Telegram, May 9, 1931.

690 _____. "Mencken Tells How He Tried to Reform Dreiser's
Writing." Chicago Sunday Tribune, March 24, 1946. Part
4, p. 4.

691 _____. "The Stoic: Third of Dreiser's Cowperwood Stories,

Coming." <u>Chicago Sunday Tribune</u>, August 31, 1947. Part
4, p. 5.

692   _____, ed. with Introduction. <u>An American Tragedy</u>, illustrated by Reginald Marsh. New York: Limited Editions Club,
1954.

693 HAPGOOD, Hutchins. "Is Dreiser Anti-Semitic?" <u>Nation</u>, 140
(April 17, 1935), 436-438; and <u>Nation</u>, 140 (May 15, 1935),
572-573.
Consists of an exchange of letters between Hapgood and
Dreiser in 1933 and 1934. The subject was a Symposium on
the Jews arranged by the then defunct <u>American Spectator</u>,
of which Dreiser was one of the editors. Hapgood, feeling
that the symposium had an anti-Semitic slant, sent two letters
to the magazine, demanding that at least one be published.
Instead Dreiser replied. Dreiser's remarks were not actually
anti-Semitic, but were thought by Hapgood to be so. Dreiser's chief quarrel with the Jews seemed to be that they do
not integrate into the febric of the country in which they
live, they never become Americans, Germans, etc. They always remain Jews.

694   _____. <u>A Victorian in the Modern World</u>. New York: Harcourt, Brace, 1939. Dreiser, pp. 266 et passim.
Recalls meeting Dreiser sometime after the publication of
<u>Jennie Gerhardt</u>. Says: "He seemed to me to have a remark-
able power of specific observation. I never saw him without
calling my attention to things he had observed that day. He
was keenly interested in literature, but one that merely sought
to amuse was worse than of no value. He felt that critics
and publishers alike were corrupted by the necessity of business advertising...."

695 HAPKE, Laura. "The Uses of the Popular Novel: Satire and
Affinity in the Fiction of Selected American Realists and Naturalists, 1865-1910." Ph.D. diss., SUNY, 1974. <u>DA</u>, 35
(1975), 4523A.
Howells, Dreiser, and Crane used a variety of satiric methods
to provide forms for their early work: derisive critical refuta-
tion of sentimental literary tenets, parody of romantic and
sentimental plots and character types, satire on the form and
point of view of the popular novel, burlesque of typical kinds
of popular fiction. Dreiser, for example, followed the standard melodramatic stories, but felt that such moral categories
of this genre did not adequately account for human behavior
and so he ultimately reversed the stereotypes.

696 HARDWICK, Elizabeth. "Fiction Chronicle." <u>Partisan Review</u>,
15 (January, 1948), 108-117.
A review of four novels--by Sartre, Erskine Caldwell, Bellow,

and The Stoic by Dreiser. Summarizes the story in the first
two volumes of Dreiser's trilogy and concludes by saying The
Stoic is best considered with the first two novels. The writing in this last novel is worse than ever, but Cowperwood
"flourishes in the dungeon of Dreiser's rhetoric." His reality
is achieved by character in action and the three books about
him are another of Dreiser's victories over the hestitations of
any critical reader.

697 HARMAN, William C. "The Women in Theodore Dreiser's Novels,
The Financier, The Titan, and The Stoic." MA thesis, Bowling Green State University, 1966.

698 HARRIS, Frank. "Twenty Favourite Books." Academy, 80
(May 27, 1911), 653-654.

699 _____. "American Novelists Today: Theodore Dreiser."
Academy, 85 (August 2, 1913), 133-134.

700 _____. "Theodore Dreiser: Books Worth Reading." Pearson's Magazine, October 1918. Reprinted in Contemporary
Portraits: Second Series. New York: Privately printed,
1919. Pp. 81-106.
        Review-essay of Free and Other Stories. Says two of them
are really memorable: "Free," and "The Second Choice."
Comments upon the bitter irony contained in both.

701 _____. "Theodore Dreiser: Twelve Men." Pearson's Magazine, July, 1919.
        Remarks that he thinks three of the twelve portraits are
especially well done: "My Brother, Paul," "A Doer of the
Word," and the last sketch, simply called "W. L. S."

702 HARRISON, Carter H. Stormy Years: An Autobiography.
Indianapolis and New York: Bobbs-Merrill, 1935.
        Was five times mayor of Chicago. Does not discuss Dreiser
directly, but gives great details about Charles T. Yerkes,
the Chicago street-car financier on whose life Dreiser based
his trilogy of The Financier, The Titan, and The Stoic.

703 HART, I. H. "The Most Popular Books of Fiction Year by
Year in the Post-War Period." Publishers' Weekly, January
28, 1933.
        Refers to An American Tragedy.

704 HART, James D. "Dreiser, Theodore," in Oxford Companion
to American Literature. New York: Oxford University Press,
1941. Reprinted 1944. Pp. 205-206.
        Biographical details with titles and dates of major works.
Little commentary as in the following: "stimulated by reading
Balzac, and released from his crass success-worship by study-

ing Huxley, Tyndall, and Spencer, he came to see life as a
strangely magnificent composite of warring energies, having
no plan or purpose."

705 HARTER, Carol Clancy. "Strange Bedfellows: The Wasteland
and An American Tragedy," in The Twenties: Fiction, Poetry,
Drama, edited by Warren French. Deland, Fla.: Everett-
Edwards, 1975. Pp. 51-64.
    Reviews slightly other writers who have touched on this
subject, but suggests they have not thoroughly explored it.
Perhaps because of the distinctive quality of the milieu from
which they evolved, both embody--however much they are
diametrically opposite as literary forms--many of the same
themes, symbolic motifs, and views of the human condition
as it is manifested in the modern world. Each creates a meta-
phoric fabric whose design ultimately reveals the barren landscape of man's spiritual and moral wasteland.

706 HARTWICK, Harry. "Hindenburg of the Novel," in The Fore-
ground of American Fiction. New York: American Books,
1934. Pp. 85-110 et passim.
    What he has seen has dazed him, because he refuses to use
the labels that make life endurable for other men. To apply
a moral classification to life is a thing he will not do. And
that seems to be the root of his confusion. He has tried to
swallow life whole, without cutting it up, or proportioning it
to his capacity. Humor he lacks, taste he holds finical, and
sophistication he disdains. He does stagger as he writes, as
if under the weight he has forced himself to carry alone.

707 HASTINGS, William Thomson, ed. Contemporary Essays. Boston
and New York: Houghton Mifflin, 1928. Dreiser, passim.

708 HATCHER, Harlan H. Creating the Modern American Novel.
New York: Farrar and Rinehart, 1935. Dreiser, pp. 34-57.
    Dreiser saw more of the basic America in five years than
Stuart Sherman saw in a lifetime. H. L. Mencken was at his
bear-baiting best in defending the author and Sherman was at
his sentimental Puritan best in belaboring him, while neither
was at too much pains to understand him. There is a rugged
strength about his style which seems appropriate to the matter
and mood. If one cares for his work, one wonders seriously
whether a different or more finished cadence would not rob
it of its striking power.

709 HATVARY, Laurel T. "Carrie Meeber and Clara Maugham:
Sisters Under the Skin." Notes on Modern American Literature, 5 (Fall, 1981), item 26.

710 HAVLICE, Patricia Pate. Index to American Author Bibliography.
Metuchen, N.J.: Scarecrow, 1971.

711 HAY, John. "Book of the Week: Dreiser's The Stoic." Commonweal, 47 (December 19, 1947), 260-261.
The Stoic is a step down from power, but is not without
its moving passages. Dreiser was in line of the great American authors, like Whitman or Melville, who built new art with
their own creative energy. You can reject Dreiser in part,
but you cannot reject him as a whole. He never turned aside
from the honesty and the force with which he pursued his
great conceptions.

712 HAYNE, Barrie. "Sociological Treatise, Detective Story, Love
Affair: The Film Versions of An American Tragedy." Canadian Review of American Studies, 8 (Fall, 1977), 131-153.

713 HAZARD, Lucy Lockwood. "Theodore Dreiser: Cowperwood,
the Creature of Chemistry," in The Frontier in American
Literature. New York: Crowell, 1927. Pp. 235-242. Reprinted New York: Frederick Ungar, 1961. American clas-
sics series.
The culminating portrait of the industrial pioneer is given
us in The Titan and The Financier, novels directly based
upon the notorious career of Charles Yerkes, the Chicago
railroad king. Dreiser's interpretation is colored by his experiences and the outlook upon life which they have formed.
Dreiser is haunted by the realization of the complexity of life.
Never able to reduce it to a simple formula which he finds adequate and satisfying, he contents himself with sketches of its
wonder and mystery, its beauty and terror.

714 HAZLITT, Henry. "All Too Humanism." Nation, 130 (February
12, 1930), 181-182.
Is a discussion of the current trend in criticism by a group
calling themselves "humanists" and shouting down with Mencken, down with Dreiser, down with Naturalism. Hazlitt says
these critics have cloaked themselves in a term that stood for
a genuinely liberating attitude in the fifteeenth century, and
degraded it to a synonym for a hide-bound academicism.

715 _____. "Another Book About Himself." Nation, 132 (June
3, 1931), 613-614.
Review of Dawn. Book is crowded with pointless and irrelevant details, but so is life; it is repetitious, but so is life.
It makes a hundred false starts as in life, and seems to use
no principle of selection. However, the work does have other
less dubious values: astonishing memory, amazing detail,
curiosity for common things, profound wonder. It leaves
memorable pictures of Chicago on the reader's mind.

716 _____. "Art and Social Change." Modern Quarterly, 6 (Winter, 1931), 10-15.

717 _____. "Our Greatest Authors: How Great Are They?"
    Forum, 88 (October, 1932), 245-250.

718 _____. "Literature as Propaganda." Saturday Review of
    Literature, 20 (September 16, 1937), 13-15.

718a HECHT, Ben. A Child of the Century. New York: Simon and
    Schuster, 1954. Dreiser, pp. 204-205. Discusses Dreiser's
    knowledge of Chicago, 1880-1905.

719 HEDGES, M. H. "Mr. Dreiser." Dial, 62 (April 19, 1917), 343.

720 HEIM, William J. "Letters from Young Dreiser." American Liter-
    ary Realism, 8 (Spring, 1975), 158-163.
        Consists of three letters from Dreiser to Judson Morris,
    the hunchback son of a Warsaw, Indiana, bookstore owner.
    Letters written in 1888 and 1889 when the seventeen-year-old
    Dreiser was living in Chicago. Letters afford an interesting
    glimpse into his young life.

721 HELLESNES, Nils. "Theodore Dreiser." Syn Og Segn (Oslo),
    53 (March, 1947), 116-120.

722 HENDERSON, Harry B., III. Versions of the Past: The His-
    torical Imagination in American Fiction. New York: Oxford
    University Press, 1974. Dreiser, pp. 232-237 et passim.
        Foreword by Allen Trachtenberg. Book is a study of fiction
    as a guide to the historical past. A new approach to the "his-
    torical novel," ranging from Fenimore Cooper through the
    moderns. Henderson died before the last two chapters were
    finished, and his wife and father put them together from his
    notes. Discusses Dreiser's Frank Cowperwood and says in
    conclusion: "his character is developed as a complete world,
    integrally relating his orientation to finance, success, defeat,
    politics, social change, the pace of urban life, houses, pos-
    sessions, art, women."

723 HENNESSEY, Joseph, ed., with Introduction by John Mason
    Brown. The Portable Alexander Woollcott. New York: Vik-
    ing, 1946. Dreiser, passim.
        Quotes from the New York World, October 25, 1926, in which
    Woollcott comments on the play which has been produced and
    based on An American Tragedy. He says: "I do not know
    how perceptive a playgoer Dreiser is, but I should think the
    mess the theater has made would permanently impair his health.
    It seems to me a gauche, spasmodic, almost childishly con-
    cocted melodrama, preposterously miscast."

724 HENRY, Arthur. An Island Cabin. New York: McClure and
    Phillips, 1902. Dreiser, pp. 159-236.

Arthur Henry was city editor of the <u>Toledo Blade</u>. When
Dreiser came to the <u>Blade</u> asking for a job, Henry offered
him a four-day position that included covering a streetcar
strike; Dreiser accepted because he had found nothing elsewhere and needed money desperately. The narrative in <u>An
Island Cabin</u> is an account of Dreiser's invitation from Arthur
Henry to spend a month or so on a little island Henry had
acquired just off the old fishing village of Noank, Connecticut. Dreiser is referred to as "Tom." Detailed, interesting
account of Dreiser as he tries to cope with the wilds of nature, catching and cleaning fish, etc.

725 _____. <u>Lodgings in Town</u>. New York: A. S. Barnes, 1905.
Dreiser, pp. 80-88 et passim.

726 HENSLEY, Donald M. <u>Burton Rascoe: A Biography</u>. New York:
Twayne, 1970. Dreiser, pp. 49-50 et passim.
Comments on <u>The Hand of the Potter</u>, the first three acts
of which were excellent, but were spoiled in the fourth by
a reporter commenting upon the "story." Dreiser "puts a
long disquisition, voicing his own opinions on the case at
hand, his vague and facile philosophy of chemical compounds,
and his curious jumble of current theories of perverts in general." And that, Rascoe concluded, was frequently Dreiser's
fault as an artist: "he usurps the function of Deity, and he
is so tiresomely and uninterestingly moral. He cannot resist
the temptation to preach, to advise, to comment." This tendency, Rascoe believed, caused Dreiser to "botch," "deface,"
or "weaken" much of his fiction.

727 HEROLD, Eve Griffith. "A Study of the <u>Bildungsroman</u> in American Literature." Ph.D. diss., Ohio State University, 1973.
<u>DA</u>, 34 (1973), 2562A.
Traces the growth of this idea: a vision of education as
experience and discovery which, if conducted within a diverse
and flexible social framework, will lead to the ideal end of
growth, the affirmation of the individual in his culture. At
the outset of the nineteenth century was an optimistic concept
which gradually eroded into the despair of such writers as
Dreiser and Farrell whose works reveal the problem of American youth in growing up in a country which was itself immature, and which prized its immaturity.

728 HERRMANN, Eva. <u>On Parade</u>, edited by Erich Posselt. New
York: Coward-McCann, 1929. Dreiser, pp. 46-49.
Quotes passage in which Dreiser says he can make no comment on his life or work that has any meaning. Lists Dreiser's principal works with publication dates. Drawing is of
a heavy, massive face with a great shock of hair.

729 HERSEY, Harold. "Great Novelist Dreiser." <u>New York Globe
and Commercial Advertiser</u>. November 9, 1915. P. 10.

730 HEUSTON, Dustin Hull. "The Theistic Quest in the Novels of
     Theodore Dreiser." MA thesis, Stanford University, 1960.

731 _____. "Theodore Dreiser: Naturalist or Theist." Brigham
     Young University Studies, 3 (Winter, 1961), 41-49.

732 _____. "Theodore Dreiser's Search for Control: A Critical
     Study of His Novels." Ph.D. diss., New York University,
     1968. DA, 30 (1970), 4453A.
         One of the difficulties a critic faces in working with Drei-
     ser is to discover some means of handling the frequent con-
     tradictions and shifts of attitude in his writing. This disser-
     tation suggests that if a reader once understands the under-
     lying concern that Dreiser struggled to master, then the ap-
     parent contradictions and shifting attitudes will form a mean-
     ingful pattern. This study has a dual emphasis as it simul-
     taneously traces the history of Dreiser's thought and relates
     it to a central concern in his personality.

733 HICKS, Granville. "The Gutter--and Then What?" Forum,
     80 (December, 1928), 801-810.

734 _____. "The Twenties in American Literature." Nation,
     130 (February 12, 1930), 183-185.
         Begins by saying that "a survey of the twenties is rather
     sad business." Reviews well-known names of the decade, but
     sees no real hope for anything great, certainly not Dreiser.

735 _____. The Great Tradition. New York: Crowell, Collier
     and Macmillan, 1933. Reprinted in revised edition, New York:
     Biblo and Tanner, 1967. Dreiser, pp. 227-232.
         It is a passion for truth, lodged in the deepest stratum of
     Dreiser's mind, operating in spite of conflicting interests, that
     gives his work its importance. In each of his six novels Drei-
     ser has touched the fundamental forces that shape American
     life. Whether he deals with poor girls who stray from the
     path of conventional virtue or with millionaires who dominate
     cities, whether he portrays the struggles of an artist or the
     tragedy of a factory hand, he makes us feel the importance
     of his people. Despite innumerable faults, his six massive
     novels, built on the rocks of honesty and pity, stand while
     the works of shrewder architects crumble.

736 _____. "Literature and Revolution." English Journal. 24
     (March, 1935), 219-239.
         Article is an address delivered before the College Conference
     of English in the Central Atlantic States, December 1, 1934.
     Does not deal significantly with Dreiser.

737 _____. "Dreiser to the Rescue." Saturday Review of Liter-
     ature, 23 (February 22, 1941), 13.

Review of <u>America Is Worth Saving</u>. Comments that it is
a minor work, yet gives some insight into the curiously involved workings of Dreiser's mind. Demonstrates that he has
not lost his old fondness for using ten words when one would
do as well. Yet the book does have a point: we should not
take sides in the war.

738 _____. "Theodore Dreiser and <u>The Bulwark</u>." <u>American
Mercury</u>, 62 (June, 1946), 751-756. Reprinted in Kazin and
Shapiro (1955), pp. 219-224.
It is not the best of his novels, but it is a remarkably appropriate climax to his career. Taken by itself, it would add
little to his reputation as a novelist, but it compels us to revise upward our estimate of the man. It is certainly a rejection of naturalism as a literary theory, and may be regarded
as the death knell of literary naturalism. Dreiser was the
lost, bewildered man of the turn of the century, caught between science and faith, between city and town. With the
most painful honesty he set forth the dilemmas of his generation and, by stating what he knew about men, said something
about Man.

739 _____. "A Liar in Search of the Truth." <u>Saturday Review</u>,
48 (April 24, 1965), 31-32.
A review of W. A. Swanberg's <u>Dreiser</u>. Says that Dreiser
deserves a biography of this length, because his life was full
of contradictions which any brief treatment might misrepresent.
This is the first time the whole record has been set down, and
Swanberg makes no claim to be a critic; he is simply telling
the story of a man's life in straightforward if undistinguished
prose. In getting at the facts of that life, he has done a
first-rate job of research.

740 HILFER, Anthony Channell. <u>The Revolt from the Village:
1915-1930</u>. Chapel Hill: University of North Carolina, 1969.
Dreiser, pp. 24-27.
Some fascinating documents by Theodore Dreiser illustrate
both the genuine appeal of the village myth and why a revolt
against it was essential. Refers to <u>A Hoosier Holiday</u> (1916),
and <u>Newspaper Days</u> (1922). To Dreiser the town and farm
emotionally represented the charm and appeal of childhood,
but it was an appeal the adult had to resist. The city, by
contrast, represented the appalling but vital present.

741 _____. <u>The Ethics of Intensity in American Fiction</u>. Austin:
University of Texas Press, 1981. "Dreiser: Pathos as Ethos,"
pp. 103-142.
Long article in six parts. Dreiser does not lack moral purpose; rather he inverts the paradigm, valorizing his characters for the intensity of their pathos rather than for the
clarity of their ethos. Pathos becomes ethos. For the verti-

cal world of ethos--rise and fall, heaven and hell, higher
self and lower self--Dreiser substitutes the horizontal world
of pathos--expansion and contraction, broadening and narrow-
ing, fulfillment and constraint.

742 HIRSH, John C. "The Printed Ephemera of Sister Carrie."
     American Literary Realism, 7 (Spring, 1974), 171-172.
     Discusses "the wealth of paper ephemera through which
     Carrie moves and which, at certain critical moments, defines
     her progress." Is referring to such items as train tickets,
     menus, paper money, advertising and business cards, and
     newspapers. Intrinsically worthless, such ephemera has value
     only because of what it represents to society. It has all of
     the impermanence of a cut flower, and none of the beauty,
     and thus is an appropriate symbol for the urban and mater-
     ial world of sentimental values and failed idealism.

743 _____. "Tragic America: Dreiser's American Communism
     and a General Motors Executive." Dreiser Newsletter, 13
     (Spring, 1982), 10-16.
     A general evaluation of the influence of a book Onward
     Industry! published by the President of General Motors Over-
     seas, James D. Mooney. One of the most direct uses of this
     book comes in Chapter 22, "Suggestions Towards a New State-
     craft," which deals with the remedies to the social ills Dreiser
     has spent over 400 pages describing. It is not without irony
     that it was to a book written by an executive of General Mo-
     tors that Dreiser turned in seeking to redress the evident
     inequalities before him.

744 _____. "Dreiser and a Financier: James D. Mooney." Drei-
     ser Newsletter, 14 (Spring, 1983), 19-20.
     Refers to James D. Mooney, author of Onward Industry!
     a work which influenced Dreiser's book Tragic America, pub-
     lished in 1932. This article furthers the connection between
     Dreiser and Mooney by examining Mooney's letters to Dreiser
     during the period of their friendship, and also notes the 13
     copies of his books which Dreiser gave to Mooney.

745 HIRSHFIELD, Robert. "The Success Ethic in America and Its
     Effect upon Four American Novelists." Ph.D. diss., Univer-
     sity of Nebraska (Lincoln), 1974. DA, 35 (1974), 2991A-
     2992A.
     Devoted to works of Jack London, Theodore Dreiser, Robert
     Herrick, and F. Scott Fitzgerald, insofar as they demonstrate
     a bias for or against the success ethic. The criteria employed
     for evaluation are comprised of the author's treatment of the
     American city in his fiction; the author's treatment of Darwin
     and Spencer as applied to social conduct; the author's attitude
     toward money, material possessions, and social status; the
     author's attitude toward women.

746 HOCHMAN, Barbara Ann. "The Moral Realism of Theodore Drei-
    ser." Ph.D. diss., Rutgers University (State University of
    New Jersey), 1982. DA, 43 (1982), 163A.
        Comments on the use Dreiser makes of typical naturalist
    material, but continues by showing how Dreiser makes use of
    these materials to his own purposes. These purposes are
    strongly humanistic if not explicitly moral and do not depend
    upon Dreiser's interest in evolution, determinism, or social
    theory. Dissertation examines all of Dreiser's major novels,
    and concludes by saying his last two, The Bulwark and The
    Stoic, recapitulate the issues of the first six.

747 _____. "Self-Image and Moral Judgement in Sister Carrie."
    Hartford Studies in Literature, 10 (1982), 108-137.

748 _____. "Dreiser's Last Work: The Bulwark and The Stoic--
    Conversion or Continuity?" Dreiser Newsletter, 14 (Fall,
    1983), 1-15.
        In Dreiser's last novels, the vague intermittent doubt which
    plagued Carrie in her rocking chair becomes a pervasive skep-
    ticism. Such skepticism dominates these novels, and finally
    vitiates them. At the same time, the "hope and zest and
    youth" which was seen in An American Tragedy to be at the
    bottom of all the constructive energy of the world everywhere
    is replaced by a longing for the ideal which tends to seize
    upon less outrageous objects of aspiration. Hence the last
    novels lose in passion and drama what they seem to gain in
    equanimity. The tolerance and love of man which were every-
    where implicit in Dreiser's earlier work come to the fore in
    The Bulwark and The Stoic. Yet because that love is isolated
    from its all-too-human, its erring objects, it becomes too the-
    oretical for effective fiction.

749 HODGINS, Francis, Jr. "The Dreiser Letters." Journal of
    English and Germanic Philology, 59 (October, 1960), 714-720.
        Review of Letters of Theodore Dreiser, edited by Robert
    H. Elias, and Letters to Louise, both published in 1959. Re-
    gards the volumes as extremely important additions to Dreiser
    material, and handsomely done by their editors. Letters are
    a real contribution to understanding how the novelist thinks.

750 HOFFMAN, Frederick J. The Modern Novel in America: 1900-
    1950. Chicago: Henry Regnery, 1951. Reprinted Chicago:
    Gateway Editions, 1956. "Pre-War Naturalism, 1900-1915,"
    pp. 41-51.
        An American Tragedy is a naturalistic "tour de force."
    The method is saturation by overemphasis and detail, rather
    than enlightenment through selection and discrimination. There
    is nothing that quite escapes being crude in this novel. The
    more refined its setting, the cruder its achievement. As the
    novel proceeds the character of Clyde gains in everything but

depth: scarcely anywhere in fiction do we know so many
facts about a character--but Clyde neither has nor deserves
dimension. He is what others say he is. He has no feeling
or insight that is not borrowed. He is a creature of an in-
defatigable and an earnestly exhaustive omniscience.

751 _____. The Twenties. New York: Viking, 1955. Dreiser,
pp. 353-354 et passim.
Discusses Dreiser's relationship to Russia and his visit to
that country in 1927. His sensitivity to the needs and hopes
of the proletariat qualified every remark he had to make about
the imperfections of both rule and economic conditions in Russia. The propaganda, for example, distressed him, the cease-
less and repetitious instruction in communist aims, the myriad
pamphlets, the garish posters; yet Dreiser called this not lying, but pardonable exaggeration of a hoped-for reality. At
the end of his visit Dreiser remained convinced not only of
the vitality of the Russian Revolution but also of its fundamental correctness in terms of human values.

752 _____. "The Scene of Violence: Dostoevsky and Dreiser."
Modern Fiction Studies, 6 (Summer, 1960), 91-105. Reprinted
in Hoffman, The Mortal No (1964), pp. 179-201. Also reprinted
in Salzman (1971), pp. 26-31.
Dostoevsky and Dreiser stand in extreme opposition as
sources of the literary comprehension of modern violence. Two
areas of metaphor are necessary in this connection: the first
ought to bring to the history of violence a set of terms that
makes it available to critical discussion; the other should consider the severe threats to the creative consciousness caused
by the acceleration of destructive means in the twentieth century.

753 _____. The Mortal No: Death and the Modern Imagination.
Princeton, N.J.: Princeton University Press, 1964. Reprints
"The Scene of Violence...," pp. 179-201.

754 HOFFMAN, Michael J. "From Realism to Naturalism: Sister
Carrie and the Sentimentality of Nihilism," in The Subversive
Vision. Port Washington, N.Y.: Kennikat, 1972. Pp. 139-
153.
Sister Carrie is the first major American work of pure Naturalism, and it is in many ways still the best. Dreiser displays the underbelly of American society that is rare in our
fiction, and he creates a set of unforgettable characters and
a form that somehow seems to balance perfectly the various
parts of the book. Every line contains a resounding cliché
that one can read only with pain. The failure of Dreiser's
Naturalism--and of almost all works in that mode--is the self-
pity that seems to find its way between the lines of the bleak
narrative; it is a necessary outgrowth of a vision that denies
the significance of both man and his institutions.

755 HOFSTADTER, Richard. Social Darwinism in American Thought: 1860-1915. Philadelphia: University of Pennsylvania Press, 1944. Reprinted New York: George Braziller, 1959. Dreiser, p. 34 et passim.
Dreiser referred to in chapter "The Vogue of Spencer," pp. 31-50. Spencer's impact upon the common man in the United States is impossible to gauge, although its effects are dimly perceptible. Was widely read by persons who were partly or largely self-educated. This is suggested by casual references to him in the lives of men who later achieved some fame. Dreiser, London, Garland, etc. have given intimations of Spencer's influence on their formative years.

756 _____. "Native Sons of Literature: Theodore Dreiser." Nation, 172 (April 28, 1951), 398.
Review-essay of F. O. Matthiessen's Theodore Dreiser. Says it is an unhappy task to comment on this last work by the great critic and does not believe that Dreiser and Matthiessen exactly belong together. The result is a summary view of Dreiser's life and work which reaches some high points, as in the chapter on Sister Carrie, but which in "most of its sequences conveys chiefly a sense of weary desperation." What the book lacks above all is a focal organizing vision of the writer as a whole.

757 HOMMA, Kenshiro. "Tayama Katai and Theodore Dreiser-- Naturalism and Its Metamorphosis." Doshisha Studies in English (Kyoto), 11 (June, 1975), 144-175.

758 HOPPE, Ralph H. "The Theme of Alienation in the Novels of Theodore Dreiser." Ph.D. diss., University of Denver, 1969. DA, 31 (1970), 389A-390A.
Throughout his life Dreiser felt himself to be an outsider, alienated and estranged from many aspects of American life. Creatures of Dreiser's experiences, observations, and imagination, most of Dreiser's characters are as isolated and as lonely as he was. Three forces especially contribute to the alienation which Dreiser's characters experience: the breakdown of the family, the rise of the city, and capitalism.

759 HOROVITZ, Sydney. "Theodore Dreiser: Basic Patterns of His Work." Ph.D. diss., University of Pittsburgh, 1951.

760 HORTON, Rod W., and Herbert W. Edwards. Backgrounds of American Literary Thought. New York: Appleton-Century-Crofts, 1952. "Literary Naturalism," pp. 246-261.
In all of this naturalistic thought, the paradox lies in the fact that understanding did not bring peace and satisfaction. It was no comfort to know that moral sense was an anomaly in a world governed only by the law of survival; it was even less inspiring to understand that man was, in Dreiser's words, "a wisp in the wind." After centuries of seeing life along tra-

ditional theological, moral, and ethical patterns, man could
not easily bring himself to agree that all of these patterns
were false and the God of our Fathers a fraud.

761 HORWILL, Herbert W. "London Discusses Mr. Dreiser." New
York Times Book Review, January 9, 1927. P. 8.

762 HOVEY, Richard B., and Ruth S. Ralph. "Dreiser's The Genius: Motivation and Structure." Hartford Studies in Literature, 2 (1970), 169-183.

763 HOWARD, June Marie. "Slumming in Determinism: The Generic
Structures of American Literary Naturalism." Ph.D. diss.,
University of California (San Diego), 1980. DA, 40 (1980),
4596A.
    This dissertation argues that naturalism is constituted as
a distinctive genre by its characteristic structures in three
areas: the semantic, the verbal, and the syntactic aspects
of narrative. Three chapters define the theoretical content
of those categories and develop analyses of the specific qualities of naturalist narrative viewed in those terms. Each chapter includes discussion of particular works: Theodore Dreiser and Sister Carrie, and books by Frank Norris, Jack London, and Upton Sinclair.

764 HOWARD, Leon. Literature and the American Tradition. Garden
City, N.Y.: Doubleday, 1966. Dreiser, pp. 242-246.
    Dreiser worked himself upward from the position of a com-
mon laborer to that of a newspaper reporter and magazine editor before he became a successful novelist. An early convert
to the theory of social evolution, he was more impressed than
most Spencerians by the concept of the mysterious life force,
which the English philosopher had called "the Unknowable,"
and seems to have felt that the business of the literary artist
was to find this life force in the raw materials of human life.

765 HOWE, Irving. "Dreiser Undone." Nation, 168 (February 5,
1949), 159-160.
    Review of Robert Elias' Theodore Dreiser. Points up all the
advantages which Elias had--access to Dreiser papers, acquaintance with Dreiser, etc.--and "yet has failed almost completely." His is a failure of method, a curious procedure of
writing a book about a novelist without discussing his novels.
Dreiser, more than most American writers, needs fresh criticism. Mr. Elias blandly says that whether "Dreiser is a genius or a giant, and whether he wrote great novels, the present book does not attempt to decide." This is not a modest
statement of limitation; it is a confession of irrelevance.

766 _____. "The Stature of Theodore Dreiser." New Republic,
151 (July 25, 1964), 19-21.

767 _____. "Dreiser and the Tragedy." New Republic, 151
(August 22, 1964), 25-28. This article and the one above
were reprinted together in Lydenberg (1971), pp. 141-152;
also reprinted in Salzman (1971), pp. 32-44; reprinted in
Pizer (1981), pp. 292-302.
Other naturalists, when they show a character being destroyed by overwhelming forces, frequently leave us with a
sense of littleness and helplessness, as if the world were col-
lapsing. This is not true of Dreiser. Clyde is pitiable, his
life and fate are pitiable; yet at the end we are not persuaded
that human existence need be without value or beauty. What
makes Dreiser so absorbing a novelist is that he remains endlessly open to experience. He is marvelous in his devotion to
whatever portion of life a man can have; marvelous in his convictions that something sacred resides even in the transience
of our days; marvelous in his feeling that the grimmest of
lives retain the possibility of a mystic something of beauty
that perennially transfigures the world.

768 _____. "Dreiser: The Springs of Desire," in The Decline of
the New. New York: Harcourt, 1970. Pp. 137-150. Similar
to item listed above.

769 _____, ed. with Afterword. An American Tragedy. New
York: New American Library, 1964. Same as two articles
(1964) listed above.

770 HOWELL, Eileen. "Theodore Dreiser's Development as a Naturalist." MA thesis, New York University, 1950.

771 HUBBELL, Jay B. Who Are the Major American Writers? Durham, N.C.: Duke University Press, 1972. Dreiser, pp. 171-
172 et passim.
Comments mainly on the relationship of Dreiser and Mencken,
whom he calls "the ablest champion of Theodore Dreiser and
one of his best critics." Mencken was fully aware of Dreiser's shortcomings as an artist: his lack of humor, the ex-
asperating rolling up of irrelevant facts, whole scenes spoiled
by bad writing. When Mencken reviewed An American Tragedy, he called it a colossal botch as a work of art, but as
a human document "it is searching and full of solemn dignity,
and at times it rises to the level of genuine tragedy."

772 HUDDLESTON, Eugene L. "Herndon's Lincoln and Theodore
Dreiser's An American Tragedy." Midwest Quarterly, 22
(Spring, 1981), 242-254.
The parallels between the young Abe Lincoln of William H.
Herndon's famed Herndon's Lincoln (1887), and the figure of
Clyde Griffiths in An American Tragedy (1925) illuminate a
pervasive theme in American literature--the American dream,
which holds out material success to all who work hard, seize

opportunities, and remain virtuous. Even though it cannot
be proven that Herndon's Lincoln influenced the novel, it is
likely that Dreiser, a voracious reader, would have read this
highly publicized biography.

773 HUMBOLDT, Charles. "The Novel of Action." Mainstream, 1
     (Fall, 1947), 440.

774 HUNEKER, James Gibbons. "Old Philadelphia, Paris Forty Years
     Ago." Philadelphia Press, August 2, 1918. P. 8.

775 HUNT, Everett L. "The Social Interpretation of Literature."
     English Journal (College edition), 24 (March, 1935), 214-219.
     Dreiser, passim.

776 HUSSMAN, Lawrence E. "The Spiritual Quest of Theodore Drei-
     ser." Ph.D. diss., University of Michigan, 1964. DA, 25
     (1965), 3573.
          In the late 1930's Dreiser began to see order and meaning
     in creation and to feel differently about moral problems. His
     changed outlook went largely unnoticed until the posthumous
     publication of The Bulwark and The Stoic. These two novels
     project the author's final testimony of his deepest beliefs, and
     in them he professed a devout if undisciplined faith in a be-
     nign Creative Force, an ethic of self-immolation and dedication
     to the human community.

777 _____. "Dreiser's Emotional Power." Dreiser Newsletter,
     4 (Spring, 1973), 12-13.
          Academic criticism with its predilection for close analysis
     focuses on the shallowest portion of all the argument in Drei-
     ser's novels, hence the long line of attacks on his style and
     defenses of his naturalism. But Dreiser's extraordinary em-
     pathy for modern man's seemingly hopeless pursuit of the
     ultimate defies the word by word analysis advocated by some
     critics.

778 _____. "Foreword." The Bulwark. Portway Bath, England:
     Cedric Chivers, Ltd., 1973. Pp. 5-15.

779 _____. "Thomas Edison and Sister Carrie: A Source for
     Character and Theme." American Literary Realism, 8 (Spring,
     1975), 155-158.
          Refers to the character of Bob Ames, a young inventor
     who lectures Carrie on the vanity of human wishes. Appears
     in two short scenes, and seems to function as spokesman for
     Dreiser's more mature values, downgrading Carrie's theatri-
     cal success and urging her to heed a higher artistic calling.
     Critics have often remarked the inventor's role, but none has
     identified Thomas Edison as the source of many of Ames' ideas
     and as an influence in the evolution of one of the novel's ma-
     jor themes.

780 _____. "A Measure of Sister Carrie's Growth." <u>Dreiser</u>
<u>Newsletter</u>, 11 (Spring, 1980), 13-23.
Reviews critical views on Carrie's growth and change, and
concludes that Dreiser did not altogether handle this aspect
of the novel to any real advantage. The key figure in any
assessment of change in Carrie is Bob Ames, who appears
late in the novel and has a small part in only two chapters.
This article studies all the evidence that Dreiser intended
Ames to function as a kind of guide to Carrie's maturity and
growth.

781 _____. <u>Dreiser and His Fiction</u>. Philadelphia: University
of Pennsylvania Press, 1983.
Consists of 215 pages with introduction and index. The
novelist, despite his widespread reputation as an objective
determinist and hard-line naturalist, always led with his heart,
thereby identifying the split in Dreiser's personality which
has held the attention of critics for decades. All of Dreiser's
fiction may be fitted rather neatly into the developing pattern
of the give-take dichotomy.

782 HUTCHENS, John K., ed. <u>The American Twenties: A Literary</u>
<u>Panorama</u>. Philadelphia: Lippincott, 1952. Reprinted New
York: Cooper Square, 1972. Prints "My Brother Paul," from
<u>Twelve Men</u> (1919), pp. 425-437.

783 HUTCHINS, T. A. "Talking Things Over: The Dreiser Aftermath." <u>El Paso Herald</u>, May 8, 1930. P. 4.
Letter to editor.

784 HUTH, John F., Jr. "Theodore Dreiser: 'The Prophet.'"
<u>American Literature</u>, 9 (May, 1937), 208-217.
Much material on Dreiser's first twenty-three years and
following <u>Sister Carrie</u> in 1900. Little material from 1894-
1900. This article is about that period, with emphasis on
Dreiser's editorship of the periodical <u>Ev'ry Month</u>, first issue
of which appeared in October, 1895. Published ballads by
Dreiser's brother Paul Dresser, and also stories by Stephen
Crane and Bret Harte among others. Dreiser also wrote edi-
torials, labeled "Reflections" and signed "The Prophet." Re-
signed in the fall of 1897, claiming he was forced out of his
post over the handling of the periodical. Never referred to
the magazine in his writings and avoided discussion of that
period of his life.

785 _____. "Theodore Dreiser: Success Monger." <u>Colophon</u>,
3 (Winter, 1938), 120-133.
Refers to a magazine edited by one Dr. Orison Swett Marden, <u>Success</u> which had used many of Dreiser's articles in
and after 1898. <u>Success</u> had, in fact, been one of Dreiser's
chief markets. Dreiser knew what readers wanted, and ground

out messages from the omnipotent gods of finance and from
leaders in art, science, and literature, like so much pork
sausage. Critics who have professed astonishment at the hundreds of thousands of words Dreiser exudes in building a book
will find in these pages evidence that his ability to fill paper
was an early acquired habit.

786   _____. "Dreiser and Success: An Additional Note." Colo-
       phon, 3 (Summer, 1938), 406-410. See also Avary article.
       Says, "my article was intended to be complete; it was com-
       plete, so far as I knew at the time it was printed. But I
       have since found that Dr. Marden published other collections
       containing Dreiser contributions, and it is to detail these that
       this supplementary account, the result of further digging in
       publishing records of thirty-odd years ago, is offered."

787   INGE, M. Thomas. "Theodore Dreiser's Sister Carrie: Essay
       Topics." Exercise Exchange, 16 (Summer-Fall, 1969), 2-3.

788   ISH-KISHOR, Sulamith, ed. with Introduction. Moods: Philo-
       sophical and Emotional (Cadenced and Declaimed). New York:
       Simon and Schuster, 1935. Pp. v-viii.

789   JACKSON, Charles. "Theodore Dreiser and Style." Book Find
       News, 2 (March, 1946), 16-17.

790   JACOBS, Johan Uys. "The Alter Ego: A Study of the Dual
       Persona of the Artist in the Late Nineteenth and Early Twen-
       tieth Century American Novel." Ph.D. diss., Columbia Uni-
       versity, 1980. DA, 41 (1981), 3107A.
       Studies Dreiser's The "Genius."

791   JAMESON, R. D. "Puritanic Taboos." New Republic, 16 (Sep-
       tember 28, 1918), 260.
       This letter to the editor scoffs at the notion that it was
       the Puritans who gave America its present day moralism and
       taboos over which "Mr. Dreiser and his friends are growling
       today." Indeed these ideals arose in the insurgent middle
       and lower classes of the nineteenth.

792   JOHNS, Orrick. The Time of Our Lives. New York: Stack-
       pole, 1937. Dreiser, pp. 325-329. Reprinted New York:
       Octagon Books, 1973.
       Recalls the period around 1935 when Dreiser came to San
       Francisco to be the principal speaker at a big Tom Mooney
       meeting. These conferences drew in more and more trade
       union, socialist, anarchist and liberal elements until they al-

most became mass meetings themselves. These great meetings
were successful in bringing thousands of workers and unem-
ployed people into class conscious activity. I do not think
that Dreiser ever realized the immense amount of work that
had gone on before he arrived to take the star part; but he
played the star part well, and without him the newspapers
would hardly have given us a line.

793 JOHNSON, A. Theodore. "Realism in Contemporary American
Literature: Notes on Dreiser, Anderson, Lewis." Southwest-
ern Bulletin (Memphis, Tennessee), September 1929. Pp. 3-
16.

794 JOHNSON, Given. "The Satirical Elements in Jennie Gerhardt."
MA thesis, Brigham Young University, 1966.

795 JOHNSON, Mary Dillon. "Dreiser's Naturalistic Novels of Compassion." Ph.D. diss., University of California (Berkeley),
1974. DA, 36 (1975), 316A-317A.
    Studies Sister Carrie, Jennie Gerhardt, and An American
Tragedy in terms of the particular form in each novel. Dreiser alters the plot form of conventional sentimental fiction by
inverting its desert-fate formula. This is what allows Dreiser
to achieve a naturalistic effect. He maximizes the potential
of the form to make the reader feel compassion for characters
whose fates do not accord with their deserts. The plots turn
on change of fortune, not of character or thought.

796 JOHNSON, Merle, and F. M. Hopkins. "American First Editions ... Theodore Dreiser, 1871--." Publishers' Weekly,
107 (December 22, 1923), 1925-1926.

797 _____. American First Editions, revised by Jacob Blanck.
New York: Bowker, 1942.
    Lists some 65-70 items--books, pamphlets, articles--primary
materials by Theodore Dreiser.

798 JOHNSON, Oakley. "Theodore Dreiser--Critic of Capitalist Society." People's Daily World, December 31, 1940. P. 5.

799 JONES, A. E., Jr. "Darwinism and ... American Fiction, 1860-
1890." Drew University Bulletin, 38 (December, 1950), 9-11.

800 JONES, Alan K. "The Family in the Works of Theodore Dreiser." Ph.D. diss., Texas Tech College, 1968. DA, 29 (1969),
2265A.
    This dissertation suggests that the family as an institution
is a major theme in all of Dreiser's novels, and for the most
part they demonstrate the disintegration of the family in American life. In Dreiser the extramarital affair is the major cause
of disintegration, as in Sister Carrie, forward through An

American Tragedy. The last chapter focuses on changing
values in America. The deterioration of religion, the movement to the city, and the emergence of the new woman are
aspects of American life which Dreiser recorded with amazing
absorption.

801 JONES, Howard Mumford. "Theodore Dreiser--A Pioneer Whose
     Fame Is Secure." New York Times Book Review, January 13,
     1946. P. 6.

802 _____. "Dreiser Reconsidered." Atlantic Monthly, 177
     (May, 1946), 162-170.
     Review of The Bulwark. As one toils through its cumbrous
     pages, they do, indeed, take one back to the twenties, when
     the wine of the puritans was being spilled on the ground.
     Any estimate of Dreiser must be based upon the revolt of
     which he was the embodiment and which conditions even his
     latest fiction. Take from Dreiser his naturalistic philosophy,
     and what you have left curiously resembles Dickens. Like
     Dickens, Dreiser never comprehended and could not portray
     cultivated life. They moved sympathetically among the lower
     middle classes, the poor, and the shabby-genteel denizens of
     that half world between the slums and success.

803 _____, and Walter Rideout, eds. Letters of Sherwood Ander-
     son. Boston: Little, Grown, 1953.
     Contains eight letters to Dreiser, and other references.

804 JONES, Lawrence W. "Canadian Graduate Studies in American
     Literature: A Bibliography of Theses and Dissertations, 1921-
     1968." Canadian Review of American Studies, 1 (Fall, 1970),
     116-129.

805 JONES, Llewellyn. "Men and Ghosts: A Review of Plays of
     the Natural and the Supernatural." Chicago Evening Post,
     March 24, 1916.
     For the most part Dreiser's seven plays in this volume are
     not actable. As a playwright Dreiser does not stand in the
     position of the critic. He photographs the condition as he
     sees it and, having an X-ray attachment to his artistic camera,
     he at the same time gives us the drama of unseen forces play-
     ing about his characters ... the volume must not be taken too
     seriously as a contribution to the theatre. He has a long road
     to travel.

806 _____. "Mr. Dreiser's English and An American Tragedy."
     Chicago Evening Post, January 22, 1926, and January 29,
     1926. Reprinted in Current Reviews, edited by Lewis Worth-
     ington Smith. New York: Holt, 1926. Pp. 203-212.
     In An American Tragedy there is a sheer ugliness of style
     exactly comparable to the ugliness of a woman who covered

herself with picked-up remnants. And where Dreiser does
not pick up a soiled remnant of language he distorts our ordinary language ... and so, in estimating Dreiser's chances
for immortality we must recognize two great handicaps: an
inadequate, and entirely fallacious psychology; and a total
lack of discrimination in the use of his medium.

807 _____. "Contemporary Fiction," in American Writers on Amer-
    ican Literature, edited by John Macy. New York: Liveright,
    1931. Pp. 488-502.
        "The first thing we notice in the literature of the first
    thirty years, is the betrayal into sentimentality of the novelist
    who begins by taking a hard-boiled view of the world. This
    does not mean that I oppose the Norrises and Dreisers to the
    Harold Bell Wrights. It simply means that Norris and Drei-
    ser do not write out of their naive or direct experiences, but
    write about what their mechanistic pre-suppositions permit
    them to perceive, which is not enough to satisfy the artist
    in them ... and so the artist, cheated out of what he could
    observe were he functioning without philosophical spectacles,
    falls back on sentimentality to fill the breach."

808 JOSEPHSON, Matthew. Zola and His Times. New York: Ma-
    caulay, 1928. Dreiser, passim.
        Does not treat Dreiser directly. Book is valuable for back-
    ground material on Zola, the father of naturalism, whom Drei-
    ser is said to have succeeded as the foremost naturalist of
    American twentieth-century literature.

809 _____. "Dreiser, Reluctant, in the Films." New Republic,
    68 (August 19, 1931), 21-22.
        Discusses the suit which Dreiser brought against Paramount
    Company for the film of An American Tragedy produced by
    Josef von Sternberg. It was, in fact, a very slight film,
    and one cannot blame Dreiser for the botch which they made
    of his 840-page novel which had been designed as "an indict-
    ment of society." The film was no more an indictment than
    the common tabloid serial. Dreiser lost the suit, but if more
    authors would raise hell, the movies might get pulled out of
    their rut.

810 JURNAK, Sheila Hope. "A Study of Dreiser's Autobiographies:
    Dawn and Newspaper Days." Ph.D. diss., Tulane Univer-
    sity, 1971. DA, 32 (1972), 4004A.
        Shows similarities of these two works to novels in the themes
    of family relationships, man's ability to control his destiny,
    and the continual search for happiness. Also share the basic
    organizational pattern of straight-line chronology. Dreiser
    uses symbolism extensively in both sets of books, the three
    most characteristic being the city, clothing and cultural ref-
    erences such as paintings, plays, and books. Dreiser's im-

agery is drawn from water, animals, and magic in both autobiographies and novels. Dawn and Newspaper Days (first
published as A Book About Myself) contribute factual knowledge about Dreiser and offer insights into his personality.
They deserve a place beside his best fiction.

811 _____. "Popular Art Forms in Sister Carrie." Texas Studies in Language and Literature, 13 (Summer, 1971), 313-320.
Dreiser's references to popular art forms function both directly and ironically. They serve three main purposes: to
produce verisimilitude by means of detail; to become cultural
emblems for the major character; to represent a cultural hierarchy symbolizing Carrie's material and cultural rise. Article contains a partially annotated list of these cultural references. Conclusion seems to be that while popular culture
incorporates the common man's daily fictions into literary form,
true art strips away illusion and displays the actual. He uses
popular art form references to dramatize both the fictional
and the actual.

812 KANE, Patricia. "Reading Matter as a Clue to Dreiser's Character." South Dakota Review, 8 (Winter, 1970-1971), 104-
106.

813 KAPLAN, Amy Beth. "Realism Against Itself: The Urban Fictions of Twain, Howells, Dreiser, and Dos Passos." Ph.D.
diss., Johns Hopkins University, 1982. DA, 43 (1982), 169A.
Dissertation seeks to develop a theory of American realism
that is grounded in an historical context. Written during a
time of social change, the novels shape the meaning and the
experience of the very social context that informs them. They
all engage in a search for a community and a common language
to make sense of social conflict and dislocation. A central
tension emerges in each novel between the desire to forge a
community and a homogeneous reality and the fear of fragmen-
tation and the incoherence of urban life. Studies Dreiser's
Sister Carrie.

814 KAPLAN, Harold. Power and Order: Henry Adams and the
Naturalistic Tradition in American Fiction. Chicago: University of Chicago Press, 1981. Pp. 85-99 et passim.
Discusses Sister Carrie, with emphasis on the city as "an
overwhelming quantification of power, a roar of life" that
dominates its human agents and objects. It is the city that
seduces Carrie, is later responsible for her rise, and is responsible for Hurstwood's fall. The novel is totally about
money, the symbol of power, nowhere better demonstrated
than in the city.

815 KARIM, N. A. "Theodore Dreiser and the Quest for a Spiritual
     Identity," in Literary Studies: Homage to Dr. A. S. Aiyer,
     edited by K. P. K. Menon et al. Trivandum, India: Dr.
     Aiyer Memorial Committee, 1973. Pp. 141-148.
     Argues that The Bulwark is the culmination of the spiritual
     quest which Dreiser began with his first published work, and
     embodies the complete account of his final religious position.

816 KARNATH, David L. "Motive in the Novels of Theodore Drei-
     ser." MA thesis, Stanford University, 1960.

817 KARSNER, David. "America's Literary Sphinx." New York
     Evening Post, October 19, 1918. Book section, p. 8.

818 _____. "Theodore Dreiser's Short Stories." New York Call
     Magazine, October 27, 1918. P. 11.
     Review of Free and Other Stories. Says, "there is no hum-
     bug about Dreiser. He is not in any sense an intellectual
     cheap skate, word monger or paragraph panderer.... In these
     stories are all the qualities that have given Dreiser a vogue.
     Short stories are as interesting as his novels."

819 _____. "Theodore Dreiser's Twelve Men." New York Call
     Magazine, April 27, 1919. P. 10.
     These twelve men are not exceptional. Twelve others would
     be just as interesting to Dreiser, and he has proved once
     again that human life, wherever it is found, is most precious,
     most fascinating, most true, most dear. Twelve Men is a
     permanent book. Its appearance is an event in the year's
     literature, and Dreiser has earned one more gold service
     stripe.

820 _____. "A Tragedy: The Hand of the Potter." New York
     Call Magazine, December 6, 1919. P. 10.
     Dreiser has done much better writing than is presented
     here. As a play to be produced, the American public would
     not stand for it. It is too horribly real. Its lights, when
     they do shine, are a melancholy yellow. The picture is too
     gruesome, yet it is commonly true.

821 _____. "Theodore Dreiser: A Portrait." New York Call
     Magazine, July 18, 1920. Pp. 6-7.

822 _____. "The Romance of Two Hoosier Brothers." New York
     Call Magazine, December 5, 1920. Pp. 6-7.

823 _____. "Here and There and Everywhere." New York Call
     Magazine, February 10, 1923. P. 8.
     Review of A Book About Myself. Says he is very partisan
     toward Dreiser, and "thoroughly enjoys, admires, and appre-
     ciates" 90 percent of his literary product. Chides other re-
     viewers who have not been so favorable toward Dreiser.

824 _____. "Dreiser's Tableaux." New York Tribune Magazine
and Book Section, January 27, 1924. P. 19.
Review of The Color of a Great City. Many of these sketches
have been published elsewhere. All of them are authentic and
bear the impress of a man alive and responsive to the cacoph-
onies of his swirling city. The majority of them have been
gleaned from those dark and drab passages in our labyrin-
thine life, but a great deal of Dreiser's writing is the product
of our darksome side.

825 _____. "Dreiser, the Daddy of American Realists." New
York Herald Tribune, June 20, 1926. Section 7, pp. 3-4,
8-9.

826 _____. "Theodore Dreiser," in Sixteen Authors to One: Intimate Sketches of Leading American Story Tellers. New York:
Lewis Copeland, 1928. Pp. 3-24.
Quotes much from what Dreiser had to say about his parents
and homelife, his early work in Chicago, his attending the
University of Indiana. Comments on one of Dreiser's idiosyncrasies: "the way he toys with his handkerchief and
plaits it as he talks. The critics write columns about this,
and then borrow from more erudite writers to describe how
badly he writes. They say he has no humor, when they mean
he is not witty. He thinks he is hard, but he is not. He
thinks he has a tough skin, but he has not. Underneath
his brusque exterior is one of the most sensitive men that
ever contemplated the mystery, the terror, and the wonder
of life."

827 KATOPE, Christopher G. "Sister Carrie and Spencer's First
Principles." American Literature, 41 (March, 1969), 64-75.
Begins with a review of what other critics have said about
Dreiser and Spencer, and what Dreiser himself has said with
regard to his reading the British philosopher, but says "there
has been no detailed examination of the specific nature of that
influence on Dreiser's first novel, written while Dreiser was
still under the profound impact of Spencer's mechanism."
Concludes that critics, "in their eagerness to stress Dreiser
the artist have tended to denigrate the philosopher. Much
effort has been expended on showing that Dreiser was not
really a complete mechanist or a determinist or a naturalist.
But Dreiser's art is inseparable from his view of reality; and
that view was markedly influenced by the laws of nature which
Herbert Spencer described in his First Principles."

828 KATZ, Joseph. "Theodore Dreiser at Indiana University."
Notes and Queries, n.s., 13 (March, 1966), 100-101.
Points up that numerous biographers and critics have overlooked the actual records of Dreiser's enrollment at the University of Indiana. It is generally said that he agreed to go

one year, at the expense of Miss Fielding, a high school
teacher who believed he would benefit greatly from a year of
higher education. What is generally overlooked is that Dreiser became interested in a college career, with a special interest in language and literature.

829 _____. "Theodore Dreiser: Enter Chicago, Hope, and Walt
Whitman." Walt Whitman Review, 14 (December, 1968), 169-
171.
Reviews critical remarks which have been made with regard
to Dreiser and Whitman and points out that even if Dreiser
"could not really be expected to find in Whitman a literary
parent" there were occasions on which Dreiser made use of
Whitman's poetry. Quotes passages from The "Genius" and
The Titan in which the similarity to Whitman is unmistakable.

830 _____. "The 'Genius' by Theodore Dreiser." Proof: The
Yearbook of American Bibliographical and Textual Studies,
edited by Joseph Katz. 1 (1971), 330-357.
Study is based on the publisher's "dummy" of The "Genius,"
with which he develops a theory of the textual evolution of
Dreiser's novel. Included are facsimiles of Dreiser's manuscript and pages of the edited typescript for comparison with
the publisher's pages.

831 _____. "Dreiser's 'Notes on Life.' " Library Chronicle,
38 (Winter, 1972), 44-45.

832 _____. "Theodore Dreiser's Ev'ry Month." Library Chronicle, 38 (Winter, 1972), 46-66.

833 _____. "Theodore Dreiser and Stephen Crane: Studies in
a Literary Relationship," in Stephen Crane in Transition:
Centenary Essays, edited by Joseph Katz. DeKalb: Northern
Illinois University Press, 1972. Pp. 174-204.
Despite his obvious debts to Crane, despite his early acquaintance with a spectrum of Crane's work, and despite the
intimacy of his response to it, Dreiser came to deny any significant relationship between his career and Crane's. The re-
visionary process was gradual, and it seems to be tied in
some way to both Dreiser's struggle for recognition and Crane's
posthumous reputation. Illustrates article with a printing of
Dreiser's and Crane's "The Men in the Storm." Details of
composition are almost identical, and it is conclusive that Dreiser borrowed it from Crane. The collected edition of Crane
published in 1925-1927 was a heavy blow to Dreiser, who became nearly obsessed with the idea of a uniform edition of
his own works. He was never given that honor, but he did
become increasingly cool on the subject of Crane's influence
on him.

834 KAUN, Alexander S. "Choleric Comments." <u>Little Review</u>, 2
     (November, 1915), 20-23.

835 KAZIN, Alfred. "The Lady and the Tiger." <u>Virginia Quarterly
     Review</u>, 17 (January, 1941), 111-119. Reprinted in <u>On Native
     Grounds</u>. New York: Reynal & Hitchcock, 1942, as "Two
     Educations: Edith Wharton and Theodore Dreiser," pp. 73-90.
     Reprinted in part in Kazin and Shapiro (1955), pp. 155-160,
     as "Theodore Dreiser: His Education and Ours." Also re-
     printed in <u>Criticism: Some Major American Writers</u>, edited
     by Lewis Leary. New York: Holt, 1971. Pp. 261-267.
        There was stamped upon Dreiser from the first a sense of
     the necessity, the brutal and clumsy dispensation of fate, that
     imposed itself upon the weak. He hated something nameless,
     for nothing in his education had prepared him to select events
     and causes; he hated the paraphernalia of fate--ill luck, the
     shadowy and inscrutable pattern of things that ground effort
     into the dust. He did not rebel against it as one who knows
     what the evil is and how it may be destroyed; he was so over-
     powered by suffering that he came to see in it a universal
     principle.

836 _____. "Dreiser." <u>New Yorker</u>, 25 (February 26, 1949),
     91-93. Reprinted in <u>The Inmost Leaf</u>. New York: Harcourt,
     Brace, and World, 1955. Pp. 236-241.
        Is principally a review of Elias' <u>Theodore Dreiser</u>. As for
     its worth Kazin says: "despite its portentous subtitle, is not
     an interpretation but an almost unnaturally objective biography,
     by a young scholar who has devoted himself for years to a-
     massing the necessary facts with a kind of professional zeal
     not usually spent on anyone so out of style as Dreiser. It
     is about as detailed and reliable a life of Dreiser as we are
     likely to get for some time. Mr. Elias is so concerned with
     Dreiser's 'ideas'--the least original side of a writer more not-
     able for his tragic grip on life than for the coherence of his
     thinking--that from his account it is hard to see why one
     should read the novels at all...."

837 _____. "American Naturalism: Reflections from Another
     Era," in <u>The American Writer and the European Tradition</u>,
     edited by Margaret Denny and William H. Gilman. Minneapo-
     lis: University of Minnesota Press, 1950. Pp. 121-131.
        With us naturalism was not so much a school as a climate
     of feeling. It was almost in the air of modern America. The
     French may have conceived <u>le roman naturalist</u>, but Chicago
     was its incarnation. Naturalism in America is not easily re-
     duced to a well-known formula of determinism with its pre-
     tensions to "laws" of human behavior, its severe air of neces-
     sary meanness. Crane and Norris were writing naturalism
     before Dreiser but with them it was still in the experimental
     stage. With <u>Sister Carrie</u> we find a writer for whom natural-

ism is the only way of addressing himself in life. He found
an impalpable emotion arising from the very commonplace-
ness of human existence.

838 _____. "Theodore Dreiser, 1871-1945: Introduction," in
Major American Writers, 2 vols., general editor Perry Miller.
New York: Harcourt, Brace, 1962. Vol. 2, pp. 461-472.
Biographical details with some commentary: "Dreiser grew
up to think of American society as a cruel and often sense-
less arrangement which he would have to dominate in order
to share in. Life is simply the great flood carrying us along,
and our highest relation to the universe lies in our submis-
sive recognition that our petty human wishes count for nothing in the world process that creates and destroys us with
the same indifference."
Also reprints short story "Nigger Jeff," a study of the
individual when he is alone entirely with himself.

839 _____. Starting Out in the Thirties. Boston: Little, Brown,
1965. Dreiser, passim.
Refers briefly to Dreiser's association with the Communist
Party.

840 _____. "A Century of Realism in American Literature," in
John Garraty, Interpreting American History: Conversations
with Historians, 2 vols. New York: Macmillan, 1970. Vol.
2, pp. 289-311. Slightly abridged version printed in American Heritage, 21 (June, 1970), 12-15, 86-90.
In this interview Kazin traces the history of the American
novel from the time of Twain, Howells, and Henry James to
the present. Of Dreiser, he says: "he is still one of the
most neglected figures in American literature. All sorts of
literary professors are still afraid of him. In his own time
he was treated with the most incredible contempt and hostility
by the literary establishment. It was not really his bad writing, but his attitude toward society that they didn't like, his
conviction that there wasn't fundamentally, any real design to
life."

841 _____, Reader with commentary. The Writer and the City.
16mm Color Film. University at Large Programs, 1970.

842 _____. "Restoring Sister Carrie." New York Review of
Books, February 19, 1981. Pp. 12-14.

843 _____, ed. with Introduction. The Titan. New York:
Laurel Dell, 1959. Introduction same as Dell edition of Sister
Carrie (1960). See below.

844 _____, ed. with Introduction. An American Tragedy. New
York: Laurel Dell, 1959. Introduction same as Dell edition
of Sister Carrie (1960). See below.

845   _____, ed. with Introduction. <u>Sister Carrie</u>. New York:
       Laurel Dell, 1960. Pp. 9-21. Reprinted in Kazin, <u>Contem-</u>
       <u>poraries</u>. Boston: Little, Brown, 1962. Pp. 87-99 as "Drei-
       ser: The Esthetics of Realism."
           The novels of Dreiser have survived most of the other
       novels published during his own generation, and they have
       survived almost all concern with Dreiser himself. There are
       still many people who believe that Dreiser's novels have lasted
       only as records of a vanished period. The truth is that Drei-
       ser's books belong to a period in which the individual is still
       large, epochal, heroic, not crushed. More and more the con-
       temporary novel is stocked with individuals who are engulfed,
       taken over, hardly exist. Dreiser's individuals have an enor-
       mous capacity for suffering.

846   _____, ed. with Introduction. <u>The Financier</u>. New York:
       Laurel Dell, 1961. Introduction same as Dell edition of <u>Sister</u>
       <u>Carrie</u> (1960). See above.

847   _____, ed. with Introduction. <u>Jennie Gerhardt</u>. New York:
       Laurel Dell, 1963. Introduction same as Dell edition of <u>Sister</u>
       <u>Carrie</u> (1960). See above.

848   _____, and Charles Shapiro, eds. <u>The Stature of Theodore</u>
       <u>Dreiser: A Critical Survey of the Man and His Work</u>. Bloom-
       ington: Indiana University Press, 1955. Reprinted, 1965.
       Introduction by Alfred Kazin, "The Stature of Theodore Drei-
       ser," pp. 3-12. Reprinted in Lydenberg (1971), pp. 11-21;
       also reprinted in Pizer (1981), pp. 47-56.
           This is what makes Dreiser so painful--in his atheism, his
       cosmology; this is what dismays us in our sensible culture,
       just as it bothered a generation that could never understand
       Dreiser's special bitterness against orthodox religion, against
       the churches; this is what drove Dreiser to look for God in
       the laboratories, to write essays on "My Creator." He may
       have been a naturalist, but he was certainly not a material-
       ist. What sticks in our throats is that Dreiser is outside the
       agreed boundaries of our concern, that he does not accept
       our society as the whole of reality, that he may crave after
       its fleshpots, but does not believe that getting along is the
       ultimate reach of man's effort.
           <u>The Stature of Theodore Dreiser</u> contains 300 pages of re-
       printed reviews, criticism, letters, and other materials. Con-
       cludes with a Selected Bibliography, pp. 271-303, of biography
       and criticism. Also a listing of Book Reviews and Notices
       arranged chronologically is an excellent compilation, but is
       far outweighed by the Salzman volume of 1972 of Reviews.
       Reprinted material consists of the following:
           I. Reminiscences:
              "Theodore Dreiser" by Edgar Lee Masters (poem), pp.
              15-16.

"An American Memory," by Ludwig Lewisohn, pp. 17-20.
"Portrait of Dreiser," by Ford Madox Ford, pp. 21-35.
"Some Correspondence with Theodore Dreiser," by James
    T. Farrell, pp. 36-50.

II. Early Newspaper Reviews, pp. 51-68

III. The Critical Battle:
    "The Barbaric Naturalism of Mr. Dreiser," by Stuart
        P. Sherman, pp. 71-80.
    "An Apology for Crudity," by Sherwood Anderson, pp.
        81-83.
    "The Dreiser Bugaboo," by H. L. Mencken, pp. 84-91.
    "The Art of Theodore Dreiser," by Randolph Bourne,
        pp. 92-95.
    "Aspects of a Pathfinder," by Thomas K. Whipple, pp.
        96-110.
    "Our Formula for Fiction," by Sinclair Lewis, pp. 111-
        112.
    "An American Tragedy: A Humanistic Demurrer," by
        Robert Shafer, pp. 113-126.
    "Theodore Dreiser Remembered," by John Chamberlain,
        pp. 127-131.
    "Reality in America," by Lionel Trilling, pp. 132-145.
    "Dreiser and the Triumph of Art," by Saul Bellow, pp.
        146-148.
    "Dreiser's Imagination," by John Berryman, pp. 149-153.
    "Theodore Dreiser: His Education and Ours," by Alfred
        Kazin, pp. 154-160.
    "Dreiser's Difficult Beauty," by Alexander Kern, pp.
        161-170.

IV. Studies:
    "Sister Carrie: Her Fall and Rise," by Malcolm Cowley,
        pp. 171-181.
    "Dreiser's Sister Carrie," by James T. Farrell, pp. 182-
        187.
    "The Survival of the Fittest," Chapter IX from Theodore
        Dreiser, by Robert H. Elias, pp. 188-203.
    "Of Crime and Punishment," Chapter from Dreiser by
        F. O. Matthiessen, pp. 204-218.
    "Theodore Dreiser and The Bulwark," by Granville Hicks,
        pp. 219-224.
    "Dreiser and Naturalism Revisited," by David Brion
        Davis, pp. 225-236.
    "Dreiser, an Inconsistent Mechanist," by Eliseo Vivas,
        pp. 237-245.
    "Theodore Dreiser and the Divided Stream," by Charles
        C. Walcutt, pp. 246-269.

849 KEHL, Del G. "Dreiser and the Winebrennarians." Dreiser
Newsletter, 5 (Fall, 1974), 5-9.

Reference is to a religious organization which is located near Grass Lake, where Clyde plans to take Roberta Alden and drown her, making it appear as an accident. Roberta sees it as an opportunity for them to be married right away, whereas Clyde immediately perceives that the lake is not isolated enough for the deed he is planning. The question arises as to why this particular sect. Several ideas suggest themselves, but perhaps the real meaning is contained in the fact that this sect believed strongly in "free will."

850 _____. "An American Tragedy and Dreiser's Cousin, Mr. Poe." Rocky Mountain Review of Language and Literature, 32 (Autumn, 1978), 211-221.

851 KELLER, D. H. "Dreiser's Concerning Dives and Lazarus." Serif, 8 (1971), 31-32.
Refers to a leaflet, printed under "The Soviet-Finnish Treaty and World Peace." Soviet Russia Today, 8 (April, 1940), 8-9.

852 KELLY, Claude. "American Victory or Tragedy: The Fallacy of Theodore Dreiser's Theories as Demonstrated by the Personal Victory of Ulysses S. Grant over the Power of Circumstance," in 2 parts. National Republic, 17 (March and April, 1930), 16-17, 44; 28-29, 46.

853 KEMLER, Edgar. "How Dreiser Was Managed," in The Irreverent Mr. Mencken. Boston: Little, Brown, 1950. Pp. 70-84.
Reviews the Dreiser-Mencken relationship, but adds nothing new to the story, except to emphasize that Mencken knew he must align himself to an unsuccessful author who would someday be famous, and that he found just the right candidate in Dreiser.

854 KENNEDY, Gail, ed. Evolution and Religion: The Conflict Between Science and Theology in Modern America. Boston: D. C. Heath, 1957. Dreiser, passim.
Dreiser not treated directly. Good background on subjects related to Dreiser, particularly theories of evolution.

855 KENNELL, Ruth Epperson. Theodore Dreiser and the Soviet Union, 1927-1945: A First-Hand Chronicle. New York: International Press, 1969.
Author was Dreiser's secretary and translator. Consists of 300 pages based upon letters from Dreiser during the years following 1927-1928; and other personal material which she had kept in her files for twenty years. In the Foreword, Dreiser is named as one of the three most widely read American authors in the Soviet Union, Mark Twain and Jack London being the others. Young and old are familiar with his books. His wide popularity among this cultured, socially enlightened people

afforded him deep comfort during the last years of his life.
Kennell's book reveals a definite Soviet bias on her part as
well as Dreiser's.

856 _____. "Airmail Interview." Dreiser Newsletter, 5 (Spring,
1974), 6-11.
Answers a variety of questions, perhaps most dominated by
Dreiser's relation to the Soviet Union and his Socialistic-
Communistic ideas. Other questions relate to the current
critical assessment of Dreiser, the actual prototype of some
of his characters, and Dreiser's relation to women.

857 KENTON, Edna. "Review of Sister Carrie." Chicago Daily
News, November 30, 1900.
Consists of a good critical summary of the novel, showing
how easily one event leads to the next, how there are no sur-
prises in the novel. There is something remorseless in the
way Dreiser shows step by step the sinking of the once prosperous manager into a listless seeker for work, a penniless
vagrant, a tattered hopeless Bowery tramp and beggar, and
his final horrible end. There is nothing melodramatic about
it--it is too logical and photographic to own one unreal note.
The book is well worth reading simply for this account of
Hurstwood.

858 _____. "Some Incomes in Fiction." Bookman, 34 (October,
1911), 147-152.

859 KERN, Alexander C. "Dreiser's Difficult Beauty." Western
Review, 16 (Winter, 1952), 129-132. Reprinted in Kazin and
Shapiro (1955), pp. 161-168.
The critical problem in Dreiser's case is not to ascertain
what gradually gained him popularity, for it is obvious that
he can tell a story. The problem is rather to recognize what
elements he has to offer in addition to the most obvious. His
work shows the ability to convey the meaning of a serious if
unsubtle view of life, to create a convincingly real world
peopled with human characters, to project their emotions with
a power which engages our affections, and to wrest a kind of
difficult beauty from unpromising materials despite a technique
which only partially served its purpose.

860 _____. "Dreiser and Fitzgerald as Social Critics." Papers
of the Midwest Modern Language Association, No. 2 (1972),
80-87.
Study is based on An American Tragedy and The Great
Gatsby. Although radically different in nearly every way
possible, Dreiser and Fitzgerald both create powerful indict-
ments of the American dream of success. Coincidentally, both
novels were published in 1925.

861 KEYSSAR, Helene. "Theodore Dreiser's Dramas: American Folk Drama and Its Limits." Theater Journal, 33 (October, 1981), 365-376.

862 KING, Wyncie. "Theodore Dreiser." New York Book Review. December 23, 1923. P. 6. Caricature.

863 KINGSLEY, Grace. "Hobnobbing in Hollywood." Los Angeles Times, December 13, 1932. Part 2, p. 7.

864 KIRK, Clara Marburg. "The Marxist Dogma in Literature." The English Journal (college edition), 24 (March, 1935), 209-214.

Relates to Dreiser in that it raises the question of how far should the teacher of literature go in permitting selections which are pro-Soviet, Marxist, etc. Upton Sinclair, for example, has frequently been cited as too revolutionary, too incendiary.

865 KLIMAN, Bernice. "An American Tragedy: Novel, Scenario and Films." Literature/Film Quarterly, 5 (Summer, 1977), 258-268.

866 KLISE, Thomas, reader. Dreiser's Tragic America. Sound filmstrip. Peoria, Ill.: Thomas S. Klise Co., 1972.

867 KLOPF, Dorothy. "Theodore Dreiser's The 'Genius': Much Matter and More Art." Modern Fiction Studies, 23 (Fall, 1977), 441-448.

Reviews what several other critics have said about The "Genius," but disagrees that there is no controlled structure in the book. Says in contradiction: "For those who, like Shakespeare's Queen Gertrude, demand 'more matter, with less art,' the absence of the finely turned phrase and le mot juste does not impede appreciation of The 'Genius'. Indeed a careful scrutiny of the novel reveals a Dreiser who takes imaginative possession of his subject, devises a form appropriate to his now clearly realized subject, and, finally defines his role as an artist."

868 KNIGHT, Arthur. "Dreiser, Carrie, and William Wyler." Saturday Review, 35 (July 12, 1952), 25-26.

Unlike most films, it is not the incident that is important here but rather the revelation of character that these incidents make possible. The characters are full-length and three dimensional. No one has been turned into a conventional villain; Carrie is neither glamorized nor sentimentalized. We are struck by the humanity of these people, not their virtue.

869 KNIGHT, Grant C. "Fiction: A Gallery of Women." Bookman, 70 (November, 1929), 320-321.

This is not Dreiser's most important book; it is, however,
a further groping to know all and forgive all, to apprehend
if not to unriddle personality. Several stories convince us
that no American writer has equal capacity to reflect the var-
iegated emotional patterns of our current civilization.

870 _____. The Novel in English. New York: R. R. Smith,
       1931. Dreiser, pp. 338-346.
       He has no philosophy of life, and writes with no fixed moral
       point of view. His favorite idea is that we are creatures of
       vagrant temperaments which are given us at birth, which we
       seemingly cannot change, and which are responsible for our
       selfishness, our cruelty, our baseness. His philosophy, if
       it can be called that, would justify us in putting self-pity
       upon a monument. No other of our novelists has so poign-
       antly presented the agony of American life; the struggling,
       the laboring toward some better future, we know not what;
       the torturing effort to become something physically and spir-
       itually.

871 _____. American Literature and Culture. New York: Ray
       Long and Richard R. Smith, 1932. "Literature of Realism:
       Theodore Dreiser," pp. 400-413.
       Reading his novels is almost the equivalent to reading a
       social history of the United States for their years. One gets
       a bird's-eye view of American life in them. Upon this mad
       world Dreiser looks with bewilderment as well as pity. Not
       despising it, but hearing the still sad music of the human
       race and having no pitch with which to set it in tune with
       the infinite. He has no remedy for the ills, neither Com-
       munist nor Tory. Sees things on the surface, says they are
       thus and so, but prescribes no panacea.

872 _____. The Strenuous Age in American Literature. Chapel
       Hill: University of North Carolina Press, 1954. "Dreiser's
       Sister Carrie," pp. 36-39.
       Uncovering the roots of the American woman's discontent
       is a task that may be left to the psychologist. Dreiser had
       no intention of assuming this task in Sister Carrie, yet that
       novel has more to say about the friction of the female per-
       sonality upon that of the male, and Dreiser is more important
       as a psychological novelist than American criticism has yet
       conceded.

873 KNOPF, Alfred A. "H. L. Mencken, George Jean Nathan, and
       the American Mercury Venture." Menckeniana, 78 (Summer,
       1981), 1-10.

874 KORES, Maryjo A. "The Search for Personal Identity and Mean-
       ing in Sister Carrie, Winesburg, Ohio, and the Novels of
       Herbert Gold." MA thesis, Ohio State University, 1960.

875 KRAFT, Hy. "Foreword." The Tobacco Men, by Borden Deal.
     New York: Holt, 1965. Pp. 11-13.
       Is called "a novel based on notes by Theodore Dreiser and
     Hy Kraft, with a foreword by Hy Kraft." From the pub-
     lisher's note the following: "In 1932 Theodore Dreiser and
     Hy Kraft traveled to Kentucky to investigate an important and
     dramatic episode of American history which had never fully
     been treated in fiction, the Tobacco Wars of the turn of the
     century. The results were some twenty pages of notes on
     the tobacco industry between 1860 and 1910 and a preliminary
     script for a motion picture. Dreiser never made further use
     of this material. Recently, after reading these notes, Borden
     Deal wrote The Tobacco Men, a new entirely original work of
     fiction."

876 _____. "Inside Dreiser," in On My Way to the Theater.
     New York: Macmillan, 1971. Pp. 59-103.
       Reviews his acquaintance with Dreiser from the time they
     met in 1928, when Kraft was proposing a Broadway production
     of Sister Carrie. At the time a dramatization of An American
     Tragedy was doing well on Broadway. Concludes with Drei-
     ser's death and funeral in 1945 in Hollywood, saying: "He
     was lonely, suffering a loneliness that must have been beyond
     his own powers to describe. He tried to understand life, to
     find out why, what, and how.... He didn't enjoy wealth any
     more than he enjoyed poverty. He lived and died 'a Proces-
     sion of One.' "

877 KRAMER, Dale. "Dreiser, Masks of the Monster-Hero." Chi-
     cago Renaissance. New York: Appleton-Century, 1966.
     Pp. 128-139.
       Discusses Dreiser's career after the disaster publication of
     Sister Carrie, and the difficulty with which he finally suc-
     ceeded in getting Doubleday to bring the novel into print.
     Other aspect of the discussion deals with Dreiser's marriage
     to Sarah White, which was never a happy one, thanks to her
     disposition and nagging and his inclination to extramarital
     affairs.

878 KRANIDAS, Thomas. "The Materials of Theodore Dreiser's
     An American Tragedy." MA thesis, Columbia University,
     1953.

879 KRIEG, Joann. "Theodore Dreiser and the Penitentiary System."
     Dreiser Newsletter, 8 (Fall, 1977), 5-8.
       Study is based on Dreiser's portrayal of the prison to which
     Frank Cowperwood is sentenced and the one to which Clyde
     Griffiths is sent to await execution. It has been said that
     Dreiser overdid himself in describing these prisons "brick by
     brick." Dreiser maintained a steady interest in the prison
     system and the forms of enforced labor which they demanded.

880 KRIEG, Louis W. "The Dreisers." Commonweal, 18 (July 28, 1933), 330. See article by Haley, C. O'Neill.

881 KRIGER, Sybil. "Determinism in the Writing of Theodore Dreiser." MA thesis, Kent State University, 1967.

882 KRIM, Seymour. "Theodore Dreiser." Hudson Review, 4 (Autumn, 1951), 474-477.
Review-essay on Matthiessen's posthumous volume on Theodore Dreiser. Says it would be pleasant to report that the book does credit to both men, but such is not the case: "As a whole, this is a pale, conservative, unimaginative and frequently boring book. It is adequate as an introduction to Dreiser only in that it is objective and can give the reader a general notion of the novelist's stature. It does not give us the penetrating, digging kind of criticism that Dreiser needs and that might have been expected from Matthiessen in view of his earlier work."

883 _____. "Dreiser and His Critics." Commonweal, 64 (June 1, 1956), 229-231.

884 KRUTCH, Joseph Wood. "Crime and Punishment." Nation, 122 (February 10, 1926), 152. Reprinted in Salzman (1971), pp. 10-12.
Dreiser's new novel is the crowning achievement of the work which he began a quarter of a century ago. To him it seemed then that novelists had lost themselves in their own refinement, that, enamored of moral delicacy and psychological subtleties, they had forgotten the simple motives by which the vast majority of mankind are moved; so with a single shrug he sloughed off once and for all the implications of the theory that man is primarily a moral animal, and he did this much as the behaviorists in psychology sloughed off the soul.

885 _____. "Literature and Propaganda." English Journal, 22 (December, 1933), 793-802.

886 _____. "Dreiser Simplified." Nation, 142 (April 1, 1936), 427-429.
Refers to another stage version of An American Tragedy which flourished briefly on Broadway a few years ago. This is another one, "The Case of Glyde Griffiths," which is also a thin hurried synopsis of the huge novel. Seems to have missed all points of the novel except that Clyde was not wholly to blame for what he did: in this play he is not at all to blame.

887 _____. "In These Days Our Literature in All Its Might Came of Age." New York Times Book Review, October 7, 1956. PP. 6-7, 40.

888 KRYLOVA, L. "Theodore Dreiser and His Influence on the
     Progressive Aesthetic Thought in the USA," in Proceedings
     of the VIIth International Congress of Aesthetics, held in
     Bucharest, August 28-September 2, 1972. Bucharest: Edi-
     tura Academiel Republicii Socialista Romania, 1976. Pp. 993-
     995. In English.

889 KUNITZ, Stanley J., Jr. "Theodore Dreiser," in Living Au-
     thors: A Book of Biographies. New York: Wilson, 1931.
     Pp. 109-111.

890 _____, and Howard Haycraft. "Theodore Dreiser," in Twen-
     tieth Century Authors. New York: Wilson, 1931. Pp. 378-
     379. Revised edition, 1942. Pp. 398-399.
     Biographical detail with slight comment: "it is as a novelist
     that he will live. The man himself, big, slowmoving, his
     blond shock of hair turned white, with strangely blazing steel
     gray eyes, is like one of his own characters."

891 KUNKEL, Fran Rita. "The Critical Approaches to the Novels
     of Theodore Dreiser, 1900-1969." Ph.D. diss., University
     of California (Los Angeles), 1971. DA, 32 (1971), 1517A.
     Reviews Dreiser criticism according to dominant methodolo-
     gies, formulating the main arguments and underlying assump-
     tions of these approaches, and pointing out their limitations
     in explaining and evaluating Dreiser's art. Among the var-
     ious critical approaches are "mimetic" and "socio-cultural"
     criticism.

892 KUSELL, Sally. "Dreiser's Style." New York Times Book Re-
     View, April 8, 1951. P. 26.
     Letter to editor.

893 KUTTNER, Alfred B. "The Lyrical Mr. Dreiser." International
     Magazine, 5 (January, 1912), 21-22.

894 KWIAT, Joseph J. "Dreiser and the Graphic Artist." American
     Quarterly, 3 (Summer, 1951), 127-141.

895 _____. "Dreiser's The 'Genius' and Everett Shinn, 'The Ash
     Can Painter.' " PMLA, 67 (March, 1952), 15-31.
     Article establishes that Dreiser knew the work of the en-
     tire Ash-Can school of painters, and had a special interest
     in and knowledge of Everett Shinn. Shinn also knew Dreiser
     as a friend and as a colleague on magazines. Dreiser's novels,
     although largely autobiographical, also incorporate details
     from Shinn's life. Various phases of Shinn's personal life,
     his art student days, his career as a newspaper artist and
     magazine illustrator, and his hostility toward the National
     Academy are retold in Witla's own career. And the similari-
     ties between Witla and Shinn are extended to include their
     parallel artistic theory and practice.

896 _____. "The Newspaper Experience: Crane, Norris, and
Dreiser." Nineteenth-Century Fiction, 8 (September, 1953),
99-117.
This experience was invaluable in formulating many of their
unconventional attitudes toward life, their selection of subject matter, even their technique. The loud and ephemeral
demands of the city room were actually a richly rewarding
and fertile one for the men who were to lead the revolt against
the ideals of the genteel tradition. No doubt the bohemian
nature of newspaper life in the nineties contributed to this
opposition to bourgeois values. But more important was the
intimate relationship with life, the variety and contrast, which
a newspaper assignment made necessary.

897 _____. "Theodore Dreiser: The Writer and Early Twentieth-
Century American Society." Sprache und Literatur, 2 (1956),
13-50.

898 _____. "The Social Responsibilities of the American Painter
and Writer: Robert Henri and John Sloan; Frank Norris and
Theodore Dreiser." Centennial Review, 21 (Winter, 1977),
19-35.
From about 1890 until the end of the 1920's American political life was quickened by a sense of social responsibility.
Industrial unrest in the early years culminated in trust-busting,
muckraking, the municipal reform movement, the popular primary, woman's suffrage, limitation of working hours, etc. All
of these tendencies represented a new emphasis upon the wel-
fare of the common man. The artistic effects of these powerful currents were profoundly expressed by two painters and
two novelists in their individual books, essays, articles, diaries, letters, and manuscripts.

899 _____. "The American Painter and Writer's Credo of 'Art
for Truth's Sake': Robert Henri and John Sloan; Frank Norris and Theodore Dreiser." Journal of American Culture, 1
(Summer, 1978), 285-300.

900 _____. "The Education of Theodore Dreiser in the World of
the City: 'Exercises' for the Early Novels." Americana-
Austriaca, 5 (1980), 91-109.

901 _____. "Theodore Dreiser's Creative Quest: Early 'Philosophical' Beliefs and Artistic Values." Arizona Quarterly, 37
(Autumn, 1981), 265-274.
Dreiser's "philosophical" beliefs were sophomoric and experi-
mental and his artistic theories were, admittedly, haphazard
and contradictory. With all his limitations as a philosophical
and esthetic thinker, nevertheless, the critic is impressed
with Dreiser's struggle to discover a rationale for his early
labors as a practicing novelist. There is a sense that he
was seriously aware of his literary-historical role of translat-

ing the confusing and even traumatic changes in American
society in the early years of the twentieth century. He attempted to mirror those changes with uncompromising, if not
always consistently successful, dramatic efforts.

902 _____, and Mary C. Turpie, eds. Studies in American Culture: Dominant Ideas and Images. Minneapolis: University
of Minnesota Press, 1960. Prints two essays related to Dreiser: "Dreiser and Veblen and the Literature of Cultural
Change," by David W. Noble, pp. 139-152; and "The 'Theonomous Analysis' in American Culture," by Charles H. Foster, pp. 189-206.

903 LABRIE, Rodrigue E. "American Naturalism: A View from
Within." Ph.D. diss., Pennsylvania State University, 1964.
DA, 26 (1965), 1044.
   This study traces the evolution of American naturalism--
1886-1945--as revealed in the critical writings, autobiographical works, and personal correspondence of Hamlin Garland.
Stephen Crane, Frank Norris, and Theodore Dreiser, all of
whom played a direct part in the movement. Previous studies
of this subject tend to view the contribution of these authors
in terms of their fiction exclusively, rarely making use of the
other forms of material available.

904 _____. "American Naturalism: An Appraisal." Markahm
Review, 2 (February, 1971), 88-90.

905 LAIT, Jack. "Protests Against Damning Dreiser, Who Wrote
The 'Genius': Attorney Says Censors Hunt 'Smut.'" Chicago Herald, November 7, 1916. P. 18.

906 LAMONT, Corliss. Humanism as a Philosophy. New York:
Philosophical Library Publications, 1949. Dreiser, pp. 95
et passim.
   We can take as further representative of the Humanist view-
point in America the realistic novels of Theodore Dreiser,
Sinclair Lewis, etc. Scientific discoveries and the scientific
temper have done much to revise, in the direction of Humanism, traditional ideas and methods in religion and and philosophy.

907 LANE, John. "Theodore Dreiser." London Times Literary
Supplement. January 20, 1921. P. 44.
   Letter to editor.

908 LANE, Lauriat, Jr. "The Double in An American Tragedy."
Modern Fiction Studies, 12 (Summer, 1966), 213-220.
   Reviews what early reviewers said about An American Trag-

edy being "a vast, sloppy, chaotic thing," and later critics who have since pointed out the use of many of the most effective techniques of prose fiction. The subject of this article is "another technique that Dreiser used: the anthropological, psychological, and literary tradition known as the Doppelganger, or double."

909 LANG, Hans-Joachim. "Dreiser: Jennie Gerhardt," in Der Amerikanische Roman, edited by Hans-Joachim Lang. Dusseldorf: August Bagel Verlag, 1972. Pp. 194-218. In English.

910 LANGE, W. W. "American First Editions: Theodore Dreiser, 1871--." Publishers' Weekly, 104, December 22, 1925. Reprinted in Merle Johnson, American First Editions. New York: Bowker, 1929. Revised editions, 1932, 1936, 1942; 1936 and 1942 by Jacob Blanck.

911 LAWSON, John Howard. "Dreiser: 20th-Century Titan." Sunday Worker, February 3, 1946. Magazine section, p. 9.

912 _____. "Tribute to Theodore Dreiser." Book Find News, 2 (March, 1946), 19.

913 _____. "Dreiser Discusses Sister Carrie." Masses and Mainstream, 8 (December, 1955), 20-22. Letters of Lawson and Dreiser, August 10--October 10, 1928.

914 LAYMAN, Richard, et al. "Theodore Dreiser, 1871-1945," in First Printings of American Authors. Detroit: Gale Research Center, 1979. Vol. 4, pp. 155-171.

915 LEAF, M. "Techniques of Naturalism in the Works of Dreiser, Crane, and Norris." MA thesis, Nottingham University, England, 1970.

916 LEARY, Lewis. "Theodore Dreiser," in Articles on American Literature, 1900-1950. Durham, N.C.: Duke University Press, 1954. Pp. 73-75. Cites 90 articles.

917 _____. "Theodore Dreiser," in Articles on American Literature, 1950-1967. Durham: Duke University Press, 1970. Pp. 116-120. Cites 110 articles.

918 _____, with John Auchard. "Theodore Dreiser," in Articles on American Literature, 1968-1975. Durham, N.C.: Duke University Press, 1979. Pp. 126-129. Cites 137 articles.

919 LEAVER, Florence. "Theodore Dreiser: Beyond Naturalism."
     Mark Twain Quarterly, 9 (Winter, 1951), 5-9.
     Discusses the folly of pasting a label on a writer, as when
     Dreiser is called a naturalist. When one has thus described
     him, the spirit of the man has been violated. Article reviews
     several principles of naturalism which do apply to Dreiser,
     but then points out that he is not typically naturalistic in that
     he manifests many humanitarian ideals and also advances sev-
     eral theories of the supernatural.

920 LEAVIS, Frank R. "Arnold Bennett: American Version," in
     For Continuity. Cambridge, England: Fraser, 1933. Re-
     printed Freeport, N.Y.: Books for Libraries, 1968. Pp.
     97-101.
     Essay-review of Dreiser and the Land of the Free by Dorothy
     Dudley (1932). Calls the book "a document of unusual inter-
     est." Saying, "that is not to pronounce it a good book. In-
     deed, its badness is an essential part of its documentary
     value: it is unintentionally a fascinating document of cultural
     dissolution. An intelligent account of Dreiser's career might
     have been very interesting, but it could hardly have been so
     convincing or have told us more. Miss Dudley's central pre-
     occupation is an account of Dreiser's obsession with recogni-
     tion as a writer, embodied with the theme of hostility of the
     American environment towards the artist."

921 LE BLEU, Cynthia C. "Contrasts in American Literary Natural-
     ism: A Comparison of the Degeneration Novels of Stephen
     Crane, Frank Norris, and Theodore Dreiser." MA thesis,
     Southwest Texas State College, 1968.

922 LE GALLIENNE, Richard. "Certain Literary Sins of Theodore
     Dreiser." Literary Digest International Book Review, Febru-
     ary, 1923. Pp. 10-11, 70-71.
     Review of A Book About Myself, of which Le Gallienne says:
     "This is a dull, distasteful and quite unnecessary book. Drei-
     ser has wasted time he might have been writing a novel. Only
     reviewers, whose time is paid for, can afford to read it. As
     a pioneer in the fight for naturalism, Dreiser deserves our
     respect and support, and he has had both to something like
     excess. The value of his work has been exaggerated."

923 _____. "The 'Genius': A Review." The Literary Review,
     October 6, 1923.
     Sidney Lanier once called Walt Whitman's poetry "raw col-
     lops off the rump of literature." The "Genius" seems just
     that. Dreiser unfolds life as a huge panorama, slowly, clum-
     sily, colorlessly presents a spectacle. Seems to write an epic
     of dullness. Deep seeing is not enough for an artist.

924 _____. "The 'Genius': A Review." The Austin Statesman,
     October 28, 1923.

More than a year after publication and the sale of thousands of copy, the New York Society for Suppression of Vice
notified the publishers that the book was in violation of laws
against obscene literature. The novel was withdrawn in July,
1916. Concludes that "no one who would be harmed by such
a book is likely to read its 736 pages, when he can get what
he wants with much less effort. Vice is not made attractive
in this book: Witla suffers as few of us would care to suffer."

925 _____. "An American Tragedy: A Review." Atlantic Monthly,
March, 1926.
Begins by saying Dreiser's method of "creation resembles
that of the oyster: begins with a hard, sharp grain of fact."
He has included a more detailed, absorbing, realistic account
of a murder trial than has hitherto found its way into fiction.
He has translated this story of a weak and commonplace boy
into an American epic comparable to Jude the Obscure and
The Brothers Karamazov. It is Dreiser's greatest novel and
one that must be reckoned with in any history of American
literature.

926 LEHAN, Richard. "Dreiser's An American Tragedy: A Critical
Study." College English, 25 (December, 1963), 187-193. Reprinted in The Modern American Novel: Essays in Criticism,
edited by Max Westbrook. New York: Random House, 1966.
Pp. 21-33.
In this article, Lehan says: "I try to suggest in what ways
there is a relationship between (1) the setting of the novel
and a character's psychological state of mind, (2) the meaning
of one scene and another which it foreshadows, (3) the meaning of one character and the meaning of his 'ratio' equivalent,
(4) the key symbols and themes, (5) the use of irony and the
meaning of the novel, and (6) the style and the meaning of
action and of character in An American Tragedy."

927 _____. "Levels of Reality in the Novels of Albert Camus."
Modern Fiction Studies, 10 (1964), 232-244.
Begins study with a comparison of Clyde Griffiths and
Meursault of The Stranger. Soon abandons this approach
in favor of comparing Meursault with The Postman Always
Rings Twice.

928 _____. Theodore Dreiser: His World and His Novels. Carbondale: Southern Illinois University Press, 1969. Reprinted
New York: Arcturus Books, 1974. Excerpt, pp. 45-53, reprinted in Pizer (1981), pp. 136-143 as "The Romantic Dilemma."
Consists of 250 pages with short bibliography, notes to
chapters, and a comprehensive index. In the Introduction
the author says that his work "is primarily a critical study

of Dreiser's novels. My concern is with the genesis and
evolution of the novels, their pattern, and their meaning."
Also examines some of the influences which most shaped Dreiser's imagination--especially his family, the city, his work as
a journalist and free-lance writer, his reading, and his reaction to the politics and the scientific ideas of his times. Concludes with the discussion that Dreiser's novels stood at the
"cross-roads" of the genteel tradition and the modern novel.

929   _____. "Assessing Dreiser." Dreiser Newsletter, 1 (Fall,
       1970), 1-3.
       A general estimate of Dreiser addressed principally to teach-
       ers of literature, "who spend most of their time discussing
       the meaning of literary texts." Attacks the so-called "New
       Criticism" because it is too limited, and in the case of Drei-
       ser, does not always work. One simply cannot apply Jamesian
       criteria to Dreiser, as Lionel Trilling did, and accomplish any-
       thing worthwhile.

930   _____. "Airmail Interview." Dreiser Newsletter, 2 (Spring,
       1971), 11-17.
       Responds to a variety of questions, including those which
       deal with Dreiser as an artist. Thinks that comparison of a
       Dreiser novel with one by James is to miss the point: novels
       should be judged on their own merits or with regard to an-
       other novel whose aims and objectives are the same. One
       question has to do with Dreiser's popularity in India, to which
       Lehan replies that he thinks a good deal of confusion exists
       as to Dreiser's mysticism.

931   _____, reader. An American Tragedy, audio tape. Twentieth
       Century American Novel Series. Deland, Fla.: Everett-
       Edwards, 1971.

932 LEISY, Ernest Edwin. American Literatuare: An Interpretive
     Survey. New York: Crowell, 1929. Dreiser, pp. 209-210.
       Characters are irresponsible followers of their desires. In
       efforts at self-realization they evade penalties and so chal-
       lenge every law and custom. The author is bewildered by all
       this chaos, but feels pity that people exist thus and he must
       portray them candidly. The style is heavy and uncertain.
       Dreiser is a slow, confused thinker. Plots are amorphous and
       the details frequently blur outline of story.

933   _____. "Dreiser's Mennonite Origin." Mennonite Life, 9
       (October, 1954), 179-180.
       Dreiser's mother belonged to a Mennonite faith before her
       marriage. Her father objected to her marrying John Paul
       Dreiser, a Catholic, but in spite of parental protests she
       eloped with him at age sixteen.

934 LENGEL, William C. "The 'Genius' Himself." Esquire, 10 (Sep-
     tember, 1938), 55 et passim.

935 _____, ed. with Introduction. Twelve Men. Greenwich,
     Conn.: Fawcett, 1962. "The Thirteenth Man," pp. vii-x.

936 _____, ed. with Introduction. A Gallery of Women, 2 vols.
     Greenwich, Conn.: Fawcett, 1962.

937 LEONARD, Neil. "Theodore Dreiser and the Film." Film Heri-
     tage, 2, No. 1 (Fall, 1966), 7-16.
     Discusses An American Tragedy.

938 _____. "Theodore Dreiser and Music," in Challenges in
     American Culture, edited by Ray B. Browne et al. Bowling
     Green, Ohio: Bowling Green University Popular Press, 1970.
     Pp. 242-250.
     We have studies of his concern with painting, with the
     theater, with the film, and several scholars have commented
     on his poetry. But we know little of his interest in music.
     He made small contribution to that field, yet music held an
     important place in his sensibility. Concludes with an important
     passage from the sketch about brother Paul: "mere bits and
     scraps of sentiment and melodrama, yet with something about
     them, in the music at least, which always appealed to me in-
     tensely. They bespoke a wistful, seeking, uncertain tempera-
     ment, tender and illusioned, with no practical knowledge of
     any side of life, but full of true poetic feeling for the mys-
     tery of life and death...." In varying degrees the feelings
     expressed in Paul's songs are those of Dreiser himself and
     the characters of his novels.

939 LERNER, Max. "On Dreiser." New York PM, December 31,
     1945. P. 2. Reprinted in Actions and Passions. New York:
     Simon and Schuster, 1949. Pp. 43-46.
     The fact is that Dreiser was the greatest American writer
     we have had in this twentieth century. He came out of our
     people, out of our soil, out of the granite rock of the Ameri-
     can experience and the American plight. It took him half
     a century to hew his sculpturings out of that rock, but now
     they are there they will stand every change of the climate
     of ideas, every buffeting of the political tempests. He was
     not a fancy craftsman, but because he was an honest one,
     his chisel was governed by a passion of his brain and heart.

940 LE VERRIER, Charles. "Un Grand romancier Americain: The-
     odore Dreiser." Revue Hebdomadaire, 42 (January 21, 1933),
     280-294.

941 LEVIN, Harry. "What Is Realism?" Comparative Literature,
     3 (Summer, 1951), 193-199.

Discusses the range of definitions for "realism" and concludes that the term is relatively meaningless except in relation to a particular author. Uses a wide variety of authors--
Zola, Flaubert, Defoe, Hardy, Dreiser--to illustrate the article.

942 LEVINE, Richard. "Characterization in Dreiser's Fiction."
     MA thesis, New York University, 1951.

943 LEVINSON, Andre. "Avant-Propos," in Une Tragedie Ameri-
     caine, translated from English into French by Victor Llona.
     Paris: Fayard, 1929. Pp. 7-16.

944 LEVITT, Albert. "Was Clyde Griffiths Guilty of Murder in the
     First Degree." Mimeographed pamphlet, Lexington, Kentucky,
     November, 1926.

945 LEWIS, Robert E. "Unified Reality: A Study of the Novels
     of Theodore Dreiser." MA thesis, University of Idaho, 1951.

946 LEWIS, Sinclair. "The Literary Zoo: Editors Who Write."
     Life, 50 (October 10, 1907), 414-415.

947 _____. "Intimate Travel Talks by World-Famed Writers."
     St. Louis Republic, February 21, 1914.
         A review of A Traveler at Forty. Comments with numerous
     examples of the extraordinary details with which Dreiser fills
     his book. Says that everywhere Dreiser goes "he watches
     people with a terrible intentness and a curiosity about them
     that never rests until he has their secrets."

948 _____. "Nobel Prize Speech of 1930." New York Times,
     December 13, 1930. P. 12. Reprinted in part in Kazin and
     Shapiro (1955), pp. 111-112.
         Pays tribute to Dreiser by saying, "Dreiser, more than any
     other man, is marching alone. Usually unappreciated, often
     hounded, he has cleared the trail from Victorian Howellsian
     timidity and gentility in American fiction, to honesty, boldness,
     and passion of life. Without his pioneering, I doubt if any
     of us could, unless we liked to be sent to jail, seek to ex-
     press life, beauty and terror."

949 LEWIS, Wyndham. "The Propagandist in Fiction." Current
     History, 40 (August, 1934), 567-572.

950 LEWISOHN, Ludwig. "Portrait of an Artist." Nation, 116 (April
     4, 1923), 394.
         Review of A Book About Myself. Begins with general ac-
     count of Dreiser's inability to write and concludes that this
     book confirms these observations, yet "even these pages are
     saved by a presence in them of the author's boundless ap-

petite for life and the interpretation of life. Here, as in
his other works, he does not try to interpret life by a rule
of thumb, by an anterior theory unrelated to the facts."

951 _____. "Culture and Barbarism," in Cities and Men. New
York: Harper Brothers, 1927. Pp. 2-18. Reprinted in part
in Kazin and Shapiro (1955), pp. 17-20.
  Points out that Dreiser was largely responsible for a new
literature to "come stalking in." At the time the East was
hopelessly cultured" and refined, writers like Dreiser, who
came from the Middle West, were "like rain on parched earth."

952 _____. Expression in America. New York: Harper and Row,
1932. Pp. 473-482.
  Launches an especially heated attack against Dreiser: "His
style grew more and more slovenly, his solecisms more and
more grating and monstrous. He broke through; he came out
of the jungle into the open with all his literary sensibilities
stone-dead.... He is the worst writer of his eminence in the
entire history of literature. He is matchless in badness.
That he is so, is the gift to the culture of their country of
the polite and conservative critics of the more or less Cal-
vinistic persuasion."

953 LIBMAN, Valentina A. "Draizer, Teodor," in Rissian Studies
of American Literature: A Bibliography, edited by Clarence
Gohdes, translated by Robert V. Allen. Chapel Hill: University of North Carolina Press, 1969. Pp. 65-76.
  Lists some 150 items in chronological order, 1925-1963, published in Russia in the Russian language. Titles are translated into English.

954 LIMON, John Keith. "Imagining Science: The Influence and
Metamorphosis of Science in Charles Brockden Brown, Edgar
Allan Poe, and Nathaniel Howthorne." Ph.D. diss., University of California (Berkeley), 1981. DA, 42 (1982), 5122A-
5123A.
  Dissertation is based on the premise that science grew in
intellectual prestige even as it grew forbiddingly recondite;
the result is that writers found themselves in an intellectual
world they decreasingly understood. Study based on Brown,
Poe, and Hawthorne to show the relationship of literature and
intellectual history, clear examples of the artist as half-
intellectual. In the conclusion of the study, Limon compares
works by Brown, Poe, and Hawthorne with modern works by
Dreiser (Sister Carrie), Pynchon, and Mailer.

955 LINCOLN, Selma Walden. "An Answer to One of the 'Gallery
of Women.'" Chicago Daily News, February 26, 1930. P. 18.
  Letter to the editor.

956 LINDBORG, Mary Anne. "Dreiser's Sentimental Heroine: Aileen
Butler." American Literature, 48 (1977), 590-596.
In Aileen Butler, of the Cowperwood trilogy, Dreiser would
create a heroine who would pattern her actions after those of
the sentimental heroines in the fiction she read. The novels
which Dreiser chose for Aileen's reading were probably representative of what he called "the sentiment and mush" which
he confessed to having read. Aileen's tragedy is that she
tries to live by this romantic fiction, in a world dominated
by such "hard-headed realism" as that of Frank Cowperwood.

957 LINDSAY, Julia I. "The Indictment of America in 1925: A
Comparative Study of The Great Gatsby and An American
Tragedy." MA thesis, University of North Carolina, 1970.

958 LINGEMAN, Richard, edited with Introduction. The Stoic.
New York: Signet-New American Library, 1981.

959 LION, Vernon M. "An Analysis of the Reputation of Theodore
Dreiser." MA thesis, University of Nebraska, 1948.

960 LIPTZIN, Sol. The Jew in American Literature. New York:
Bloch, 1966. Dreiser, pp. 159-166.
Dreiser's reputation as a great liberal was justified because
of his stand on many political and social issues. It was not
justified on the basis of his attitude toward Jews. Not until
1944, a year before his death, when the war against the
Nazis was drawing to a successful conclusion, did Dreiser
speak out against the German treatment of Jews. In a broad-
cast beamed to the German people, he mentioned the thousands upon thousands of helpless and often heroic Jews. By
that time, however, the consequences of anti-semitism were
apparent in the extermination camps, and every American liberal had dissociated himself from the philosophy underlying
the Nuremberg race laws.

961 LOEWENBERG, Bert J. "Darwinism Comes to America, 1859-
1900." Mississippi Valley Historical Review, 28 (December,
1941), 258-271.

962 LOGGINS, Vernon. "Dominant Primordial: Theodore Dreiser,"
in I Hear America ... Literature in the U.S. Since 1900.
New York: Crowell, 1937. Pp. 125-134.
Dreiser's other writings (autobiographical books, essays,
travel sketches, plays, many short stories, and a volume of
poems), when compared with his novels, are of negligible importance. He has been a pioneer in American literature, like
Zola in France and Hardy in England. In the battle into which
his first novel drew him and kept him for a quarter of a century, he proved himself a bold, uncompromising, and fearless
warrior. All sorts of silly and false charges were brought

against him--German monstrousness, private immoralities, gross,
taste, ignorance, and an illiterate style. But his steady habits
and his confidence in his art prevailed. An American Tragedy
put an end to the namecalling crusade waged against him.

963 LOJEK, Helen Heusner. "Ministers and Their Sermons in Amer-
     ican Literature." Ph.D. diss., Denver University, 1977. DA,
     38 (1977), 787A-788A.
         American novels contain a wide variety of portraits of min-
     isters, portraits which reflect historical trends observable in
     the American church. Three basic themes are discernible in
     these fictional treatments, and this study considers each theme
     in the period during which it rose to greatest prominence.
     In the third period, since World War I, the dominant tone of
     American fiction toward religion becomes one of disillusion and
     frequently despair. This last category includes Dreiser's
     An American Tragedy.

964 LOMBARDO, Agostino. "Lettere de Dreiser," in La Ricerca
     del Vero: Saggi sulla Tradizione Letteraria Americana. Rome:
     Edizione de Storia e Letteratura, 1961. Pp. 309-315. In
     Italian.

965 LONG, Robert Emmet. "Sister Carrie and the Rhythm of Failure
     in Fitzgerald." Fitzgerald Newsletter, No. 25 (Spring, 1964),
     146-147.

966 _____. "Dreiser and Frederic: The Upstate New York Exile
     of Dick Diver." Fitzgerald Newsletter, No. 37 (Winter, 1967),
     1-2.
         Reference is to Dick Diver, of Tender Is the Night, who
     leaves the French Riviera for the obscurity of upper New
     York State, drifting from one small town in Upstate New York
     to another. It is known that Fitzgerald had read Dreiser's
     An American Tragedy, and Harold Frederic's The Damnation
     of Theron Ware, both of which are novels of social realism,
     depicting with unblinking exactness the sterility of life in the
     little towns of upstate New York.

967 LONGSTREET, Stepehn. Chicago: 1860-1919. New York:
     David McKay, 1973. Dreiser, pp. 79-80 et passim.
         Dedicated to the memory of the one who first suggested
     this book, "To Theodore Dreiser." Longstreet says: "once
     I was talking with Dreiser along a Los Angeles street--in
     his last days--and his thoughts turned to his memories of
     Chicago as he once knew it; he began to recite for me some-
     thing from one of his novels: 'The city of Chicago. This
     singing flame of a city, this all America, this poet in chaps
     and buckskin, this rude, raw Titan, this Burns of a city!
     By its shimmering lake it lay, the kind of shreds and patches,
     a maundering yokel with an epic in its mouth, a tramp, a hobo

among cities, with the grip of Caesar in its mind, the dramatic force of Euripides in its soul. A very bard of a city this, singing of high deeds and high hopes, its heavy brogans buried deep in the mire of circumstance....' Later I learned that he was quoting from The Titan."
Good review of book in Dreiser Newsletter, 5 (Spring, 1974), pp. 27-28, by Frederic E. Rusch.

968 LOOMIS, Roger Sherman. "A Defense of Naturalism." International Journal of Ethics, 29 (January, 1919), 188-201. Reprinted in Becker, ed. (1963), pp. 535-548.
Is a philosophical rather than literary discussion. Draws a distinction between realism and naturalism, the first of which has become acceptable and the second which has not because of its insistence on pessimism and bestialism and its denial of the demi-god in man. Defends naturalism as "a cosmic order without justice, a morality without sanction or stability, and a will, free within limits to choose what it likes best, but determined as to what it likes best." Does not discuss Dreiser, but is informative for excellent background ideas.

969 LORD, David. "Dreiser Today." Prairie Schooner, 15 (Winter, 1941), 230-239.

970 LOVING, Jerome M. "The Rocking Chair Structure of Sister Carrie." Dreiser Newsletter, 2 (Spring, 1971), 7-10.
The repetitive use of the rocker is subtle yet most effective. The rocking chair was a common object--well-known at all levels of economy, and Dreiser used it at all levels from the most poverty stricken to the most opulent. The plot of Sister Carrie is structured around the rocking-chair scenes, with each successive one becoming more crucial. The subject matter of the novel concerns two individuals tossed up and down, and their agony is most effectively dramatized as they rock and dream and wonder what went wrong.

971 LUCCOCK, Halford Edward. Contemporary American Literature and Religion. Chicago: Willett, Clark, 1934. Dreiser, pp. 62-67.
Three aspects of Dreiser may be selected as having particular importance for the religious and moral thinking and life of our day: (1) the underlying philosophy which pervades the whole of his work; (2) his great mass of description of the effects of the industrial system on human life has far more of a positive value for religion and morals; and (3) the aspect of deeply felt pity relates his work to religion: he does not affix guilt, he does not condemn.

972 LUDINGTON, Townsend. "Century's Ebb: The Thirteenth Chronicle--A Review." New Republic, 173 (November 22, 1975), 23-25.

Refers to the last novel by John Dos Passos, finished some
three months before he died in September 1970. Is not called
a "finished" piece of work, but it does contain some good Dos
Passos writing. It often paints a dark, often savage picture,
but it also reflects Dos Passos' pleasure and amusement in
his fellow men, who may scurry about foolishly and self-
importantly, but who serve as well their moments of tragedy,
compassion and of greatness. Dreiser and Dos Passos shared
many of the same interests, philosophies, activities, and much
of the same period of time in which they created their works.

973 _____, ed. The Fourteenth Chronicle: Letters and Diaries
of John Dos Passos. Boston: Gambit, 1973.
Includes two letters from Dos Passos to Dreiser, dated
September 10, 1933; and November 27, 1934. In the first
Dos Passos apologizes for not sending an article for the Spectator and comments on the world situation. In the other he
asks Dreiser to sign a petition to the Spanish government on
behalf of the painter Luis Quintanilla.

974 LUDLOW, Francis. "Plodding Crusader." College English, 8
(October, 1946), 1-7.

975 LUNDEN, Rolf. "The Antithetic Pattern of Theodore Dreiser's
Art." American Studies in Scandinavia, No. 7 (Summer,
1972), 39-56.

976 _____. "The Inevitable Equation: The Antithetic Pattern
of Theodore Dreiser's Thought and Art." Ph.D. diss., University of Uppsala, 1973. Also published as book, Stockholm:
Almqvist & Wiksell, 1973.
Based on a study of Dreiser's Notes on Life.

977 _____. "The Scandinavian Reception of Theodore Dreiser."
Dreiser Newsletter, 6 (Spring, 1975), 1-8.
Before 1925 Dreiser was virtually unknown, and the general
status of American literature was very low. After the publication of An American Tragedy and Dreiser's trip to Scandinavia in 1926, when he met publishers in Sweden and Den-
mark, translations started one after the other, which helped
convince the obstinate critics of the value of American fiction.

978 _____. Dreiser Looks at Scandinavia. Stockholm: Almqvist
& Wiksell, 1977.

979 _____. "Theodore Dreiser and the Nobel Prize." American
Literature, 50 (1978), 216-229.
Reviews the honor of the Nobel award and shows how desperately some writers seek it. Dreiser and Sinclair Lewis,
who received the award in 1930, were two of these seekers,
and it is thought that Dreiser's wound was deep in being passed

over. In the years that followed many other writers and critics came to believe that Dreiser, not Lewis, should have received the award, among them Eugene O'Neill, who re-received it three years later.

980 LUNDKVIST, Artur. Tre Amerikaner: Dreiser, Lewis, Anderson. Stockholm: A. Bonnier, 1939. Dreiser, passim.

981 LUNDQUIST, James. Theodore Dreiser. New York: Ungar, 1974. Modern Literary Monographs.

Consists of 150 pages: a chronology, six chapters, notes on each chapter, a short bibliography of best-known sources, and an index. Is brief, but adequate for a beginner's understanding of Dreiser. In conclusion: "He was a man of contradiction and great inconsistency in his own output. He could weld together a giant novel like An American Tragedy and follow it up by botching what could have been an important book, Tragic America. In his personal life he could sometimes be viciously cruel to his mistresses and associates. At other times the compassionate streak that is present in his fiction would overcome him. He could devote himself with great energy to contemporary developments in politics and science, yet his verse collections show little awareness of what was happening in poetry at that time...."

982 LYDENBERG, John. "Theodore Dreiser: Ishmael in the Jungle." Monthly Review, 7 (August, 1954), 124-136. Reprinted in American Radicals, edited by Harvey Goldberg. New York: Monthly Review Press, 1957. Pp. 37-52. Also reprinted in Lydenberg (1971), pp. 22-35.

"I was an Ishmael, a wanderer," Dreiser spoke of himself during his homeless newspaper days in the 1890's. Did he think of himself as an outcast too? His birth on the wrong side of the Terre Haute tracks marked him as drastically as did Ishmael's birth in the wrong tent. If not an outcast, Dreiser was at least an outsider. He did not write beautiful or pleasing novels, and hence was the target of "taunts, arrows, and stick bombs." This Ishmael had, in his old age, tried on the mantle of Isaac, but what we will remember and cherish is the bitter fruit of his days as Ishmael the outcast, wandering alone in the desert, telling the truths that the orthodox and well-born saw not or dared not tell.

983 _____, ed. Dreiser: A Collection of Critical Essays. Englewood Cliffs, N.J.: Prentice-Hall, 1971.

Contains 182 pages with Introduction by Lydenberg and reprinted criticism. Articles as follows:

"The Stature of Theodore Dreiser," by Alfred Kazin, pp. 11-21.
"Ishmael in the Jungle," by John Lydenberg, pp. 22-35.

"Dreiser and the Success Dream," by Kenneth Lynn, pp. 37-44.

"Dreiser and the Sentimental Novel," by Leslie A. Fiedler, pp. 45-51.

"Sister Carrie's Brother," by Malcolm Cowley, pp. 52-62.

"The Barbaric Naturalism of Mr. Dreiser," by Stuart P. Sherman, pp. 63-72.

"The Dreiser Bugaboo," by H. L. Mencken, pp. 73-80.

"The Art of Theodore Dreiser," by Randolph Bourne, pp. 81-85.

"Reality in America, Part II," by Lionel Trilling, pp. 87-95.

"Dreiser's Moral Seriousness," by Gerald Willen, pp. 96-103.

"Theodore Dreiser and the Divided Stream," by Charles Child Walcutt, pp. 104-128.

"An American Tragedy," by Robert Penn Warren, pp. 129-140.

"Dreiser and Tragedy: The Stature of Theodore Dreiser," by Irving Howe, pp. 141-142.

"The Finesse of Dreiser," by Ellen Moers, pp. 153-162.

"Mr. Trilling, Mr. Warren, and An American Tragedy," by Charles Thomas Samuels, pp. 163-173.

984 LYNN, Kenneth S. "Theodore Dreiser: The Man of Ice," in The Dream of Success: A Study of the Modern American Imagination. Boston: Little, Brown, 1955. Pp. 16-26. Excerpt reprinted in Lydenberg (1971), pp. 37-44 as "Dreiser and the Success Dream."
Dreiser asserted with a bluntness which no other American writer at the turn of the century could match that pecuniary and sexual success were the values of American society. The indebtedness to Dreiser expressed by later American writers is a formal acknowledgment of the fact that his was the most significant exploration made by any novelist in his generation of the themes of money and sex, the two themes which have become so very much the major concern of our modern literature.

985 _____, ed. with Introduction. Sister Carrie. New York: Holt, Rinehart, 1957. Rinehart edition. Introduction reprinted in Pizer, ed., Sister Carrie (1970), pp. 509-518. Also reprinted in Lynn, Visions of America. Contributions in American Studies, No. 6. Westport, Conn.: Greenwood Press, 1973. Pp. 137-148.
The people in Sister Carrie are vulgar, sometimes vicious; their dreams are paltry, and they do not even know it. But because they do not know it, their commitment to those dreams is total and they long for what they are sure is happiness with an energy and an intensity that invests their careers with an importance that transcends their intrinsic meaning. There is nothing wholehearted about these people except their worship of money and luxury; they are as dehumanized as

the artificial city, and their hearts are as cold as the glittering lights that hypnotize them. In the slow measured manner
of Hurstwood's preparation for suicide, Dreiser reveals to us
the essential dignity as well as the tragedy of man.

986 LYON, Harris Merton. "Theodore Dreiser's 'Sister Carrie.' "
     Houston Post, June 9, 1907. Pp. 26-27. Reprinted in Pizer
     (1981), pp. 162-165.
         Is, for today at least, a book for the few, not the many.
     It would never have run as a serial in one of the 15-cent,
     popular magazines. It has been adjudged immoral by some.
     There is nothing in the book to offend any serious thinking
     person; it is not an esoteric, a lubricious, a salacious book
     in any way whatsoever. It is simply the calm, impassioned,
     impersonal statement that such and such forces worked thus
     and so about a man and a woman, and produced such and
     such results.

987 LYONS, Eugene. The Red Decade: The Stalinist Penetration
     of America. Indianapolis: Bobbs-Merrill, 1941. Dreiser, pp.
     80 et passim.
         This book does not pretend to be an academic and compre-
     hensive history of communism in America. It is intended as
     an informal account of Bolshevism in our country, the strange
     Bolshevism that reached a bizarre climax in the amazingly
     successful People's or Popular Front phase of Muscovite ac-
     tivity outside its Russian homeland. It relates various writ-
     ers, including Dreiser, to the cause of Communism.

988 MABIE, Hamilton W. "A Few Books of To-Day." Outlook, 102
     (November 23, 1912), 643-652. Comments on Sister Carrie
     and Jennie Gerhardt.

989 McAFEE, Helen. "The Literature of Disillusion." Atlantic
     Monthly, 132 (August, 1923), 225-234.

990 McALEER, John J. Theodore Dreiser: An Introduction and
     Interpretation. New York: Barnes and Noble, 1968.
         Consists of 161 pages with Index and selected bibliography.
     Is contained in 12 chapters, chronologically discussing the
     works of Dreiser. In a preface, the author says: "It shows
     how his personal history molded his vigorous spirit of inquiry.
     It distinguishes, in a blend of influences that extend from
     crises which bruised his psyche in boyhood, to his systematic
     pursuit, in his adult years, of philosophical maturity and
     spiritual integrity, the genesis of his major works. It traces
     the connection between plot, image, and idea in his novels
     and reveals how his interests and experience relate to, and
     even explain, his form, his style, and his art. It offers de-

finitive assessment of his extensive use of symbols, and explains how certain symbols--notably, his abundant motion sym-
bols--are tied, in their recurrence and interaction, to a functional purpose. The moving world of Theodore Dreiser did
not rest on an effervescent compassion, but on a dynamic
theory of flux. Finally, the study gives an account of Dreiser's architectonic genius and of those lurking currents of
transcendentalism which, throughout his works, are a sus-
taining force."

990a _____. "Dreiser's 'Notes on Life': Responses to an Impen-
etrable Universe." Library Chronicle, 38 (Winter, 1972), 78-
91.

990b _____. "An American Tragedy and In Cold Blood." Thought,
47 (Winter, 1972), 569-586.
   Reviews a cross-section of critical opinion about each novel,
indicating that the critics were about equally divided as to
the excellence and the failure of each novel. After a thorough
analysis of both novels, as to characters, their motivation,
their actions, etc., and a rather comprehensive comparison of
the two works, McAleer concludes that An American Tragedy,
although based on actual events, undergoes the process of
becoming art; whereas Capote's work is locked into a form--
the nonfiction novel--which ultimately renders it almost without meaning.

990c _____. "Flux Metaphors in Sister Carrie." Dreiser Newsletter, 15 (Spring, 1984), 1-9.
   Reviews briefly the history of the idea that Nature is in a
constant state of flux. Dreiser evidently came upon the idea
in the works of Emerson. In Sister Carrie, among several
flux allusions generating from Carrie, the rocking chair allusions stand preeminent. Tidal allusions, however, are of
comparable importance and are less conspicuous only because
they blend more thoroughly into the fabric of the narrative.
They, in turn, are organically allied to bird and ship allusions which relate to the very essence of the novel.

990d MACAULEY, Robie. " 'Let Me Tell You About the Rich.' "
Kenyon Review, 27 (Autumn, 1965), 645-671.
   Title is derived from F. Scott Fitzgerald's short story "The
Rich Boy," and is a discussion of the rich in fiction. This,
of course, would include Dreiser's Frank Cowperwood, "the
strangest picture of a robber baron we have and probably
the best we shall ever get." Reviews Cowperwood's career
and character, saying "he has a genius for manipulation--both
of money and of people. He lives in the midst of scandal and
accusation without the slightest internal effect on him." Dreiser did not paint a hateful picture of Cowperwood: he is not
cruel and dangerous. He is neat, smiling, resolute, fairspoken,

well-mannered, persuasive, and courageous even in defeat.
Above all, he is supremely intelligent.

990e McCall, Raymond G. "Attitudes Toward Wealth in the Fiction
of Theodore Dreiser, Edith Wharton, and F. Scott Fitzgerald."
Ph.D. diss., University of Wisconsin, 1957.

990f McCOLE, C. John. "The Tragedy of Theodore Dreiser." Catholic World, 132 (October, 1930), 1-7.

990g _____. "Theodore Dreiser and the Rise of American Realism,"
in Lucifer at Large. London and New York: Longmans,
Green, 1937. Reprinted Freeport, N.Y.: Books for Libraries
Press, 1968. Pp. 17-54.
In his achievements, Dreiser does represent something colossal, yet there is doubt that anything lasting will spring
out of "that barren rock of Naturalism" upon which he has
taken his position. Furthermore Dreiser has never worried
about his grammar. He writes so badly that not long ago the
editorial column of a large newspaper suggested using his
lumbering, clumsy, ungrammatical sentences to teach classes
just how badly the King's English can be written.

990h MacCOLLOUGH, Martin (pseudo. of Samuel W. Tait, Jr.). Letters on Contemporary American Authors. Boston: Four
Seas Press, 1921. Dreiser, pp. 81-87.
Does not share any favorable response to Dreiser. Says,
"first, let me tell you what you no doubt have already discovered, namely that as a craftsman, a worker with lath and
plaster and paint, Dreiser is very deficient. The maltreat-
ment of English, in particular, has become traditional with
him.... This failing shows most glaringly in his selection of
words and phrases. Nor is he much more adept at construct-
ing a narrative."

990i McCOY, Esther. "Theodore Dreiser Talks to a Friend." People's
Daily Word, January 3, 1946. P. 1.

990j McDONALD, Edward D. "Dreiser Before Sister Carrie." Bookman, 67 (June, 1928), 369-374.
Reviews the chronology of Dreiser's major works and sees
some kind of emerging pattern. The purpose of the article,
however, is to focus attention to the body of writing Dreiser accomplished under his own name, outside the newspapers,
during the three years immediately preceding the first publication of Sister Carrie in 1900.

990k _____. A Bibliography of the Writings of Theodore Dreiser,
with a Foreword by Theodore Dreiser. Philadelphia: Centaur
Bookshop, 1928. Reprinted New York: Burt Franklin, 1968.
Consists of 130 pages, mostly listing copies of books by

Dreiser, with a briefer listing of Dreiser's contributions to
books and periodicals. Concludes with 30 pages of studies
and reviews of Dreiser's works, in books, pamphlets, and
periodicals. Items have no commentary. In the Introduction
Dreiser said: "On thinking back over the books I have written, I can only say: Ladies and Gentlemen, this has been
my vision of life. This is what living in my time has seemed
to be like--life with its romance and cruelty, its pity and terror, its joys and anxiety, its peace and conflict. You may
not like my vision, ladies and gentlemen, but it is the only
one I have seen and felt, therefore, it is the only one I can
give you."

991 McDONALD, James L. "Dreiser's Artistry: Two Letters from
An American Tragedy." Dreiser Newsletter, 7 (Fall, 1976),
2-6.
     Refers to the letters which Clyde receives from Sondra
Finchley and Roberta Alden in Chapter 42 of An American
Tragedy. These letters, coming as they do, side by side,
offer a "finely wrought presentation and dramatization of the
characters of the two women," the glittering, unreal world
of the rich girl which Clyde hopes to enter, and the simple,
yet dedicated world of the lower-class world which he is trying to escape.

992 McDOWELL, Arthur. Realism: A Study in Art and Thought.
London: Constable, 1918.

     At the bottom of realism, in all its variations, seems
to be the sense of actual existence; an acute awareness of it,
and a vision of things under that form. Sometimes realism
is to blame for the lack of artistic effect, as in the case of
the American novelist, Theodore Dreiser.

993 McDOWELL, Margaret B. "The Children's Feature: A Guide to
the Editors' Perceptions of Adult Readers of Women's Magazines." Midwest Quarterly, 19 (Autumn, 1977), 36-50.
     Focuses on two magazines, 50 years apart: The Delineator
beginning about 1906 and McCall's beginning in 1954. Dreiser
was editor of The Delineator from 1906 to 1911. Both magazines dramatically shifted editorial emphasis and moved mili-
tantly into campaigns to stabilize family relationships, to cut
divorce rates, and to discourage women from seeking careers
outside the home. Both magazines consistently appealed to
the woman's fears through columns on beauty, health, discipline of children, and marital adjustment.

994 McFADDEN, James G. "A Book About Myself: A Review."
Literary Digest International Book Review, 1 (March, 1923),
79.
     Letter to editor.

995 McILVAINE, R. M. "A Literary Source for Caesarean Section in A Farewell to Arms." American Literature, 43 (November, 1971), 444-447.

Suggests that the death of Catherine Berkley bears a resemblance to the climactic episode of Dreiser's novel The "Genius," the death of Angela Witla following a Caesarean operation. This scene is one of the most vivid in Dreiser's generally rather gray and drab novel. There are many more significant differences than similarities between the two scenes, and it is not meant to imply that Hemingway in any way plagiarized from Dreiser. However, it would seem that Dreiser's scene, consciously or unconsciously, furnished a partial model for Hemingway's novel.

996 _____. "A Literary Source for Hurstwood's Last Scene." Research Studies (Washington State University), 40 (1972), 44-46. Relates Sister Carrie to Stephen Crane's "The Men in the Storm."

997 McINTYRE, O. O. "Dinner with Dreiser." Cosmopolitan, 95 (December, 1933), 56-57.

998 MacMILLAN, Duane J. "Sister Carrie, Chapter IV: Theodore Dreiser's 'Tip-of-the-Hat' to Stephen Crane." Dreiser Newsletter, 10 (Spring, 1979), 1-7.

Sees Chapter IV as very nearly a complete "Crane" short story--it simply takes Carrie the rest of the novel to fail to recognize the reality which had met her at the train upon her arrival in Chicago. Dreiser may have been more cynical than even Crane regarding man's ability to "accept his place" in the real world; but the limitations of both Carrie and her creator do not, in any way, detract from Dreiser's kudo to Crane.

999 McTAGUE, Sylvia H. "Dreiser the Iconoclast: His Attack on Marriage." MA thesis, University of Mississippi, 1968.

1000- MACY, Baldwin. "New York Letter." Chicago Evening Post
1   Friday Literary Review, May 10, 1912. P. 6.

1002 MACY, John, ed. American Writers on American Literature. New York: Liveright, 1931. "Contemporary Fiction," by Llewellyn Jones, pp. 488-502.

1003 MADISON, Charles A. Irving to Irving: Author-Publisher Relations, 1800-1974. New York: R. R. Bowker, 1974. "Dreiser's Troubles with Publishers," pp. 94-110.

Title of book refers to Washington Irving and Clifford Irving, with twenty-five other authors between. Says at the outset that "no other major American writer had such unfortunate experiences with publishers as Theodore Dreiser."

His entire life was charged with the pain of frustration, suffering from anguished poverty in childhood, subjected to the quirks of a troubled personality. Discusses the numerous publishers with whom Dreiser was associated, and his various difficulties with them. Does not make a case that it was all the publishers' fault.

1004 MAILER, Norman. "Modes and Mutations: Quick Comments on the Modern American Novel." Commentary, 41 (March, 1966), 37-40. Reprinted in Mailer, Cannibals and Christians. New York: Dial Press, 1966. Pp. 53-57.
There was something going on in American life which was either grand or horrible or both, and Dreiser and Wolfe labored as titans to capture the phenomenon. They were able to describe society, and Dreiser in particular came closer to understanding the social machine than any American who ever lived, but he paid an unendurable price: he was forced to alienate himself from manner in order to learn the vast amount he learned. Manner insists one learn at a modest rate, that one learn each step with grace before going on to the next. Dreiser was in a huge hurry, he had to learn everything--that was the way he must have felt his mission, so there is nothing of manner in his work; which is to say nothing of tactics.

1005 MAILLARD, Denyse. "L'Enfant Américain dans le Roman du Middle-West." Ph.D. diss., University of Paris, 1935.

1006 MANCHESTER, William. Disturber of the Peace: The Life of H. L. Mencken, with Introduction by Gerald W. Johnson. Harper, 1951. Dreiser pp. 36 et passim.
In the spring of about 1905 one of the last of the potboiling ventures brought him a friendship which was to ultimately shake to its foundations the national literature. He had agreed to ghost a series of scientific articles for a Baltimore physician. The doctor broached the matter to Theodore Dreiser, then editor of the Butterick publications, and Dreiser, said he would wait to look at the manuscript before deciding. When the first piece arrived Dreiser was so pleased that he bought it on the spot. A few weeks later the ghoster himself called to discuss the rest of the series.

1007 MANLY, John Mathews, and Edith Rickert. Contemporary American Literature. New York: Harcourt, Brace, 1922. Reprinted 1929. Dreiser, pp. 161-163 in 1929 edition.
Consists of biographical sketch, bibliography, and study outline. Comments are brief: "Hey, Rub-a-Dub-Dub should be read by every student of Dreiser for his attitude toward humanity, and his failure to think out a point of view." The ideal of the naturalists was to record what they saw, without moral or ethical bias; to set down all the facts they could col-

lect, with as little artistic selection as possible. Actually most of them tended to see human life in terms of animal life.

1008 MARBLE, Annie Russell. "Revolt and Escape," in A Study of the Modern Novel, British and American, Since 1900. New York: Appleton, 1928. Pp. 366-372.
Mainly biographical details. Quotes what several other critics have said: "The lack of humor, so apparent in his novels, was responsible for many hours of loneliness and frustration until he found himself as a novelist. This expression of his art has been a spiritual outlet for him, but his fiction is ponderous and depressing for the average reader. The student notes the static quality of his mind, with little change in his literary methods or philosophy. His creative gifts lack evidence of growth."

1009 MARCUS, Mordecai. "Loneliness, Death, and Fulfillment in Jennie Gerhardt." Studies in American Fiction, 7 (Spring, 1979), 61-73.
Reviews some of the revisions which Dreiser made in the manuscript of Jennie Gerhardt, and shows how these revisions made for a much better novel. In the novel's final published version, recurrent loneliness and looming death feed an overwhelming tension between the drive for inner integrity and fulfillment in such people as Jennie and the unconscious self-division in people like Lester, which baffles integrity and holds off fulfillment.

1010 MARKELS, Julian. "Dreiser and the Plotting of Inarticulate Experience." Massachusetts Review, 2 (1961), 431-448. Reprinted several times: Salzman (1971), pp. 45-55; Wegelin (1972), pp. 315-324; Pizer, ed., Sister Carrie (1970), pp. 528-541; Pizer (1981), pp. 186-199.
Thinks the source of Dreiser's power and his meaning lies in his method of arranging the episodes of his plots in order to dramatize with perfect coherence that absence of foreordained purpose in the universe, and its corollary, the hegemony of chance, of which he speaks so awkwardly in his philosophical writings. Not consistently but in long and powerful sequences, Dreiser's plot construction results in a fully credible image of human experience as an amoral process. It implies the possibility of human purpose and dignity arising out of a necessary immersion in this process. Hence Dreiser's method excludes the deterministic pathos of the conventional naturalistic novel, which conceives of human experience as the closing of a trap rather than the unfolding of a process.

1011 MARKEY, Gene. Literary Lights: A Book of Caricatures. New York: Knopf, 1923. Contains a caricature, "Two Great Realists--Theodore Dreiser and E. Phillips Oppenheim," p. 8.

Shows a typical, paunchy, lop-sided face of Dreiser; does
not add anything new to the stereotyped concept.

1012 MARQUIS, Don. "205 Words." Saturday Review of Literature,
      9 (October 15, 1932), 174.
      Admits to having tried to read seven or eight of Dreiser's
      books, but could not get through them. His admirers admit
      that he can't write but insist that he is a genius. Marquis
      says, "I don't find what he has to say worth his sufferings
      to get it said, or my sufferings to get it read. All I can
      get out of his books is a sense of the vast accumulation of
      commonplace details dully presented. I do not consider this
      monumental and unkempt rubbish heap a representation of life;
      if it is anything at all, it is a representation of the junk life
      left behind when it departed."

1013 MARSHALL, Donald Ray. "The Green Promise: Greenness as
      a Dominant Symbol in the Quest of Eden in American Fiction."
      Ph.D. diss., University of Connecticut, 1971. DA, 32 (1971),
      925A.
      Traces the symbolical associations of green with freshness,
      fertility, life, immortality, resurrection, youth and innocence.
      The color became a natural symbol for the New World, and
      as time has passed the diminishing of America's verdure has
      become for the writer of fiction a gauge by which to measure
      its spiritual decline. By the end of the nineteenth century,
      the disappearance of America's physical greenness, in writers
      such as Dreiser, Norris, etc., is pointed up as parallel to
      the deterioration of its spiritual terrain.

1014 MARTIN, Jay. "The Visible and Invisible Cities," in Harvests
      of Change: American Literature, 1865-1914. Englewood
      Cliffs, N.J.: Prentice-Hall, 1967. Pp. 252-263.
      Dreiser continued the tradition of the urban novel into the
      twentieth century and was able to rescue the city for fiction
      by presenting it undistorted by literary or ethical conven-
      tions. He restored the city to the uses of the American im-
      agination by attempting to see neither the badness of the
      city, nor its goodness, but rather its "beauty and its ugli-
      ness, and to find a beauty in its ugliness."

1015 MARTIN, Quinn. "The Magic Lantern: A Book That Would
      Make a Great Film." New York World, March 7, 1926. Metro-
      politan section, p. 4m.

1016 MARTIN, Ronald E. "Theodore Dreiser: At Home in the Uni-
      verse of Force," in American Literature and the Universe of
      Force. Durham: Duke University Press, 1981. Pp. 215-
      255.
      The works of Dreiser are expressions of a value system
      that is basically and generally in keeping with the universe

of force. His view of the causes, consequences, and significance of man's actions as represented in Dreiser's fiction
is fundamentally compatible with his view of the universe as
a mechanistic, deterministic welter of forces. Dreiser projects the universe of force with none of the intellectual irony,
the bitter tones of absurdity and rejection that Henry Adams
had, and he seldom gave the sense, as Frank Norris and
Jack London did, that in describing the universe of force
he was repeating a well-learned but imperfectly assimilated
lesson. Of the four writers, Dreiser most fully internalized
the universe of force; he was at home there if he was at
home anywhere.

1017 MARX, Caroline. "Book Marks." New York World-Telegram,
September 25, 1936.

1018 MARX, Leo. "The Teacher." Monthly Review, 2 (October,
1950), 205-210.

1019 MASTERS, Edgar Lee. "An American 'Genius.'" Chicago
Evening Post, October 22, 1915.
Review of The "Genius." In this book Dreiser's clear eye
and patient, accurate hand display themselves in all the elab-
orateness that we have been taught to expect in his work.
The book ends rather abruptly after 700 pages, and the tragedy of Eugene Witla seems far too great for the weak back
which bore it.

1020 _____. "Theodore Dreiser--a Portrait." New York Times
Book Review, October 31, 1915. P. 424. Reprinted many
times.

1021 _____. "Theodore Dreiser," in The Great Valley. New
York: Macmillan, 1916.

1022 _____. "Theodore Dreiser's 'A Book About Myself.'" Chicago Evening Post Literary Review, March 16, 1923. P. 4.

1023 _____. Across Spoon River. New York: Farrar & Rinehart, 1936. Dreiser, pp. 145 et passim.

1024 _____. "Dreiser at Spoon River." Esquire, 11 (May, 1939),
66 et passim.

1025 MATHESON, Terence J. "The Two Faces of Sister Carrie:
The Characterization of Dreiser's First Heroine." Ariel: A
Review of International English Literature, 11 (1980), 71-86.

1026 MATTHIESSEN, F. O. "God, Mammon, and Mr. Dreiser."
New York Times Book Review, March 24, 1946. Pp. 1, et
passim.

Review of The Bulwark. The novel is as bare as a par-
able. Its style avoids some of the problems that have always
confronted Dreiser's readers. As though in response to his
Quaker material, he writes with greater simplicity and spare-
ness, with fewer clumsy and broken-backed sentences than he
used to grope his way through. But his word-sense can still
be as cumbersome as ever.

1027 _____. "Of Crime and Punishment." Monthly Review, 2
(October, 1950), 189-204. Reprinted as Chapter 11 of Matthiessen's Theodore Dreiser (1951).

1028 _____. "Dreiser's Politics." Tomorrow, 10 (January, 1951),
10-17. Reprinted in Matthiessen's Theodore Dreiser, Chapter 12 (1951).

1029 _____. Theodore Dreiser. New York: William Sloane Associates, 1951. Reprinted Westport, Conn.: Greenwood
Press, 1973. Excerpt reprinted in Pizer (1981), pp. 169-
185 from Chapter 5, "A Picture of Conditions."
        Consists of 267 pages with Index of Works and a General
Index. Also has bibliographical notes to chapters. In 13
chapters as follows:
        An Indiana Boyhood
        Chicago, Chicago!
        Newspaper Days
        A Young Man of the Provinces in New York
        A Picture of Conditions
        Ten Years on the Desert
        The Large, Truthful Lines of Life
        The Business Novel
        The Genius Himself
        The Essential Tragedy of Life
        Of Crime and Punishment
        Dreiser's Politics
        Dreiser's Philosophy
This work was finished when Matthiessen died in the spring
of 1950. It was published with few changes in the manuscript. However, it is uneven in execution and is not Matthiessen at his best. He does not seem to understand this
author as he did James and T. S. Eliot.

1030 MAURICE, Arthur B. "Makers of Modern American Fiction
(Men): Dreiser and Dixon." Mentor, 6 (September 1, 1918),
1-11.

1031 MAY, Armand. "Things to Consider." New York Times, May
27, 1931. P. 26.
        Letter to editor.

1032 MAY, Henry P. The End of American Innocence: A Study of

the First Years of Our Own Time, 1912-1917. New York:
Knopf, 1959. Dreiser, pp. 187-191 et passim.
Of the turn-of-the-century naturalists, only Dreiser refused to either die young, disappear, or reform. Changing
little, learning little, he hung on through several stages of
cultural revolution until pessimism got another hearing.
From beginning to end of his career, he embodied all the elements of naturalism that dominant opinion feared most. Dreiser was almost the ultimate underdog. His career fits neither
the conventional pattern of the struggle out of the depths nor
the radical stereotype of the oppressed but battling proletarian. Clearly Dreiser needed no education beyond that ef-
forded by Terre Haute and Chicago slums to make him a pessimist.

1033 MAYBERRY, George. "Dreiser: 1871-1945." New Republic,
114 (January 14, 1946), 46.
There is little to be said of the man or the artist. His
faults may bar his work from full title of greatness, but it
remains a fact that almost alone of our novelists his books
were broadly conceived, minutely executed, large in theme
and peopled with dimensional characters. In an age in which
so many of the currents of education and in general culture
are anti-naturalistic and anti-humanitarian, Dreiser and his
work are an heritage of all who stand against naturalism in
the arts and surrealism in religion and morals.

1034 _____. "Dreiser: The Last Chapter." New Republic, 114
(April 1, 1946), 449-450.
Review of The Bulwark. Although shorter than Dreiser's
other novels, this one sprawls with characters and overflows
with incident. The structural failures of The Bulwark high-
light successful parallels in Dreiser's earlier work and suggest again that it is from the cumulative effect of infinitely
wrought details that much of his art as well as his power
derives.

1035 _____, ed. with Introduction. An American Tragedy. New
York: New American Library, 1949. Good abridged version,
suited for undergraduate or high-school classroom use.

1036 MAYFIELD, Sara. "Another Fitzgerald Myth Exploded by Menck-
en." Fitzgerald Newsletter, No. 32 (Winter, 1966), 1.

1037 MAYHALL, Fan. "Religion and Morality in the Works of Theodore Dreiser." MA thesis, Mississippi State University, 1963.

1038 MELLETT, Sue. "Indiana in Literature." Indianapolis Star,
June 3, 1945. Section 4, p. 18.

1039 MENCKEN, H. L. "A Novel of the First Rank." Smart Set,
35 (November, 1911), 153-155.

Is convinced that Jennie Gerhardt is the best American novel he has ever read, with the exception of Huckleberry Finn. "Yet in the face of them, and in the face of all the high authority, constituted and self-constituted, behind them, it seems that Jennie Gerhardt stands apart from all of them, and a bit above them. It lacks the grace of this one, the humor of that one, the perfect form of some other one; but taking it as it stands, grim, gaunt, mirthless, shapeless, it remains, and by long odds, the most impressive work of art we have yet to show in prose fiction."

1040 _____. "Dreiser's Novel: The Story of a Financier Who Loved Beauty." New York Times Book Review, November 10, 1912. P. 654. Reprinted in Pizer (1981), pp. 229-232.
Leaves a less vivid impression than the two books preceding it. Attributes this to the fact that a man is the main character, and that this volume for all its 780 pages is incomplete. Principally discusses the characterization of Frank Cowperwood, and the background of the story, the world of high finance and politics. Dreiser works his way through that maze with sure steps, and leaves order and understanding where confusion reigned.

1041 _____. "Anything but Novels." Smart Set, 42 (February, 1914), 153-154.
Review of A Traveler at Forty. Dreiser's volume is an astounding mixture of the common place and the unprecedented. It differs enormously from the customary travel books; it is not a mere description of places and people, but a revelation of their impingement upon an exceptional and almost eccentric personality. It is, in a sense, a free commentary upon those novels, a sort of epilogue in mufti. It makes a bit clearer the Dreiser philosophy and the Dreiser view of life.

1042 _____. "Adventures Among the New Novels." Smart Set, 43 (August, 1914), 153-157. Reprinted in Pizer (1981), pp. 237-242.
Review of The Titan. The art of Dreiser is almost wholly representative, detached, aloof, unethical. He makes no attempt whatever to provide that pious glow, that soothing escape from reality which Americans are accustomed to seek and find in prose fiction. But what of The Titan? It comes closer to the Dreiser ideal than any other story he has done. Here he has thrown overboard all the usual baggage of the novelist, making short and merciless shrift of "heart interest," "sympathy," and even romance.

1043 _____. "A Literary Behemoth." Smart Set, 47 (December, 1915), 150-154. Reprinted in Pizer (1981), pp. 247-252.
Review of The "Genius." For all his long-windedness, for all his persistent refusal to get about his business, for all

his mouthing of things so small that they seem to be nothings,
this Dreiser is undoubtedly a literary artist of very respectable rank, and nothing proves it more certainly than this,
the last, the longest, and one is tempted to add the damned-
est of his novels. The thing is staggering, alarming, madden-
ing and yet one sticks to it. It is rambling, formless, chaotic, and yet there emerges out of it a picture of almost
blinding brilliancy, a panorama that will remain in the mind
so long as memory lasts. Here is the Hindenburg of the
novel.

1044 _____. "A Soul's Adventures." Smart Set, 49 (June, 1916),
154.

Review of Plays of the Natural and Supernatural. Finds
the seven pieces interesting, although Dreiser lacks technique
for writing plays, and probably none of them will be produced or would be attended if they were. The plays will
offer nothing for the "smut hounds" to pounce upon.

1045 _____. "Theodore Dreiser." Baltimore Evening Sun, July
26, 1916. P. 6.

1046 _____. "More Dreiseriana." Baltimore Evening Sun, August
1, 1916. P. 6.

1047 _____. "Two Dreiser Novels." Baltimore Evening Sun,
August 4, 1916. P. 8.

1048 _____. "The Creed of a Novelist." Smart Set, 50 (October,
1916), 138-143.

Review of A Hoosier Holiday. Is a volume of mingled reminiscence, observation, speculation, and confession of faith.
It should be of service to Dreiser's reputation, for it shows
the man as he actually is, stripped of all the scarlet trap-
pings hung on him by horrified reviewers.

1049 _____. "Sister Carrie's History." New York Evening Mail,
August 4, 1917. P. 7.

1050 _____. "The Dreiser Bugaboo." The Seven Arts, 2 (August, 1917), 507-517. Reprinted in Kazin and Shapiro (1955),
pp. 84-91. Also reprinted in Lydenberg (1971), pp. 73-80;
and in Pizer (1981), pp. 19-26. Further reprinted in The
Young Mencken, edited by Carl Bode. New York: Dial
Press, 1973. Pp. 552-561.

Attacks those who attack Dreiser for his pessimistic, bleak
view of humanity. Asserts that Dreiser will remain. Fears
that Dreiser could begin to respond to criticism by trying to
please the howling mob. That would be a terrible fall, to
abandon his honest reflections on life and start writing what
people wanted to hear.

1051 _____. "Theodore Dreiser," in A Book of Prefaces. New
York: Knopf, 1917. Pp. 67-148. Reprinted in The Shock
of Recognition, edited by Edmund Wilson. Garden City,
N.Y.: Doubleday, 1943. Pp. 1160-1208.
Compares Dreiser with Joseph Conrad. Both take refuge
in "I don't know." Man is not only doomed to defeat but
denied any glimpse or understanding of his antagonist. One
half of Dreiser's brain wars with the other. He is intelligent,
thoughtful, in many ways a sound artist, but at times a dead
hand falls upon him and he is nothing but an Indiana peasant.
Dreiser is at his best when he deals with old men. In their
tragic helplessness they stand as symbols of that unfathomable
cosmic cruelty which he sees as the motive power of life itself.

1052 _____. "Dithyrambs Against Learning." Smart Set, 57
(November, 1918), 143-144.
Review of Free and Other Stories. They range from experiments in the fantastic to venture into realism, and, in
tone, from the satirical to the rather laboriously moral. In
the midst of many reminders of his high talents, Dreiser's
worst failing as a practical writer appears with painful vivid-
ness in this book.

1053 _____. "Dreiser's New Book." New York Sun, April 13,
1919. P. 4.
Review of Twelve Men. In more than one way he has done
nothing better since The Titan. It shows a deliberate return
to his first manner--the manner of pure representation, of
searching understanding, of unfailing gusto and contagious
wonderment. There are a dozen sketches of character, ro-
tund, brilliantly colored, absolutely alive.

1054 _____. "The Human Face," in Prejudices: Second Series.
New York: Knopf, 1920. Reprinted New York: Octagon
Books, 1977. Pp. 206-208.
Remarks on "the best portrait that I have ever seen in
America is one of Theodore Dreiser by Bror Norfeldt. Who
this artist may be I haven't the slightest notion--a Scandinavian, perhaps. He has painted Dreiser in a capital manner. The portrait not only shows the outward shell of the
man; it also conveys something of his inner spirit, his simple-
minded wonder at the mystery of existence, his constant effort to argue himself out of a despairing pessimism, his genuine amazement before life as a spectacle."

1055 _____. "More Notes from a Diary." Smart Set, 62 (May,
1920), 138-140.
Review of Hey, Rub-a-Dub-Dub. Earnestly pursuing the
true, he too often unearths the merely obvious, which is
sometimes not true at all. One misses the jauntiness of the

accomplished duellist; his manner is rather that of the honest householder repelling burglars with a table-leg. In
brief, it is enormously serious and painstaking stuff, but
seldom very interesting stuff and never delightful stuff.

1056 _____. "Footnote on Criticism," in Prejudices: Third Series. New York: Knopf, 1922. Pp. 84-104. Reprinted in
Criticism in America: Its Function and Status, edited by
Irving Babbitt. New York: Harcourt, Brace, 1924. Pp.
261-286.
Speaks in first person of his efforts to write about Dreiser, and believes that he was uniformly misunderstood. "My
idea was simply and solely to sort out and give coherence
to the ideas of Mr. Mencken, and to put them into suave
and ingratiating terms, and to discharge them with a flour-
ish."

1057 _____. "Adventures Among Books--II." Smart Set, 70
(March, 1923), 143-144.
Review of A Book About Myself. It deals with the author's
years as a newspaper reporter, and despite his usual dis-
cursiveness and undistinguished English, it is a work full
of fascination. Dreiser's career as a reporter was not distinguished, and the tale he has to tell is thus not very
startling. Absolutely nothing is left out; it is on the surface, obvious, unimportant, dull; it is underneath, full of
strange eloquence.

1058 _____. "Dreiser's New York." Baltimore Evening Sun, January 12, 1924.
Review of The Color of a Great City. The New York that
Dreiser deals with in this stately book (tall, blackbound,
creamy paper; sketches in brown ink by C. B. Falls) is not
the city of today, but that of two decades or more ago.
Dreiser is not much interested in gilded revelries. It is
the life of humble folk that attracts him. Here he presents
it in his patient, painstaking manner, as it was at the turn
of the century. It is not a very exciting book, but there is
in it something of the glamor and something of the poetry of
the New York that is no more.

1059 _____. "The American Novel," in Prejudices: Fourth Series. New York: Knopf, 1924. Pp. 278-293. First published
in part in Voices (London), 5 (November, 1921), 115-121.
It was probably Dreiser who chiefly gave form to the movement, despite the fact that for eleven long years he was
silent. He was the storm-center of a battle-royal that lasted
nearly twenty years. The man himself was solid, granite,
without nerves. Very little cunning was in him and not
much bellicose enterprise, but he showed a truly appalling
tenacity.

1060 _____. "The Case of Dreiser." Chicago Tribune, March
15, 1925. Part 8, pp. 1, 7. Reprinted in A Book About
Theodore Dreiser and His Work (c. 1925), pp. 6-13.

1061 _____. "Dreiser in 840 Pages." The American Mercury,
7 (March, 1926), 379-381. Reprinted in somewhat different
form in A Mencken Chrestomathy. New York: Knopf, 1926.
Pp. 501-505. Also reprinted in Salzman (1971), pp. 12-17.
Whatever else this vasty double-header may reveal about
its author, it at least shows brilliantly that he is wholly devoid of what may be called literary tact. A more artful and
ingratiating fellow, facing the situation that confronted him,
would have met it with a far less difficult book. How did
Dreiser meet the challenge? He met it by throwing out the
present shapeless and forbidding monster--a heaping cart-
load of raw materials, with rubbish of all sorts intermixed.
Such is scientific salesmanship as Dreiser understands it.

1062 _____. "An American Literary Phenomenon--Theodore Dreiser." Vanity Fair, 26 (May, 1926), 50.

1063 _____. "Ladies, Mainly Sad." American Mercury, 19 (February, 1930), 254-255.
Review of A Gallery of Women. Dreiser draws the fifteen
sketches with a surety of hand that seldom falters. He is
at his best in just such character sketches, and he has a
special skill of getting under the skins of women. His writing continues to be painful. What ails him is simply an in-
capacity to let anything go. This makes, at times, for hard
reading, although it distinguishes Dreiser from other novelists with his astounding fidelity of observation.

1063a _____. "Footprints on the Sands of Time." American Mercury, 23 (July, 1931), 383.
Review of Dawn. In the end the record that he produces
is seen to have the quality of a really impressive human document. The man himself is extraordinary, and his account
of his youthful hopes and agonies is a piece of literature.
One rejoices that it offers new glimpses of his heroic and
tragic mother, and of his incomparable Brother Paul.

1064 _____. "That Was New York: The Life of an Artist."
New Yorker, 24 (April 17, 1948), 64-71.

1065 _____. "Minority Report: Third Series." Menckeniana,
No. 38 (Summer, 1971), 1-2. Reprinted in Dreiser Newsletter, 5 (Spring, 1974), 5, as "Mencken on Dreiser."
Says "he was typical, in more ways than one, of a whole
generation of Americans--a generation writhing in an era of
advancing chaos. He renounced his ancestral religion at the
end of his teens, but never managed to get rid of it. If he

had lived another five or ten years he would have gone back to Holy Church, the path followed before him by many other such poor fish. His last book was a full-length portrait of a true believer, like Dreiser himself, flabbergasted by the apparent lack of common sense and common decency in the cosmos, but in the end yielding himself to the God who had so sorely afflicted him."

1066 _____, ed. with Introduction. An American Tragedy, illustrated by Grant Reynard. Cleveland: World Publishing Co., 1946. Reprinted 1948. Also reprinted New York: Thomas Y. Crowell, 1974, Apollo editions; and Cambridge, Mass.: Robert Bentley, 1978.

1067 MEYER, Avis Edward. "Literary Journalism: A Chronicle of Influence and Association from Addison and Steele to Dreiser, Anderson, and Hemingway." Ph.D. diss., St. Louis University, 1979. DA, 40 (1979), 2665A.
    This dissertation examines the relationship between literature and journalism in America, establishing a significant bond between the presumably disparate pursuits. Chapters one and two explore the origins of the journalistic style in America, appropriated from Addison and other London journalists and perpetuated by Franklin and early American writers. Chapters three, four, and five explore the work and experience of Dreiser, Anderson, and Hemingway as representative of twentieth-century literary journalists.

1068 MEYER, George Wilbur. "The Original Social Purpose of the Naturalistic Novel." Sewanee Review, 50 (October-December, 1942), 563-570.
    Article concerned principally with Zola and his original expressions of naturalism. With Zola determinism was not synonymous with fatalism: he did believe in the possible elimination of social evils. It was with pessimists like Dreiser that determinism became fatalism, and the sores and wounds of society are inevitable, like the revolutions of the earth and the wetness of rain.

1069 MICHAELS, Walter Benn. "Sister Carrie's Popular Economy." Critical Inquiry, 7 (1980), 73-90.

1070 MICHAUD, Régis. "Theodore Dreiser: L'homme et sa philosophie," in Le roman Américain d'aujourd'hui: Critique d'une civilization. Paris: Boivin, 1926. Pp. 55-79. Reprinted in translation as The American Novel of Today: A Social and Psychological Study. Boston: Little, Brown, 1928. Pp. 71-127.
    At the bottom of his philosophy there is a calm and serene, but disenchanted individualism. He sees life as a struggle of the great individuals against the masses. The fact that a

few emerge from the mass does not justify higher expecta-
tions of the future of mankind. Life is a struggle, but not
necessarily toward the better. Pity plays no part in Dreiser's
stories. Few writers have known the art of penning through
thousands of pages without one single ray of hope and few
could operate a guillotine with the sangfroid found in the
execution of Clyde Griffiths.

1071 _____. "Theodore Dreiser," in Panorama de la Littérature
     Américaine Contemporaine. Paris: Kra, 1928. Pp. 165-
     170.

1072 MICKELSON, Joel C. "Correlations Between Art and Litera-
     ture in Interpreting the American City: Theodore Dreiser
     and John Sloan," in Images of the American City in the Arts,
     edited by Joel C. Mickelson. Dubuque, Iowa: Kendall-Hunt,
     1978. Pp. 20-25. Also reprints Chapter 1, Sister Carrie,
     "The Magnet Attracting: A Waif Amid Forces."
         Reviews elements which Sloan, the painter, and Dreiser,
     the novelist, have in common: general agreement as to the
     realistic approach in what they wanted to say and how they
     wanted to say it; both encountered censorship trouble; both
     frequently pictured street beggars, slum settings, railroad
     yards, and dreary winter streets. Above all they both con-
     tributed to the battle for artistic freedom in the United States.
     Perhaps their most important contribution was their belief
     that there can be significance and sometimes even beauty in
     any area of life, even that considered trivial or sordid.

1073 MICKLUS, Carla Mulford. "An American Tragedy: or, The
     Tragedy of the Adamic Myth." American Literary Realism,
     14 (Spring, 1981), 9-15.
         Most critics suggest that the "tragedy" of the novel lies
     in Clyde's betrayal by the ideals promoted by writers like
     Horatio Alger who imply that any man can become a success
     materially. But Dreiser attacks an ideal more fundamental
     to American experience: he explodes the myth of the Amer-
     ican Adam. This myth, according to R. W. B. Lewis, "saw
     life and history as just beginning. It described the world
     as starting up again under fresh initiative, in a divinely
     granted second chance for the human race." In the depic-
     tion of Clyde and in the overall pattern of An American
     Tragedy, Dreiser explodes the implicit hopefulness of this
     American myth and shows the futility of one's attempting to
     escape his past.

1074 MILLER, Henry. "Dreiser's Style." New Republic, 46 (April
     28, 1926), 306. Letter in response to a review by T. K.
     Whipple, March 17, 1926.
         Objects to the application of the same criteria to novels
     as one might apply to essays or philosophical works. Drei-

ser's effects are not achieved in spite of but because of his style. The "cheap, trite, and tawdry" enable him to present a world which a more elegant and precise style could only hint at.

1075 _____. The Books of My Life. London: P. Owens, 1952. Reprinted New York: New Directions, 1957. Dreiser, pp. 217-221.

Says that before either Anderson or Dos Passos "had swum into my ken, I had read and adored Theodore Dreiser. I read everything of his, in those early days, that I could lay hands on. I even modelled my first book on a book of his called Twelve Men. I loved his brother, too, whom he portrayed so tenderly in this book: Paul Dresser, the song writer. Dreiser gave a tremendous impetus to the young writers of his day. His big novels--we call them 'huge, cumbersome, and unwieldly' today--carried a tremendous impact. They were somber, realistic, dense, but never dull."

1076 MILLER, James McDonald. An Outline of American Literature. New York: Farrar and Rinehart, 1934. Dreiser, pp. 194 et passim.

This naturalism is scathing social criticism, decidedly pessimistic in temper. Development came with the passing of the Frontier, which also awakened America to the realization that there was no gold at the foot of the rainbow, that natural resources were limited, and that our birthright had been squandered. Thus, two valuable contributions of the Frontier--optimism and independence--passed from our literature. Then, too, the consciousness of the city as a formative influence on social life, and not a very beautiful or satisfying city, began to express itself. American horizons were restricted from the broad sweep of prairie and mountain skyline to the harsh rooftops of the narrow street.

1077 MILLER, Jerry L. "Journey into the Twentieth Century: A Study of Theodore Dreiser's Development as a Poet." MA thesis, Indiana University, 1963.

1078 MILLER, Juanita M. "Honore de Balzac's Influence on Theodore Dreiser as Revealed in the Similarities of Le Père Goriot and Sister Carrie." MA thesis, Atlanta University, 1969.

1079 MILLER, Perry, ed. with Introduction. American Thought: The Civil War to World War I. New York: Rinehart, 1954. Dreiser, passim.

Dreiser not treated directly; good background material on naturalistic and evolutionary philosophy.

1080 MILLER, Ralph N. A Preliminary Checklist of Books and Ar-

ticles on Theodore Dreiser. Kalamazoo, Mich.: Western
Michigan College Library, 1947. Pamphlet, 11 pages, mimeo-
graphed.

1081 MILLER, Raymond A., Jr. "Representative Tragic Heroines
in the Work of Brown, Hawthorne, Howells, James, and Dreiser." Ph.D. diss., University of Wisconsin, 1957. DA, 17
(1957), 2612.
Considering tragedy to be universal, it possesses meaning
for the modern American. What the meaning is in its varia-
tions and its vitality, seen in representative works of five
American novelists, is both the purpose and theme of this
dissertation. Dreiser narrows tragedy, or supplies at least
another basis. Dreiser shows that man's powers are limited,
that life is mean or a trap. His women never achieve total
insight, but their blind struggle inspires pity and terror
which is the heart of tragedy.

1082 MILLER, William E., and Neda M. Westlake, editors. "Essays
in Honor of Theodore Dreiser's Sister Carrie." Library
Chronicle, 44 (1979), 7-93.
Articles by Berkey and Winters, Hakutani, Riggio, West,
and Westlake.

1083 MILLETT, Fred B. "Theodore Dreiser, 1871--," in Contemporary American Authors: A Critical Survey and 219 Biographies and Bibliographies. New York: Harcourt, 1940. Pp.
332-337. "Toward Naturalism," and "Beyond Naturalism,"
pp. 29-48.
Bibliography is brief but well chosen. It is in the novels
of Dreiser that naturalism of the traditional continental variety
is most perfectly illustrated. Like the great French naturalist, Emile Zola, Dreiser appreciates the terrible complexity
of modern industrial society. In the intense economic struggle,
he sees strong-willed financiers or geniuses forcing their
ways to positions of transient eminence. But he has also
seen hundreds of men fail, through inner weakness or outer
circumstance, to exact what they desire from the indifferent
or hostile social organism.

1084 MILLGATE, Michael. "Theodore Dreiser and the American
Financier." Studi Americani, 7 (1961), 133-145. Reprinted
in Millgate, American Social Fiction: James to Cozzens.
New York: Barnes and Noble, 1964. Pp. 67-86.
As an artist, Dreiser presents considerable difficulties.
Yet it is almost impossible for the reader to reconcile himself to the sheer badness of Dreiser's writing: few writers
have been so insensitive to language, so ignorant of the possibilities of their craft. Nor is it simply that Dreiser has
no ear for colloquial speech, that his grammar is faulty, his
rhetoric ludicrously high-flown, his image-making power al-

most nonexistent. Much more serious is his frequent inability to say clearly what he means, the sheer imprecision
and inconsistency of much of his writing.

1085 _____, ed. with Introduction. Sister Carrie. London:
Oxford University Press, 1965.

1086 MILLS, Nicolaus. "Class and Crowd in American Fiction."
Centennial Review, 24 (Spring, 1980), 192-217.
In the works of Howells, Dreiser, and Steinbeck, when
the crowd acts, it does not matter if its target is a street-
car company, an apple grower, or a bank. By virtue of
the social threat it represents, it takes on the police and
the government, and although it may, as in Sister Carrie,
hold its own for a while, that is the best it can do. In the
fiction of America's social realists, the poor do not win victories so much as sympathy, and in the end they are victims, whether they struggle alone or try as a class and a
crowd to change their lives.

1087 MIZENER, Arthur. "The Innocence of Dreiser." New Statesman, 58 (July 4, 1959), 20.

1088 _____. The Sense of Life in the Modern Novel. Boston:
Houghton Mifflin, 1964. Dreiser, pp. 9-12.
Dreiser's "peculiar and ever-changing philosophy" as he
himself called it, is in itself incredibly silly. But if it is
arguable that the expressions of this philosophy constitute
what is worst in Dreiser's work, it is also arguable that
only his interminable thinking about it could bring to the
surface of his consciousness those powerful feelings that
give his best work its awkward impressiveness. All his
life he philosophized in his inimitable way over the sensitive and seeking individual in his pitiful struggle with nature. Yet it was apparently the painstaking elaboration of
this doctrine that released from the depth of his imagination
all his best characters.

1089 MODERN FICTION STUDIES, 23 (Autumn, 1977), 339-488.
Special Theodore Dreiser Issue, with guest editor Jack Salzman.

1090 MOERS, Ellen. "The Finesse of Dreiser." American Scholar,
33 (Winter, 1963), 109-114. Reprinted in Lydenberg (1971),
pp. 153-162; also reprinted in Pizer (1981), pp. 200-208;
and in Pizer, ed., Sister Carrie (1970), pp. 558-567.
The writing in the seduction scene of Sister Carrie is
careful to the point of finesse, a word that challenges the
old and worn-out complaints against his style. In one of
the recent favorable statements about Dreiser, Saul Bellow
asked a useful question about the nature of "bad writing"
by a powerful novelist, but moved away from the answer

with the lamest recommendation: that Dreiser's "Fine" writing often fails on slow and close examination, while the coarse,
dense, uneven language of the more subtle novelists yields
surprising rewards, and explanations of the art of fiction,
to the careful reader.

1091 _____. "New Light on Dreiser in the 1890's." Columbia
Library Columns, 15 (May, 1966), 10-24.

1092 _____. The Two Dreisers: The Man and the Novelist as
Revealed in His Two Most Important Works. New York:
Viking, 1969. Excerpt from Chapter 2, Part 4, reprinted in
Salzman (1971), pp. 73-84.
In her Preface Moers says: "I soon found that Dreiser
did straddle two worlds of time, our own and the past."
Points to Sister Carrie and An American Tragedy as indic-
ative of the "two Dreisers." Consists of some 300 pages
with reference notes to each chapter and an index of great
detail. The chapters cover the following subjects:

Part I. Apprenticeship in the 1890's
Introduction: The Blizzard
1. Newspapers and the Bowery
2. Magazines and Pictures
3. What to Do?
4. "Curious Shifts of the Poor"

Part II. Sister Carrie
Introduction: Summer Song
1. Broadway Realism
2. Theater Lights
3. Midwest Time and Talk
4. Plants and Insects

Part III. Turn of the Century
Introduction: Transition
1. New Psychology
2. Aftermath
3. Twelve Men
4. Toward An American Tragedy

Part IV. An American Tragedy
Introduction: A Case of Murder
1. Mr. Badman
2. Clyde Griffiths: "The Mechanism Called Man"
3. On the Frontiers of Consciousness
4. Chemism and Freudianism
5. Arabian Nights
6. Pure Religion and Undefiled

1093 _____. "Airmail Interview." Dreiser Newsletter, 1 (Fall,
1970), 4-10.

Answers a number of questions, principally concerning
her own book, The Two Dreisers (1969), in which she vows
not to become trapped in the "either Dreiser or James" syndrome. Concludes by enumerating several items which need
attention in the field of Dreiser studies, among which a good
bibliography, primary and secondary sources.

1094 _____. A Century of Dreiser: Sound Seminar Audio Tape.
New York: McGraw-Hill, 1970.

1095 _____. "When New York Made It." New York Times Book
Review, May 16, 1971. Pp. 31-32.

1096 _____. "A 'New' First Novel by Arthur Henry." Dreiser
Newsletter, 4 (Fall, 1973), 7-9.
Refers to a novel published in 1890 by Arthur Henry,
Nicholas Blood, Candidate. Has never been mentioned by
biographers as the first novel of Henry. Raises the question of Dreiser's knowing about the novel. Was he aware
of its existence, and are the annotations those of Dreiser
in a copy of the novel at the library of the University of
Texas (Austin)? Perhaps the answer to several questions
lies in the novel itself: it is a smoothly written piece of
rabid anti-Negro propaganda; the main character is a bes-
tial, drunken, degenerate, dangerous Black man, the candidate of the Negro community in a Memphis election.
In "A Further Note on the 'Dreiser' Annotations" (pp. 9-
10), D. Gene England concludes that the annotations are
not Dreiser's and there is no evidence to justify calling them
his.

1097 _____. "The Survivors. Into the Twentieth Century."
Twentieth Century Literature, 20 (January, 1974), 1-11.
Comments in passing on a number of authors who were
born in the 1870's and were therefore "old" or in their
thirties by the turn of the century. Comments on the phenomenon of these writers who survived well into the Twentieth-
Century, and who still seem modern even after a century.
Dreiser was one of the great survivors: "Dogged" in manner,
attitude, style. "But they all had it, those tough old men
who make up the generation of survivors, a certain thick-
ness of hide and toughness of constitution."

1098 _____, ed. "Virginia Woolf on Dreiser." Dreiser Newsletter, 7 (Fall, 1976), 7-9.
Reprints "A Real American," from Contemporary Writers
by Virginia Woolf, edited by Jean Guiguet. New York:
Harcourt, Brace & Jovanovich, 1965. First appeared, un-
signed, in the Times Literary Supplement of August 21, 1919.
Is a review of Twelve Men and Free and Other Stories. Comments that "perhaps Dreiser gets a great deal too much of

it in, but, together with the colour and the pathos, there
is another quality which excuses his sins of taste, and perhaps explains them. He has genuine vitality. His interest
in life, when not impeded by the restriction of a definite
form, bubbles and boils over and produces Twelve Men, a
much more interesting work than Free."

1099 _____, and Sandy Petrey. "Critical Exchange: Dreiser's
       Wisdom ... or Stylistic Discontinuities." Novel 11 (Fall,
       1977), 63-69. On Moers' Two Dreisers and Petrey's "The
       Language of Realism ... " (see 1977) below.

1100 MONROE, Harriet. "Comment: Dorothy Dudley's Frontiers."
       Poetry, 43 (January, 1934), 208-215.

1101 MONTEIRO, George. "Addenda to the Bibliographies of Cather,
       Conrad, Dreiser, etc." Papers of the Bibliographic Society
       of America, 73 (1979), 478-481.

1102 MONTESER, Frederick. The Picaresque Element in Western
       Literature. Studies in the Humanities, No. 5. University:
       University of Alabama Press, 1975.

1103 MONTGOMERY, Judith. "Pygmalion's Image: The Metamorpho-
       sis of the American Heroine." Ph.D. diss., Syracuse Uni-
       versity, 1971. DA, 32 (1972), 4623A-4624A.
           Traces the growth and change in the American fictional
       heroine from the beginning when she was the creation of
       and the ultimate possession of a husband, male-directed in
       education, religion, economics, and legal rights. Dreiser's
       Carrie Meeber is the beginning of the new image of heroine:
       when her dependence on two men is mocked by their neglect,
       she seeks to make it on her own; and although she never
       attains any real happiness she does survive. In the future,
       novelists such as F. Scott Fitzgerald would create heroines
       who made men their possessions, the Pygmalion myth reversed.

1104 MOOKERJEE, R. N. "An Embarrassment of Riches: Dreiser
       Research." Indian Journal of American Studies (Hyderbad,
       India), 1 (July, 1969), 91-96.

1105 _____. "Victims of a 'Degrading Doctrine': Dreiser's An
       American Tragedy." Indian Journal of American Studies,
       1 (July, 1970), 23-32.

1106 _____. "The Literary Naturalist as Humanist: The Last
       Phase of Theodore Dreiser." Midwest Quarterly, 12 (Summer,
       1971), 369-381.
           For the greater part of his life Dreiser remained to his
       countrymen an uncompromising naturalist who wholly believed
       in mechanical determinism, to whom life meant chaos and dis-

order, and men and women, driven by uncontrollable biological forces, were no better than animals. But an examination
of Dreiser's less known writings and less publicized statements made during the same period would lead one to believe that he also incorporated traits which could hardly be
reconciled with strict naturalism. Even in his major works,
his naturalism was tempered with spiritualism and humani-
tarianism.

1107   _____. "Dreiser's Ambivalent Naturalism: A Note on Sister
Carrie." Rajasthan University Studies in English, 5 (1971),
36-48.

1108   _____. "Dreiser's Use of Hindu Thought in The Stoic."
American Literature, 43 (May, 1971), 273-278.
The last volume of Dreiser's trilogy is the only work in
which he is concerned with Hindu thought in a major way.
The novelist's solution to the vexing questions raised by his
protagonist's career is given in terms of the philosophy of
the Bhagavad Gita, the greatest of the Hindu philosophical
works. During Dreiser's last days of working on The Stoic,
Helen Dreiser became deeply interested in the philosophy of
the Hindus and had begun to make a systematic study of the
subject. The introduction of Hindu ideas into the last chapters of the novel in the character of Berenice is therefore
not difficult to guess.

1109   _____. "The Emerging Social Critic: The Plays of Theodore Dreiser," in Asian Response to American Literature,
edited by C. D. Narasimhaiah. Delhi, India: Vikas, 1972.
Pp. 151-157.
As specimens of dramatic art, these attempts have not been
regarded highly. Refers to Plays of the Natural and the
Supernatural (1916) and The Hand of the Potter (1918). As
expressions of Dreiser's ideas on life, death, society, and
its treatment of the poor and the abnormal, they provide
very valuable insight into the working of Dreiser's mind.
Of particular significance is the important perspective the
plays offer on his social criticism at a time when he was being
hailed as the champion naturalist who believed only in the
survival of the fittest and showed no concern for the poorer
and the socially oppressed classes.

1110   _____. Theodore Dreiser: His Thought and Social Criticism. Delhi, India: National Publishing House, 1974.

1111   _____. "The Bulwark: Dreiser's Peace with the World,"
in Indian Studies in American Fiction, edited by M. K. Naik,
et al. Delhi, India: Macmillan India, 1974. Pp. 115-124.

1112   _____. "Dreiser's Views on Art and Fiction." American
Literary Realism, 12 (Autumn, 1979), 338-342.

It is heartening to note that in recent years, instead of
labelling him as the leader of the naturalistic school of writing and leaving him there, earnest and unbiased efforts are
being made to study Dreiser as a complex creative writer
and analyze his novels as works of art. It would therefore
be of interest to know what Dreiser himself had to say about
art in general and the work of the novelist in particular.
This article is "an attempt in that direction."

1113 _____. "Dreiser's Interest in India's Struggle for Independ-
ence." Dreiser Newsletter, 10 (Spring, 1979), 20-22.
His sympathy and crusading zeal were not confined to his
own country. This dedication is evident from an examination of his correspondence with freedom fighters from India
who had organized themselves in the United States to continue their struggle against the British and attain independ-
ence for the country. Dreiser never made any secret of his
aversion to British Imperialist policies. A major part of a
chapter in America Is Worth Saving is devoted to an account
of the grim conditions brought about by the British rule in
India.

1114 MOORE, Harry T. "The American Novel Today." London
Mercury, 31 (March, 1935), 109-114.

1115 _____. "Dreiser: The Greatest? Tedious Bore? Sex Fiend?
Trail Blazer? Hard Rock? Hypocrite?" Chicago Tribune
Books Today, April 25, 1965. P. 2. Reprinted in Moore,
Age of the Modern and Other Literary Essays. Carbondale:
Southern Illinois University Press, 1971. Pp. 73-76, as "Dreiser and the Inappropriate Biography."
Review of Swanberg's Dreiser. Even though Swanberg may
be essentially sympathetic to the often blundering Hoosier
he writes of here, Dreiser comes out of these pages a monster, and in their context he is a monster. But he deserves
a hearing on behalf of his genuine accomplishment, the kind
of hearing that a literary critic writing a biography of Dreiser would have given him. Thinks too much emphasis on
Dreiser's women and sexual affairs.

1116 MORACE, Robert A. "Dreiser's Contract for Sister Carrie:
More Fact and Fiction." Journal of Modern Literature, 9
(May, 1982), 305-311.

1117 MORAND, Paul. "Paris Letter." Dial, 82 (March, 1927), 233-
238.

1118 MORDELL, Albert. "With a Persecuted Author." Philadelphia
Press, September 9, 1917. Magazine section, pp. 17, 19.

1119 _____. "My Relations with Theodore Dreiser." Critic and
Guide, 5 (March, 1951), 1-7. Reprinted in Haldeman-Julius

as a Writer on Free Thought ... , edited by Emanuel Haldeman-Julius. Girard, Kansas: Haldeman-Julius, 1951. Pp.
3-18.

1120 MORE, Paul Elmer. "Modern Currents in American Literature,"
in The Demon of the Absolute. Princeton, N.J.: Princeton
University Press, 1928. Dreiser, pp. 64-69. Reprinted in
Pizer (1981), pp. 27-29.
Finds A Book About Myself more significant than any of
his novels. It has the telling straightforward style and
method natural to a trained reporter. When he tries to be
literary, it is of the mongrel sort to be expected from a mis-
cegenation of the gutter and the psychological laboratory.
If only he knew the finer aspects of life as he knows its
shabby underside, if only he had had a chance, he might
possibly have produced that fabulous thing, the Great American novel.

1121 _____. "A Revival of Humanism." Bookman, 71 (March,
1930), 1-11.
Review of Humanism and America, edited by Norman Foerster. Contains a list of articles and authors, among which
is "An American Tragedy" by Robert Shafer.

1122 MORGAN, H. Wayne. American Writers in Rebellion from Mark
Twain to Dreiser. New York: Hill and Wang, 1965. "The
Naturalist as Humanist," pp. 146-189.
Reviews Dreiser's life and publications with an aim toward
revealing his philosophy as it evolved during his career.
Dreiser's life almost uniquely illustrated the pain and time
which the sensitive mind consumes in seeking meaning in
existence. For that arduous task he will always be vivid
in American letters. His warmth of character, his probing
questions, and the sympathy with which he treated all he
touched will make him respected. Few men in our time came
upon life so hungry to know its essence and so filled with
the conflicts that beset most men.

1123 MORRIS, Lewis Randolph. "Philosophical Concepts in American
Short Stories." Ph.D. diss., Howard University, 1971.
DA, 33 (1972), 1692A.

1124 MORRIS, Lloyd R. "Skepticism of the Young: Puzzled Iconoclast," in Postscript to Yesterday: America the Last Fifty
Years. New York: Random House, 1947. Pp. 121-130.
To the generation that grew to maturity between 1925 and
1945, Dreiser seemed less a living contemporary than an Olym-
pian of the remote past. How could they be aware of the
derision, persecution, and bitter disappointment which, for
nearly a lifetime, had been endured by this tall, grey, lonely
man whose appearance was as awkward and anxious and earn-

est as his cumbersome novels? Honors came to him late,
but when he died it was as if something primary had disap-
peared from the American scene.

1125 _____. "Heritage of a Generation of Novelists." New York
Herald Tribune Books, 26 (September 25, 1949), 12-13, 74.

1126 MORRIS, Wright. About Fiction. New York: Harper and
Row, 1975. Dreiser, pp. 117 et passim. Refers briefly to
Dreiser in chapter called "The Decline of Fiction--If There
Is One."

1127 MORSBERGER, Robert E. " 'In Elf Land Disporting': Sister
Carrie in Hollywood." Bulletin of the Rocky Mountain Modern Language Association, 27 (1973), 219-230.
Comments on poor quality of 1952 movie, which turns the
novel into a soap opera and ignores Dreiser's grim realities.

1128 _____. "Dreiser's Frivolous Sal." Dreiser Newsletter, 7
(Spring, 1976), 9-15.
Reference is to a movie "My Gal Sal," which Dreiser al-
lowed to be made based on the life of his brother Paul, his
music and Dreiser's story from Twelve Men, "My Brother
Paul." The main motive in his cooperation was financial.
Though it uses much of Paul's music, its scenario bears
little resemblance to Dreiser's reminiscence or to his brother's
life. This film was made in 1942.

1129 MOTTRAM, Eric. "The Hostile Environment and the Survival
Artist," in The American Novel and the Nineteen Twenties,
edited by Malcolm Bradbury and David Palmer. Stratford-
Upon-Avon Studies, No. 13. London: Arnold Publishers,
1971. Pp. 233-262.
Dreiser is central to the search for equilibration, that
equilibrium between what Dreiser called "chemic impulses
and appetites," "instinct toward individuality" and the "law
of balance and equation" over none of which, separately or
in combination, no man and no society has any control whatever. In 1925 Dreiser managed to allow Clyde Griffiths a
measure of stoic pathos as he goes to the chair, but nothing
more. Even the boy's defiance is blurred. The novel is
a confession of bewilderment, honest and impressive.

1130 MOULTON, Phillips P. "The Influence of the Writings of John
Woolman." Quaker History, 60 (Spring, 1971), 3-13.

1131 MOURI, Itaru. "Reconsideration of Sister Carrie--The Significance of the Latent World." Studies in English Literature,
47 (1971), 199-215. Article in Japanese; abstract in English.

1132 MOYLES, Robert G. "Theodore Dreiser: The Reluctant Nat-
      uralist." MA thesis, Memorial University, 1967.

1133 MOYNE, Ernest J. "Baroness Gripenberg Writes an Article
      for Theodore Dreiser's Delineator." Scandinavian Studies,
      48 (Winter, 1976), 85-93.

1134 MUKHERJEE, Arum Prabha. "Pursuit of Wealth as a Quest
      Metaphor in the American Novel: A Study of Dreiser and
      Some of His Contemporaries." Ph.D. diss., University of
      Toronto, 1981. DA, 43 (1982), 4450A.
      Begins by examining the historical shift in attitudes toward
      "the gospel of wealth" consisting largely of the vocabulary
      in which it was described. The pursuit of wealth came to
      be cloaked in religious terms, and lost much of its former
      association with disease and darkness. Most of Dreiser's
      works are analyzed in this manner, and finally other works
      by Howells, Norris, Herrick, etc. are compared with Drei-
      ser.

1135 MULLER, Herbert J. "Impressionism in Fiction: Prism vs
      Mirror." American Scholar, 7 (Summer, 1930), 355-367.
      Reviews a variety of definitions of Impressionism and con-
      cludes that perhaps the best approach to literature is to con-
      sider the definition which Cézanne adopted for his own paint-
      ings: "I have not tried to reproduce Nature: I have rep-
      resented it; in other words, art should not imitate nature,
      but should express the sensations aroused by nature."
      Names and discusses authors who are clearly impressionists;
      excludes Zola and Theodore Dreiser who operated on a mech-
      anistic laboratory philosophy and formula.

1136 _____. Modern Fiction: A Study of Values. New York:
      Funk & Wagnalls, 1937. "Naturalism in America: Theodore
      Dreiser and Proletarian Fiction," pp. 199-222.
      Neither Crane nor Norris made a deep impression upon
      their audience. Both died young before the battle of nat-
      uralism was really fought. Dreiser bore the brunt of this
      battle, which ultimately concerned the artist's right to make
      an honest, unaffected study of American life. Dreiser oc-
      cupies a melancholy position. He is thought of by youth in
      the past tense. With An American Tragedy he became gen-
      erally regarded as a foremost American novelist of his gener-
      ation. He is now regarded as a curious relic. Time has
      marched on; Dreiser as an artist stood still. He has writ-
      ten doggedly, perspiringly, ponderously, as if he could not
      help himself.

1137 _____. "The New Psychology in Old Fiction." Saturday Re-
      view of Literature, 16 (August 21, 1937), 3-4, 11.

1138 MULQUEEN, J. E. "Sister Carrie: A Modern Pilgrim's Prog-
      ress." C.E.A. Critic, 31 (March, 1969), 8-20.

1139 MUMFORD, Lewis. "The Shadow of the Muckrake," in The
      Golden Day. New York: Boni & Liveright, 1926. Reprinted
      New York: Norton, 1934. Pp. 233-269. Dreiser, passim.
      Dreiser has a power and reach which set him well above
      his immediate contemporaries. Across the panorama of the
      mid-American prairie, where Chicago sits like the proverbial
      spider in the midst of her steel web, Dreiser flung his can-
      vas; his Philadelphia, too, is spiritually part of that Chi-
      cago. Dreiser's books reflect a bulk and multitudinousness.
      They are as full of details as a day's shopping: you may
      find in his books the wages of laundry wagon drivers in
      1894, the style of women's gloves in 1902, how one cashes
      a check at a bank, the interior arrangements of a modern
      hotel, the details of a criminal prosecution.

1140 MUNSON, Gorham Bert. "Odds and Ends." Saturday Review
      of Literature, 3 (June 25, 1927), 928.
      Review of Chains: Lesser Novels and Stories. Says this
      volume, a collection of odds and ends of short stories and
      novelettes, will not add to Dreiser's reputation. The writ-
      ing is as wasteful and cumbersome as ever, though it is not
      often pointed out that Dreiser writes a banal sentence as
      though he had discovered it.

1141 _____. "The Motivation of Theodore Dreiser," in Destina-
      tions: A Canvass of American Literature Since 1900. New
      York: J. H. Sears, 1928. Reprinted New York: AMS,
      1970. Pp. 41-56.
      The expectation is that Dreiser will outlast his generation.
      Chance has so arranged that he, and not Norris or Crane,
      should be usually regarded as the initiator of the naturalistic
      novel in America. Thereby Dreiser gains a position in our
      literary history, and his historical position is fortified by his
      typicality as a member of his generation. Later students
      wishing to know that period can find its heart at once by
      plunging into his fiction, plays, poems, and essays. But
      he will be read by them not alone for a literary historical
      understanding. The American environment of his day is in
      books, amply and meticulously reported, and so his works
      become basic documents of social history.

1142 _____. "Prose for the Drama: William Vaughn Moody, Theo-
      dore Dreiser, and Eugene O'Neill," in Style and Form in
      American Prose. Garden City, N.Y.: Doubleday, Doran,
      1929. Pp. 234-255.
      Dreiser's aim is to copy the speech of everyday life, and
      one might say that he flatly succeeds. Quotes from The
      Hand of the Potter to illustrate point. This is prose as un-

distinguished as a street-corner discussion, and not a whit
more buoyed up by aesthetic energy. The prose of Dreiser's plays is mean, however clear it may be.

1143 _____. "Our Post-War Novel." Bookman, 74 (October,
1931), 141-144.
Thinks the American novel is mainly under the influence
of four men: Dreiser, Lewis, Fitzgerald, and Hemingway.
Dreiser is a naturalist. His temperament is somber and
brooding, although tempered with pity, and sometimes an
outburst of moral indignation. He is a fact-teller on a rather
large scale, and his novels are a species of fictitious journalism. He represents a strong impulse in many Americans to
see the facts of our society, starkly and in all their crudity.

1144 _____. "The Magic of the Short Story." Connotation, 1
(1962), 2-9.

1145 MURAYAMA, Kiyohiko. "The Road to An American Tragedy."
Hitotsubashi Journal of Arts & Sciences, 19 (November,
1978), 40-51.

1146 _____. "Dreiser in Japan." Dreiser Newsletter, 12 (Spring,
1981), 9-11.
Does not enjoy the great reputation he deserves in Japan.
Is known there to only a small part of the reading public
who in general are fairly familiar with American literature.
There are even complete works in Japanese translation of
some major writers, including Hemingway and Faulkner.
Dreiser's works have been translated into Japanese, too, but
Dreiser is a mere name to many Japanese. Recently a Japanese publisher has announced that they will publish a 20-
volume Works, limited to 200 copies. While his reputation
in Japan is still meager, he is gaining it slowly but surely.

1147 MURPHY, John J. " 'Presumptuous Girls' of Cather, Dreiser,
and James." Platte Valley Review, 9 (April, 1981), 83-95.

1148 MURRAY, Edward. The Cinematic Imagination: Writers and
the Motion Pictures. New York: Frederick Ungar, 1972.

1149 MURRAY, George. "Poison Tongue of Mr. Dreiser." London
Daily Mail, September 22, 1942. P. 1.

1150 MYERS, Walter. The Later Realism. Chicago: University of
Chicago Press, 1927. Does not treat Dreiser directly; presents good background material on realism.

1151 NAGAWARA, Makoto. "Dreiser at the Turn of the Century:

Sister Carrie." Ritsumeikan Bungaku, No. 212 (February, 1963), 17-36.

1152 NANCE, William L. "Eden, Oedipus, and Rebirth in American Fiction." Arizona Quarterly, 31 (Winter, 1975), 353-365.

1153 NATHAN, George Jean. The Intimate Notebooks of George Jean Nathan. New York: Knopf, 1932. "Theodore Dreiser," pp. 38-53. Reprinted as The World of George Jean Nathan, edited by Charles Angoff. New York: Knopf, 1952. "Dreiser," pp. 66-79.
One always finds Dreiser surprised and amazed at what has long been familiar to most persons. When he sees something for the first time, it is discovered to the world so far as he is concerned. Once, returning from a trip through the West, he hotly demanded why no one had ever remarked on the majesty of the Grand Canyon. Going to Europe for the first time at forty, he subsequently delivered himself of a book full of wide-eyed marvelings at various Continental cities, peoples and customs that had already been written about by hundreds of men before him and that were subjects of long-standing knowledge to almost everybody else.

1154 _____. "Editorial Conference," in The American Spectator Yearbook, edited by George Jean Nathan, Ernest Boyd, Theodore Dreiser, Sherwood Anderson, James Branch Cabell, Eugene O'Neill. New York: Stokes, 1934. Pp. 346-359.

1155 _____. "Three Friends: Lewis, O'Neill, Dreiser," in The Borzoi Reader, edited by Carl Van Doren. New York: Knopf, 1936. Pp. 579-615. Reprinted Garden City, N.Y.: Garden City Publishing Company, 1938. Originally published in The Intimate Notebooks (1932). See above.

1156 _____. "Memories of Fitzgerald, Lewis, and Dreiser." Esquire, 50 (October, 1958), 148-154.

1157 NELLIGAN, George J. "Talking Things Over: Dreiser-- Failure." El Paso Herald, April 30, 1930. Pp. 4, 9. Letter to editor.

1158 NELSON, John Herbert, ed. Contemporary Trends: American Literature Since 1914. New York: Macmillan, 1933. Dreiser, pp. 64-66. Reprints excerpt from A Book About Myself, "Discouraging Days in New York."

1159 NEWMAN, Louis I. "Dreiser and Haman." Nation, 140 (May 15, 1935), 572. See under Trachtenberg, Joshua.

1160 NICHOLSON, Guy H. "Dreiser, No Tennis Expert." New York Times, August 6, 1938. P. 9.

1161 NILON, Charles H. Bibliographies of American Literature
      (B.A.L.). New York: Bowker, 1970.
      Lists 13 bibliographies of Dreiser.

1162 NOBLE, David W. "Dreiser and Veblen and the Literature
      of Cultural Change." Social Research, 24 (Autumn, 1957),
      311-329. Reprinted in Studies in American Culture: Domin-
      ant Ideas and Images, edited by Joseph Kwiat and Mary C.
      Turpie. Minneapolis: University of Minnesota Press, 1960.
      Pp. 139-152.
         Veblen wrote that life is without ultimate meaning, but he
      ordered it with a rigid discipline. Middle-class mores were
      the solid facts of barbarian behavior. Members of the lower
      class carried the instincts of workmanship, of idle curiosity,
      of parental bent, which would provide the ultimate criteria
      for the meaning of existence.... Dreiser presented two char-
      acters who can serve as symbols for Veblen's class traits.
      Sister Carrie is concerned with the decline of Hurstwood, a
      middle-class man, and the rise of Carrie, a lower-class girl.
      Somehow it was Dreiser, who had no theory of the social
      nature of man, who provided a much more compelling portrait
      of the condition of man in the new world of the city; some-
      how it was Dreiser who provided the histories of individuals
      caught up in a society that had lost its capacity to believe
      in the values that gave it order and continuity.

1163 _____. The Paradox of Progressive Thought. Minneapolis:
      University of Minnesota Press, 1958. Dreiser, passim. See
      Chapter II, "The Heavenly City of the New Republic," pp.
      34-54.

1164 _____. The Eternal Adam and the New World Garden. New
      York: Braziller, 1968. Dreiser, pp. 124-132.
         Dreiser was obsessed by the problem of innocence within
      the context of the new national faith in an evolutionary uni-
      verse. For Dreiser the suffering of the individual was im-
      portant; uncertainty and tragedy must remain part of the
      human situation until evolution in some far distant time should
      have brought man and his environment into harmony. His
      faith in progress seems never to have reached rocklike cer-
      tainty. He was haunted by thoughts of the universe toward
      the tragedies of individual lives, but he accepted the pos-
      sibility of the survival of innocence in a world that does
      move, even if in an exceedingly slow and confused fashion,
      toward an ultimate spiritual fulfillment.

1165 NOLTE, William H. H. L. Mencken: Literary Critic. Middle-
      town, Conn.: Wesleyan University Press, 1966. Dreiser, pp.
      210-227 et passim.
         In their long friendship Mencken appears to have been the
      stronger and more influential of the two. Mencken knew
      what he believed; Dreiser searched for belief, for a Rock.

By the time Mencken met Dreiser the general outline of his
own skeptical view of things was drawn. Dreiser's mental
journey was a groping in the dark. Mencken insisted that
it was impossible to pigeonhole Dreiser: he did not fit any
contemporary theories of realism and naturalism. To read
Dreiser unmoved, Mencken said, is to confess that there is
nothing moving in the eternal tragedy of man.

1166 NORRIS, Charles G. "My Favorite Character in Fiction."
    Bookman, 62 (December, 1925), 410-411. Sketched by
    George A. Picken.
        Raises the question of how one chooses the best character.
    Is it one whom you admire as likable, stimulating, etc.; or
    is it the character you deem the best drawn, the most bril-
    liantly conceived. Chooses the latter and says "I must sub-
    mit Hurstwood because there is no truer portrait--man or
    woman--in any book I've read." Choice is Hurstwood be-
    cause his moral degradation, his slow crumbling, and the
    disintegration of his soul, spirit, and body as the direct
    result of his crime is masterly conceived, masterly presented,
    and masterly worked out.

1167 NORTH, Sterling. "Dreiser's Last Testament." New York
    Post, March 21, 1946.
        Review of The Bulwark. Dreiser was an old man when he
    dictated the final sentence of this novel. But he had watched
    and studied humanity for three-quarters of a century. He
    had explored capitalism, socialism, communism in his search
    for the greater good of the greater number. Readers of
    this novel will wonder whether or not he ended life as a
    member of the Society of Friends.

1168 NOSTWICH, Theodore D. "The Structure of Theodore Drei-
    ser's Novels." Ph.D. diss., University of Texas, 1968. DA,
    29 (1969), 3617A.
        This study demonstrates that the so-called formless novels
    of Dreiser employ sound structural principles and have ade-
    quate form. All eight novels are examined, An American
    Tragedy and The Bulwark more briefly than the others.
    Several principles of study are used: the stages of composi-
    tion; Dreiser's intention in writing it; the organization of
    the plot; the choice and arrangement of episodes; the struc-
    tural function of characterization; the use of conventional
    unifying devices.

1169 _____. "The Source of Dreiser's 'Nigger Jeff.' " Resources
    for American Literary Study, 8 (Autumn, 1978), 174-187.
        Has been generally thought that Dreiser based his story
    on a lynching which he had witnessed sometime between May
    1893 and March 1894 and had been covered for the St. Louis
    Republic by the young reporter. But there is another less

problematic source. On January 17 and 18, 1894, the Republic's front pages told of the lynching of John Buckner
for allegedly raping two women. Based on an examination
of this story, reprinted in this article from a microfilm in
the Library of Congress, it seems likely that Dreiser derived
much of his short story from this newspaper account.

1170 NOTMAN, Otis. "Talks with Four Novelists: Mr. Dreiser."
New York Times, June 15, 1907. P. 393. Reprinted in
Pizer, ed., Sister Carrie (1970), pp. 474-475.
Dreiser said, "I simply want to tell about life as it is.
Every human life is intensely interesting. If the human being has ideals, the struggle and the attempt to realize those
ideals, the going back on his own trail, the failure, the success, the reasons for the individual failure, the individual
success--all these things are interesting, interesting even
where there are no ideals, where there is only the personal
desire to survive, the fight to win, the stretching out of
the fingers to grasp."

1171 NUGENT, Walter. "Carter H. Harrison and Dreiser's 'Walden
Lucas.'" Newberry Library Bulletin, 6 (September, 1966),
222-230.

1172 NYREN, Dorothy, ed. "Dreiser, Theodore (1871-1945)," in
A Library of Literary Criticism. New York: Ungar, 1960.
Pp. 145-150.
Excerpts from 15 articles.

1173 OAK, V. V. "The Awful Dreiser." Nation, 122 (June 2, 1926),
610.
This letter to the editor complains of the way Dreiser's
books are not permitted on the shelves of big city and big
state university libraries, even Sister Carrie or Jennie Gerhardt. Was very surprised when he asked for a copy of
"The Hand of the Potter" and was told that he had to get a
permit from "his instructor" before that book could be checked
out. At the time Oak was a 30-year-old graduate student.

1174 O'BRIEN, Edward J. The Advance of the American Short
Story. New York: Dodd, Mead, 1923. Revised edition,
1931. Dreiser, pp. 222.
As a short story writer, he is less significant than as a
novelist. The memorable poignancy of "The Lost Phoebe"
ensures it a place beside the best American legends, and it
is likely to become a memory among the people until it is absorbed into their folk-lore. Otherwise Dreiser's stories appear as studies for larger paintings, rugged in their naturalism and craggy in their style. They have power, insight,
and sweep, and they are very badly written.

1175 OKANO, Hisaji. "Sister Carrie and Morality," in Annual Reports of Studies, Vol. 23. Kyoto: Doshisha Women's College of Liberal Arts, 1972. Pp. 189-216. In Japanese; abstract in English.

1176 _____. "A Spiritual Meaning in Jennie Gerhardt," in Annual Reports of Studies, Vol. 24. Kyoto: Doshisha Women's College of Liberal Arts, 1973. Pp. 82-109. In Japanese; abstract in English.

1177 OLDANI, Louis Joseph. "A Study of Theodore Dreiser's The 'Genius.'" Ph.D. diss., University of Pennsylvania, 1972. DA, 33 (1973), 6926A.
      This study approaches the novel on two points: a literary history, accounting for the genesis of the work, and a printing and publishing history. It traces Dreiser's use of personal and family experience and additonal sources, both real and imaginary, to produce what is, finally, a work of fiction with elements of autobiography. The second part of the dissertation reconstructs a printing and publishing history of the novel inasmuch as the records will allow.

1178 _____. "A Bibliographical Description of Dreiser's The 'Genius'." Library Chronicle (University of Pennsylvania, where the manuscript of Dreiser's novel is housed), 39 (Winter, 1973), 40-55.

1179 _____. "Dreiser and Paperbacks: An Unpublished Letter." Dreiser Newsletter 6 (Fall, 1975), 1-9.
      Traces Dreiser's problems with first one publisher and then another, and his efforts to interest someone in bringing out his books in paperback form, hoping to bring his books "back to life." The letter in this article is addressed to Mr. Will Lengel who had become his literary agent. Lengel made many attempts from 1939 to 1945 to bring about the inexpensive edition, but to no avail.

1180 _____. "The Lively State of Dreiser Bibliography." Research Studies, 44 (December 1976), 253-257.
      Review of Theodore Dreiser: A Primary and Secondary Bibliography by Donald Pizer, Richard W. Dowell, and Frederic E. Rusch. Thinks the work is definitive in some sections, in all sections extensive and instructive. "It is not likely to be superseded, but merely supplemented as further items come to light."

1181 _____. "Two Unpublished Pound Letters: Pound's Aid to Dreiser." Library Chronicle, 42 (Spring, 1977), 67-70.

1182 OLD NORTHWEST: A Journal of Regional Life and Letters. Special Dreiser edition, projected for late in 1983. Edited by Jack E. Wallace.

Note: "The special issue of the Old Northwest did not
materialize. There were not enough satisfactory articles for
a single issue. The articles we did accept will appear later
this year in regular issues of Old Northwest." Jack Wallace.

1183 OLSEN, Humphrey A. "Vincennes an Interlude in Famous
Novelist's Life." Vincennes Sun-Commercial (Indiana), December 29, 1965. P. 11.

1184 O'NEILL, John. "The Disproportion of Sadness: Dreiser's
The Financier and The Titan." Modern Fiction Studies, 23
(Autumn, 1977), 409-422.
If Dreiser's great theme was "the disproportion between
man and his world," it first appears that he departed from
this theme in the two Cowperwood novels. In obvious ways
at least, Frank Cowperwood seems capable of overcoming any
disproportion between will and world, by sheer force if necessary. A more careful examination of these two novels leads
to the conclusion that once again Dreiser conceived of his
subject as the puzzling disparity between individual and
milieu. The Financier and The Titan are not great novels,
but they should be of interest to the student and critic of
Dreiser because here is an attempt to expand his range as
a writer and to complicate his sense of the "disproportion
between man and his world."

1185 OPPENHEIM, James. Behind Your Front. New York: Harper, 1928. Dreiser, pp. 59-63.
Is a book aimed at enabling the reader to psychoanalyze
himself or perhaps some public figure. Contrasts Dreiser
with Thomas Edison, both extraverted men who operate largely on feeling. Edison and Dreiser, however, are almost exact opposites, or appear to be so, the difference being that
Edison is largely guided by Intuition and Dreiser by Sensation. For Dreiser he says: Pessimistic, careful of personal
appearance, naive about many things, pities mankind but
thinks it beyond much help. Sensation is defined as the experience of the five or more senses, including the whole
sexual system.

1186 ORAVETS, Andrew Joseph J. "Out of Kings: An Inquiry
into the Americanness of the Classic American Novel." Ph.D.
diss., Ohio State, 1975. DA, 37 (1976), 972A-973A.
Examines six American novels in order to establish that
the affinities among them are a reflection of certain pressures within American culture. The main characters in the
classic American novels share one common characteristic: they
are frustrated or defeated and their plight results from ad-
herence to abstract visions that they imbibe from their culture. The visions they follow divide them from themselves
and from others.

1187 ORLANSKY, Claire B. "The Impact of Nineteenth-Century
      Scientific Thought on Tennyson, Dreiser, and Faulkner."
      MA thesis, University of Utah, 1967.

1188 ORLOV, Paul Avrum. "The Subversion of the Self: Anti-
      Naturalistic Crux in An American Tragedy." Modern Fiction
      Studies, 23 (Fall, 1977), 457-472.
          Criticism of An American Tragedy, liberated from the as-
      sumption that the work is a naturalistic depiction of man objec-
      tively viewed as a helpless victim of heredity and environ-
      ment, has begun to examine the novel in ways that imply a
      humanistic orientation--in particular a concern with Dreiser's
      artistic treatment of the idea of individual identity.

1189 _____. "Dreiser's Defense of the Self: A Reading of Sister
      Carrie and An American Tragedy." Ph.D. diss., University
      of Toronto, 1978. DA, 40 (1979), 859A.
          This study has a twofold purpose: to show that Dreiser's
      ideas about selfhood is the key to understanding how he
      transcends his "inconsistent mechanism" to write novels of
      humanistic significance and affective power, and to offer
      close textual readings of what are generally considered his
      two finest novels to demonstrate that his art is based on a
      fundamental belief in the self and reflects an impassioned con-
      cern about the erosion of personal identity by the force of
      distorted values in a modern, mechanized, materialistic so-
      ciety.

1190 _____. "Plot as Parody: Dreiser's Attack on the Alger
      Theme in An American Tragedy." American Literary Real-
      ism, 15 (Autumn, 1982), 239-243.
          An American Tragedy can be regarded as a bitterly ironic
      inversion of a Horatio Alger story, but it has not been no-
      ticed that Dreiser heightens the ironic disparities between
      Clyde Griffiths' story and an Alger hero's by introducing
      plot elements that suggestively mirror those in a typical
      "bound-to-rise" book. And Dreiser's novel is a powerful
      indictment of the American success-myth embodied in the
      works of Alger precisely because it parodies their most dis-
      tinctive plot-devices in its portrayal of an ambitious youth's
      tragic failure.

1191 ORTON, Vrest. Notes to Add to a Bibliography of Theodore
      Dreiser. Perth Amboy: Mosquito Press, 1928. 21-page
      pamphlet.

1192 _____. Dreiserana: A Book About His Books. New York:
      Chocorus Bibliographies, 1929. Reprinted New York: Has-
      kell House, 1973. Also reprinted Norwood, Pa.: Norwood
      Editions, 1976; and Philadelphia: Richard West, 1977. 84
      pages.

In four parts, listing 62 primary items; Dreiser's contributions to periodicals; Dreiser's manuscripts; and reviews and
studies about Dreiser. Work is very incomplete.

1193 OUSBY, Ian. A Readers' Guide to Fifty American Novels.
      New York: Barnes and Noble, 1979. Dreiser, pp. 170-
      183. Discusses Sister Carrie and An American Tragedy.
      Despite its stylistic flaws, Carrie remains a powerful docu-
      ment. Probably one reason for its success is that Dreiser,
      who spent so much of his own life struggling to attain money
      and status, could identify with all three of the major char-
      acters. Of An American Tragedy he says: "Although based
      on his own first-hand knowledge, Dreiser still handles Clyde's
      drive towards wealth and power as an objective study. Even
      in the final pathetic moments of the novel, Dreiser does not
      indulge in either sentimental sympathy or moralizing about
      his hero. It was, no doubt, this clinical attitude of the au-
      thor that was the real affront to conventional morality."

1194 OVERHULS, Barbara S. "Theodore Dreiser's Novels: A Sty-
      listic Study." MA thesis, University of Oklahoma, 1951.

1195 ØVERLAND, Orm. "The Inadequate Vehicle: Dreiser's Financier,
      1912-1943." American Studies in Scandinavia, 7 (Summer,
      1971), 18-38.

1196 OVERTON, Grant M. "Dreiser," in An Hour of the American
      Novel. Philadelphia: Lippincott, 1929. Pp. 104-108.
      Somewhere between Sister Carrie (1900) and An American
      Tragedy (1925) a tremendous battle was fought, or perhaps
      only wound its way to a termination, and a complete victory
      perched at last on the Dreiserian banner. But by this time
      the banner was black. Candor about sex, however, was
      merely one of the objectives in the 25 years' battle. Candor
      itself, whether involving sex or not, was fought for, candor
      and a creed.

1197 PAGETTI, Carlo. Theodore Dreiser. Firenze, Italy: La
      Nuova Italia, 1978. In Italian; has not been translated.

1198 PALEY, Alan L. Theodore Dreiser: American Editor and
      Novelist. Charlottesville, N.Y.: Sam Har Press, 1973.
      Outstanding Personalities Series, No. 55; 30-page pamphlet.

1199 PALMER, Erwin C. "Symbolistic Imagery in Theodore Dreiser's
      An American Tragedy." Ph.D. diss., University of Syra-
      cuse, 1952.

1200 _____. "Theodore Dreiser: Poet." South and West, 10
      (Fall, 1971), 26-44.

1201 PARKER, Dorothy. "Reading and Writing: Words, Words,
     Words." New Yorker, 7 (May 30, 1931), 69-72. Reprinted
     in Parker, The Constant Reader. New York: Viking, 1970.
     Pp. 138-143.
         Has nothing good to say about Dreiser's book Dawn. Ad-
     mits that after years of keeping quiet about Dreiser, she
     will now say it out loud: "To me Dreiser is a dull, pompous
     dated, and darned near ridiculous writer."

1202 PARRINGTON, Vernon Louis. "The Development of Realism,"
     in The Re-interpretation of American Literature, edited by
     Norman Foerster. New York: Harcourt, Brace, 1928. Re-
     printed New York: Russell and Russell, 1959, with a Pref-
     ace by Robert P. Falk. Pp. 139-159.
         The old teleological foundations of American optimism were
     disintegrating, and the intellectual backgrounds were prepar-
     ing from which was to emerge a realism amoral, deterministic,
     tic, dark with pessimism. From such a background emerged
     in the nineties three writers, Crane, Norris, and Dreiser,
     who were to create in America the type of realism to which
     Zola had given the name naturalism. It was impersonal and
     objective, and equipped with a philosophy derived from the
     physical sciences. It conceived of man as a complex of physi-
     cal drives, dwelling in a mechanistic world, caught and de-
     stroyed in a web of internal and external forces.

1203 _____. Main Currents in American Thought, 3 vols. New
     York: Harcourt, Brace, 1927-1930. "Theodore Dreiser:
     Chief of American Naturalists," Vol. 3, pp. 334-359.
         Howells said in 1899: "Whoever should strike a note so
     profoundly tragic in American fiction as was struck in Dos-
     toevsky's Crime and Punishment would do a false and mis-
     taken thing." In 1925 came An American Tragedy, not too
     unlike this Russian novel. The most detached and keenly
     observant of all our writers, Dreiser was a heavy-footed
     peasant, with curiosity and boundless pity, to examine cri-
     tically this "animal called man." Not since Whitman has there
     been such a great projection of reality.

1204 PARRISH, Anne, and Josiah Titzell. "Writer's Reply to Mr.
     Dreiser." New York Herald Tribune, October 14, 1942. P. 22.

1205 PATERSON, Isabel. "Reading with Tears." Bookman, 64
     (October, 1926), 192-197.
         Article is a response to a reader who complained that he
     no longer enjoyed modern fiction and wonders if he is wholly
     lacking in taste or if the critics who recommend such works
     are wholly sincere. Answer is that the novel has become de-
     personalized and sociological. We no longer have a hero, but
     now society playing the principal part as the villain of the
     piece. In Dreiser's An American Tragedy this tendency is
     carried to its ultimate conclusion.

1206 _____. "Books and Other Things," Column. New York
Herald Tribune, November 13, 1928. P. 23. Review of
Dreiser Looks at Russia.

1207 _____. "Books and Other Things." New York Herald Tribune, November 29, 1929. P. 15.
Review of A Gallery of Women. Thinks Dreiser is a curiosity of literature, "and he grows curioser and curioser."
He cannot write a tolerable paragraph, a passable sentence.
But he can write a novel. And he is at his best in portrait
sketches, such as in Twelve Men and A Gallery of Women.

1208 _____. "Books and Other Things." New York Herald Tribune, May 8, 1931. P. 21.
Review of Dawn.

*1209 PATTEE, Fred Louis. "Theodore Dreiser," in The New Ameri-
can Literature, 1890-1930. New York: Century, 1930. Pp.
180-192.
To follow the tide of realism as it left the boundaries set
by Howells and Norris and Crane is to come upon the figure
of Dreiser, just as in poetry we eventually come to Whitman.
With no thought of doing so, he became the central figure
in what is now called "extreme realism" or naturalism. The
novels of disillusion and gloom were bound to come from some
pen. The American period of adolescence had reached the
doubt-everything stage. From earliest times the attitude of
American literature had been optimistically Romantic.

1210 PATTERSON, Eric Haines. "The Most Stately Mansions: An
Analysis of Domestic Architecture Among the Affluent in
America in the Later 19th-Century ... " Ph.D. diss., Yale,
1977. DA, 39 (1978), 1680A-1681A. In two volumes.
Study is based on three novelists--Edith Wharton, Henry
Blake Fuller, and Theodore Dreiser--important in the first
major period in American literature in which fiction was conceived as social history. All of them share a concern for
the effects of new affluence as it involves the family, and
as it manifests itself in certain material artifacts--the house
they live in and the furnishings with which they decorate it.

1211 PAVESE, Cesare. "Dreiser e la sua battàglia sociale." La
Cultura, 12 (April-June, 1933), 431-437. Reprinted in Pavese,
American Literature: Essays and Opinions, translated by
Edwin Fussell. Berkeley: University of California Press,
1970. Pp. 107-116, as "Dreiser and His Social Battle."
Dreiser's intention was not only to be brutal in the word,
in the created work of art, but objectively to represent a
world which lives brutally, which is badly made. Dreiser,
describing the life, not even too immoral, of his Carrie who
ruins a successful average man of Chicago, running off with

him and then abandoning him in misery, found his originality in the fact that none of the characters is evil, but life is evil.

1212 PEARSON, Norman Holmes. "Idealist in Conflict with Society." Saturday Review of Literature, 32 (January 29, 1949), 14-15.
Review-essay of Theodore Dreiser: Apostle of Nature, by Robert H. Elias. Regards the work as "unusually frank and honest" in the spirit of Dreiser's powerful belief in the faithful presentation of life. The book slowly and convincingly traces Dreiser's stumbling climb up the ladder and gives more insight to the writer than we have had before.

1213 PERKINS, George, ed. The Theory of the American Novel. New York: Holt, 1970. Dreiser, pp. 249-251.
Reprints an essay "Unpublished Realism" (title supplied by editor), by Theodore Dreiser from A Book About Myself.

1214 PERSONS, Stow, ed. Evolutionary Thought in America. New Haven, Conn.: Yale University Press, 1950. Reprinted New York: George Braziller, 1956. Prints "Naturalism in American Literature," by Malcolm Cowley, pp. 300-333.

1215 PETERSON, Sandra Marny. "The View from the Gallows: The Criminal Confession in American Literature." Ph.D. diss., Northwestern University, 1972. DA, 33 (1972), 2947A.
Study is based principally on four novels: The Scarlet Letter, Billy Budd, An American Tragedy, and The Confessions of Nat Turner. This discussion uses the criminal confession as a touchstone with which to examine the relationships between man, society, and a divine order. These relationships are seen to change over the years. In Dreiser's novel, for example, Divinity is wholly missing, and the individual is subordinate to powerful social forces. His formal confession is simply another capitulation to society.

1216 PETREY, Sandy. "The Language of Realism, The Language of False Consciousness: A Reading of Sister Carrie." Novel: A Forum on Fiction, 10 (Winter, 1977), 101-113.
Recalls the question which Saul Bellow asked about what bad writing in a powerful novel signified. Says he "would like to explore the possibility that the way out of the quandary is to concentrate neither on the good nor the bad writing but on the effects produced by combining the two in a single text."

1217 PETRIE, Dennis W. Ultimately Fiction: Design in Modern American Literary Biography. West Lafayette, Ind.: Purdue University Press, 1981. Dreiser, pp. 124-125, 137-145.

Discusses W. A. Swanberg's biography of Dreiser, beginning with a quick review of the critical comments which the
book received when it was first published. Concludes, however, that ultimately the biography sounds just like the Dreiser novels, and despite Swanberg's aim of capturing the whole
man, he has created a selective portrait.

1218 PHELAN, James. Worlds from Words: A Theory of Language
in Fiction. Chicago: University of Chicago Press, 1981.
Dreiser, pp. 67-115, 148-152.
Examines Sister Carrie in terms of the language Dreiser
uses and concludes that the language here fits the objective
of the author. In conclusion he says: "Though created out
of language, the worlds we experience in novels are more
than worlds of words; they are, more accurately, worlds
from words, worlds that contain the elements of character
and action, which are essentially nonlinguistic and which
are more central to our experience of those worlds than the
words which create them."

1219 PHILLIPS, William L. "The Imagery of Dreiser's Novels."
PMLA, 78 (December, 1963), 572-585. Reprinted in Salzman
(1971), pp. 85-92; and in Pizer (1981), pp. 104-126. Also
reprinted in Pizer, ed., Sister Carrie (1970), pp. 551-558.
Examines the dominant image patterns in five novels: Sister
Carrie, The Financier, The Titan, An American Tragedy, and
The Bulwark. Quotes extensively to show how Dreiser's imagery enriches the total effect of the novels and helps to
discriminate individual incidents and characters. Also points
out the ways in which the major groups of images--water,
animals, and fairyland--have shifted in their suggestions
through the course of his career, and have reflected the
central meanings of the novels.

1220 PICHEL, Irving. "Revivals, Re-issues, Remakes, and 'A Place
in the Sun.' " Quarterly of Film, Radio, and Television, 6
(Summer, 1952), 388-393.
Compares the 1931 version of Dreiser's novel with the
1952 film by George Stevens. Emphasizes how the story has
changed, not so much in the line of action as in the motivation of the characters. It is now the story of individuals,
not society.

1221 PIECHOWSKI, Marjorie Pauline. "Social Classes and Upward
Mobility in American Urban Fiction from Howells to Cather."
Ph.D. diss., University of Wisconsin (Milwaukee), 1978.
DA, 39 (1979), 5515A.
Study is based on a variety of authors, all presenting the
diverse occupational and social divisions within American
cities, and the difficulties encountered by ambitious persons
attempting to establish a financial and social position in the

new urban frontier. Four social groupings repeatedly occur
in the novels as characters attempt to find a place within
the theoretically classless, democratic American society. Dreiser's spectrum of characters may be found in all four categories, with most of them trying to cross economic lines from
lowest to upper-middle class.

1222 PIPER, Henry Dan. "Social Criticism in the American Novel
of the Nineteen Twenties," in The American Novel and the
Nineteen Twenties, edited by Malcolm Bradbury and David
Palmer. Stratford-Upon-Avon Studies, No. 13. London:
Arnold Publishing Co., 1971. Pp. 59-83.
Dreiser was America's first proletarian novelist. By 1920,
more than any other living American, he represented for the
postwar generation of younger writers the triumph of that
native literary tradition of social protest and criticism that
had its origins in the fiction of Flaubert and Zola, as well
as in the methodology of the new quantitative social sciences
of economics and sociology. When An American Tragedy appeared in 1925, its spectacular success marked the belated
triumph of the naturalistic method. By the laborious, powerful accumulation of factual detail, Dreiser's fiction revealed
the tragic contradictions lying beneath the prosperous surface of American life.

1223 PIRINSKA, Pauline. "Theodore Dreiser, 1871-1945," in Six
Writers and Their Themes: Theodore Dreiser, Sinclair Lewis,
Scott Fitzgerald, Ernest Hemingway, John Steinbeck, and
William Faulkner. Sofia: 1971. Pp. 1-23.
Entire book consists of 117 pages typescript copy, secured
on loan from the Library of Congress. In the Dreiser section, as in the others, biographical information is reviewed
with brief remarks about his work. The analysis concludes
with a letter which Dreiser wrote to James T. Farrell in 1943.
Sees this letter as a fitting summary of the man. It also
reveals the helpful understanding attitude Dreiser had to
younger writers, struggling as he had had to do, in pre-
serving the integrity of their art.

1224 _____. "Theodore Dreiser and America." Abstracts of English Studies, 16 (October, 1972), item 539.

1225 PIZER, Donald. "Nineteenth-Century American Naturalism: An
Essay in Definition." Bucknell Review, 13 (December, 1965),
1-18. Reprinted in Pizer, Realism and Naturalism in Nineteenth-Century American Literature. Carbondale: Southern
Illinois University Press, 1966. Revised edition, 1984. Pp.
11-32, as "Late Nineteenth-Century American Naturalism."
Also reprinted in Pizer, ed., Sister Carrie (1970), pp. 567-
573.
Suggests that the naturalistic novel usually contains two

tensions or contradictions, and the two in conjunction with
each other constitute the theme and form of the naturalistic
novel. The fictional world is that of the commonplace and
unheroic in which life would seem to be chiefly the full round
of daily existence. The naturalist, however, discovers in
this material the extraordinary and excessive in human nature.

1226   _____. "Theodore Dreiser's 'Nigger Jeff': The Development of an Aesthetic." American Literature, 41 (1969), 331-
341.
An opportunity to study Dreiser's developing aesthetic
lies in the existence of several versions of the short story
"Nigger Jeff." The three extant versions of this story reveal with considerable clarity and force Dreiser's changing
beliefs concerning the nature of fiction.

1227   _____. "The Problem of Philosophy in the Novel." Bucknell Review, 18 (Spring, 1970), 53-62. Reprinted in part
in Pizer, ed., Sister Carrie (1970), pp. 583-587.
Philosophical ideas are often inadequate guides to the interpretation of the novel in which they appear. Although
the novelist may seem to be supplying an interpretative key
to the events he is portraying, he may have a false or superficial discursive grasp of the meaning of these events. An
artist is often an unsatisfactory commentator on the meaning
of his own work, and hence the critic may serve in shedding
light on the creation.

1228   _____. "Dreiser Studies: Work to Be Done." Dreiser
Newsletter, 1 (Spring, 1970), 10-13.
In this initial issue of the Newsletter, Pizer indicates that
work should be done on Manuscripts and Bibliography (the
Dreiser holdings at the University of Pennsylvania are so
large that a catalog is very far in the future). In the area
of Text and Editions there is an especial need for publications of Dreiser's uncollected works. Biographical and Historical studies are needed, and so are fresh critical approaches
which abandon that naturalistic straight-jacket approach.

1229   _____. "The Publications of Theodore Dreiser: A Checklist." Proof: The Yearbook of American Bibliographical
and Textual Studies, 1 (1971), 247-292. Edited by Joseph
Katz. Columbia: University of South Carolina Press. Includes three plates.
Lists Dreiser's separate publications, contributions to
separate publications, and his contributions to journals and
newspapers. Arranged chronologically.

1230   _____. "Dreiser's Novels: The Editorial Problem." Library
Chronicle (University of Pennsylvania), 38 (Winter, 1972), 7-
24.

1231 _____. "A Summer at Maumee: Theodore Dreiser Writes Four Stories," in Essays Mostly on Periodical Publishing in America: A Collection in Honor of Clarence Gohdes, edited by James Woodress. Durham, N.C.: Duke University Press, 1973. Pp. 193-204.

Is based upon an episode of the summer of 1899, during which Dreiser spent the time with Arthur Henry, "the now obscure writer who played such an important role at this turning point in Dreiser's life." Dreiser claimed, although somewhat inaccurately, that this was the beginnings of his career as a writer of fiction. He said he wrote four or five short stories: "Of the Shining Slave Makers," "The Door of the Butcher Rogaum," "The World and the Bubble," "Nigger Jeff," and "When the Old Century Was New."

This article discusses the relationship between each story, and the magazine in which it appeared, although no trace of "The World and the Bubble" survives and apparently it was never published.

1232 _____. " 'Along the Wabash': A 'Comedy-Drama' by Theodore Dreiser." Dreiser Newsletter, 5 (Fall, 1974), 1-4.

What Dreiser did in the ten months between his arrival in New York in late November 1894 and the appearance of his magazine Ev'ry Month in October 1895 has never been totally established. He has said that he was attempting to write short stories. Also a group of letters in the Copyright Office of the Library of Congress reveals for the first time that he was attracted by the idea of becoming a playwright. There is no evidence that he actually wrote the play for which he requested a copyright.

1233 _____. "Nineteenth Century American Naturalism: An Approach Through Form." Forum (Houston), 13 (Winter, 1976), 43-46.

1234 _____. The Novels of Theodore Dreiser: A Critical Study. Minneapolis: University of Minnesota Press; Ontario: Burns & MacEachern, 1976.

Contains 346 pages with notes for each chapter. In four parts, covering all eight novels. Is scholarly, authoritative in every respect. In his Preface, Pizer says: "My book has two major aims--to establish the facts of the sources and compositions of each of Dreiser's novels and to study the themes and form of the completed work. My intent has not been to construct a genetic history of each novel merely to make available such a history, but rather to relate what can be discovered about the factual reality of a novel to its imaginative reality. If I write fully about matters of composition or theme, I do so out of a conviction that there is profit in attempting to establish the history and quality of each novel at some length in order to present a foundation of fact and opinion for correction or amplification by future scholars and critics."

1235 _____. "American Literary Naturalism: The Example of Dreiser." Studies in American Fiction, 5 (1977), 51-63. Reprinted in American Fiction: Historical and Critical Essays, edited by James Nagel. Boston: Northeastern University Press, 1977. Also reprinted in Pizer, ed. (1981), pp. 144-155.

One of the major conventions in the study of American naturalism is that naturalistic belief is both objectionable in its own right and incompatible with fictional quality. But the example of Dreiser reveals that the strength often found in the naturalistic novel rests in the writer's commitment to the distinctive form of his naturalistic beliefs and in his ability to transform these beliefs into acceptable character and event. Until we are willing to accept that the power of a naturalistic writer resides in his naturalism, we will not profit from the example of Dreiser.

1236 _____, and Jack Salzman. "'A Dreiser Industry'?" Modern Fiction Studies, 24 (1978), 255-256.

Pizer objects to the reference of Dreiser studies and scholarship as a "Dreiser Industry"--the implication that with so many colleges and universities adopting a "publish or perish" policy, that much of what is published on Dreiser is rubbish. Salzman replies that he meant no such thing exclusively of Dreiser; it is a rampant practice throughout the land, and "we write too much and we publish too much." Admits to having published some items simply for the value of keeping his academic career afloat.

1237 _____, ed. Hamlin Garland's Diaries. San Marino, Calif.: Huntington Library Press, 1968. Dreiser, pp. 123-124 et passim.

Refers to two references to Dreiser: February 7, 1904, in New York City. Dreiser had been recovering from a nervous breakdown by working with a railroad gang on the upper tip of Manhattan: "Dreiser turned out to be a tall, thin, ugly and very uncouth fellow of serious not to say rebellious turn of mind. He was bitter over his treatment by Doubleday. He became a bit tiresome at last, and we were glad when he went back to his work as boss of a gang of excavators."

January 21, 1913, in Chicago. Dreiser was in Chicago for research on The Titan. In 1916 Garland refused to sign a statement protesting the suppression of The "Genius," and the two men were enemies from that time. "He is a pessimist. 'A mad world, my masters,' is his favorite quotation. A big awkward, blundering yet amiable mind, with a certain largeness of perception and honesty of purpose. Not highly polished but sturdy and bold in action."

1238   , ed. with Introduction and Notes. <u>Sister Carrie</u>.
New York: Norton, 1970. Norton Critical edition.
Consists of 1900 Doubleday, Page, first edition text, with
explanatory footnotes throughout the text; about 100 pages
of Backgrounds and Sources Material; and about 100 pages
of modern Criticism. Concludes with a Chronology of <u>Sister
Carrie</u> and an excellent short bibliography.

1239   , ed. <u>American Thought and Writing: The 1890's</u>.
Boston: Houghton Mifflin, 1972.
Reprints the following items related to Dreiser:

"The Real Howells," from <u>Ainslee's</u>, 5 (March, 1900). Pp.
62-68.
"Curious Shifts of the Poor" which first appeared in <u>Demor-
est's</u>, 36 (November, 1899). Pp. 288-297.
"Nigger Jeff," from <u>Ainslee's</u>, 8 (November, 1901). Pp.
531-545.

1240   , ed. with Introduction. <u>Theodore Dreiser: A Selection of Uncollected Prose</u>. Detroit: Wayne State University
Press, 1977. 340 pages; Introduction, pp. 13-27.

1241   , ed. with Introduction. <u>Critical Essays on Theodore
Dreiser</u>. Boston: G. K. Hall, 1981.
Contains 341 pages of reprinted criticism and other materials, with subject and author idex. Is clearly the best book
of its kind recently published. Contains the following items:

General Essays:
"Theodore the Poet," by Edgar Lee Masters, p. 3.
"The Naturalism of Mr. Dreiser," by Stuart P. Sherman,
pp. 4-12.
"Dreiser," by Sherwood Anderson, pp. 13-14.
"The Art of Theodore DReiser," by Randolph Bourne, pp.
15-18.
"The Dreiser Bugaboo," by H. L. Mencken, pp. 19-26.
"Modern Currents," by Paul Elmer More, pp. 27-29.
"Dreiser: An Inconsistent Mechanist," by Eliseo Vivas,
pp. 30-37.
"Reality in America," by Lionel Trilling, pp. 38-46.
"The Stature of Theodore Dreiser," by Alfred Kazin, pp.
47-56.
"Theodore Dreiser: The Wonder and Terror of Life," by
Charles C. Walcutt, pp. 57-91.
"Theodore Dreiser's Transcendentalism," by Roger As-
selineau, pp. 92-103.
"The Imagery of Dreiser's Novels," by William L. Phillips
pp. 104-126.
"Heathen Catacombs," by David Weimer, pp. 127-135.
"The Romantic Dilemma," by Richard Lehan, pp. 136-143.

"American Literary Naturalism: The Example of Dreiser,"
by Donald Pizer, pp. 144-156.

Sister Carrie:
  "Sister Carrie," by W. M. Reedy, pp. 157-159.
  "With the Novelists," Anonymous, pp. 160-161.
  "Theodore Dreiser's Sister Carrie," by Harris Merton Lyon,
     pp. 162-165.
  "Sister Carrie," by Joseph H. Coates, pp. 166-168.
  "A Picture of Conditions," by F. O. Matthiessen, pp. 169-
     185.
  "Dreiser and the Plotting of Inarticulate Experience," by
     Julian Markels, pp. 186-199.
  "The Finesse of Dreiser," by Ellen Moers, pp. 200-208.

Jennie Gerhardt:
  "A Novel of the First Rank," by H. L. Mencken, pp. 209-
     212.
  "Pathos and Dreiser," by Warwick Wadlington, pp. 213-
     228.

The Cowperwood Trilogy:
  "Dreiser's Novel," by H. L. Mencken, pp. 229-232.
  "Recent Reflections of a Novel-Reader," Anonymous, pp.
     233-234.
  "Dreiser and His Titan," by E. F. Edgett, pp. 235-236.
  "The Titan," by H. L. Mencken, pp. 237-242.

The "Genius":
  "Desire as Hero," by Randolph Bourne, pp. 243-246.
  "A Literary Behemoth," by H. L. Mencken, pp. 247-252.

An American Tragedy:
  "Theodore Dreiser: An American Tragedy," by T. K.
     Whipple, pp. 253-257.
  "An American Tragedy," by Robert Shafer, pp. 258-270.
  "Homage to Theodore Dreiser on the Centenary of His
     Birth," by Robert Penn Warren, pp. 271-291.
  "An American Tragedy," by Irving Stone, pp. 292-302.
  "Mr Trilling, Mr. Warren, and An American Tragedy,"
     by Charles T. Samuels, pp. 303-312.
  "An American Tragedy: Theme and Structure," by Shel-
     don Norman Grebstein, pp. 313-322.

The Bulwark:
  "Theodore Dreiser's The Bulwark: A Final Resolution,"
     by Sidney Richman, pp. 323-336.

1242   _____; Richard W. Dowell; and Frederic E. Rusch. Theo-
        dore Dreiser: A Primary and Secondary Bibliography. Bos-
        ton: G. K. Hall, 1975.

Contains over 500 pages in three parts. (1) Works by
Dreiser, which seems complete and accurate enough; is the
best listing of its kind to date; (2) Works on Dreiser, which
is divided into seven sub-parts, Books and Pamphlets, Articles in Newspapers and Journals, Tapes, etc.; and (3)
Miscellanea, consisting of production of plays and adapta-
tions of works. Concludes with an Index to authors and
titles. Works are all listed in chronology, with a system
of numbering that is cluttered and meaningless. It is without annotation, and has no subject index to criticism.

1243 POIRIER, Richard. A World Elsewhere: The Place of Style
      in American Literature. New York: Oxford University Press,
      1966. "Panoramic Environment and the Anonymity of the
      Self," pp. 235-252. Reprinted in Pizer, ed., Sister Carrie
      (1970), pp. 574-583.
         That creative and shaping force which earlier American
      writers found in nature or in the composite man called the
      Poet is located by Dreiser in the objects that fill what were
      the free spaces of America. It is compelling how Dreiser can
      be intimidated by the Things he describes, even by the ba-
      nalities of conversation he reports. Anything for Dreiser is
      part of the hieroglyph of "the race." It is nagging to ask
      that in the face of this there should be in his style anything
      like a firmly consistent individual presence.

1244 POMEROY, Charles William. "Soviet Russian Criticism, 1960-
      1969, of Seven Twentieth-Century American Novelists." Ph.D.
      diss., University of Southern California, 1971. DA, 32 (1971),
      449A.
         Study focuses on Dreiser, Steinbeck, Hemingway, Faulkner,
      Salinger, Fitzgerald, and John Updike. Most Russian critics
      interpret Clyde Griffiths of An American Tragedy as a typi-
      cal American, psychologically mutilated and driven to crime
      by his country's degenerate environment. The conclusion
      profiles Soviet critics, three of the doctrinaire type, three
      who combine socio-cultural commentary with esthetic discrim-
      ination, and three who emphasize such elements familiar in
      American-style criticism as style, unity, narrative technique,
      and latent meaning.

1245 POSSELT, Erich, ed. "Statements of Belief." Bookman, 68
      (September, 1928), 25-27. Reprinted in Herrmann, Eva,
      On Parade, edited by Erich Posselt (1929), pp. 46-49.
         Quotes the often-quoted passage in which Dreiser says he
      can make no comment that holds either interest or import for
      himself. He says: "In short I catch no meaning from all I
      have seen, and pass quite as I came, confused and dismayed."

1246 POUND, Ezra. "Dreiser Protest." Egoist, 3 (October, 1916),
      159.

Powers   218

1247 POWERS, Margaret Ellen. " 'The Unstrung Balloon': A Study
      of Narrative Devices in Nineteenth-Century American Fiction."
      Ph.D. diss., University of Minnesota, 1981. DA, 42 (1982),
      5123A.
          Dreiser referred to as an example of the realistic mode
      of fiction.

1248 POWNALL, David E. "Theodore Dreiser," in Articles on
      Twentieth-Century Literature: An Annotated Bibliography,
      1954-1970, 2 vols. New York: Kraus-Thomson, 1973. Drei-
      ser, Vol. 2, pp. 702-717.
          Contains 72 items, arranged in several categories: General,
      An American Tragedy, The Bulwark, Jennie Gerhardt, The
      "Genius," The Hand of the Potter, "Nigger Jeff," and Sister
      Carrie. Annotations are brief, but excellent.

1249 POWYS, John Cowper. "Theodore Dreiser." Little Review,
      2 (November, 1915), 7-13. Reprinted in The Powys Review,
      2 (Winter, 1979), 33-37.
          Review of The "Genius." Dreiser has achieved a very
      curious and a very original work. It has the epic rather
      than the dramatic quality. It is quite properly in accord-
      ance with the epic attitude of mind, this reduction of the
      more purely human episodes to a proportionate insignificance
      compared with the general surge and volume of the life-stream.

1250 _____. "Theodore Dreiser: The Titan," in One Hundred
      Best Books. New York: G. A. Shaw, 1916. Reprinted
      New York: American Library Service, 1922. P. 29.

1251 _____. "Real American Book by Genius Is Star in Literary
      Heavens." San Francisco Bulletin, August 23, 1919.
          Review of Twelve Men. It is more than a personal achieve-
      ment. It is a landmark, a memorable mile-stone in the his-
      tory of American literature. In this book Dreiser has really
      found himself.

1252 _____. "An American Tragedy: A Review Essay." Dial,
      80 (April, 1926), 331-338. Reprinted in The Powys Review,
      2 (Winter, 1979), 38-42.
          The greatness of this work lies in the fact, among other
      things, that it covers so much ground. No one except Drei-
      ser seems strong enough to swallow the whole chaotic spec-
      tacle and to disgorge it into some form of brain-stuff. His
      vision of things blames no one, lets no one off, reduces all
      benevolence and righteousness to sorrowful humility; pitiful,
      patient, dumb. For at the back of the world, as he sees
      it, is neither a Devil nor a Redeemer; only a featureless
      mulungu, that murmurs forever "Om! Om! Om!"

1253 _____. "Modern Fiction," in Sex in the Arts: A Symposium,

edited by J. F. McDermott and K. B. Taft. New York:
Harper's, 1932. Excerpt reprinted in The Powys Review, 2
(Winter, 1979), 43-45.

1254 _____. Autobiography. New York: Simon and Schuster,
1934. Reprinted New York: New Directions, 1960. Dreiser, pp. 411 et passim.

1255 _____. "Introduction," in Notes on Life by Theodore Dreiser, edited by Marguerite Tjader and John J. McAleer. University: University of Alabama Press, 1974. Introduction
reprinted in The Powys Review, 2 (Winter, 1979), 46-49.
Material derived from earlier publications; Powys died in
1963.

1256 POWYS, Llewelyn. The Verdict of Bridlegoose. New York:
Harcourt, Brace, 1926. "Good Friends," pp. 38-45 and
"Certain Celebrities," pp. 88-93.
Biographical sketches of Dreiser and others, including his
brother John Cowper Powys.

1257 PRESTON, John Hyde. "True Style." Saturday Review of
Literature, 2 (May 22, 1926), 814.
Letter to editor. Style comes inevitably when men of
genius have labored and toiled long enough. Dreiser seems
not to have reached this point as yet, and it is doubtful that
he ever will, when one takes into account his irritating indifference, and his endless pages of useful but incoherent
material which a better artist in style would have boiled
down from mere colored water to a thick delicious syrup.

1258 PRICE, Lawrence Marsden. The Reception of United States
Literature in Germany. Chapel Hill: University of North
Carolina Press, 1966. Dreiser, pp. 441 et passim.
Asserts that three times as many Anglo-Saxon books as
French books are now displayed for sale in the German book-
stores. Names several German authors almost assured of
translation into English. Dreiser and others of his period
are certain to appear in German translation.

1259 PRICE, Richard Alan. "The Culture of Despair: Characters
and Society in the Novels of Edith Wharton and Theodore
Dreiser." Ph.D. diss., University of Rochester, 1976. DA,
37 (1976), 315A.
Both novelists present a view of American culture in their
major novels which is responsible for the disillusionment and
destruction of their characters. Their protagonists are
atomistic--cut off from family and friends in an urban world
where the meretricious tokens of success no longer produce
a sense of personal fulfillment. Those characters who are
not orphans soon cut themselves off from families which they

find suffocating and social ties which they find hypocritical
and limiting.

1260 _____. "Dreiser at the Aquarium." Dreiser Newsletter, 8
(Spring, 1977), 1-5.
Article discusses a short piece entitled "A Lesson from the
Aquarium" which Dreiser published in 1906 in a magazine
called Tom Watson's Magazine. The article by Dreiser discusses the observed behavior of stort minnows, hermit crabs,
and shark suckers. He extends his description, however,
to make some criticisms of human behavior as well. Is interesting because it provides a probable germ for the lobster
and squid episode in The Financier and says some things
about Dreiser's own thinking after his breakdown and before
his success in magazine editing and publishing.

1261 _____. "Lily Bart and Carrie Meeber: Cultural Sisters."
American Literary Realism, 13 (Autumn, 1980), 238-245.
Draws a comparison of Edith Wharton's heroine from The
House of Mirth and Dreiser's Carrie Meeber. Among the
conclusions reached are those that the novels have a similar
structure, and both women are portrayals of rootless alienated individuals. "Both heroines find that a fulfilled life
is impossible in the culture of late hineteenth-century America."

1262 PRITCHARD, John Paul. Return to the Fountains. Durham,
N.C.: Duke University Press, 1942. Dreiser, pp. 176 et
passim.
Tragedy must have the cathartic effect of purging off as
well as the arousing of certain emotions. An American Tragedy fails to accomplish the enlargement of spirit that true
tragedy has. It is hardly worthwhile to struggle through
eight hundred or more pages to be left at the end with a
feeling of sheer oppression.

1263 PROSSER, F. D. "Mr. Dreiser's Remedy." New York Times,
May 16, 1931. P. 16.
Letter to editor.

1264 PURDY, Strother B. "An American Tragedy and L' Etranger."
Comparative Literature, 19 (1967), 252-268.
Begins by pointing out the similarities in theme and event
between An American Tragedy and The Stranger, but the
subject has never been developed or studied in any detail
because the two novels seem totally too far removed from
each other. This article explores the similarities in the two
novels primarily in terms of their naturalistic-existentialist
philosophy and concludes that both "reveal the great strength
they share, the portrait of twentieth-century man as the victim of his own crime, a victim collaborating in the crime that
is his own death."

1265 PUTZEL, Max. "Dreiser, Reedy, and 'De Maupassant Jr.' "
      American Literature, 33 (January, 1962), 466-484.
      Reviews Dreiser's relations with Reedy, and the support
      which Reedy generally gave Dreiser. They also shared a
      protégé, Harris Merton Lyon, the "De Maupassant Junior,"
      of Dreiser's Twelve Men. Lyon died early. Reedy and Drei-
      ser remained associates until near Reedy's death in 1920.

1266 _____. The Man in the Mirror: William Marion Reedy and
      His Magazine. Cambridge, Mass.: Harvard University Press,
      1963. Dreiser, pp. 120-131 and pp. 255-264.
      "Dreiser," pp. 120-131 similar to article above in which
      Dreiser's relation to Reedy is reviewed over the years.
      Quotes a good many passages from Reedy's reviews of Drei-
      ser's novels through 1915. See Reedy below.
      "Dreiser and Harris Merton Lyon," pp. 255-264, brings
      further discussion of Harris Merton Lyon, the young writer
      who died prematurely in 1916. Later Dreiser used his char-
      acter and his almost obsessive drive for fame as the basis
      for "De Maupassant, Junior," one of the biographical sketches
      in Twelve Men. The story is successful in bringing to life
      the writer of the so-called "farmhouse" letters. It is told
      by a magazine editor, who relates how the talented young
      writer came to him as an arrogant youth, became spoiled by
      the magazine's publisher, was lost or cast off when the edi-
      tor took another job, re-appeared from time to time as a
      would-be man of letters and gentleman farmer, and died leav-
      ing suitcases full of old manuscript. Poignant as the tale
      is, it tells more of Dreiser than it does its hero, identified
      simply as "L___."

1267 QUIN, Mike (pseudo. of Paul William Ryan). "Dreiser Tells
      'Em," in More Dangerous Thoughts, with Introduction by
      Theodore Dreiser; illustrations by Rosalie Todd and Chuck.
      San Francisco: People's World Press, 1941. Pp. 97-99.
      Says quite openly, that "if you'll go into any commercial
      book store you will find that three-fourths of the books on
      sale consist of elaborate efforts of the upper class to con-
      vince themselves of lies or pawn off their lies on the people.
      Dreiser doesn't belong to them. He belongs to us. He's
      the greatest living writer in America and he belongs to the
      working people. That makes the upper class sore as hell.
      Nothing makes a capitalist madder than the existence of
      something he can't buy with his money, confuse with his
      lies, or scare with his wrath."

1268 QUINN, Arthur Hobson. American Fiction: An Historical and
      Critical Survey. New York and London: D. Appleton-
      Century, 1936. Dreiser, pp. 642-652.

No one cares about Hurstwood, in fact there is no reason to care about Carrie. Dreiser tries at the end to depict her as a seeker after beauty, but nothing she does or says indicates it. Her aspirations are purely material, and she lets Hurstwood starve while she has plenty without a thought. As to The "Genius" it is "an encyclopedic revelation of the lives of male and female sensualists whose standards have an aroma of the barnyard."

1269 _____, ed. The Literature of the American People. New York: D. Appleton-Century-Crofts, 1951. "Dreiser," by George F. Whicher, pp. 847-851.

Mostly biographical detail. Critical comments on the major novels. Says in conclusion "Seldom has so drastic a movement been accomplished with so little fanfare. It took a full decade for critics to realize what was going on, but when the realization came the nature of the party underwent a complete 'bouleversement.' "

1270 QUINN, Vincent G. "Religion and Ethical Attitudes in Theodore Dreiser's Fiction." MA thesis, Columbia, 1950.

1271 QUINTAL, Claire-H. "Emile Zola et Theodore Dreiser." MA thesis, University of Montreal, 1958. In French.

1272 RADIN, Edward. "The Original American Tragedy." New York Sunday Mirror Magazine Section, January 26, 1947. Pp. 12-13.

1273 RAHV, Philip. "Proletarian Literature: A Political Autopsy." The Southern Review, 4 (January, 1939), 616-628.

The period of the proletarian mystification of American letters is now definitely over. Dreiser belonged to certain organizations that were clearly aligned with the Communist Party, but none of his major fiction can be classified in this manner.

1274 _____. "On the Decline of Naturalism." Partisan Review, 9 (November-December, 1942), 483-493. Reprinted in Rahv, Image and Idea. Norfolk, Conn.: New Directions, 1949. Pp. 128-138. Revised and enlarged in 1957. Pp. 141-154. Also reprinted in Becker (1963), pp. 579-590.

Theodore Dreiser comes as close as any American writer to plotting the careers of his characters strictly within a determinative process. For whatever its past accomplishments, it cannot be denied that its present condition is one of utter debility. What was once a means of treating material truthfully has been turned, through a long process of depreciation, into a mere convention of truthfulness, devoid of

any significant or even clearly definable literary purpose
or design.

1275 RANDALL, Alvia L. W. "Dreiser's Women." MA thesis, At-
      lanta University, 1969.

1276 RANDALL, Gray M. "The Short Story Technique of Theodore
      Dreiser." MA thesis, University of Washington, 1951.

1277 RAPIN, Rene. "Dreiser's Jennie Gerhardt. Chapter 62."
      Explicator, 14 (May, 1956), item 54.
      Based on an analysis of what apparently was a publisher's
      error in which was printed "impression imperial," instead of
      "colorful, impressive, imperial," which shows in the manu-
      script. The first phrase makes no sense, whereas the sec-
      ond adds dignity and significance to the otherwise solemn
      and beautiful passage.

1278 RASCOE, Burton. "Dreiser Gives Us His Best Effort in Twelve
      Men." Chicago Tribune, May 3, 1919.
      In all these portraits there is that same sincere attempt
      to present these men as they are. Here is wondrous, in-
      scrutable, fascinating life as revealed in the diversity. It
      is one of the most unusual books in our literature, and cer-
      tainly one of the best that Dreiser has given us.

1279 _____. "Dreiser Shakes the Potter's Hand." Chicago Trib-
      une, October 11, 1919.
      Review of Dreiser's play, "The Hand of the Potter." His
      power as a dramatic technician is evident in the suspense
      and outcome of the scene where the perverted youth ap-
      proaches the little girl, and again in the scene where the
      family accepts slowly and terrifyingly the evidence that the
      boy has committed a hideous crime.

1280 _____. "The Books of the Week." Chicago Tribune, April
      10, 1920.
      Review of Hey Rub-a-Dub-Dub! The title sketch of this
      volume is one of the finest, most moving, and most poignant
      things Dreiser has ever written. The mood of heavy sorrow
      and troubled forebodings never leaves him. But he expres-
      ses a phase of American life and temperament with a sin-
      cerity and veracity almost unknown before him; he has re-
      corded our growth and groping with profound fidelity.

1281 _____. "Reviewing the Reviewer." Freeman, 2 (January
      26, 1921), 473-474.
      Letter to editor.

1282 _____. "The Interesting Dullness of Dreiser's Life." New
      York Tribune Book News and Reviews, December 31, 1922.
      P. 17.

Review of <u>A Book About Myself</u>. The most interesting aspect of this book is its uneventfulness. But here he has given us a book of tenderness and truth, humbly and sincerely told, the poignantly interesting history of a not unusual life, which in its very common-placeness may serve as a representative record of the barrenness of the average life in elements of adventure and ecstasy.

1283   _____. "A Bookman's Day Book" (title of column). <u>New York Tribune Magazine and Books</u>, December 31, 1922. P. 20. Reprinted in Rascoe, <u>A Bookman's Daybook</u>, edited by C. Hartley Grattan. New York: Liveright, 1929. Pp. 59-60, as "Dreiser, Conservative Editor."

Comments on Dreiser's policy of publication when he was editor of a woman's magazine: he would publish nothing that was even slightly off, "afraid of new ventures," etc. Later in life Rascoe recalls Dreiser's criticism of editors for lacking the courage to publish "anything new, unusual, out of the regular run of stuff."

1284   _____. "A Bookman's Day Book." <u>New York Tribune Magazine and Books</u>, April 29, 1923. P. 30. Reprinted in <u>A Bookman's Daybook</u> (1929), p. 97, as "Dreiser's Proper Story."

Recalls an incident with Arthur Vance, editor of the <u>Pictorial Review</u> in which Vance made Dreiser a proposition: "If you will write a story that hasn't a prostitute or a kept woman in it, I promise to buy it and pay our top price for it." Dreiser accepted the dare, and "made good on it." Vance called it "a corking story, with a real plot, humor and beauty in it...." The title of the story was "Glory Be! McClathery," later published as "St. Columba and the River."

1285   _____. "A Bookman's Day Book." <u>New York Tribune Magazine and Books</u>, November 25, 1923. P. 32. Reprinted in <u>A Bookman's Daybook</u> (1929), pp. 163-164 as "Arthur Henry, Whitlock, and Dreiser."

Recalls the old days of Chicago journalism when Arthur Henry was working at <u>The Daily News</u>, and later when he covered the political news with Brand Whitlock, who was then mayor of Toledo, Ohio. Henry was managing editor of <u>The Blade</u>. One day a tall, lanky youth with a funny face drifted into the office and asked for a job. "There's a street-car strike," replied Henry, "and nobody here wants to take a chance." The youth didn't even ask where, turned on his heel, went out--and came back with a whale of a story. The youth was Theodore Dreiser.

1286   _____. "Contemporary Reminiscences." <u>Arts and Decorations</u>, 20 (April, 1924), 28, 57, 62.

1287   _____. <u>Theodore Dreiser</u>. New York: R. M. McBride,

1925. Reprinted New York: Haskell House, 1972. Also reprinted Norwood, Pa.: Norwood Editions, 1977; and Philadelphia: Richard West, 1978.

Consists of 83 pages, brief, uncritical study, but author recognizes the work as such. Says: "Among authors of the present day he is one of the very few who have never troubled themselves to answer critics, never bothered to correct false impressions about themselves, never sought reprisals against those who have maligned and misrepresented them. He has gone on, living obscurely, keeping out of the factional fights of the day, away from the gatherings of writers."

1288 _____. "An American Tragedy." New York Sun Saturday Book Reviews, January 9, 1926. P. 10.

Is a novel of such breadth, depth and significance as only Dreiser could write. Dreiser's already towering stature among modern realists increases with this tragedy.

1289 _____. "Dreiser's Early Youth." New York Sun, May 9, 1931.

Review of Dawn. It is a record of his associations with people, the trials of his family, the beginnings of his thirst for knowledge and beauty and understanding. It is a great book, a memorable and valuable one, destined to become a classic of self-revelation.

1290 _____. "Dreiser Sees Red." New York Sun, January 29, 1932.

Review of Tragic America, which he does not think will be acceptable to the general reader of the bourgeois type. Nor will it be acceptable to the Communists. Suggests it is a good book for American capitalists to take a peek into, if only to be reminded that this book is a symptom of something more than the psychic effects of the depression in the "business cycle."

1291 _____. "Theodore Dreiser," in Prometheans, Ancient and Modern. New York and London: Putnam's, 1933. Pp. 241-269.

After An American Tragedy Dreiser began to take an active part in social and economic reform and published a heavily documented indictment of capitalism under the title Tragic America. It is jumbled, impressive, and angry, but his métier is to make the reader see and feel, not to lead a cause. He has been the great incorruptible among American novelists in reflecting what he knows and has experienced and observed.

1292 _____. "Does Dreiser's Final Novel Reveal Spiritual Creed?" Chicago Sunday Tribune, March 24, 1946. Part 4, pp. 3, 8.

Believes that the novel was finished many years before
its publication and represents some kind of religious or emotional experience which he came to doubt and so did not publish the novel. It is unlike everything he wrote, bare and
matter-of-fact. Many Dreiserians, on the other hand, will
say it is both the invocation and the nunc dimittis of the
whole testimony about his life as embodied in his troubled
and tortured search for meaning in what he had seen and
thought and felt.

1293 _____. We Were Interrupted. Garden City, N.Y.: Doubleday, 1947. Dreiser, pp. 146 et passim.
Slight reference to Dreiser as a serious writer who was
writing in a period of frivolity and wisecracks, in the later
years of the 1920's.

1294 _____, ed. with Introduction. Sister Carrie, illustrated
by Reginald Marsh. New York: Limited editions club, 1939.

1295 RECCHIA, E. J. "Naturalism's Artistic Compromises in Sister
Carrie and The Octopus." Literatur in Wissenschaft und
Unterricht, 5 (1972), 277-285.

1296 REEDY, William Marion. "Sister Carrie: A Strangely Strong
Novel in a Queer Milieu." St. Louis Mirror, 10 (January 3,
1901), 6-7. Reprinted in Pizer (1981), pp. 157-159.
It is photographically true, and yet there is an art about
it that lifts it often above mere reporting. And there grows
upon the reader the impression that there lurks behind the
mere story an intense, fierce resentment of the conditions
glimpsed.

1297 _____. "Reflections: Dreiser's Great Book." Reedy's Mirror, 21 (January 2, 1913), 2.
Review of The Financier. Calls it a "great story of Self
in a half hundred manifestations--Self bent on Self's ends
to the end of everything. Voice of the narrator is very
dim in this novel as he guides you through this hell which
is only the life of Self."

1298 _____. "Reflections: Dreiser's 'Titan.'" Reedy's Mirror,
22 (May 29, 1914), 3.
Review of The Titan.

1299 _____. "The Genius of Theodore Dreiser." Reedy's Mirror, 23 (October 8, 1915), 166.
Review of The "Genius."

1300 _____. "Review of Plays of the Natural and Supernatural."
Reedy's Mirror, 24 (July 14, 1916), 8.

1301 _____. "Review of A Hoosier Holiday." Reedy's Mirror, 24
    (December 14, 1916), 839-840.

1302 _____. "Dreiser's Short Stories." Reedy's Mirror, 26 (De-
    cember 13, 1918), 641.
    Review of Free and Other Stories.

1303 REFFETT, Sid Shannon. "Visions and Revisions: The Nature
    of Dreiser's Religious Inquiry." Ph.D. diss., University of
    Notre Dame, 1972. DA, 33 (1973), 5195A.
    Dreiser did not resolve the dilemma in terms of an accep-
    table orthodox faith. Consequently the word religion cannot
    be limited to a dogmatic resolution of a search for faith;
    rather it must be interpreted as a descriptive term which
    indicates, however broadly, the spiritual nature and devo-
    tional character of Dreiser's inquiry into the ultimate mean-
    ings of being.

1304 REGAN, Patricia. "Realism--Or Is It?" Catholic World, 167
    (June, 1948), 235-242.

1305 REYNOLDS, Quentin. The Fiction Factory: Or From Pulp
    Row to Quality Street. New York: Random House, 1955.
    Dreiser, pp. 147-151.
    Deals with Dreiser in 1898, then 27 years old, who walked
    into the office of Street & Smith looking for a job and was
    handed the editorship of Smith's Magazine, the most unlikely
    choice in the world for editor of a magazine created to at-
    tract the interests of John Smiths all over the country. He
    approached the task of editing the magazine on a strictly
    professional level and not as the tortured artist he was. He
    had a strong mother-fixation and a deep hatred for his father,
    yet none of this was ever evidenced in either the fiction or
    the articles he bought and edited for Smith's.

1306 RICE, Diana. "Terrible Typewriter on Parnassus." New York
    Times Magazine, April 27, 1924. P. 11.

1307 RICHARDS, Edmund C. "As to Theodore Dreiser." Chicago
    Evening Post Friday Literary Review, November 29, 1912.
    P. 4.

1308 RICHARDS, Grant. Author Hunting by an Old Literary Sports-
    man. London: Hamish Hamilton; New York: Coward-Mc-
    Cann, 1934. Dreiser pp. 170-206 (American edition; different
    pagination in English and American editions). Also published
    as Author Hunting: Memories of Years Spent Mainly on Pub-
    lishing. New York: Coward-McCann, 1934. Reprinted Lon-
    don: Unicorn, 1960.
    Met Dreiser in 1911 at the time Harper's had brought out
    Jennie Gerhardt. At the time Dreiser was working on The

<u>Financier</u> but had no money to make a European tour, which
he thought necessary in doing research on the figure of
Frank Cowperwood. Richards arranged an advance and Dreiser went to Europe. The result of this tour was <u>A Traveller</u>
<u>at Forty</u>, a manuscript initially over a million words. Grant
cut and cut, and once published did not try exceedingly
hard to promote it. Says in conclusion: "On the whole I
do not regret the publication, and in the course of time Dreiser has more than fulfilled my belief in him, my belief in
him both as a writer and as a potential best-seller which in
Paris he had thought so exaggerated."

1309 RICHARDS, Hodee. "Dreiser's <u>Bulwark</u>: Summary of a Use-
      ful Life." <u>People's Daily World</u>, May 8, 1946. P. 6.

1310 RICHARDS, Robert Fulton. "Dreiser, Theodore," in <u>Concise</u>
      <u>Dictionary of American Literature</u>. New York: Philosophical
      Library, 1955. Pp. 69-71.
      Brief, biographical coverage. Says: "No other writer of
      our time has faced such a barrage of criticism or misunder-
      standing, and no other writer in American letters has so
      often been acknowledged as the pioneer of the contemporary
      novel."

1311 RICHMAN, Sidney. "The World and the Dream: An Analysis
      of the Pattern of Ideas in the Novels of Theodore Dreiser."
      Ph.D. diss., University of California (Los Angeles), 1960.

1312 _____. "Theodore Dreiser's <u>The Bulwark</u>: A Final Resolu-
      tion." <u>American Literature</u>, 34 (May, 1962), 229-245. Re-
      printed in Pizer (1981), pp. 323-336.
      One of the more vexing problems in modern American liter-
      ature surrounds Dreiser's activities in the final year of his
      life. In that year he completed <u>The Bulwark</u>, a novel which
      in content and tone sits squarely in the transcendental tra-
      dition, owing nothing at all to Herbert Spencer and every-
      thing to Thoreau and John Woolman. And as if this were
      not enough, a few months earlier he had joined the Communist
      party. Taken together the two acts are so strikingly opposed
      to the popular image of Dreiser the naturalist, and are in
      themselves so paradoxical, that even now they await a co-
      herent explanation.

      RIDDELL, John <u>see</u> FORD, Corey (pseudo.)

1313 RIDEOUT, Walter B. <u>The Radical Novel in the United States,</u>
      <u>1900-1954</u>. Cambridge, Mass.: Harvard University Press,
      1956. Dreiser, pp. 115 et passim.
      Uses the term "radical" in a political sense, and relates
      most of the writers discussed to the far left-wing, or Com-
      munism. Dreiser does not really belong to this classification.

In An American Tragedy the author clearly gives overtones
of class justice, but it cannot be called a radical novel.

1314   RIGGIO, Thomas Pasquale. "The Education of Theodore Drei-
       ser." Ph.D. diss., Harvard University, 1972.

1315   _____. "Another Two Dreisers: The Artist as 'Genius.' "
       Studies in the Novel, 9 (1977), 119-136.
          Sees The "Genius" as the turning point in Dreiser's fic-
       tion, but the generally negative appraisals of this novel--
       even by people who like Dreiser--have obscured its central
       place in Dreiser's work. In his shift from fictional biography
       of his sisters to fictional autobiography, Dreiser attempted
       to understand his characters from the inside, and to grad-
       ually discover a character and a set of issues that dominated
       his writing for a decade.

1316   _____. "Europe Without Baedeker: The Omitted Hanscha
       Jower Story--from A Traveller at Forty." Modern Fiction
       Studies, 23 (Fall, 1977), 423-440.
          Article is based on the story of a German streetwalker,
       Hanscha Jower, which was excised by the editors of Century
       Company from the manuscript of A Traveller at Forty. Con-
       tains very good Dreiser composition and is printed here for
       the first time.

1317   _____. "The Divided Stream of Dreiser Studies." Studies
       in the Novel, 9 (1977), 2110216.
          Review-essay of Vera Dreiser's My Uncle Theodore and
       Donald Pizer's Novels of Theodore Dreiser: A Critical Study.
       Sees the two works as perpetuating the split between biog-
       raphy and criticism that has characterized Dreiser studies
       for decades and which has impeded a real understanding of
       Dreiser.

1318   _____. "American Gothic: Poe and An American Tragedy."
       American Literature, 49 (1978), 515-532.
          Article is based on a study of Chapters 42-48 in Book II
       of An American Tragedy in which there are numerous im-
       ages that reflect the Gothic tradition. It has been assumed
       that Dreiser derived this mode of imagery from Freud, the
       nightmares, the voices, etc., but this article proposes that
       it was Edgar Allan Poe to whom Dreiser turned at a critical
       point in his composition. Quotes many passages, particularly
       from Poe's poetry, to demonstrate this hypothesis.

1319   _____. "Dreiser on Society and Literature: The San Fran-
       cisco Exposition Interview." American Literary Realism, 11
       (1978), 284-294.
          Prints an interview, transcribed from an unmarked record-
       ing in the Dreiser collection at the University of Pennsyl-

vania. This item has not been included in any bibliography.
The event took place in San Francisco during the 1939 Golden
Gate International Exposition. The interview gives a rare
glimpse into late Dreiser reflections on American society and
on his own recent reading experiences.

1320   _____. "Mark Twain and Theodore Dreiser: Two Boys Lost
          in a Cave." Mark Twain Journal, 19 (1978), 20-25.
              Neither Twain nor Dreiser scholarship has had much to
          say about the relationship between the two American realists.
          Dreiser's correspondence shows a long and serious interest
          in Twain, and in two 1935 articles Dreiser spoke of a series
          of personal encounters with the older writer. It had not
          been noticed that Twain had a part in shaping Dreiser's
          writing in at least one instance: a key chapter in Dawn
          for which Dreiser drew extensively on chapters 31 and 32
          of Tom Sawyer.

1321   _____. "Notes on the Origins of Sister Carrie." Library
          Chronicle, 44 (Spring, 1979), 7-26.

1322   _____. "The Dreisers in Sullivan: A Biographical Revision."
          Dreiser Newsletter, 10 (Fall, 1979), 1-12.
              Dreiser's record of the Sullivan, Indiana, years (1879-
          1882) focuses on events that influenced his life and shaped
          his literary imagination, particularly the success and subse-
          quent failure of his father. Is now thought that Dreiser
          somewhat exaggerated his father's propensity for failure.

1323   _____. "Dreiser in the Making." Review, 3 (1981), 175-
          180. Review article.

1324   _____. "Dreiser's Early Labors." Dreiser Newsletter, 15
          (Spring, 1984), 10-13.
              Review of An Amateur Laborer, edited by Richard Dowell
          et al., 1983. Says the editors "deserve high marks for trans-
          forming a motley, truncated manuscript into a finely edited
          book." One complaint, however, is that there is no index.
          The last word must be one of appreciation to the editors for
          providing a valuable addition to the Dreiser canon. One
          wishes only for more, and if they had decided to add to this
          book the later companion piece "Down Hill and Up," no one
          would have complained.

1325   _____; James L. W. West, III; and Neda Westlake; eds.
          American Diaries of Theodore Dreiser, 1902-1926. Philadel-
          phia: University of Pennsylvania Press, 1982.
              Consists of 471 pages, covering seven diaries of 24 years.
          Shows Dreiser in many roles: the disconsolate neurasthenic
          struggling to save his career and marriage, the author jump-
          ing from manuscript to manuscript as the market and his in-

spiration dictate, the lover demanding fidelity from his women
while jumping from bed to bed himself. The volume is a valuable contribution to Dreiser scholarship, making a rich and
interesting fund of autobiographical material easily accessible
for the first time. Editor Riggio points out that even in the
autobiographies, Dreiser was prone to don a mask. In the
diaries, he does not.

1325a ROBERTS, John V. "The Design of Theodore Dreiser's Sister
      Carrie." MA thesis, Columbia University, 1950.

1326 ROBERTS, Joseph B., Jr. "Dreiser's Social Consciousness."
      MA thesis, University of North Carolina, 1954.

1327 ROBINSON, William J. "An American Tragedy." Critic and
      Guide, 25 (October, 1926), 391-398.

1328 ROCHESTER, Anna. "Dreiser was Right." New Republic, 70
      (April 20, 1932), 275.
      Letter to editor. Objects to the fiction that Morgan, Mellon,
      and Insull, Corp., have no interests in the coal mines in
      Harlan County, Kentucky. Dreiser had maintained that such
      big interests were operating in Kentucky, and he had been
      held up--in reviews of Tragic America--as being wrong. He
      was not wrong, as Rochester found in doing research for
      her book Harlan Miners Speak.

1329 ROCKWELL, Kenneth. "A Call on Dreiser." Dallas Daily Times
      Herald, November 23, 1947. Part 6, p. 5.

1330 RODMAN, Selden. "Common Sense Protests." Nation, 140
      (May 15, 1935), 572.
      Letter to editor. See under Trachtenberg, Joshua.

1331 ROLFE, Edwin. "Theodore Dreiser." Poetry, 68 (June, 1946),
      134-136.

1332 ROLO, Charles J. "Dreiser's America." Tomorrow, 7 (Febru-
      ary, 1948), 55-59.

1333 ROSE, Alan Henry. "Sin and the City: The Uses of Disorder
      in the Urban Novel." Centennial Review, 16 (1972), 203-
      220.
      Focuses on Dreiser's Sister Carrie and four other urban
      novels as the basis for a discussion that these novels mark
      the beginning of the collapse in the myth that the American
      city was the answer to the American dream of success: from
      1900 it became the symbol of Fall, defeat, and alienation.

1334 _____. "Dreiser's Satanic Mills: Religious Imagery in An
      American Tragedy." Dreiser Newsletter, 7 (Spring, 1976),
      5-8.

For the most part critics have either ignored or discussed in negative terms the influence of Dreiser's Catholic
upbringing upon his fiction. This article explores the Ly-
curgus period in Clyde's life and shows Dreiser uses of
vivid, almost medieval, images of hell and damnation.

1335 ROSENBERG, Bernard. "Mr. Trilling, Theodore Dreiser, and
      Life in the United States." Dissent, 2 (Spring, 1955), 171-
      178.

1336 ROSENBLATT, Paul. John Woolman: A Biography. New
      York: Twayne, 1969. "Woolman and Dreiser," pp. 122-125.
      In Woolman's impact upon men like Coleridge, Lamb, Chan-
      ning, and Emerson we have a touchstone for the quality of
      his achievement. It seems, however, that not until the twen-
      tieth century was Woolman's influence directly felt by a ma-
      jor writer--Theodore Dreiser. Without Dreiser's emerging
      consent to Quaker ideals, if not religion, The Bulwark (1946),
      his final novel, could not have been written. Woolman's
      Journal provided much of the inspiration for the book, per-
      haps its very conception.

1337 ROSENMAN, Mona Gail. "The Adamsean Prototype for the Anti-
      Hero in the Modern American Novel." Ph.D. diss., Kent
      State University, 1970. DA, 31 (1970), 4179A-4180A.
      In The Education of Henry Adams, Adams established a
      basic pattern for anti-heroic thought and behavior in the
      modern American novel. This dissertation studies novels
      by Sherwood Anderson, Dos Passos, Farrell, Hemingway,
      and An American Tragedy. The hypocrisy and immorality
      of society are revealed by the experiences of Clyde Griffiths,
      the victim. His treatment by the public and the injustice of
      his trial bear witness to the truth of Adams' 1869 statement
      that the moral law and the Constitution had both expired.

1338 _____. "An American Tragedy: Constitutional Violations."
      Dreiser Newsletter, 9 (Spring, 1978), 11-19.
      In a rather technical article Rosenman shows that Clyde's
      Fourteenth Amendment rights were violated, and that he was
      convicted of a capital crime on circumstantial evidence. Com-
      pares the fictional case of Clyde, the real case of Chester
      Gillette (who was also electrocuted), and the more recent
      murder trials of Dr. Sam Sheppard, who was defended by
      F. Lee Bailey and was acquitted of the murder of his wife.
      Concludes that Clyde would now also be acquitted.

1339 ROSENTHAL, T. G., ed. with Introduction. The Financier.
      London: Panther, 1968.

1340 _____, ed. with Introduction. The Titan. London: Pan-
      ther, 1968. Same as The Financier.

1341 _____, ed. with Introduction. <u>Jennie Gerhardt</u>. London: Panther, 1970.

1342 ROSS, Danforth. <u>The American Short Story</u>. Minneapolis: University of Minnesota Press, 1961. "The Lost Phoebe," and "Typhoon," pp. 28-29.

Dreiser believed that man's chemistry determines his actions and that a kind of social chemistry operates in society. In a story called "Typhoon" the human being to be examined is Ida Zobel, who is attractive but has been brought up by strict German parents. A young man conditioned by society to accept the double standard for men and women easily seduces her, then refuses to take responsibility when she becomes pregnant. She kills him, and she and her family are ruined. Ida never asks if she has done wrong. She is simply concerned with her predicament and is striving helplessly to get out of it.

In "The Lost Phoebe" a farm couple have achieved a kind of osmosis through years of living together. The wife dies and the old husband begins to suffer hallucination. He pursues his "lost Phoebe" over the countryside until he meets his death.

1343 ROSS, Woodburn O. "Concerning Dreiser's Mind." <u>American Literature</u>, 18 (November, 1946), 233-243.

Purpose of this article is to determine whether Dreiser, chief of the naturalists, was also a mystic. Continues with numerous examples of mysticism in Dreiser but concludes: "Dreiser should never be called a mystic. A mystic is one who places his faith in nonrational means of apprehending reality, who seeks through contemplation truth which is denied to the scientist. One is not a mystic who sings of the beauty and brevity and disillusionment of life. One must keep in mind the difference between a writer's exhibiting an understanding of a certain point of view and his adopting it himself."

1344 ROTHWEILER, Robert Liedel. "Ideology and Four Radical Novelists: The Response to Communism of Dreiser, Anderson, Dos Passos, and Farrell." Ph.D. diss., Washington University, 1960.

1345 ROTTENBERG, Abraham. "Dreiser's Chauvinism." <u>Nation</u>, 140 (May 15, 1935), 572.

Letter to editor. See under Trachtenberg, Joshua.

1346 ROULSTON, Robert. "The Libidinous Lobster: The Semi-Flaw in Dreiser's Superman." <u>Rendezvous</u>, 9 (Spring, 1974), 35-40.

1347 ROVIT, Earl. "Theodore Dreiser," in <u>20th-Century American</u>

Literature, edited with Introduction by Warren French. New York: St. Martin's Press, 1980. Pp. 175-179.

Book is in effect a dictionary (arranged alphabetically) of notable American authors of the twentieth century. Contained in each entry is a list of the author's publications, a list of bibliographies about the author, and a brief biographical profile of the author. Rovit concludes for Dreiser: "There is a sense in which his achievement may seem crude, but it required something stronger than gentility to clear a continent in which his successors could pursue their vision of truth unimpeded by the barriers of hypocrisy, reticence, and prudential caution. The momentum of history was in this direction, of course, but yet some of the richness and power of the modern American novel is due to Dreiser's sweeping redefinition of the novelist's task."

1348 RUBIN, Louis D., Jr. and John Rees Moore, eds. *The Idea of an American Novel*. New York: Crowell, 1961. Dreiser, pp. 280-296.

Contains evaluations about Dreiser by Mencken, Benchley, Trilling, and Farrell, balanced pro and con. Also prints "The Moral Hypocrisy of the American Mind," from *A Book About Myself*, by Dreiser.

1349 _____. "Dreiser and *Meet Me in the Green Glen*: A Vintage Year for Robert Penn Warren." *Hollins Critic*, 9 (April, 1972), 1-12.

Is a tribute to Robert Penn Warren in the year of his publishing an important new novel and "a masterful critical study of an important novelist." In commenting on the Dreiser study, Rubin praises Warren for having "the breadth of imagination to recognize that his own conception of style isn't the only possible way of looking at the matter, and that style is not something that adorns a work of literature, but the medium in which the work of literature exists. Warren discusses each of the novels, but it is worth noting that it is about *An American Tragedy* and the Cowperwood novels that he gets the best effect.

1350 RUBINSTEIN, Annette. "A Pillar of Society." *New Masses*, 59 (April 30, 1946), 23-24.

A review of *The Bulwark*.

1351 RULAND, Richard. *The Rediscovery of American Literature: Premises of Critical Taste, 1900-1940*. Cambridge, Mass.: Harvard University Press, 1967. "Exemplum: The Sherman-Mencken Debate," pp. 137-165.

Reviews the Dreiser criticism of these two and shows that it was not so much Dreiser that interested either critic, but an irreconcilable point of view and the novelist served their purposes. The debate eventually ended in a kind of recon-

ciliation due mainly to the logical fruition of views that were
developing from the earliest days of Sherman's career, but
also due to the across-the-board triumph of Mencken's literary position and his consequent lack of interest in extending
the exchange.

1352 RUNYON, Damon. "Runyon Tells of Changing Broadway."
      New York American, October 25, 1920. P. 14.

1353 _____. "Dreiser's Other Tragedy." Modern Fiction Studies,
      23 (Fall, 1977), 449-456.
      Article is based upon an analysis of The Hand of the Pot-
      ter: A Tragedy in Four Acts. This play has as its subject
      a young man who sexually molests and then kills an eleven-
      year-old girl, and finally kills himself. This play, like An
      American Novel, was based upon actual newspaper accounts
      of a similar crime, but the play is not simply a documentary
      account. Dreiser has structured his characters and incidents
      to emphasize the forces and the society which led to such an
      atrocity in crime and its subsequent results in the suicide
      of the retarded main character.

1354 RUSCH, Frederic E. Has compiled and edited "A Dreiser Check-
      list," for the following years: 1970, 1971, (Parts I and II),
      1972, 1973, 1974, 1975, 1976, 1977, 1978, 1979, 1980, 1981,
      1982. Each bibliography is divided into several sections:
      New editions, translations, etc.; Dreiser studies and studies
      that include Dreiser; Reprints of earlier Dreiser studies; and
      Abstracts of dissertations on and including Dreiser.
      The bibliographies have appeared in the following issues
      of The Dreiser Newsletter:

      1970--3 (Spring, 1972), 13-21.
      1971, Part I--3 (Fall, 1972), 12-19.
      1971, Part II--4 (Spring, 1973), 5-11.
      1972--4 (Fall, 1973), 12-23.
      1973--5 (Fall, 1974), 12-20.
      1974--6 (Fall, 1975), 17-24.
      1975--7 (Fall, 1976), 10-16.
      1976--8 (Fall, 1977), 9-18.
      1977--10 (Spring, 1979), 14-19.
      1978--10 (Fall, 1979), 17-20.
      1979--11 (Fall, 1980), 15-22.
      1980--12 (Fall, 1981), 17-19.
      1981--14 (Spring, 1983), 12-20.
      1982--15 (Fall, 1984), 18-24.

1355 SAALBACH, Robert Palmer. "The Philosophy of Theodore
      Dreiser." MA thesis, University of Chicago, 1939.

1356 _____. "Collected Poems": Theodore Dreiser, edited with
Introduction and Notes. Ph.D. diss., University of Washington, 1951. Published in item 1361.

1357 _____. "The Dreiser Centennial." Dreiser Newsletter 1
(Fall, 1970), 19.
Note announcing that the August 1970 workshop on Dreiser
is going forward and that plans for the Dreiser Centennial
celebration are shaping up. As editor of the Newsletter,
Saalbach makes an appeal for ideas and money.

1358 _____. "Note: Airmail Interview of Neda Westlake." Dreiser Newsletter, 3 (Fall, 1972), 6-11.
Recalls meeting Miss Westlake when he visited the Dreiser
collection to gather material for an edition of Dreiser's poems.
See Westlake, Neda M., for further material.

1359 _____. "Dreiser's Social Criticism." Dreiser Newsletter,
6 (Spring, 1975), 14-20.
Review of Mookerjee, Theodore Dreiser: His Thought and
Social Criticism. Calls it a book that should give pleasure
to all Dreiserians. It is a biography with emphasis on books
that concentrate on Dreiser's social commentary, Dreiser Looks
at Russia, Tragic America, and America Is Worth Saving.
Book is based largely on primary materials in the Dreiser
collections and is therefore very accurate.

1360 _____. "Dreiser and the Powys Family." Dreiser News-
letter, 6 (Fall, 1975), 10-16.
Begins with a quotation from the Introduction to Notes
on Life by John Cowper Powys, and continues by relating
Dreiser to other members of the family, and pointing out how
Dreiser felt an especial love for the family.

1361 _____, ed. with Introduction and Notes. Selected Poems
(from Moods) by Theodore Dreiser. New York: Exposition
Press, 1969. Contains 160 poems.
Not all of Dreiser's verse is of equal merit. His earliest
attempts at poetry, which go back as far as some unpublished verses written in 1895 are, for the most part, quite
conventional in thought and style and hardly worthy of no-
tice. Sometime between 1907 and 1910, he shifted from
rhymed verse to free verse in the manner of Walt Whitman.
Not until 1926, though, did any of these moods, as he called
them, appear in book form. Still, as late as 1935, when the
fourth edition of Dreiser's poems was being prepared (edited
by Sulamith Ish-Kishor), Dreiser felt that he had been misunderstood.

1362 SAIDLOWER, Sylvia. "Moral Relativism in American Fiction of
the Eighteen Nineties." Ph.D. diss., New York University,
1970. DA, 31 (1970), 6631A.

The writers of the nineties share a sense of moral paradox. In the process they use a range of organic experi-
mental techniques not explainable by the philosophy or style
of any given school. They are a generation cut short largely
by chance. But their decade marks no hiatus in the American mainstream: they are still moral fabulists. Their work
forms a bridge to the twentieth century. Uses Dreiser's
Sister Carrie and a score of other novels to illustrate the
thesis.

1363 SALPETER, Harry. "The Boswell of New York." Bookman,
     71 (March-August, 1930), 383.
     "For the first minute of my interview with Theodore Drei-
     ser he struck me as a bad-mannered, glowering Titan, but
     he gradually thawed out and during the interview folded and
     unfolded a handkerchief, a characteristic gesture of his by
     which some of his nervous energy seems to be absorbed.
     He is decidedly one of our heaviest intellectuals."

1364 SALZMAN, Jack. "Sister Carrie: A History of Dreiser's Novel."
     Ph.D. diss., New York University, 1966. DA, 27 (1967),
     783A.
     Believes that the story of Dreiser's attempt to have his
     first novel published has become somewhat distorted. This
     dissertation is based upon an attempt to present an accurate
     picture leading up to the publication and a subsequent history
     of the novel and also comments on the general trend of the
     reviews the novel got when it was published. Concludes
     that none of the real details were quite so bad as Dreiser
     was given to asserting.

1365 _____. "The Publication of Sister Carrie: Fact and Fic-
     tion." Library Chronicle, 33 (1967), 119-133.

1366 _____. "Dreiser and Ade: A Note on the Text of Sister
     Carrie." American Literature, 40 (January, 1969), 544-548.
     Based on the supposition that Dreiser had used part of
     George Ade's fable "The Two Mandolin Players and the Will-
     ing Performer" in one of the early chapters of Sister Carrie.
     In 1907 when the novel was re-issued, Dreiser re-wrote the
     offending lines, fitting the new ones into the place of the
     original lines. These lines, written to cover up the apparent
     plagiarism, have appeared in all subsequent editions of Sis-
     ter Carrie and mark the only significant alteration made in
     the published American text of Dreiser's first novel.

1367 _____. "The Critical Recognition of Sister Carrie: 1900-
     1907." Journal of American Studies, 3 (1969), 123-133.
     Reviews some of the early legends surrounding the first
     publication of Dreiser's novel and concludes--based on the
     sales records--that Carrie was neither suppressed nor with-
     drawn. Nor were the reviews as harsh as Dreiser and leg-

end would have it. According to the most recent research, the favorable reviews outnumbered the negative ones. The novel's history was one of slow acceptance, but it now ranks as one of the major American novels.

1368 _____. "Theodore Dreiser, 1871-1945." American Literary Realism, 2 (Summer, 1969), 132-138.
Good overall review of Dreiser criticism, beginning around 1915 and coming into the present. Also contains a short listing of primary and secondary bibliographies, editions and published manuscript material, manuscript collections, and a listing of recent important articles. Of particular interest is the conclusion in which "Areas Needing Further Attention" are enumerated.

1369 _____. "Dreiser Then and Now." Journal of Modern Literature, 1 (1971), 421-430.
Review-essay of four recent books on Dreiser: Kennell, Dreiser and the Soviet Union; Lehan, Dreiser: His World and His Novels; McAleer, Dreiser; Moers, Two Dreisers. Compares Dreiser criticism with that of some other authors and finds Dreiser somewhat behind the times.

1370 _____. "'I Find the Real American Tragedy,' by Theodore Dreiser." Resources for American Literary Study, 2 (Spring, 1972), 3-74. Reprinted from Mystery Magazine, 11 (1935).
This is a reprint of Dreiser's discussion of the murder of Freda McKechnie by Allen Edwards that appeared in the February-June 1935 numbers of Mystery Magazine. Salzman gives some background on Dreiser's interest in the case.

1371 _____. "The Curious History of Dreiser's The Bulwark." Proof, 3 (1973), 21-61.

1372 _____. "Criticism of Theodore Dreiser: A Selected Checklist." Modern Fiction Studies, 23 (Fall, 1977), 473-487.
Is relatively brief, but very well selected. Consists of a General section, and Studies of Individual Works of Fiction.

1373 _____, ed. with Introduction. Sister Carrie. New York: Johnson Reprint Publishers, 1969. Facsimile of 1901 Heinemann edition (London).

1374 _____, ed. with Introduction. Sister Carrie. Indianapolis: Bobbs-Merrill, 1970.

1375 _____, ed. with Introduction. The Merrill Studies in An American Tragedy. Columbus, Ohio: Charles E. Merrill, 1971.
Consists of some 100 pages of reprinted criticism with In-

troduction that gives a brief review of the background of
An American Tragedy. The following items are included:

"Dreiser," by Sherwood Anderson, pp. 2-4.
"Touching a Terrible Tragedy," by Clarence Darrow, pp.
5-9.
"Crime and Punishment," by Joseph Wood Krutch, pp. 10-
11.
"Dreiser in 840 Pages," by H. L. Mencken, pp. 12-16.
"Mr. Dreiser in Tragic Realism," by Stuart Sherman, pp.
17-25.
"The Scene of Violence: Dostoevsky and Dreiser," by Fred-
derick J. Hoffman, pp. 26-31.
"An American Tragedy," by Irving Howe, pp. 32-44.
"Dreiser and the Plotting of Inarticulate Experience," by
Julian Markels, pp. 45-55.
"Of Crime and Punishment," by F. O. Matthiessen, pp. 56-
72.
"Clyde Griffiths: 'The Mechanism Called Man.'" by Ellen
Moers, pp. 73-84.
"The Imagery of Dreiser's Novels," by William L. Phillips,
pp. 85-91.
"An American Tragedy," by Robert Shafer, pp. 92-98.
"An American Tragedy," by Robert Penn Warren, pp. 99-
111.

1376 _____, ed. with Introduction. Theodore Dreiser: The
Critical Reception. New York: David Lewis, 1972.
    Contains 738 pages with Index to names of Reviewers and
Critics. Is arranged chronologically, beginning with reviews
of Sister Carrie in 1900 and concluding with The Stoic in
1947. Lists 24 works by Dreiser with publication dates and
original publishers. Each section concludes with a listing of
a Checklist of additional reviews on the work. Authors of
these reviews are given when known. This work is superbly
edited and arranged to be the best possible scholarship of
its kind.

1377 _____, ed. with Preface. Modern Fiction Studies, 23 (Fall,
1977), 339-487, special Dreiser issue.
    Thinks the present issue says much about the state of
Dreiser criticism. Hopes that Dreiser will not become "an
industry," caught up in the publish or perish syndrome of
American universities.

1378 SALZMAN, Maurice. Plagiarism: The "Art" of Stealing Literary Material. Los Angeles: Parker, 1931. Dreiser, pp.
202-205.
    Is an analytical comparison of passages from Dreiser's
Dreiser Looks at Russia and The New Russia by Dorothy
Thompson. Dreiser claims that "both of us got material from

common sources.... We were in Russia together. I talked
to her about my travels and gave her lots of my material."
The plagiarism, if one calls it that, is not taken seriously.

1379 SAMPSON, Ashley. "Religion in Modern Literature." Contemporary Review, 147 (April, 1935), 462-470.

1380 SAMUELS, Charles Thomas. Death Was the Bridegroom. New
York: n.p., 1955. Dreiser, pp. 20-21.

1381 _____. "Mr. Trilling, Mr. Warren, and An American Tragedy." Yale Review, 53 (Summer, 1964), 629-640. Reprinted
in Lydenberg (1971), pp. 163-173; and in Pizer (1981), pp.
303-312.
        Trilling riddled the body (referring to An American Trag-
edy), but Matthiessen, turning it into a period piece, neatly
interred it. But in the autumn of 1962, The Yale Review
staged an exhumation by, of all people, Robert Penn Warren.
After the battles and the insults, after Trilling's brilliant
attack and Matthiessen's more damning defense, Mr. Warren
finds all Dreiser's well-known selling points. And because
Mr. Warren can write, they now appear more palatable than
anyone had thought them.

1382 _____. "The Irrepressible Dreiserian." New Republic,
161 (July 19, 1969), 25-26, 30-31.
        Review article of Ellen Moers' The Two Dreisers (1969).
Does not think the work brings any new insight or stimulat-
ing evaluation of Dreiser's novels. Says: "Although the
book took six years to research and write, its facility belies
such authorial exertion and seems to spare ours."

1383 SAPORTA, Marc. "Theodore Dreiser, 1871-1945," in Histoire
du Roman Americain. Paris: Seghers, 1970. Pp. 130-134.
In French.
        Consists of biographical detail with slight comment on
works.

1384 SASAKI, Midori. "The Theme of Seduction in the Novels of
Theodore Dreiser: The Fallen Woman No Longer Fallen."
Studies in Américan Literature (Japan), 12 (1976), 9-18.

1385 SASAKI, Takashi. "Dreiser's Antipodal Attitude toward the
American Dream of Success in the Progressive Period: Sister
Carrie and Jennie Gerhardt." Doshisha Literature (Japan),
29 (1979), 53-82.

1386 SATŌ, Shōhei. "The World of Theodore Dreiser." Gakuen,
No. 280 (April, 1963), 18-40. In Japanese; abstract in
English.

1387 SAWICKI, Robert M. "Theodore Dreiser and <u>An American</u>
      <u>Tragedy</u>: From the American Dream to the American Night-
      mare." MA thesis, Columbia University, 1965.

1388 SAYLER, Oliver M. "Theodore Dreiser, Hoosier, Serves as
      Preceptor for the Younger Artists and Writers of Modern
      America." <u>Topics</u> (Indianapolis), 1 (August 18, 1920), 5-6.

1389 SAYRE, Kathryn K. "The Themes of Dreiser." MA thesis,
      Columbia University, 1929.

1390 SCHARNHORST, Gary. "A Possible Source for <u>Sister Carrie</u>:
      Horatio Alger's <u>Helen Ford</u>." <u>Dreiser Newsletter</u>, 9 (Spring
      1978), 1-4.
          Alger's work was published in 1866 and at least two edi-
      tions of the novel would have been available to Dreiser as
      late as 1899. It is possible that Dreiser modeled one chapter
      in <u>Sister Carrie</u> upon a similar chapter in the Alger novel.
      Prints parallel passages to demonstrate the similarities in
      which both young heroines frantically search for a job in
      a New York theatre.

1391 SCHELLING, Felix Emmanuel. "The Greatest Play Since Shakes-
      peare," in <u>Appraisements and Asperities</u>. Philadelphia:
      Lippincott, 1922. Pp. 120-125.
          Refers to "Caius Gracchus," a play by Odin Gregory.
      Dreiser wrote an introduction for its publication, in which
      he called it "the greatest play since Shakespeare." Com-
      ments on Dreiser's ignorance and lack of taste, in apparently
      not recognizing the play for what it is--commonplace and
      trashy.

1392 SCHERMAN, David E., and Rosemarie Redlich. "Theodore
      Dreiser," in <u>Literary America</u>. New York: Dodd, 1952.
      Pp. 134-135.
          Consists of photographs of the American scene which re-
      late to well-known writers and their work. Good picture of
      Big Moose Lake in the Adirondacks, which was the scene of
      <u>An American Tragedy</u>. Comments that "after Dreiser had
      devoted considerable thought and several novels to the theme
      of the 'survival of the fittest'--studies of American business
      magnates--he came to believe that the struggle of the unfit,
      the semiconscious, and the helpless against the forces that
      shaped their destinies was more typical of American life than
      the occasional success of a genius or a tycoon."

1393 SCHIFFHORST, Gerald J. <u>Theodore Dreiser's An American</u>
      <u>Tragedy</u>. Woodbury, N.Y.: Barron's Educational Series,
      1965. Barron's Simplified Approach.
          Consists of 107 pages of a biographical sketch, a chapter

called "Naturalism and the Dreiserian Synthesis," "Dreiser and the Critics," and a detailed summary by books of An American Tragedy. Concludes with a brief and superficial reading list. May be an acceptable aid for undergraduate classes in American literature. The closing comment, after covering eleven years in the pitiful life of Clyde Griffiths, is worth noting: "Dreiser ends as he began--with a picture of futility, of an American family plagued by the inevitable. Now the scene is San Francisco, where 'a little band of five' is preaching at dusk on a summer night. Passersby feel sorry for the little boy. The poignancy of Clyde's destruction is intensified by the universal implications of this scene with its picture of eternal and unenlightened defeat. A generation has passed, and nothing has been learned. Incomprehensible forces have destroyed his mother's hopes, but her 'hard, fighting faith' lives on. The cycle has come full circle."

1394 SCHMIDBERGER, Loren Francis. "The Structure of the Novels of Theodore Dreiser." Ph.D. diss., Fordham University, 1965.

1395 SCHMIDT-VON BARDELEBEN, Renate. "Dreiser on the European Continent: Part I, Theodore Dreiser, The German Dreisers, and Germany." Dreiser Newsletter, 2 (Fall, 1971), 4-10.

Surveys the information concerning the German Dreisers, for whom Theodore had absolutely no use; it was the German in America, the immigrant, who is an important figure in his work, not the German in Germany. For Dreiser, Germany was an emotional experience, a set of values and grievances attached to the figure of his father. He rightly considered himself an American and generally held the same opinions on Germany and typical German characteristics as the average American.

1396 _____. "Dreiser on the European Continent: Part II, The Reception of Dreiser in Western Europe." Dreiser Newsletter, 3 (Spring, 1972), 1-8.

Surveys the reception of Dreiser in France, Italy, and Germany. Dreiser fared far better in France than elsewhere, and in Italy he was practically unknown until after World War II. Then the Italian press made up for all the years of neglect, and no American was more popular in translation and in scholarly publications. In Germany Dreiser has been generally ignored, and even after World War II, when his works were once again published, they were in old translations and thoroughly out of date.

1397 SCHNEIDER, Isidor. "Theodore Dreiser." Saturday Review of Literature, 10 (March 10, 1934), 533-535.

Discovers Dreiser when he was reading Twelve Men. Could
not really appreciate it, nor could he totally put it aside.
Led to further exploration of the writer, following his career
from the earliest time when Dreiser was considered little
more than a pornographer to the 1930's when he became
closely associated with the New Deal and the fight for the
common man's rights.

1398 _____. "Dreiser: A Man of Integrity." Book Find News,
      2 (March, 1946), 18-22.

1399 SCHNEIDER, Ralph Thomas. "Dreiser and the American Dream
      of Success: The Early Years." Ph.D. diss., Kansas State
      University, 1969. DA, 30 (1970), 5456A-5457A.
      The dream of material success was shared alike by Dreiser
      and many of the characters he created. Although the fact
      does not square well with his reputation as a determinist,
      Dreiser was an aspirant. His autobiographies and early mag-
      azine articles clearly indicate that his early years were times
      of privation and of a consequent desire for material success.
      But Dreiser's attitude underwent a major reversal. By the
      time he was forty, he had changed his mind about the value
      of material success: instead of regarding it as the best pos-
      sible goal in life, he came to see it as an illusion capable
      of misleading those unwary enough to pursue it.

1400 SCHNEIDER, Robert W. "Theodore Dreiser: The Cry of De-
      spair," in Five Novelists of the Progressive Era. New York:
      Columbia University Press, 1965. Pp. 153-204.
      Man, for Dreiser, was an insignificant atom in a vast cos-
      mos where neither he nor his society was considered to be
      important. There was a plan in nature, perhaps even a
      master planner, but this plan or planner took no notice of
      the hopes and aspirations of the individual, who was but a
      slave, a tool, to be utilized by nature, then cast aside.
      Even though man could not interfere with the plan of the
      universe, a plan which Dreiser conceived of as a tendency
      toward equilibrium, he could "rough hew" the edges of his
      own life. Thus man was endowed with a very limited free-
      dom to act, and his acts took place in a social context where
      he was hedged about with unnatural restrictions, yet forced
      to take part in an almost unmitigated battle for life.

1401 SCHOENBERG, Philip. "Making the Jews Responsible." Na-
      tion 140 (May 15, 1935), 572-573. See under Trachtenberg,
      Joshua.

1402 SCHORER, Mark. Sinclair Lewis: An American Life. New
      York: McGraw, Hill, 1961. Dreiser, pp. 277-278, 561-563,
      et passim. Contains many references to Dreiser; see Index.
      Recounts the more familiar stories relating Lewis and Drei-

ser, including the slapping incident (over Dorothy Thompson's book), and the Nobel award in which Lewis acknowledged that perhaps Dreiser should have won it. Not too well known, however, is the incident of 1944, in which year the American Academy presented a special award to a distinguished American novelist. Lewis, demonstrating his generosity and inability to nurse grudges, argued that the award must go to Dreiser, and proceeded to draw up the letter that offered it to him. Almost without change this letter went to Dreiser over the signature of Walter Damrosch, the president of the Academy.

1403 SCHRIFTGIESSER, Karl. "Boston Stays Pure." New Republic, 58 (May 8, 1929), 327-329.

Article is based on the incident in Boston in which the former vice-president of Boni and Liveright sold a copy of An American Tragedy to an undercover Boston police lieutenant during the famous battle of books in 1927, and was charged with selling a book containing obscene, indecent, and impure language and manifestly tending to corrupt the morals of youth. The incident resulted in a trial, the outcome of which was quite expected: the book could not be sold in Massachusetts.

1404 SCHWAB, Arnold T. James Gibbons Huneker: Critic of the Seven Arts. Stanford: Stanford University Press, 1963. Dreiser, pp. 199-201, discusses Jennie Gerhardt.

At the request of Dreiser, at that time a successful editor of pulp magazines and women's fashion journals, Huneker read, in the late spring of 1911, the manuscript of Jennie Gerhardt, and sent Dreiser a detailed criticism of it. Grateful for this "excellent criticism," Dreiser soon replied to Huneker that he had removed nearly all the objectionable repetitions and moralizings, and later that year sent him an inscribed copy of the book. Dreiser came to rank Huneker with Mencken and Charles B. DeCamp as superior critics, "as grim critically as any I know."

1405 SCHWARTZ, Jacob. "Dreiser (Theodore)," in 110 Obscure Points: The Bibliographies of 25 English and 21 American Authors. London: Ulysses Bookshop Press, 1931. Pp. 50-51.

Chronologically lists 18 items, primary works, with analytical descriptions.

1406 SCHYBERG, Frederick. Moderne Americansk: Litterature, 1900-1930. Copenhagen: Gyldendaske, 1930. Dreiser, pp. 38-45. In Danish; has not been translated.

1407 SCOTT, Kenneth W. "Did Dreiser Cut Up Jack Harkaway?" Markham Review, No. 2 (May, 1968), 1-4.

1408 SCULLY, Frank. "Theodore Dreiser," in Rogues' Gallery:
      Profiles of My Eminent Contemporaries. Hollywood: Murray,
      1943. Reprinted Freeport, N.Y.: Books for Libraries Press,
      1972. Pp. 108-124.
         In describing Dreiser he says: "Having been assigned by
      life to be its grief commissioner (without portfolio) it was
      only natural that I should have met Theodore Dreiser when
      he was on the downbeat, and in Hollywood. There is no
      place where the downbeat can be so melancholy or the up-
      beat so delightful, as in Hollywood. I first picked him up
      one Sunday morning. He was trying to crawl out of being
      himself, the Great American Tragedy--a best seller at fifty
      and the forgotten man at seventy. Nearing seventy at the
      time, he was nursed and attended by a wife about half his
      years. A huge lumbering man, with thick lips and irregular
      teeth, he had chewed his way from the wrong side of the
      street in Terre Haute to the top ant hill of American letters."

1409 SEARS, Donald A., and Margaret Bourland. "Journalism Makes
      the Style." Journalism Quarterly, 47 (Autumn, 1970), 504-
      509.
         Article examines eight novelists, four trained in journalism
      --Crane, Dreiser, Hemingway, John Hersey--and four non-
      journalistic--Henry James, Wharton, Wolfe, Capote--and
      scores them on "observable and countable features of basic
      journalistic style." Some of these features are length of
      sentences, use of active or passive voice, etc. Concludes
      that "each of the eight authors has a style of his own, and
      it is impossible to say which is better.... However, it is
      possible to say that elements of compressed syntax, clear
      and active word choice, and concrete objective detail in
      Crane, Dreiser, Hemingway, and Hersey are related to their
      common journalistic background with its emphasis on the
      elimination of semantic noise."

1410 SEAVER, Edwin. "Theodore Dreiser and the American Novel."
      New Masses, 1 (May, 1926), 24.

1411 _____. "American Writers and Kentucky." New Masses,
      7 (June, 1932), 9-10.

1412 SEBASTYEN, Karl. "Theodore Dreiser at Home." Living
      Age, 339 (December, 1930), 375-378.

1413 SEE, Fred G. "The Text as Mirror: Sister Carrie and the
      Lost Language of the Heart." Criticism, 20 (1978), 144-166.
         Long, detailed study of the language in Dreiser's novel,
      leading to the conclusion that "in Sister Carrie we see de-
      sire expressing itself in a language whose range is no more
      than the assembly of a sheerly material world.... Carrie's
      consciousness and the language of Dreiser's novel can mir-

ror nothing but the individual isolated amid fragments unrelated in any ontological sense."

1414 SELTZER, Leon F. "Sister Carrie and the Hidden Longing
      for Love: Sublimation or Subterfuge?" Twentieth-Century
      Literature, 22 (May, 1976), 192-209.

1415 SEQUEIRA, Isaac J. E. "A Note on the Influence of Dreiser's
      Tropistic Theory of Life on His Naturalistic Fiction." Os-
      mania Journal of English Studies, 8 (1971), 29-35.

1416 SERWER, Harry. "Racial Solidarity--A Myth." Nation, 140
      (May 15, 1935), 573. See under Trachtenberg, Joshua.

1417 SHAFER, Robert. "An American Tragedy: A Humanistic De-
      murrer," in Humanism and America: Essays on the Outlook
      of Modern Civilization, edited by Norman Foerster. New
      York: Farrar and Rinehart, 1930. Pp. 149-169. Reprinted
      in the following: Kazin and Shapiro (1955), pp. 113-126;
      Salzman (1971), pp. 92-98; and Pizer (1981), pp. 258-270.
      Reviews life and career of Dreiser, then comments on An
      American Tragedy, "by all odds the best of Dreiser's novels,
      though perhaps not the most interesting." All of his novels
      are tales of human irresponsibility, constructed to illustrate
      life's contradictions of the hollow conventions of society, and
      life's obedience to blind laws which make the individual's
      experience a chaos with an end unrelated to desert. This
      is the theme of An American Tragedy.

1418 _____, ed. American Literature. New York: Odyssey
      Press, 1926. Dreiser, pp. 497-498 et passim.
      Volume consists of selections with brief, biographical and
      critical introductions to each author. A Dreiser short story,
      "The Second Choice," from Free and Other Stories (1918)
      is printed in this collection. Of Dreiser Shafer says: "Some
      rebellious spirits praise him for the very ignorance and con-
      fusion which have led into a largely unconscious skepticism
      concerning all of the cohesive forces of society. Has been
      praised too for a tender comprehension of his characters
      which has enabled him to picture them with an altogether
      remarkable completeness and truthfulness, and for a quality
      of deep and sustained feeling which he seldom fails to com-
      municate to his readers despite all of his difficulties with
      his medium."

1419 SHANE, Marion L. "Spiritual Poverty in Selected Works of
      Four American Novelists: Twain, Crane, Fitzgerald, and
      Dreiser." Ph.D. diss., Syracuse University, 1953.

1420 SHAPIRO, Charles Katz. "The Role of Attitudes in the Novel."
      Folio, 18 (November, 1952), 15-20.

1421 _____. "Dreiser and the American Dream." MA thesis,
Indiana University, 1953.

1422 _____. "Jennie Gerhardt: The American Family and the
American Dream," in Twelve Original Essays on Great American Novels, edited by Charles Shapiro. Detroit: Wayne
State University Press, 1958. Pp. 177-195.
Each of Dreiser's novels illustrates a different aspect of
what he felt was a crucial misdirection of American energy.
In his first two books, Dreiser studies the failure of the
American as an individual and of Americans as a family group,
and his theme provides a valid and compassionate foundation
for the novels. He was writing out of the misery and passion of his own experience. Dreiser's works, while explor-
ing many sides of a problem, would adhere to a single point
of view, and the focus, often shifting, from book to book,
in various economic and philosophical directions, would origin-
ate in what he believed at the moment to be the deepest
roots of American unhappiness.

1423 _____. "A Critical Study of the Novels of Theodore Dreiser." Ph.D. diss., Indiana University, 1959. DA, 20 (1959),
1369-1370.
A careful study of Dreiser's novels shows that though he
was an uneven writer, Dreiser was conscious of his craftsmanship, and his lengthy fictional works were carefully
planned and carefully written. They were part of his lifelong inquiry, his continual grabbing at what he considered
to be the vital problems inherent in American life. Dreiser's novels all have an important design, significant because he was a keen, if often naive observer of the social
and political realities of his day.

1424 _____. Theodore Dreiser: Our Bitter Patriot, with Preface by Harry T. Moore. Carbondale: Southern Illinois
University Press, 1962. Reprinted, 1964.
Contains 123 pages with notes to chapters and a fair index. Contents in six chapters following the order of the
novels, with An American Tragedy and the Short Stories
arranged last. In the introduction he says: "Seeing America as a country emerging from its youth, he was concerned
about a culture which was creating within itself goals which
perverted the worthwhile institutions of the society and
robbed the individuals of the chance to live up to their full,
inherent potentialities. Each of the Dreiser novels illustrates
a different aspect of this crucial misdirection of America's
energies." Of An American Tragedy he says: "The story
of young Clyde Griffiths becomes the story of all America;
and beneath the story remains a steady concentrated focus
on a society which tantalizes but never produces."

1425 _____. Guide to Theodore Dreiser. Columbus, Ohio:
Charles E. Merrill, 1969. 44-page booklet.
Superficial, but well done for undergraduate students,
perhaps. Summarizes the major biographical influences, the
plots of the novels, their critical receptions, and other critical comments regarding Dreiser's philosophical outlook on the
individual oppressed by twentieth-century America.

1426 _____. "On Our Own: Trilling vs Dreiser," in Seasoned
Authors for a New Season: The Search for Standards in
Popular Writing, edited by Louis Filler. Bowling Green,
Ohio: Popular Press, 1980. Pp. 152-156.

1427 SHEEAN, Vincent. Dorothy and Red. Boston: Houghton
Mifflin, 1963. Dreiser, pp. 147-149 et passim.
Dorothy's articles from Russia had been published as a
book in October under the name of The New Russia (1928).
In November Dreiser published a book called Dreiser Looks
at Russia, covering much the same ground. That was not
surprising: they had both been there at the same moment,
using the same interpreters, official sources, newspapers,
etc. A resemblance might have been expected. But Dreiser's book contained whole sentences and even paragraphs
which were word for word the same as those written by
Dorothy. It seems likely that Dreiser's newspaper articles
were not enough to make up a whole book and that the young
man hired by the publisher to pad them out to book length
merely reached in all directions for anything he could find
on the subject. Dreiser's publisher may not have known.

1428 SHELTON, Frank Wilsey. "The Family in the Novels of Wharton, Faulkner, Cather, Lewis, and Dreiser." Ph.D. diss.,
University of North Carolina, 1971. DA, 32 (1972), 5244A.
The five novelists dealt with are treated thematically,
with the aim of discovering how they regard and employ the
institution of family in their fiction. Each author concentrates on a different segment of society, and taken together
they provide a wide diversity of backgrounds. Dreiser concentrates on city life, and in his work can be seen most
clearly the effect of the urban environment on family.

1429 SHERMAN, Stuart P. "The Barbaric Naturalism of Theodore
Dreiser." Nation, 101 (December 2, 1915), 648-650. Reprinted in the following: On Contemporary Literature (New
York: Holt, 1917. Pp. 85-101); Contemporary Essays, edited
by William Thomson Hastings (Boston: Houghton Mifflin,
1928. Pp. 348-363); Kazin and Shapiro (1955), pp. 71-80;
Lydenberg (1971), pp. 63-72; Pizer (1981), 4-12.
The impressive unity of Dreiser's novels is due to the fact
that they are all illustrations of a crude and naively simple
naturalistic philosophy. Each book with its bewildering mass

of detail is argument on behalf of a few brutal generaliza-
tions: (1) life is a jungle, (2) the earth is populated with
giants and pygmies; giants eat pygmies if they can, (3) man
is an animal, irrational and uncontrollable, (4) courtship is
in the jungle manner, (5) men are like tigers and lions.

1430 _____. "The National Genius." Atlantic Monthly, 127
(January, 1921), 1-11. Reprinted in Sherman, The Genius
of America: Studies in Behalf of the Younger Generation.
New York: Scribner's, 1923. Pp. 1-32 as "The Genius of
America."
     When Dreiser declares that God cares nothing for the Ten
Commandments or for the pure in heart, he really means
that inanimate nature cares nothing for them, and that the
animal kingdom and he and the heroes of his books follow
nature. But he denies a faith which in some fifty millions
of native Americans survives the decay of dogma, and somehow in attenuated form, keeps the country from going wholly
to the dogs. For, of course, if it were demonstrable that
God had abandoned a charge so important, plain men of sense
would quietly assume responsibility and carry on in His stead.

1431 _____. "Mr. Dreiser in Tragic Realism." New York Herald
Tribune, January 3, 1926. Section 6, pp. 1-3. Reprinted
in Sherman, The Main Stream. New York: Scribner's, 1927.
Pp. 134-144. Also reprinted in Salzman (1971), pp. 17-24.
     In its larger features the construction of An American
Tragedy is as solid as a bank building. It is very long,
to be sure, but there is little in it which is not functional,
not a part of Dreiser's ponderous design. Metaphorically
Sherman admits: "I was very nervous for fear the roof
would fall during a couple of sagging chapters early in the
second volume; but no, he slowly swung his heavy timbers
into place, restored his tension and maintained it to the end.
The structure of a novel he has mastered. It is the structure of the sentence which remains a mystery to him."

1432 _____. Life and Letters of Stuart P. Sherman, 2 vols.,
edited by Jacob Zeitlin and Homer Woodbridge. New York:
Farrar & Rinehart, 1929. Dreiser, Vols. I and II, p. 319
et passim.
     Compares some of Sherman's short criticism of Dreiser with
longer essay in which he does not recognize so many of Dreiser's virtues.

1433 SHERWOOD, Margaret. "Characters in Recent Fiction." Atlantic Monthly, 109 (May, 1912), 672-684.
     Comments on the characterization in about thirty novels,
recently published in 1911-1912. Most of these novels have
long ago passed from the scene, with the exception of one
by Hamlin Garland, Arnold Bennett, and Jennie Gerhardt

by Dreiser. Of this novel, Sherwood says: "In this long tale of the woman who is the victim of bitter poverty and of men's selfishness, there is a certain impression of reality, but it seems momentary, and one finishes the novel feeling that so many facts have very little meaning."

1434 SHULMAN, Irving. "A Study of the Juvenile Delinquent as Depicted in the Twentieth-Century American Novel to 1950." Ph.D. diss., University of California (Los Angeles), 1972. DA, 33 (1972), 329A-330A.
      Studies a wide variety of writers, Crane, Dreiser, Farrell, Richard Wright, Faulkner, Caldwell, and others. It is argued that the rise in juvenile delinquency is related to the failure of communities to provide for full social acceptance of all citizens, employment and other economic opportunities. The juvenile is seen as one who must throughout his lifetime be victimized by obvious and subtle discriminations.

1435 SIBLEY, W. G. "Along the Highway: Hardly a Masterpiece." Chicago Journal of Commerce, August 6, 1930. P. 14.

1436 SIEK, Edna H. "Social Darwinism in Theodore Dreiser's Novels." MA thesis, Sacramento State College, 1961.

1437 SIEVERS, Wieder David. "The Post-War Era Transition: Theodore Dreiser," in Freud on Broadway: A History of Psycho-Analysis and the American Dream. New York: Hermitage House, 1955. Pp. 66-68.
      The first American play with a thoroughly unembarrassed treatment of sex was Dreiser's The Hand of the Potter (1921). In a play that is still timely during our present wave of sex killings, Dreiser draws a picture of a sexual psychopath with authentic detail. Dreiser gave credit to Freud for influencing his philosophy of life: "A strong revealing light thrown on some of the darkest problems that haunted and troubled me and my work." Dreiser wrote no other full-length plays, and his loss to the theatre renders it all the poorer.

1438 SILET, Charles L. P. "Theodore Dreiser's Introduction to McTeague." Dreiser Newsletter, 8 (Spring, 1977), 15-17.
      In the spring of 1927 Dreiser was asked to write the introduction to McTeague for a Limited Edition of the work. Dreiser's introduction is a rambling, highly personal account of his debt to Norris, and the error of so little critical attention being paid to Norris. He bitterly attacks Crane whom he had come to despise, and makes a muddled attempt to show that Henry Blake Fuller and not Crane was the first pioneer realist in American fiction. Dreiser's dates are hopelessly wrong, but his argument has merit, and it seems appropriate that someone of Dreiser's stature should at least praise the work of the greatly neglected Henry Blake Fuller.

1439 SILLEN, Samuel. "Dreiser's J'Accuse." New Masses, 38 (January 28, 1941), 24-26.

1440 _____. "The Logic of My Life." Daily Worker, August 5, 1945. Magazine section, pp. 1, 4.

1441 _____. "His Art Led Him to Communism." Daily Worker, December 31, 1945. Magazine section, pp. 4, 9.

1442 _____. "Final Volume of Dreiser Trilogy to be Published This Fall." Daily Worker, August 1, 1947. Magazine section, p. 11.

1443 _____. "Dreiser Predicted Wall Street's Attack on America's Essential Freedoms." People's Daily World, 3 (January, 1952), no pagination.

1444 _____. "Notes on Dreiser." Masses and Mainstream, 8 (December, 1955), 12-19.

1445 SIMON, Jean. "La Génération de 1900: Theodore Dreiser," in Le Roman Américain au xxe Siecle. Paris: Bolvin, 1950. P. 19-37. In French; has not been translated.

1446 SIMPSON, Claude M., Jr. "Theodore Dreiser, Sister Carrie," in Wallace Stegner, editor. The American Novel from J. F. Cooper to William Faulkner. New York: Basic Books, 1965. Pp. 106-116.
      Sister Carrie is a historical landmark in American fiction. It represents a point of view of the late nineteenth century, but its publication was tinged with curious scandal. In one of its major plot movements it could be accounted a success story, but in this sense it appears to go counter to one of the great American myths: that hard work and perseverance, even more than natural talent and education will enable one to rise in the world. None of his books is more interesting. It announces most of his major themes; it exhibits his characteristic interest in detailed documentation, and portrays a world propelled by power and chance.

1447 _____. "Sister Carrie Reconsidered." Southwest Review, 44 (Winter, 1959), 44-53.
      The rebellious book of 1900 which was so long in finding its audience, has now become a classic. Its limitations are real, but Dreiser's power of drama and characterization is great enough to transcend the rhetorical flaws and ideological inconsistences of the novel. After several generations of the anti-heroic, as an antidote to saccharine wholesomeness, it has become a commonplace that the modern reader may find Dreiser lacking in boldness. If his characters are being tested, so is the society out of which they spring. In

these terms <u>Sister Carrie</u> continues to speak to us as a
perennially contemporary novel.

1448 _____, ed. with Introduction. <u>Sister Carrie</u>. Boston:
Houghton Mifflin, 1959. Riverside edition; same as 1959
article.

1449 SINCLAIR, Upton. <u>Money Writes</u>. New York: Albert and
Charles Boni, 1927. Chapter 25 on Dreiser, "An American
Victory," pp. 124-128.
  Theodore Dreiser is another man who has told us his own
story. In <u>A Book About Myself</u>, he makes himself known to
us on page one, and we observe that the child is father to
the man. Wandering about the streets of Chicago, a homeless, jobless, miserable youth, he reads a newspaper column
by Eugene Field. That was thirty-seven years ago, and
Dreiser is still interested in the local life of America; he is
interested in life here and now, no other time or place; he
watches street scenes, institutions, characters, functions,
and stores them up in the note-book of his memory, and when
he has a few million of them, he weaves them into a vast
pattern.

1450 _____. <u>The Cup of Fury</u>. Great Neck, N.Y.: Channel,
1956. Dreiser, pp. 116-123.
  In this evaluation, Sinclair says: "Dreiser was no reeling
drunkard, no down-and-out rot-gut drinker. My feeling is
that his perceptions were sometimes blurred by drink, often
confusing his noble heart. I recall that he came to visit
us one night, enough 'under the influence' to fall asleep in
his chair while he was talking and when people were talking
to him. At his request we had asked a prominent medium,
Arthur Ford, to demonstrate some aspects of psychic research. During the demonstration, Dreiser was asked to cor-
roborate several details about an old newspaper friend. He
seemed confused, unable to recollect important events of his
past life."

1451 _____, et al. "Theodore Dreiser: In Memoriam." <u>Book
Find News</u>, 2 (March, 1946), 8-9.

1452 SINGH, Brij Mohan. "Moods and Cadences: Dreiser's House
of Short Fiction." <u>Panjab University Research Bulletin</u>, 8
(April-October, 1977), 49-59.

1453 _____. "Dreiser's First Short Story: 'McEwen of the Shining Slave Makers': A Composite Study." <u>Panjab University
Research Bulletin</u>, 13 (April, 1982), 21-29.

1454 SINGLETON, M. K. <u>H. L. Mencken and the American Mercury
Adventure</u>. Durham, N.C.: Duke University Press, 1962.

1455 SIPPEL, Erich William. "Degeneration and Virtue in American
     Literature and Culture, 1871-1915." Ph.D. diss., Brown
     University, 1975. DA, 37 (1976), 317A.
        Part II discusses the problems created for American au-
     thors by the popular doctrine that success was the reward
     for the cultivation of virtuous character. American realists
     and naturalists, including Dreiser, developed strategies to
     criticize the doctrine of success. These strategies include
     portraying, not success and virtue, but failure and degener-
     ation; apotheosizing middle-class values; making the success-
     ful man an anarchic force in society; and regenerating the
     values and supposedly characterized pre-industrial society.

1456 SKARD, Sigmund. American Studies in Europe: Their History
     and Present Organization, 2 vols. Philadelphia: I and II,
     pp. 105 et passim. Books are organized under countries
     and universities. Authors, therefore, are scattered through-
     out.

1457 SMITH, Bernard. Forces in American Criticism. New York:
     Harcourt, Brace, 1939. Dreiser, pp. 159 et passim.
        Discusses Floyed Dell's review of The "Genius" and H. L.
     Mencken's "Theodore Dreiser" in A Book of Prefaces (1917).
     Realists have all sought to recreate the experiences of men
     living in a known or observable scene; and he is not a real-
     ist whose readers doubt that what he is depicting is con-
     sistent with their knowledge of the world they live in.

1458 SMITH, Carl S. "Dreiser's Trilogy of Desire: The Financier
     as Artist." The Canadian Review of American Studies, 7
     (Fall, 1976), 151-162.
        Most readers view Frank Cowperwood in the light of Dar-
     win, Spencer, and Nietzsche, as an illustration of Dreiser's
     belief that life is defined by a struggle among forces. While
     this approach is unquestionably valid, it does not pay suf-
     ficient attention to Dreiser's assertion that the financier is
     the ultimate creative artist of this period. The Trilogy is
     an important commentary on American culture. Dreiser's
     handling of his subject is at times contradictory and uncer-
     tain, and the books require close examination.

1459 SMITH, D. J. "The Glamor of the Glittering Rails." Midwest
     Quarterly, 11 (Spring, 1970), 311-326.
        A good analysis of the railroad in various authors, includ-
     ing Dreiser, and the uses to which it has been made. Con-
     cludes by saying: "It is in the mainstream of the American
     novel that the most telling vignettes of the railroad in Ameri-
     can life occur. There one finds the many things that the
     train meant to the people whose existence it affected: com-
     plex and dubious business dealings: anxious small-town
     people hurrying to the railway station; hot, dusty, noisy,

weary miles of travel; and for the lonely, the frustrated,
the thoughtful and romantic, the oppressed and short-changed
--for them, the long drifting call of the train whistle, and
the glamor of the glittering rails."

1460   SMITH, Edward B. "Judge Jones Exiles Some, Say Miners."
Knoxville News-Sentinel, November 7, 1931. Pp. 1, 10.

1461   _____. "Miners' Distress Seen by Writers." Knoxville
News-Sentinel, November 8, 1931. P. 6a.

1462   SMITH, Edward H. "Dreiser--After Twenty Years." Bookman, 53 (March, 1921), 27-34.
There is in Dreiser's questing still the human note of wish-
fulness. Consciously he probably does not hope to find, but
in his unconscious there labors still the pitiful deep hunger
of mankind for some satisfactory and impossible solution.
Perhaps this explains the much noted preoccupation with the
so-called unseen world, with semi-mystical subjects such as
underlie some of his minor work. Whether this is only a
mild concern of whether its hold upon the writer will aug-
ment with time, seems a matter of vital interest but one
which cannot now be discussed for lack of evidence.

1463   SMITH, Henry Nash. "The Search for a Capitalist Hero:
Businessmen in American Fiction," in The Business Establishment, edited by Earl F. Cheit. New York: Wiley, 1964.
Pp. 77-112.
Dreiser's trilogy about Frank Cowperwood contains by far
the most impressive portrait of a big businessman in American fiction. No later writer has brought to the subject anything like Dreiser's commitment, no one else has dealt with
it at such length or with such intensity. Yet in characteriz-
ing Cowperwood, Dreiser has in the main simply taken over
the familiar catalogue of the businessman's vices and presented them as virtues.

1464   SMITH, Lewis Worthington. "The Drift Toward Naturalism."
South Atlantic Quarterly, 22 (October, 1923), 355-369.
Realism is a literary method. The realist makes it his
business to tell the truth about life. The realist, however,
does not assume to believe that the truth must be pleasant,
that ugliness is not ugliness. In this respect his creed differs from that of naturalism. Realism is willing to remain
merely a literary method. Naturalism is a philosophy.

1465   _____, ed. Current Reviews. New York: Holt, 1926.
Dreiser, pp. 203-212, "An American Tragedy," reviewed
by Llewellyn Jones. Chicago Evening Post, January 22,
1926.

1466 SMITH, Martha Stribling. "A Study of the Realistic Treat-
      ment of Psychic Phenomena in Selected Fiction of Howells,
      Garland, James, Norris, and Dreiser." Ph.D. diss., Univer-
      sity of North Carolina (Chapel Hill), 1972. DA, 33 (1972),
      1743A-1744A.
        Purpose of dissertation is to examine the fictional treat-
      ment of psychic phenomena, mental experiences unaccounted
      for by contemporary knowledge. These five novelists offer
      a wide range of psychic phenomena, including ghosts, telep-
      athy, spiritualistic manifestations, and other mysterious
      events within realistic settings, leaving room for physicalistic
      interpretations as well as speculative ones. In four short
      stories, Dreiser contrasted an external perspective with the
      distorted inner reality of characters who feel the loneliness
      of grief or guilt. He also presented characters like Carrie
      Meeber, who live within the worlds of their own feelings
      where intuitions blend imperceptibly into desires and impres-
      sions.

1467 SMITH, Rebecca W. "Portrait of An American: The National
      Character in Fiction." Southwest Review, 21 (April, 1936),
      245-260.
        Article begins with the seventeenth century and surveys
      in a wide variety of novelists the belief that an American is
      a unique person, different from dwellers in other lands.
      Among those studied are James Fenimore Cooper, Mark Twain,
      Henry James, Howells, Dreiser, Thomas Wolfe. Of Dreiser
      the author says: "The most astounding of all our portraits
      of the American in any role whatever is Frank Cowperwood,
      who runs the gamut of money-making and sex. What is this
      man of the new, vast continent? He is what every American
      would wish to be--master of men and women and millions.
      The nation has never accepted Dreiser's portrait; yet, of-
      ficially rejected, it nevertheless hangs in the national gal-
      lery, shocking, irreverent, unforgettable."

1468 _____. "The Worker as Hero." American Bookman, 1 (Fall,
      1944), 35-42.

1469 SNELL, George. "Theodore Dreiser: Philosopher," in The
      Shapers of American Fiction, 1708-1947. New York: E. P.
      Dutton, 1947. Pp. 233-245.
        Perhaps we have never had a novelist who came nearer to
      Tolstoy, Fielding, and Balzac as the chronicler of Life. For
      him the novel was a vast crucible into which would be poured
      everything--his observation of manners, characterization of
      men and women, thoughts and issues of the day, his entire
      reading of the meaning of existence. The novel, in Drei-
      serian terms, was a carry-all, vast, sprawling, all-inclusive,
      to be written with sincerity, eschewing all tracks and con-
      trivance.

1470 SODERBERGH, P. A. "Theodore Dreiser in Pittsburgh, 1894."
      <u>Western Pennsylvania Historical Magazine</u>, 51 (July, 1968),
      229-242.

1471 SOLOMAN, Eric. "A Source for Fitzgerald's <u>The Great Gat-
      sby</u>." <u>Modern Language Notes</u>, 73 (March, 1958), 186-188.

1472 SOSKIN, William. "Reading and Writing." <u>New York Evening
      Post</u>, March 26, 1932. P. 7.

1473 SPANGLER, George M. "Suicide and Social Criticism: Durk-
      heim, Dreiser, Wharton, and London." <u>American Quarterly</u>,
      31 (Fall, 1979), 496-516.
          Article is an examination of <u>Suicide</u>, a book published in
      1897 by Emile Durkheim, a noted French sociologist, in re-
      lation to three important American novelists. Obviously dif-
      fering in method--the difference between statistical analysis
      and dramatized fictional case--all of them reached the same
      conclusion: modern society is a killer, the suicide its vic-
      tim. For these four writers self-destruction is one of the
      salient facts and the apt symbol of social conditions in West-
      ern Europe and the United States. Based more and more
      exclusively on the values of individualism, especially eco-
      nomic individualism, urban, industrial societies in their frag-
      mentation, their lack of true social coherence, have an ex-
      traordinary capacity to cause suicide.

1474 SPATZ, Jonas. "Dreiser's <u>Bulwark</u>: An Archaic Masterpiece,"
      in <u>The Forties: Fiction, Poetry, Drama</u>, edited by Warren
      French. Deland, Fla.; Everett-Edwards, 1969. Pp. 155-
      162.
          <u>The Bulwark</u> manages, despite its primitive style, to
      achieve an authenticity that transcends current conventions
      of language, characterization, and narrative technique. The
      novel was born long after its time, but it is not an anach-
      ronism. It is almost as if Dreiser, by-passed by the main-
      stream of modernism, was attempting to demonstrate what
      could be done not only with the assumptions of nineteenth-
      century fiction but also with the simplicities that have formed
      the basis of tragedy from the beginning.

1475 SPILLER, Robert E. "Dreiser as Master Craftsman." <u>Saturday
      Review of Literature</u>, 29 (March 23, 1946), 23.
          Review of <u>The Bulwark</u>, which Spiller calls "a major novel,
      a substantial piece of work, well conceived and carefully ex-
      ecuted, representing its author in his full creative power."
      If it may also be taken as a last will and testament, it pre-
      sents an interesting biographical problem, for here is an
      answer in faith to the spiritual doubt of his best work. Was
      this Dreiser's deathbed confession? Had the mysticism which
      always colored his dogged acceptance of the ugly with the

beautiful finally taken a form and a control in religious
awakening? His biographers must decide.

1476 _____. The Cycle of American Literature. New York:
Macmillan, 1955. "Second Renaissance: Dreiser and Frost,"
pp. 211-242. Reprinted New York: New American Library,
1957. Pp. 162-183. Also reprinted New York: The Free
Press, 1967. Pp. 158-180.
    In one sense, all that Dreiser wrote was a single long
autobiography. The struggles and conflicts of his parents,
his sisters, his brothers, and himself are told in tortuous
detail in a series of soul-searching narratives. Failure had
hung heavily over his father; the affectionate, animal-like
mother held her many children close to the uncertain home,
but even she could not prevent them from being too soon
forced out into the sea of American life. The two great
drives in all his stories, money and sex, were symbols of
successes or failures as he had known them.

1477 _____. "A Giant Still Asking to Be Accounted For." New
York Times Book Review, May 16, 1965. Pp. 4-5.

1478 _____. "The Alchemy of Literature," in The Third Dimension. New York: Macmillan, 1965. Pp. 153-171.
    The civilization of the United States in the twentieth cen-
tury presents a basic human situation in terms so new that
they require a completely new literary response. Dreiser
took a fresh look at life and said, "let's take a few simple
characters, people that we know, and present them logically
and honestly and let the story tell itself." Here was the
beginning of a new process of symbolization of actual life.
These characters were themselves, but they were generalized.
Each of them became an anybody. Because each of Dreiser's
characters has a particular and then a general meaning, they
are each a symbol of ideality as well as a semblance of reality.

1479 _____. "The Second Renaissance." Audio Tape. Great
American Writers, No. 4. Deland, Fla.: Everett/Edwards,
1970.

1480 _____. "Theodore Dreiser and the Quakers," in Spiller,
The Mirror of American Life: Essays and Reviews on American Literature, edited by Yukio Irie. Tokyo: Eichosha,
1971.

1481 _____, et al., eds. Literary History of the United States,
3 vols. New York: Macmillan, 1948. One volume edition
of Books I and II published in 1953. "Theodore Dreiser,"
by Robert E. Spiller (based, with permission, on an article
by James T. Farrell), Vol. 2, pp. 1197-1207. Bibliography
by Thomas H. Johnson, Vol. 3, pp. 474-477.

Dreiser has been upbraided because of his auctorial comments. The newness of his material and method seemed to him to need explanation, and the censorship and rejection of certain of his novels did little to convince him that such explanation was not necessary. He had no model upon which to shape his attack on the formal middle-class conventions of the times. There are many passages in these novels that rise to high levels of passionate writing. In Dreiser the subject matter is always more important than the expression. Because he reveals the very nerves of American society he has exerted a more profound, a more lasting influence than any other novelist on twentieth century realistic fiction in America.

1482 SPINDLER, Michael. "Youth, Class, and Consumerism in Dreiser's An American Tragedy." Journal of American Studies, 12 (1978), 63-79.

Begins with a slight review of several studies based on An American Tragedy, the novel which Sergei Eisenstein called "as broad and shoreless as the Hudson ... as immense as life itself." Says that most of these studies are imprecise in delineating Clyde's origins, focusing instead upon the character and his tragic fate. An analysis of Clyde's "social relations," particularly as elaborated in the closely integrated themes of youth, class, and consumerism, is a prerequisite to a more exact identification of Clyde's social representativeness.

1483 SPRAGUE, DeWitt C. "Some Picaresque Elements in the Novels of Theodore Dreiser." MA thesis, University of Iowa, 1929.

1484 SPRINGER, Anne Marie. "The American Novel in Germany; A Study of the Critical Reception of Eight American Novelists Between the Two Wars." Ph.D. diss., University of Pennsylvania, 1959. Published Hamburg, Germany: Cram & DeGruyter, 1960. Dreiser, pp. 60-74.

1485 SQUIRE, John Collings, ed. Contemporary American Authors. New York: Holt, 1928. Dreiser, by Milton Waldman, pp. 97-117.

1486 STAHL, Ben F., illustrator. Sister Carrie. Franklin Center, Pa.: Franklin Library, 1979.

1487 STALNAKER, John M., and Fred Eggan. "American Novelists Ranked: A Psychological Study." English Journal, 18 (April, 1929), 295-307.

Is an analysis of a survey made by the authors. They selected 72 "men and women who are primarily novelists of some importance and standing," and sent a request to 65 outstanding critics asking them to rank these novelists in an order

of their "general literary merit." They were asked to group
the 72 novelists into ten divisions, beginning with very best,
etc. Dreiser was ranked by 31 critics in Group 2. List
does not include classic American novelists, Melville, Hawthorne, etc. One critic replied to the authors: "The worst
thing the matter with American fiction is the blah that gets
printed about it, and here you are providing the blah-blah-
black sheep with valuable assistance in the guise of a scientific survey!"

1488 STARK, Harold, Preface. People You Know by Young Bos-
      well. New York: Boni and Liveright, 1924. "The Genius,"
      pp. 68-70.
           Is cast as an interview between Dreiser and "Young Bos-
      well," in which the author is asked questions about the cur-
      rent situation in literature. For example, when asked if any-
      thing significant will come out of the new burst of literary
      activity, Dreiser said: "I think the movement is too forced,
      too radical and too obvious an attempt to be different, but
      that radicalism will freshen the traditional methods of writing.
      If literature were not freshened periodically it would become
      mere repetition, like Chinese painting...."

1489 STARR, Alvin Jerome. "The Influences of Stephen Crane.
      Theodore Dreiser, and James T. Farrell on the Fiction of
      Richard Wright." Ph.D. diss., Kent State University, 1974.
      DA, 35 (1975), 6162A.
           Selected these three writers because their influences are
      pervasive throughout Wright's fiction and because the effect
      that each of these men had on Wright's literary career is
      clearly demonstrable. In the Dreiser chapter he studies
      the relationship between Native Son and An American Trag-
      edy in the areas of plot, theme, characterization, and style.

1490 STARRETT, Vincent. Born in a Bookshop: Chapters from
      the Chicago Renascence. Norman: University of Oklahoma
      Press, 1965. Dreiser, pp. 174 et passim.

1491 STEADMAN, R. W. "A Critique of Proletarian Literature."
      North American Review, 247 (Spring, 1939), 142-152.

1492 STEIN, Allen F. "Sister Carrie: A Possible Source for the
      Title." American Literary Realism, 7 (Spring, 1974), 173-
      174.
           Dreiser claimed he wrote down his title "at random," but
      his memory was not always too accurate when it came to choos-
      ing between the dull factual and the more dramatic. How-
      ever, a popular Civil War song entitled "Sister Carrie" may
      have unconsciously influenced him. Written in 1860 by A. P.
      Peck, it is an appeal to South Carolina not to secede, and
      warning of dire consequences if she does so. South Caro-

lina, called Carrie, is presented as a beautiful, wayward
daughter about to leave her parents' home. It is not known
whether Dreiser knew the song, but it was popular until the
1890's.

1493 STEINBRECHER, George, Jr. "Inaccurate Accounts of Sister
Carrie." American Literature, 23 (January, 1952), 490-493.
Undertakes to show that Robert Elias and F. O. Matthiessen have both made mistakes with regard to one of Dreiser's
sisters, who was the prototype of Carrie Meeber. In effect,
the error is that Dreiser's sister was far more forward and
wilful than the fictional character.

1494 _____. "Theodore Dreiser's Fictional Method in Sister Carrie
and Jennie Gerhardt." Ph.D. diss., University of Chicago,
1953.

1495 STENERSON, Douglas C. H. L. Mencken: Iconoclast from
Baltimore. Chicago: University of Chicago Press, 1971.
Dreiser, pp. 156-159 et passim.
On the whole Mencken remained faithful to his conviction
that Dreiser was "a great instinctive artist." In his letters
he tried to allay Dreiser's fears and urged him to complete
quickly whatever project he had underway. He assured Dreiser that he was winning acceptance as "the leading American
novelist." When Mencken read page proofs of A Traveler at
Forty, he called on Dreiser to follow it up at once with the
novels he was then working on. He said, "You ought to
have seven or eight volumes on the shelves instead of only
three. Once you get them there, you will be discussed
more, and also read more."

1496 STEPANCHEV, Stephen. "Dreiser Among the Critics: A Study
of American Reactions to the Work of a Literary Naturalist,
1900-1949." Ph.D. diss., New York University, 1950.
Published in Abstract: Dreiser Among the Critics. New
York: New York University Press, 1950. Reprinted Folcroft, Pa.: Folcroft Library Editions, 1972. It is the dissertation to present the results of research into the making
of Theodore Dreiser's literary reputation in the United States
during 1900-1949. The critical reception was highly contro-
versial, but no one has attempted to determine what issues
were raised, who the principals in the battle were, and what
trends in Dreiser's reputation became evident in the course
of the decades.

1497 STEPHENS, Gary. "Haunted Americans: The Endurance of
American Realism." Partisan Review, 44 (1977), 71-84.

1498 STESSIN, Lawrence. "The Businessman in Fiction." Literary
Review, 12 (Spring, 1969), 281-289.

Begins with novels by the likes of Dickens and Thackeray, progresses to Galsworthy--in The Forsythe Saga--William Dean Howells, Mark Twain, Frank Norris and finally to Dreiser who presents the "tooth and claw" theme in his Cowperwood trilogy. After Dreiser such writers as Marquand were anticlimactic.

1499 STEVENS, Bennett. "The Gnats and Dreiser." New Masses, 7 (May, 1932), 24.
Review of Tragic America, which he does not regard as an "effective book." The facetious banter which he interjects in an effort to popularize his subject, and his awkward style, obscure the significant material which the book contains. In conclusion, however, Dreiser offers a challenge to American artists and intellectuals awakened politically by the crisis to declare themselves on the side of the revolutionary workers in the fierce struggles that are taking place and in the yet more bitter ones that loom ahead.

1500 STEWART, Randall. "Dreiser and the Naturalistic Heresy." Virginia Quarterly Review, 34 (Winter, 1958), 100-116.
Dreiser, perhaps more than any other American writer of stature, came nearer to going the whole way into naturalism, and An American Tragedy best exemplifies this statement. Naturalism has now been replaced by a kind of neo-orthodoxy, thanks to the literary leadership of the South. For in the South, where the naturalistic idea never took hold, the doctrine of Original Sin was never lost sight of.

1501 _____. American Literature and Christian Doctrine. Baton Rouge: Louisiana State University Press, 1958. Dreiser, pp. 113-120. Essentially the same as article listed above.

1502 _____. "Moral Crisis as Structural Principle in Fiction: A Few American Examples." Christian Scholar, 42 (December, 1959), 284-289. Reprinted in Stewart, Regionalism and Beyond: Essays of Randall Stewart, edited by George Core. Nashville, Tenn.: Vanderbilt University Press, 1968. Pp. 185-193.
When we come to our fifth illustration, Sister Carrie, we are confronted by the question, How does a writer fare when there is no moral crisis at all? For by the tenets of naturalism, man is not a moral agent and so cannot experience a moral crisis. Dreiser is in short an amoralist. However, there are three places in the story at any one of which we should have had a quite satisfactory moral crisis if the story had been written by a moralist: where Carrie goes to live with Drouet, where Carrie allows herself to be abducted by Hurstwood, and where Carrie deserts Hurstwood. One can hardly say where Carrie "decides" because the word implies moral choice, and Carrie makes no decisions, no moral choices.

She is carried along by circumstances, and the author is
at great pains to slide over these rough places, to smooth
them out, to remove any possible feeling of crisis.

1503 STODDARD, Donald R. "Mencken and Dreiser: An Exchange
of Roles." Library Chronicle, 32 (Winter, 1966), 117-136.

1504 STOKES, Peter B. "Technique and Temperament in Dreiser's
Sister Carrie." MA thesis, Toronto University, 1964.

1505 STONE, Edward, ed. What Was Naturalism? Materials for an
Answer. New York: Appleton-Century-Crofts, 1959.
In four parts, a collection designed especially for college
students. Part I: excerpts from Darwin, Spencer, Taine,
Zola, Schopenhauer, etc. Theories and commentary. Part
II: excerpts from authors such as Melville, Garland, Crane,
London, Norris, and Dreiser (Sister Carrie, The Financier,
The Hand of the Potter, "Sanctuary" from Chains). Parts
III and IV: Aids and topics for student papers. Concludes
with a short bibliography on naturalism, with references to
Dreiser.

1506 STONE, William B., and Philip L. Gerber, comment and reply.
"Dreiser and C. T. Yerkes." PMLA, 88 (October, 1973),
1188-1190.
Stone advances theory that Cowperwood's career can be
traced in terms of his relationships with women: this man
of affairs is by no means as competent in love as he is in
business, and his "womanizing" is clearly his tragic flaw.
Gerber replies that he thinks Stone is mistaken in making
Cowperwood's need for women responsible for his series of
falls, even the one after his death when his fortune and materials are dissipated and dispersed.

1507 STOREY, Barron, edited with illustrations. The Best Short
Stories of Theodore Dreiser. Franklin Center, Pa.: Franklin Library, 1980.

1508 STORY, Suzanne. "Human Action and Responsibility in Theodore Dreiser's An American Tragedy and Richard Wright's
Native Son." MA thesis, University of Texas, 1965.

1509 STOUT, Rebecca A. "The City as Setting in Theodore Dreiser's Jennie Gerhardt: The Role of the City in the Naturalistic Tradition." MA thesis, University of North Carolina,
1966.

1510 STOVALL, Floyd. "From Idealism to Naturalism," in American
Idealism. Norman: University of Oklahoma Press, 1943.
Pp. 131-136.
In the materialism of Dreiser, American thought as expressed

in literature reached the final point in that decline from
idealism. The idealism of Emerson and the materialism of
Dreiser are at opposite poles of American philosophy. Many
factors combined to produce this change, the most powerful
being the advance of science. Science made the machine,
which enslaves the body of man by eliminating physical
strength as a power in human affairs; and science produced
the philosophy of scientific determinism, which enslaves the
mind of man by rendering impotent the individual will.

1511 STRAUMANN, Heinrich. American Literature in the Twentieth
      Century. London: Hutchinson, 1951. Reprinted New York:
      Harper and Row, 1965. Dreiser, pp. 32-34.
      Dreiser is nearer the tough-minded kind of determinist,
      and yet--as always with a great writer--it would be unfair
      to leave him with that label. It has often been noticed that
      there is a curious discrepancy between what he has to say
      and how he is actually saying it; in other words, we are
      profoundly impressed by the perspective of the ideas and
      events in his stories and the true ring of his statements,
      and at the same time vexed by his inability to attend to de-
      tails of expression and technique.

1512 STRAUSS, Harold. "Realism in the Proletarian Novel." Yale
      Review, 28 (December, 1938), 360-374.
      Thinks there is an alarming instability in literature of the
      day and that both realists and romanticists have refused to
      undertake a broad, dispassionate interpretation of human
      objectives, motives, and behavior. The younger realists
      have resorted to a diffuse, disordered, and despairing im-
      pressionism, and by implication have denied that the inter-
      pretation of human objectives falls within their duty. Does
      not relate Dreiser to this tradition, and says, "the young
      Dreiser, although troubled by inequities and injustices in
      the social organism, did not despair of seeing them abated,
      and of presenting life as a whole in an orderly and there-
      fore comprehensible pattern."

1513 STRONKS, James B. "Addenda to the Bibliographies of Stephen
      Crane, Dreiser, Frederic, Fuller, Garland...." Papers of
      the Bibliographic Society of America, 71 (1977), 362-368.

1514 _____. "Supplements to the Standard Bibliographies of
      Crane, Dreiser...." American Literary Realism, 11 (Spring,
      1978), 124-133.

1515 STRUNSKY, Simeon. "About Books, More or Less: Prose
      Poems." New York Times Book Review, June 27, 1926. P.
      4.

1516 _____. "About Books, More or Less: Said Without Flow-
      ers." New York Times Book Review, May 29, 1927. P. 4.

1517 _____. "About Books, More or Less: Paragraphs." New
      York Times Book Review, March 4, 1928. P. 4.

1518 STUART, Henry Longen. "Theodore Dreiser's A Traveler at
      Forty." Bookman, 38 (February, 1914), 673-674.
      Calls it "half-baked and served with a good deal of diluted
      language," but will no doubt contribute to the generally un-
      informed and inartistic state of our gulping-down reading
      public.

1519 _____. "Fifty 'Outstanding Novels' of the Last Six Months:
      Dreiser's Monumental An American Tragedy Leads the List."
      New York Times Book Review, June 27, 1926. Pp. 3, 24-
      25.

1520 _____. "As Usual, Mr. Dreiser Spares Us Nothing." New
      York Times Book Review, May 15, 1927. P. 2.
      Review of Chains. Says one is hardly well started on this
      series of fifteen "lesser novels and stories" before he is
      plunged into "a sea of slovenly writing." It is not likely
      that this book will unsettle the reputation of the author of
      An American Tragedy.

1521 SULLIVAN, Jeremiah J. "Conflict in the Modern American
      Novel." Ball State University Forum, 15 (Spring, 1974),
      28-36.

1522 SULLIVAN, William J. "Studies on James, Dreiser, and Faulk-
      ner." MA thesis, University of Utah, 1966.

1523 SUTTON, William A. The Road to Winesburg: A Mosaic of
      the Imaginative Life of Sherwood Anderson. Metuchen, N.J.:
      Scarecrow Press, 1972. Dreiser, pp. 294-297.
      Consists of several exchanges of letters between Anderson
      and Dreiser. There is no evidence that Anderson's admira-
      tion for Dreiser ever flagged. In 1926 he was to say in a
      casual newspaper interview: "He is really a distinguished
      literary figure of our time in America. At times he appears
      heavy and Germanic, but he has really a wonderful insight
      into life. I am a great admirer of Dreiser." And he wrote
      Dreiser late in his own life that his admiration for him had
      been growing ever "since I first picked up the first book"
      of his he had ever read. "I love your guts Teddy." As
      a postscript he added: "Anyway Teddy you are my Nobel
      Prize man."

1524 SWANBERG, W. A. "Mencken and Dreiser." Menckeniana,
      No. 15 (Fall, 1965), 6-8.

1525 _____. "Dreiser Among the Slicks." Horizon, 7 (Spring,
      1965), 54-61. Excerpt from Swanberg's biography of Drei-
      ser; see item below.

Article studies the period of Dreiser's life during which
he was "a most successful Philistine," the editor of one of
the most successful Butterick publications, The Delineator.
Was not the first job he had as editor, but it was the best
paid, and although he spent three years of mental terror in
the interest of honesty and "betterment," he finally left and
got on with the writing of "dour and realistic" novels.

1526 _____. Dreiser. New York: Scribner's, 1965. Reprinted
in paperback, New York: Bantam, 1967.
    Nearly 700 pages, in six books, with numerous chapters
in each. Concludes with notes on the chapters and an index.
For all its length and complexity, it is a simple chronological narrative covering Dreiser's life and the events of his
publications. The critics accepted the work for what the
author said it was: "intended solely as biography, not criticism. There have been many analyses of Dreiser's works,
but no attempt to study the whole man." Continues by saying: "There has been no one like him. He deserves study
simply as one of the most incredible of human beings, a man
whose enormous gifts warred endlessly with grievous flaws."
Alfred Kazin said of Swanberg's book: "The most valuable
single record of Dreiser's life.... Dreiser was an unbeliev-
ably and sometimes absurdly contradictory figure, but Mr.
Swanberg has shown us just what he was like."

1527 _____. "The Double Life of Theodore Dreiser." Critic,
29 (November-December, 1970), 20-27.
    Article explores Dreiser's lifelong grudge against God. At
68 when he moved to California his grudge against the creative force softened. He made what for him was a religious
avowal, when he wrote to Edgar Lee Masters, "God is slicker
than we are. He's always one leap ahead." In 1943, two
years before his death, the second part of his double life
seemed as complete as he could make it when he wrote an
essay, "My Creator." In it he celebrated the universal
beauty and all but gave over his suspicious thoughts of the
Almighty.

1528 _____. "Airmail Interview." Dreiser Newsletter, 1 (Spring,
1970), 2-6.
    Answers a dozen or so questions submitted by editors of
the magazine, principally on the subject of his book Dreiser
(1965). Does not know what present-day status of Dreiser
criticism is or level of acclaim of the day, but feels that his
position as a pioneer and pathfinder are secure.

1529 SWINNERTON, Frank. "A Tribute to Theodore Dreiser." New
York Times, December 15, 1926. P. 5.

1530 SZUBERLA, Guy Alan. "Urban Vistas and the Pastoral Garden:

Studies in the Literature and Architecture of Chicago
(1893-1909)." Ph.D. diss., University of Minnesota, 1972.
DA, 33 (1972), 288A.

Chicago, with its modern skyline and unlimited sprawl,
generated a new sense of urban space, and that perspective
induced a reinterpretation of the pastoral ideal. This dissertation seeks to outline and explain the process through
which the architects and the novelists--including Dreiser--
came to discover that America's pastoral ideal failed to account for the strange beauty of their city.

1531 _____. "Dreiser at the World's Fair: The City Without
Limits." Modern Fiction Studies, 23 (Fall, 1977), 369-379.

The urban landscape that Dreiser creates in Sister Carrie
symbolizes an apprehension of space and beauty. Through
his caracters' sense of scale, he expresses his vision of the
city as infinite. Chicago's skyscraper architecture and its
long, sweeping vistas provoked a feeling that might be called
the urban sublime. Dreiser derived much of his imagery
and many of his ideas from what he saw at the Columbia Exposition in Chicago, 1893. Thirty years later he proclaimed
that he saw "a lightness and an airiness wholly at war with
anything that this western world had as yet presented, which
caused me to be swept into a dream from which I did not recover for months."

1532 TAKAHASHI, Atsuko. "A Study of Theodore Dreiser's Thought."
Essays and Studies in British and American Literature (Tokyo Women's Christian College), 7 (Summer, 1959), 71-102.

1533 TALBOTT, Barbara Merlo. "The Material Ideal: Women as
Symbols of Success in Selected American Fiction." Ph.D.
diss., University of Wisconsin (Milwaukee), 1978. DA, 39
(1979), 5518A.

As the frontier receded in geographical fact--as genteel
values and great wealth replaced the rugged codes of an
earlier era--women succeeded the land as material tokens of
American idealism. The purpose of this dissertation is to
define the golden girl's mystique and to trace her evolution
in American fiction. Among women studied is Sondra Finchley of An American Tragedy.

1534 TARBUTTON, Jeanetta. "Theodore Dreiser: The Development of an American Naturalist." MA thesis, Stephen F.
Austin (Nacogdoches, Texas), 1953.

1535 TAVERNIER-COURBIN, Jacqueline. "Hurstwood Achieved:
A Study of Dreiser's Reluctant Art." Dreiser Newsletter, 9
(Fall, 1978), 1-16.

Reviews briefly several critical opinions of Hurstwood's
characterization, but does not agree that there is anything
accidental in his theft, that his downfall is personally ac-
countable, that he is a consistent and coherent character
and that the characterization of him is a brilliant moral and
psychological study.

1536 TAYLOR, Dwight. "The Life of the Party," in Joy Ride.
      New York: Putnam's, 1959. Pp. 221-233.
      Based on an account given by Burton Rascoe, in We Were
      Interrupted, of a party given by Theodore Dreiser, "Dreiser's
      Party a Flop." Says: "Dreiser's was a personality which
      was very hard to pin down. He was not particularly emo-
      tional or articulate in conversation, and one had to guess
      at a great deal which hung below the surface. But he was
      the kind of person whom most of us have met at one time
      or another of whom se say 'I don't know why I like him,
      but I do.'"

1537 TAYLOR, G. R. Stirling. "Theodore Dreiser." London Out-
      look, 58 (December 18, 1926), 607-608.

1538 _____. "The United States as Seen by an American Writer."
      Nineteenth Century, 100 (December, 1926), 803-815.

1539 TAYLOR, Gordon O. "The Voice of Want: Frank Norris and
      Theodore Dreiser," in The Passages of Thought: Psycho-
      logical Representation in the American Novel, 1870-1900.
      New York: Oxford University Press, 1969. Pp. 136-157.
      Discussion is based largely on Sister Carrie which "deals
      with romantic attachment of a sort as well as with sexual
      attraction, and as heroine Carrie is not completely without
      the vestiges of conventional roots, as her audible though
      ineffectual conscience suggests. In a sense much more im-
      portant to the novel's overall development, however, Carrie
      is portrayed as outside of the relationships on which the
      conventional love plot depends. She is 'alone' throughout,
      and those who find in her final solitude a significant element
      of moral retribution forget that she is alone in scene after
      scene, not only in the literal dramatic sense but in terms of
      Dreiser's definition of her essential identity as well."

1540 TAYLOR, Walter F. "The Maturity of Naturalism: Theodore
      Dreiser (1871--) and Sherwood Anderson (1876--)," in A
      History of American Letters. Boston: American Book, 1936.
      Pp. 365-380.
      Comments on the "success theme" in The Financier and
      The Titan. "It is the most adequate and convincing treat-
      ment in fiction of big business, and shows an understanding
      of a complicated social situation. It is a creation of a popu-
      lous world within the borders of his own fiction, where hun-

dreds of people live and struggle and enjoy and suffer together, with supreme lifelikeness, yet in accordance with a
disposing plan which causes the multitudinous, disparate
facts of actual life to take on a deeper significance."

1541 THOMAS, J. D. "The Natural Supernaturalism of Dreiser's
Novels." Rice Institute Pamphlets, 44 (April, 1957), 112-
125.

1542 _____. "The Supernatural Naturalism of Dreiser's Novels."
Rice Institute Pamphlets, 46 (April, 1959), 53-69.

1543 _____. "Three American Tragedies: Notes on the Responsibilities of Fiction." South Central Bulletin, 20 (Winter,
1960), 11-15.

1544 _____. "Epimetheus Bound: Theodore Dreiser and the
Novel of Thought." Southern Humanities Review, 3 (Fall,
1969), 346-357.

1545 THOMAS, Norman. "Dreiser as Economist." Nation, 134
(April 6, 1932), 402-403.
Review of Tragic America, which he says is Dreiser at
his worst. English teachers and economists alike can have
fun with this book, and even friendly critics will call attention to the author's glaring errors and to his extraordinary
inability to say anything. "In short, neither the student
nor the ordinary reader will turn to this book for an accurate
picture of America."

1546 THOMPSON, Alan Reynolds. "Farewell to Achilles." Bookman,
70 (January, 1930), 465-471.
The Iliad, singing the wrath of godlike Achilles, set a
literary fashion which endured all fortunes of time except
our own age of machines and test tubes. Today heroes are
so far out of fashion that their very existence is denied.
Our recent fiction has proved itself heir to all the ages in
producing such a novel as the so-called American Tragedy
in which the so-called hero is a young man of such character, or lack of it, that his final extinction in the electric
chair, despite its harrowing details, may fairly be considered
a matter rather for rejoicing than regret.

1547 _____. "Dawn: A Review." Bookman, 73 (March-August,
1931), 533-534.
Besides wordiness Dawn exhibits all the other familiar
faults of this extraordinary writer. Possesses rare psychological insight, exact powers of observation and great
human compassion, is at the same time grossly tasteless in
the use of words. The ugliness of his writing tends to loom
after a time like a monstrous symbol of the ugly civilization

which he chronicles. Only by resolutely ignoring the lin-
guistic atrocities can one get behind the expression of the
matter.

1548 _____. "The Cult of Cruelty." Bookman, 74 (January,
1932), 477-487.
America has had in Theodore Dreiser its own little Zola--
a rather sentimental and loquacious one, a Zola with a stut-
ter. And Dreiser, along with the so-called critical realists--
Mencken, Lewis, and the rest--prepared the soil for our
present crop of cruelty. We have caught up with Europe,
and will probably go beyond her. Continues with discussion
of Faulkner, Robinson Jeffers as examples of this "cult of
cruelty," in which every horrible thing imaginable is presented.

1549 THOMPSON, Harold W. Body, Boots, and Britches. Philadelphia: Lippincott, 1940. Reprinted Syracuse, N.Y.: Syracuse University Press, 1979. Contains "The Ballad of Grace
Brown and Chester Gillette," pp. 443-445.
Says in a head-note to the poem that this "is a more recent mountain-murder which Dreiser has celebrated in An
American Tragedy, the killing at Big Moose in the Adiron-
dacks of Grace Brown by Chester Gillette, a dazed young
man, who decided too late that he wished to marry another
girl. The following ballad about the case is a version sung
by a former woodsman at Gloversville."

1550 THORP, Willard. American Writing in the Twentieth Century.
Cambridge, Mass.: Harvard University Press, 1960. Dreiser, pp. 164-168.
As a thinker Dreiser was seldom to be found twice in the
same place. Now that the facts of his life are known we
begin to understand why he twisted and turned as he did,
and why shortly before he died he became a Communist, and
yet commented so oddly on what he had just done: "What
the world needs is more spiritual character. The true religion is in Matthew." Dreiser's greatest contribution was in
his discovery of the "walled city," the pinnacle of beauty
which most Americans can see into but cannot enter. Americans have falsely believed anyone can get to the stars if
only he struggles hard enough. Most of the Dreiser characters cannot get there, not because they are bad, but
simply because Nature forbids the entry.

1551 _____, ed. with Afterword. Sister Carrie. New York:
New American Library, 1961. Pp. 467-475.

1552 TIPPETTS, Sally L. "The Theatre in Dreiser's Sister Carrie."
Notes and Queries, n.s., 13 (March, 1966), 99-100.
Dreiser's selections give a representative picture of the

melodramatic theatre fare of the day, and provide realistic
detail as well as a suitable background for Carrie's career.

1553 TITTLE, Walter. "Glimpses of Interesting Americans." Century, 110 (August, 1925), 441-447.

1554 TJADER, Marguerite. "Dreiser's Last Year ... The Bulwark
in the Making." Book Find News, 2 (March, 1946), 6-7, 20.

1555 _____. "Theodore Dreiser: World Spirit." Free World, 11
(April, 1946), 56-57.

1556 _____. "Dreiser's Last Visit to New York." Twice-a-Year,
14 (Fall, 1946), 217-228.

1557 _____. Theodore Dreiser: A New Dimension. Norwalk,
Conn.: Silvermine Publishers, 1965.
      Contains 227 pages with no Index. In two parts, with
twelve chapters: encounter with Dreiser in N. Y., 1928-
1929; fighter for human equities, 1933-1934; Dreiser's last
visit to New York, 1944 ... etc. Part II, the closing years,
ends with death and funeral. Is not a critical study of
works; is personal appreciation, mostly in contrast to the
usual concept of Dreiser as a naturalistic novelist.

1558 _____. "Airmail Interview." Dreiser Newsletter, 2 (Fall,
1971), 11-17.
      Answers a number of questions, principally based upon
her firsthand knowledge of Dreiser, for whom she worked
as secretary many years during the author's residence in
Hollywood. Also includes a number of questions on her forth-
coming Notes on Life, which she feels will contribute to a
better understanding of Dreiser, who was finally one of the
most complex individuals who ever lived.

1559 _____. "John Cowper Powys and Theodore Dreiser: A
Friendship." The Powys Review, 2 (Winter-Spring, 1979-
1980), 16-23. Reprinted from August 31, 1946.

1560 _____. "Dreiser's Investigation of Nature." Dreiser Newsletter, 11 (Fall, 1980), 1-9.
      Is based upon a discussion of Dreiser's general interest
in science, and how he collected notes and fragments all his
life for what he hoped would become a definitive statement
of his philosophy. He did not achieve his goal. Notes on
Life (described above) is but a fraction of the material available on the subject of Dreiser's interest in science, nature,
which for him were the same.

1561 _____, and John J. McAleer, eds., with Introduction by
John Cowper Powys. Notes on Life. University: University of Alabama Press, 1974.

Consists of 350 pages, with notes but no index. He did
not complete this project, yet he poured so much time and
energy into its preparation that even some of the shorter
essays and fragments are rich in insights and powerful
Dreiser language. Many of the essays can well stand by
themselves. The editors have made a "reader's selection,"
using the longer pieces, excluding only the few already published. The shorter essays were chosen as the most appropriate or colorful to illustrate the chapter topics.

1562 TORRENTS, Olivella. "The Theme of Success in American
Fiction from 1900-1941, with Special Reference to Dreiser,
Lewis, Fitzgerald, and Dos Passos." MA thesis, King's Col-
lege, 1966.

1563 TORWILL, Herbert W. "London Discusses Mr. Dreiser." New
York Times Book Review, January 9, 1927. P. 8.

1564 TOTH, Emily. "Timely and Timeless: The Treatment of Time
in The Awakening (Kate Chopin) and Sister Carrie." Southern Studies: An Interdisciplinary Journal, 16 (Fall, 1977),
271-276.

1565 TOWNE, Charles Hanson. "Some Magnificent Failures." Literary Digest International Book Review, 1 (February, 1923),
12-13, 68.

1566 _____. "Behind the Scenes with Author and Editor." Literary Digest International Book Review, 4 (July, 1926), 15-
28. Reprinted in Towne, Adventures in Editing. New York:
D. Appleton, 1926. Pp. 121-153.
    "Always catholic in his tastes, Dreiser eagerly hailed the
new author, and was never too busy to talk with one who
dropped in. He was patiently sympathetic with beginners.
He had known poverty and hunger, of which he has told in
one of his volumes; and he had a supreme pity for the poor.
I have never known anyone with a more consuming curiosity
about life. And there was an undercurrent of sadness in
the man, though never any bitterness. He hated pretense;
he loved intellectual integrity. And he could spot either at
once."

1567 _____. "A Number of Things." New York American, January 11, 1932.
    Review of Tragic America, which he calls interesting, al-
though not persuasive. Dreiser has never been one to shirk
a huge task, and he has certainly set himself one in this
book. He has roamed about the country, sympathetic toward
the under dog, fearless in his criticism of systems which
crush the poor, eloquent in his righteous wrath. He hopes
for a better day when there will be a state controlled by and
giving honor and recognition to those most deserving it.

1568 TOWNSEND, Barbara Ann. "Superstitious Beliefs of Theodore
      Dreiser." Ph.D. diss., Ball State University, 1972. DA,
      33 (1973), 6377A.
          This dissertation deals with the part of Dreiser's belief
      which was not disciplined by science, charms, omens, pre-
      monitions, fortune-telling, astrology, prophetic dreams, and
      spiritualism. Three major aspects of superstition in Drei-
      ser's life and works--luck, foreknowledge, and spirits--are
      covered. His investigation of religion is discussed only
      when it is relevant to the superstitions beliefs presented,
      and his pseudo-scientific beliefs are not covered.

1569 TOWNSEND, Dabney. "Review of Free Will and Determinism,
      by Perry D. Westbrook." American Literary Realism, 13
      (1980), 154-155.

1570 TRACHTENBERG, Alan; Peter Neill; and Peter C. Bunnell;
      eds. The City: American Experience. New York: Oxford
      University Press, 1971. Prints "The Magnet Attracting: A
      Waif Amid Forces," pp. 126-132. Chapter 1, Sister Carrie.

1571 TRACHTENBERG, Joshua, et al. "Letters About Dreiser."
      Nation, 140 (May 15, 1935), 572-573.
          Contains the following: "Anti-Semites Both!" by Trachten-
      berg; "Dreiser and Haman," by Louis I. Newman; "Common
      Sense Protests," by Selden Rodmann; "Dreiser's Chauvinism,"
      by Abraham Rottenberg; "The Logical Solution," by Leonard
      D. Weil; "Making the Jews Responsible," by Philip Schoen-
      berg; and "Racial Solidarity--a Myth," by Harry Serwer.
          All of these letters constitute a cross-section discussion
      of Dreiser and his attitudes and ideas towards the Jews.

1572 TRENT, William P., et al., eds. Cambridge History of Ameri-
      can Literature, 3 vols. New York: Macmillan, 1944. Drei-
      ser, Vol. 3, p. 298.
          The little theatre has encouraged the one-act play and
      Theodore Dreiser with his Plays Natural and Supernatural
      is a surprising example.

1573 TRILLING, Lionel. "Dreiser and the Liberal Mind." Nation,
      162 (April 20, 1946), 466, 468-472. Combined with an arti-
      cle "Reality in America" (Partisan Review , January-Febru-
      ary, 1940), and reprinted as "Reality in America," in Trill-
      ing's The Liberal Imagination: Essays on Literature and So-
      ciety. New York: Viking, 1950. Pp. 3-21. Book reprinted
      in paperback, Garden City, N.Y.: Doubleday Anchor, 1954.
      Pp. 15-31. Article reprinted several times as in the follow-
      ing: Literary Opinion in America, edited by Morton Zabel
      (New York: Harper, 1951. Pp. 18-30); Kazin and Shapiro
      (1955), pp. 132-145; Lydenberg (1971), pp. 87-95; Pizer
      (1981), pp. 38-46.

Dreiser, of course, was firmer than the intellectual culture
that accepted him. He meant his ideas, at least as far as
a man can mean ideas who is incapable of following them to
their consequences. But we, when it came to his ideas,
talked about his great brooding pity and shrugged the ideas
off. Whether or not Dreiser was following the logic of his
own life, he was certainly following the logic of the liberal
criticism that accepted him so undiscriminatingly as one of
the great, significant expressions of its spirit. This is the
liberal criticism, in the direct line of Parrington, which es-
tablishes the social responsibility of the writer and then goes
on to say that, apart from the duty of resembling reality
as much as possible, he is not really responsible for anything, not even for his ideas.

1574   _____. "Dreiser and the Liberal Mind." Nation, 157 (April
            20, 1946), 466 et passim.
            Review of The Bulwark, of which he says it is a simple
            didactic story recommending a simple Christian belief, the
            virtues of self-abnegation and self-control, of belief in and
            submission to the purposes of higher powers, those "super-
            ior forces that bring it all about."

1575   _____. "Dreiser, Anderson, Lewis, and the Riddle of So-
            ciety." Reporter, 5 (November 13, 1951), 37-40.
            Calls them "three lonely men," and yet all were consciously
            and specifically American; all addressed themselves to the
            problems--or rather the problem--of American society, which
            they agreed in understanding as the securing of freedom for
            the individual personality. And yet as one looks now at
            their careers, it seems that society is the last thing in the
            world they really interested in, and that the traditional
            meaning of the world "personality" was the last thing they
            could conceive.

1576 TULEVECH, Michael C. "Dreiser's The Bulwark." MA thesis,
            Columbia University, 1952.

1577 UNTERMEYER, Louis. "In the Manner of Thomas Hardy, James
            Oppenheim, Arnold Bennett, and Theodore Dreiser." Vanity
            Fair, 2 (April, 1914), 33.
            Parody.

1578   _____. "Theodore Dreiser," in The Makers of the Modern
            World. New York: Simon and Schuster, 1955. Pp. 434-
            443.
            He added something rough-hewn and ungainly but massive
            to literature. It was said that he had no talent but a great
            deal of genius. The lack of talent made him vulnerable; but

although many of his successors wrote with far more _finesse_ than Dreiser ever achieved, it was his desperate earnestness and lifelong war with timidity and prudery that won them the prerogative to write honestly and without fear.

1579 VANCE, William L. "Dreiserian Tragedy." Studies in the Novel, 4 (Spring, 1972), 39-51.

Tragedies are concerned with the causes of suffering, suffering greater than that reconcilable with man's ideas of justice. Man incurs guilt when suffering ensues from actions he deliberately chose, when he is himself a cause. Yet the context of every choice is a webbed mat of chance and necessity beyond knowledge and control. The complexity of tragic causation--free will, chance, and necessity--is fully recognized in the novels of Theodore Dreiser. The valuable aspect of Dreiser's tragic awareness is contained in the design of the action and in the tone maintained in tracing it. The vital tragic awareness is in the author's conception of the whole and in the relation of the parts.

1580 VAN DOREN, Carl. "Contemporary American Novelists: Theodore Dreiser." Nation, 112 (March 16, 1921), 400-401. Reprinted in Van Doren, Contemporary American Novelists, 1900-1920. New York: Macmillan, 1923. Reprinted 1928. Pp. 74-83.

He gains, on the whole, as much as he loses by the magnitude of his cosmic philosophizing. These puny souls over which he broods, with so little dignity in themselves, take on a dignity from his contemplation of them. Small as they are, he has come to them from long flights, and has brought back a lifted vision which enriches his drab narratives. Something spacious, something now lurid now luminous, surrounds them. From somewhere sound accounts of an authority not sufficiently explained by the mere accuracy of his versions of life.

1581 _____. "American Realism." New Republic, 34 (March 21, 1923), 107-109.

Crane, Frank Norris, and London each a protestant in his fashion, insisted on going behind the returns in a search for truth that had been suppressed. Dreiser threw over the whole American system of thought about the meaning of existence, so far as he could manage it, and started to build his tower of doubt. H. L. Mencken braided his lash, sharpened his goad, and lifted his mocking voice against all the idealists and reticences. American life and the American view of life at large were challenged without pity and without remorse.

1582 _____. "Beyond Good and Evil." Century Magazine, 111
(April, 1926), 763-765.
Review of An American Tragedy, which he says is on so
large a scale that it exhibits certain of Dreiser's traits with
an increased clarity. It answers once and for all the charge
that he has an inadequate sense of the interwoven fabric
of human lives. This story is knit as close as canvas.

1583 _____. "Lesser Novels." New York Herald Tribune Books,
May 22, 1927. Pp. 3-4.
Review of Chains, a book of fifteen short stories and shorter novels. He says that "reading Dreiser is like looking
at a very large picture or a large actual landscape." There
is sure to be an extensive general design, but the parts
are executed with reference to their share in that design
rather than to the effects which they are individually to
make.

1584 _____. What Is American Literature? New York: Morrow,
1935. Dreiser, pp. 114-118.
The older party could say of Dreiser that his men were
vulgar, and arrogant, his women limp, his ideas clumsy,
and his style abominable. Undeterred, he piled up his creative documents on the America he knew. It was often ruthless, often shabby, often absurd in its pretensions. But
his characters were so painstakingly set forth, with so much
willingness to let them appear exactly as they were, that in
time they were seen to be not mere outlines of men and
women, but figures with the weight of life.

1585 _____. "The Nation and the American Novel." Nation, 150
(February 10, 1940), 212-214.
Reviews the basic periods of the American novel and relates the attitudes and policies the Nation expressed during
these periods. Sees the periodical as very influential in the
cause of the American novel. Between 1900 and 1918 the
Nation was more conservative and objected to the new naturalism. After 1918 the magazine had a new critical policy
which even made Dreiser a contributor and Mencken a contributing editor.

1586 _____. "Theodore Dreiser," in The American Novel: 1789-
1939. New York: Macmillan, 1940. Revised edition, 1949.
Pp. 245-259.
The burden of naturalism fell chiefly on Dreiser, more
controversy than ever on any American novelist. The truth
was that he offended by bringing the American novel a body
of material and an attitude almost wholly strange to the native tradition. Before him all the American novelists had
sprung from the older stocks among the people and had,

though with occasional dissents, taken for granted certain patterns of life which were primarily Anglo-American. Dreiser was the first of the important writers who rose from immigrants of the nineteenth century.

1587 _____, and Mark van Doren. American and British Literature Since 1890. New York: Century, 1925. Dreiser, pp. 57-60. Revised edition, New York: Appleton-Century, 1939. Though unquestionably a great novelist, Dreiser has always been handicapped by his defects as an artist. His imagination is not trustworthy when it tries to penetrate the secrets of subtle people. He loves beauty, but he appreciates only a few aspects of it, and does not always know how to reveal them. Nevertheless, he has rendered an indispensable service to American literature.

1588 VAN GELDER, Robert. "An Interview with Theodore Dreiser." New York Tribune Book Review, March 16, 1941. Pp. 2, 16. Reprinted in Van Gelder, Writers and Writing. New York: Scribner's, 1946. Pp. 164-168. See also related to Dreiser, "Notes on the Literary Life," pp. 1-19.
Comments on the typical characteristics of Dreiser as he conducts an interview, chewing on his words, twisting his handkerchief, etc. Does not say anything new on the subject.

1589 VAN VECHTEN, Carl. "Theodore Dreiser as I Knew Him." Yale Library Gazette, 25 (January, 1951), 87-92. Reprinted in Van Vechten, Fragments of an Unwritten Autobiography, 2 vols. New Haven, Conn.: Yale University Press, 1955. Vol. 2, pp. 3-15.
Says "I met him shortly after the publication of Sister Carrie and knew him all through his career. When I began to make photographs, Dreiser was one of the first authors I invited to pose. He had a wonderful head for photography and my pictures of him were superb. He came to me in the morning on his way to a train. He was in great good humor and joked all through the sitting. Indeed, one of the best pictures shows Dreiser laughing, a rare shot, which is published in Elias's biography. Dreiser's last letter to me in 1938 refers to these photographs."

1590 VIDAN, Ivo. "The Capitulation of Literature? The Scope of the 'Non-fictive Novel.'" in Yugoslav Perspectives on American Literature: An Anthology, edited by James L. Thorson. Ann Arbor, Mich.: Ardis, 1980. Pp. 157-180.

1591 VIVAS, Eliseo. "Dreiser, an Inconsistent Mechanist." Ethics, 48 (July, 1938), 498-508. Reprinted in Vivas, Creation and Discovery: Essays in Criticism and Aesthetics. New York: Noonday, 1955. Pp. 3-13. Also reprinted in Kazin and Shapiro (1955), pp. 237-245; and in Pizer (1981), pp. 30-37.

Dreiser is a better artist than his philosophy permitted
him to be. Sometimes the meaning which his novels have is
sinister, sometimes pathetic, sometimes it almost reaches
tragic heights. But meaning they usually have. In Dreiser's own life, in his enormous capacity for pity, we find
an example of a man who, through his work, gave the lie
to his own theories.

1592 VOGEL, Dan. The Three Masks of American Tragedy. Baton
Rouge: Louisiana State University Press, 1974. Dreiser,
pp. 54-60 et passim.
The three masks referred to are those of "Oedipus Tyrannos," "Christ," and "Satan." Dreiser is discussed under
the "mask of Oedipus Tyrannos" in his novel An American
Tragedy. The analysis measures Clyde Griffiths as a tragic
hero and finds that much is omitted in his characterization.
Dreiser may have had "a profoundly tragic sense of man's
fate," but this is not the same as having a profound concept
of it. His plot is simple: it depicts the fate of a young
man caught in mechanistic naturalism, without any glimpse
of purpose or morality in heaven or on earth. Without an
ostensible belief in meaning and value, Dreiser cannot depict
meaning and value. No tragedy can arise in such a fiction.

1593 VOGELBAUM, Alexandra Doris. "The New Heroines: The
Emergence of Sexuality in the Treatment of the American
Fictional Heroine, 1890-1900." Ph.D. diss., Tulane University, 1978. DA, 39 (1979), 6768A.
Examines five novelists, including Dreiser, whose work
contributed to the transformation of the American fictional
heroine. These authors sought to create heroines who would
reflect the realities of woman's life rather than the cultural
idea of woman established by the cult of the lady. Dreiser
did not waver in his determination to create wholly realistic
portraits of women. In Sister Carrie, for example, there is
a heroine whose sexuality is rendered as a unique and complex reality, affected solely by the heroine's temperament
and the specific social conditions in which she exists.

1594 VON SZELISKI, John J. "Dreiser's Experiment with Tragic
Drama." Twentieth Century Literature, 12 (April, 1966),
31-40.
If Dreiser paid anything the respect of worship, it was
Nature. His brand of Nature-dictated tragic vision is a
bizarre and fascinating reflection of both the pressures
molding his thinking and the philosophy of what constituted
tragedy which he wished to press on his society. Discusses
The Hand of the Potter, which admittedly is a wretched play,
but does demonstrate in unambiguous terms the effect of
"all-powerful Nature" in creating the lives of men.

1595 VOSS, Arthur. <u>The American Short Story: A Critical Survey</u>.
Norman: University of Oklahoma Press, 1973.

1596 WADLINGTON, Warwick. "Pathos and Dreiser." <u>Southern Re-
view</u>, 7 (April, 1971), 411-429. Reprinted in Pizer (1981),
pp. 213-227.
Defines "pathos" and shows that the word is frequently
misused as a form of tragedy that misses the heights of
tragedy. It is Dreiser's forte. "The Key to the pathetic
mode is above all suffering. In tragedy, suffering is both
a cause and result of the extreme position the hero takes at
the very boundaries of human experience, and in the end
suffering and psychic divisiveness are transcended in some
climactic epiphany. In pathos, suffering is primarily the
cause and result of the unsuccessful attempt by the unified
personality to reach an accommodation with his world either
by submission or conquest, and suffering is endless, never
to be transcended, ceasing only in death.... In pathos the
protagonist is fated to a life of unresolved repetition or to
a death which gives little or no sense of final resolution."

1597 WAGENKNECHT, Edward. <u>Cavalcade of the American Novel</u>.
New York: Holt, 1943. Revised printing, 1954. "Dreiser:
The Mystic Naturalist," pp. 281-293.
The view that Dreiser fought the battle for naturalism in
American fiction is one-sided, an oversimplification of the
Dreiser problem. Dreiser the creator broods over his world
with a vast cosmic pity; one feels of him that he "loves mankind without reservation, is incapable of hate, and finds
nothing created altogether common or unclean," that he
gathers all things, however lowly and crooked and broken,
within the love of God. If the Creator of the universe is,
in this aspect, anything like him, few souls will perish. And
he who has refused to judge must surely be justified at the
Judgment.

1598 WAGER, Willis. <u>American Literature: A World View</u>. New
York: New York University Press, 1968. Dreiser, pp. 223-
235.
In addition to novels, Dreiser wrote much in other forms,
such as short stories, essays, plays, poems, and so on.
One of his most attractive books consists of a number of
character sketches, <u>Twelve Men</u> (1919), including a heart-
warming account of his brother Paul, who was a popular song
writer. By 1930 neglect of Dreiser in America had set in--
partly because, by the second quarter of the twentieth century, American fiction had begun to adopt a poetical rather
than a historical, reportorial, or documentary aim. Interest
in Dreiser, however, continued abroad: the publication of

a complete edition of his works in Russia was regarded as
the literary event of 1930.

1599 WAGNER, Vern. "The Maligned Style of Theodore Dreiser."
      Western Humanities Review, 19 (Spring, 1965), 175-184.
      Examines a number of critics who have commented on Drei-
      ser's style and compares their evaluations with those of his
      students in Contemporary Literature who always rank Drei-
      ser as the single best writer they study. Concludes that it
      is critics, not readers, who can't stand Dreiser.

1600 WALCUTT, Charles Child. "The Three Stages of Theodore
      Dreiser's Naturalism." PMLA, 55 (March, 1940), 266-289.
      Has been frequently reprinted: Kazin and Shapiro (1955),
      pp. 246-269, as "Theodore Dreiser and the Divided Stream,"
      with revisions made for this volume; this version also re-
      printed in Lydenberg (1971), pp. 104-128.
      The naturalism of Dreiser may be approached through a
      study of his personality, the sort of experience he had in
      his formative years, and the philosophical speculations which
      grew from his experiences and reading.

1601 _____. "Naturalism in 1946: Dreiser and Farrell." Accent,
      6 (Summer, 1946), 263-268.
      Review of The Bulwark by Dreiser and Bernard Clare by
      Farrell. Of Dreiser's novel he says: "This is the first
      novel in which the author is confronted with the problem of
      advancing four or five separate actions, and the result is
      not fortunate." It is not as well constructed as the early
      straight-line naturalistic novels; it even lacks their relent-
      less movement toward disaster; it lacks the power of utter
      conviction.

1602 _____. American Literary Naturalism: A Divided Stream.
      Minneapolis: University of Minnesota Press, 1956. "Theo-
      dore Dreiser: The Wonder and Terror of Life," pp. 180-
      221. Reprinted in Pizer (1981), pp. 57-91. Contains some
      of the same material as in PMLA article (1940) above.
      Dreiser drank his inspiration from both branches of the
      divided stream. He has been described as a pessimist, a
      socialist, a communist; he has been said to embody the an-
      tithesis of American transcendentalism; he has himself ac-
      knowledged beliefs in the meaninglessness of life, in the moral
      autonomy of the superman, in the ultimate value and dignity
      of the individual. In his later works he has placed mind
      above matter. And even while he was writing his early books
      he believed in a mystical Cosmic Consciousness that one would
      hardly have expected from reading those books. His mixture
      of despair and idealism, of wonder and fear, of pity and
      guilt, of chemistry and intuition, has given us the most mov-
      ing and powerful novels of the naturalistic tradition.

Review of Walcutt's book, American Literature, 29 (January, 1958), 505-507 by Walter F. Taylor: "His accomplishment has been to pose these questions, to deal with them more profoundly and perceptively than any of his predecessors, and in so doing to provide a series of remarkably fine analyses of the interlinkage of philosophy and fictional form."

1603 _____. "Sister Carrie: Naturalism or Novel of Manners." Genre, 1 (January, 1968), 76-85.
Objects to theory that naturalism is considered at an opposite pole from the novel of manners. Suggests that the materialist rejection of freedom and responsibility was only a small fraction of the so-called naturalistic novel. Regards Dreiser's novel as a "perfect novel of manners." Its problems are typical. There is no evidence of revolt against the society, just an inchoate but overwhelming desire to get on top of it. It is false to say that the novel challenges the Victorian sexual code. On the contrary, it describes, and accepts, a very different social order.

1604 WALDMEN, Milton. "Contemporary American Authors: VII-- Theodore Dreiser." London Mercury, 14 (July, 1926), 283- 291. Reprinted in Living Age, 331 (October 1, 1926), 45- 50 as "A German-American Insurgent."

1605 _____. "Theodore Dreiser," in Contemporary American Authors, edited by John Collings Squire. New York: Holt, 1928. Pp. 97-117.
He chooses words without discrimination and they resemble a pile of leaden coins whose surfaces have been worn flat and whose bodies evoke no resonance. Commits solecisms which are incomprehensible, and constantly misuses words. He is in accord with the greatest masters of tragic writing in believing that the violation of certain laws must inevitably lead to disaster on the part of the violator. His characters violate laws which are almost universal.

1606 _____. "Tendencies of the Modern Novel." Fortnightly Review, 140 (December, 1933), 717-725.

1607 WALKER, Charles R. "How Big Is Dreiser?" Bookman, 63 (April, 1926), 146-149.
He is neither the man nor the artist his critics or defenders make him out to be. He is a conscientious artist who does his work, sometimes aided, sometimes checked by his philosophy, but succeeding ultimately in getting down a picture of human existence that is at once ugly, passionate, foolish, romantic, and profound.

1608 _____. "Business in the American Novel." Bookman, 66 (December, 1927), 401-405.

Discusses several works in which the theme of business
is prominent, but thinks Dreiser is the greatest novelist to
have made use of business and industry. All of his novels
have a background of business affairs, but of course The
Financier and The Titan are devoted totally to the details
of the stock market, buying and selling, etc.

1609 WALLACE, Inez. "Ask Inez Wallace: Must We Have Another
American Tragedy?" Cleveland Plain Dealer, October 3,
1926. Dramatic section, p. 5.

1610 WALLACE, Jack E. "The Comic Voice in Dreiser's Cowperwood
Narrative." American Literature, 53 (March, 1979), 56-71.
Reviews several adverse criticisms of the Cowperwood
novels, and concludes that the problem arises when the
critic insists that the story is meant to be experienced as
tragedy. Wallace proposes that the novel is in the comic
mode and shows how this approach considerably improves
a reader's response to it.

1611 WALLACE, Margaret. "Books--A History Takes Shape." In-
dependent Woman, 25 (July, 1946), 209.

1612 WANLESS, James Michael. "Dreiser's Way with Words." Ph.D.
diss., Wayne State University, 1977. DA, 38 (1978), 6732A.
The purpose of this study is twofold: to derive a clear
picture of Dreiser's actual ideas from the patterns discernible
in his most trustworthy kind of utterance, the prose of his
best books; and to describe the characteristic features of
his narrative manner, the forms that prevail in his most
effective texts.

1613 WARD, Alfred C. American Literature: 1880-1930. New
York: Dial Press, 1932. Dreiser, pp. 111-117.
The conscious pursuit of realism is a sign of decay, for
it endeavors to lay bare the disabilities and afflictions under
which man labors. Handicapped by a tedious sameness of
theme and weighed down by a style that is shockingly glutin-
ous and deficient in humor, Dreiser is almost the worse afflicted among authors of major importance. But anyone who
can persuade us that slabs of congealed tapioca are both
interesting and exciting is certainly a genius. Dreiser performed a feat as marvellous as that, not once only, but in
several of his vast novels.

1614 WARFEL, Harry R. The American Mind. New York: American Book, 1937. Dreiser, p. 832 et passim.
Comments on criticism of S. P. Sherman and H. L. Mencken,
who were at odds with each other over Dreiser. Quotes Dreiser who said, "All my life, someone, a critic, a publisher, a
friend has always been telling me not to go so far, not to

talk about this or that, to stay back, to keep still." Reprints "The Lost Pheobe," one of the better short stories by Dreiser.

1615 WARNER, Stephen Douglas. "Representative Studies in the American Picaresque: Investigations of Modern Chivalry (Hugh Henry Brackenridge), Adventures of Huckleberry Finn (Mark Twain), and Adventures of Augie March (Saul Bellow)." Ph.D. diss., Indiana University, 1971. DA, 32 (1972), 4582A.

The basic elelments of the picaresque are demonstrated to exist and function in the three novels named above. The final chapter briefly considers several other American novels which reflect a significant indebtedness to the picaresque, among them Dreiser's Jennie Gerhardt.

1616 WARREN, Robert Penn. "An American Tragedy." Yale Review, 52 (October, 1962), 1-15. Reprinted in Lydenberg (1971), pp. 129-140; also reprinted in Salzman (1971), pp. 99-111. Recently reprinted in The American Novel in the 19th- and 20th Centuries, edited by Edgar Lohner. Berlin: Erich Schmidt, 1974. Pp. 152-161.

Dreiser's tales of failure are his successes, and An Ameri-0 can Tragedy is his greatest success. We feel the burden of the personal pathos, and the burden of the historical moment, the moment of the Great Boom which climaxed the period from Grant to Coolidge, the half century in which the new America of industry and finance capitalism was hardening into shape and its secret forces were emerging to dominate all life. The novel can be taken as a document, both personal and historical, and it is often admired and defended, in these terms.

1617 _____. "Homage to Theodore Dreiser on the Centenary of His Birth." Southern Review, 7 (Spring, 1971), 383-410. Reprinted New York: Random House, 1971, as pamphlet. Also reprinted in Pizer (1981), pp. 271-291. Condensation printed in Brooks, Cleanth et al., eds., American Literature: The Makers and the Making, 2 vols. New York: St. Martin's Press, 1973. Vol. II, pp. 1877-1906.

Reviews Dreiser's life and works and offers comment on each published item. Most of article is analysis of An American Tragedy with emphasis on the character of Clyde. Similar to 1962 article above.

1618 _____. Democracy and Poetry. Cambridge: Harvard University Press, 1975. Dreiser, pp. 23-27.

The work of Dreiser revolved around two related themes, the central themes of his age: the nature of success and the nature of the self. Discusses Carrie, the Cowperwood novels, and An American Tragedy in this light. In the end

Clyde is the slave of dreams, and has no self, going to his
death as a representative American, in a land of fictive
values seized, or yearned after, by fictive selves.

1619 _____, ed. with Introduction. An American Tragedy. Cleve-
      land: World, 1962. Same as article in item 1616.

1620 WASSERSTROM, William. Heiress of All the Ages: Sex and
      Sentiment in the Genteel Tradition.. Minneapolis: Univer-
      sity of Minnesota Press, 1959. Dreiser, pp. 82-84.
          Editors who were afraid to publish Sister Carrie and,
      later, readers who were displeased by it were distressed
      because the novel discarded the true system. Carrie vio-
      lates order and stands outside degree. For Dreiser was
      among the first to proclaim a mode of thought which dis-
      tinguished the present from the past: desire is not so ter-
      rible as people have been taught to believe and therefore
      need not be defined, located, and supervised. Carrie is
      a foolish pleasant, accessible girl with whom a man is on
      his own.

1621 WATSON, Charles N., Jr. "The 'Accidental' Drownings in
      Daniel Deronda and An American Tragedy." English Lan-
      guage Notes, 13 (June, 1976), 288-291.
          Points up that Dreiser based his novel largely on the
      actual case of Grace Brown and Chester Gillette, but in the
      matter of Roberta's drowning he created an event which has
      much ambiguity in a mixture of conscious calculation, eleventh-
      hour hesitation, and timely accident. Suggests that one
      source for Dreiser's scene could be George Eliot's novel,
      which Dreiser had read thrity years earlier.

1622 WEBER, Diane Judith Downs. "The Autobiography of Child-
      hood in America." Ph.D. diss., George Washington Univer-
      sity, 1971. DA, 32 (1971), 936A.
          Studies five well-known autobiographies of Americans and
      pursues the question of why so many more of this genre
      are produced in America than in England. Others are stud-
      ied to a lesser degree, including those of Dreiser.

1623 WEEKS, Edward. "The Best Sellers Since 1875." Publishers'
      Weekly, 125 (February 21, 1934), 1503-1506.

1624 _____. "A Modern Estimate of American Best Sellers, 1875-
      1933." Publishers' Weekly, 125 (April 21, 1934), 1507.

1625 WEGELIN, Christof, ed. The American Novel: Criticism and
      Background Readings. New York: Free Press, 1972. Re-
      prints "Dreiser Discusses Sister Carrie." First appeared in
      Masses and Mainstream, 8 (December, 1955), pp. 307-309.

1626 WEIL, Leonard D. "The Logical Solution." Nation, 140 (May
     15, 1935), 572. See under Trachtenberg, Joshua.

1627 WEIMER, David R. "Heathen Catacombs," in The City as Meta-
     phor. New York: Random House, 1966. Pp. 65-77.
          Dreiser built to no great symbolic moments; he has memor-
     able small ones. They occur, unpretentiously, quite on the
     way to something grander, as we think of them at the time.
     But for all this he manages to convey the poignance of lives
     in which feelings always overflow the vessels built to contain
     them. In Dreiser's novels in the city desire is increased,
     made furtive, and finally destroyed. And there is no way
     out.

1628 WEIR, Sybil Barbara. "The Disappearance of the Sentimental
     Heroine Characterization of Women in Selected Novels by
     Robert Herrick, Edith Wharton, and Theodore Dreiser, 1898-
     1925." Ph.D. diss., University of California (Berkeley),
     1972.

1629 _____. "The Image of Women in Dreiser's Fiction, 1900-
     1925." Pacific Coast Philology, 7 (April, 1972), 65-71.

1630 WELLS, H. G. "Wells Assays the Culture of America." New
     York Times, May 15, 1927. Section 4, pp. 3, 20.

1631 WENTZ, John C. "An American Tragedy as Epic Theater:
     The Piscator Dramatization." Modern Drama, 4 (February,
     1962), 365-376.
          The history of the German dramatization of Dreiser's novel
     begins with one quarrel and ends with another six years
     later. Separating these disputes were six years of prepara-
     tion, frustration, friendship, hard work, qualified triumph,
     and even tragedy for the scores of people who at one time
     or another lent their energies to the play's creation and pro-
     duction. This article traces the history of this endeavor,
     and concludes with its failure.

1632 WERTHEIM, Arthur Frank. The New York Little Renaissance.
     New York: New York University Press, 1976. "Mencken,
     Dreiser, and The Smart Set," pp. 187-199.
          Dreiser was hailed by the social critics as a realist who
     wrote honestly about American life. His work was backed
     by various groups in the Little Renaissance, and editors
     rallied around Dreiser as a precursor of the new American
     writing. Dreiser was also lionized by the Greenwich Village
     crowd. Dreiser lived in a small studio on West 10th Street,
     with the actress Kirah Markham, and held open house on
     Sunday evenings. Young writers gravitated around him and
     tended to venerate him as the father of American realism.

1633 WEST, Anthony. "Man Overboard." New Yorker, 25 (April 25, 1959), 169-174. Review of Letters, 3 vols., edited by Robert Elias (1959).

1634 WEST, James L. W., III. "Nicholas Blood and Sister Carrie." Library Chronicle, 44 (Spring, 1979), 32-42.

1635 _____. "John Paul Dreiser's Copy of Sister Carrie." Library Chronicle, 44 (Spring, 1979), 85-93.

1636 _____. "Dreiser and the B. W. Dodge Sister Carrie." Studies in Bibliography, 35 (1982), 323-331.

1637 WEST, Ray B., Jr. The Short Story in America, 1900-1950. Chicago: Regnery, 1952. Dreiser, pp. 33-44. Reprinted, Freeport, N.Y.: Books for Libraries Press, 1968.
      Even the best of Theodore Dreiser's short stories are limited. Almost any of Dreiser's stories might have been expanded into novels, for they are confined neither in space nor in time. They are seldom based upon incidents, or when they are, the incidents are usually culminating events in a long series of injustices, misunderstandings, and intolerances which must be rehearsed in order to lend credibility to what is generally a final catastrophe. Calls "The Lost Phoebe" Dreiser's most popular "because it secceeds, as most of his stories do not, in getting at this essential quality of human existence."

1638 WESTBROOK, Max. "Dreiser's Defense of Carrie Meeber." Modern Fiction Studies, 23 (Fall, 1977), 381-393.
      Dreiser thought of himself as a meticulous observer, as one who learned from life rather than from books; but in spite of this self-image Dreiser was no scientiest, not in spirit and not in method. Frequently he used the awkward and much discussed technique of inserting authorial sermons. While awkward, they can be seen to make a good deal of sense when Dreiser wants to defend a particular character.

1639 WESTBROOK, Perry D. Free Will and Determinism in American Literature. Rutherford, N.J.: Fairleigh Dickinson University Press, 1979. Dreiser, pp. 141-160. Review by Dabney Townsend, American Literary Realism, 13 (1980), 154-155.
      Reviews several of Dreiser's works--Sister Carrie, An American Tragedy, The Financier, Hey, Rub-A-Dub-Dub, and The Bulwark--in light of the assertion that Dreiser is doubtless the most complex, the most thoughtful, and the most influential of American naturalists. Toward the end of his life, Dreiser had come to modify his stand that matter was the only reality, but this new aspect of his thought left no more room for freedom of the will than did his earlier very thoroughgoing materialsim.

1640 WESTBROOK, Wayne W. <u>Wall Street in the American Novel</u>.
New York: New York University Press, 1980. "The Devil
and the Dollar," pp. 152-158.
Dreiser often criticized America for its economic structure
of subjects and sovereigns. Six years after he wrote <u>The</u>
<u>Titan</u> (1914), a portrayal of the American capitalist at <u>his</u>
most powerful and corrupt, the novelist was directly comparing the country to ancient commercial Rome, which was a
material welter ruled by emperors. Any assumption that
Dreiser held the businessman or financier in undiminished
admiration is false. He wrote without moral condemnation,
but pictured the financier as the coldest, most selfish, yet
strangely the most useful of all phenomena.

1641 WESTLAKE, Neda M. "Theodore Dreiser's <u>Notes on Life</u>."
<u>Library Chronicle</u>, 20 (Summer, 1954), 69-75.

1642 _____. "Theodore Dreiser Collection--Addenda." <u>Library</u>
<u>Chronicle</u>, 25 (Summer, 1959), 55-57.

1643 _____. "<u>Twelve Men</u> by Theodore Dreiser." <u>Proof: The</u>
<u>Yearbook of American Bibliographical and Textual Studies</u>, 2
(1972), 153-174. Edited by Joseph Katz. Columbia: University of South Carolina Press, 1972.

1644 _____. "Airmail Interview." <u>Dreiser Newsletter</u>, 3 (Fall,
1972), 6-12.
Questions relate principally to the Dreiser collection at
the University of Pennsylvania, where Miss Westlake is li-
brarian in charge of this collection. Answers the question
of how the Dreiser manuscript papers came to Pennsylvania,
the extent of the collection, etc.

1645 _____. "The Complete Works of Theodore Dreiser: An
Announcement." <u>Dreiser Newsletter</u>, 7 (Spring, 1976), 15-
16.
The University of Pennsylvania, custodian of the extensive
Dreiser Collection, announced that it will sponsor "The Com-
plete Works of Theodore Dreiser" for publication. Neda West-
lake was named General Editor of the project, and James
L. W. West will be the Textual Editor.

1646 _____. "The <u>Sister Carrie</u> Scrapbook." <u>Library Chronicle</u>,
44 (1979), 71-84.

1647 _____. "Japanese Publish Collected Edition." <u>Dreiser News-</u>
<u>letter</u>, 14 (Spring, 1983), 10-11.
A review of <u>The Works of Theodore Dreiser in Twenty</u>
<u>Volumes</u>, published in Kyoto, Japan. Is described as "an
impressive achievement." Accompanied by a brochure, in
Japanese, giving a summary biography of Dreiser, and sug-

gesting that Dreiser's determinism in conflict with his compassion is the key to his popularity in Japan.

1648 _____, and Jack Salzman, eds. "An Unpublished Chapter
from An American Tragedy." Prospects: Annual of American Cultural Studies, 1 (1975), 1-6.
Published from the manuscript, which with some others
were later condensed into the first chapter of the published
novel. Editors say: "we have attempted a faithful representation of the text ... Dreiser was obviously writing rap-
idly, feeling his way into the early life of Clyde Griffiths,
as though trying several possible tunes before the melody
would become clear to him."

1649 _____, ed. with Preface. Theodore Dreiser: Centenary
Exhibition. Philadelphia: University of Pennsylvania Library, 1971. 27-page pamphlet.

1650 _____, general editor. Sister Carrie. Textual editor,
James L. W. West; Historical editors John C. Berkey and
Alice M. Winters. Philadelphia: University of Pennsylvania
Press, 1981.

1651 WHICHER, George F. "Respectability Defied," in The Literature of the American People: A Historical and Critical Sur-
very, edited by Arthur Hobson Quinn. New York: Appleton, 1951. Pp. 847-851. See under Quinn, Arthur Hobson.

1652 WHIPPLE, Thomas K. "Theodore Dreiser: An American Tragedy." New Republic, 46 (March 17, 1926), 113-115. Reprinted in Pizer (1981), pp. 253-257.
The source of Dreiser's greatness seems to be his emotional endowment, not so much an intensity as a tremendous,
steady, unfailing flood of feeling. He is distinguished from
ordinary men by extraordinary strength and volume of passion. Chiefly it shows itself in his tragic sense, in his profound consciousness of the tragedy inherent in all existence,
in the very scheme of things--tragedy inescapable, essential,
universal, perceived by many, but by very few so overwhelm-
ingly felt.

1653 _____. Spokesmen: Modern Writers and American Life.
New York: Appleton-Century, 1928. "Theodore Dreiser,"
pp. 70-92. Reprinted in Kazin and Shapiro (1955), pp. 96-
110 as "Aspects of a Pathfinder."
One thing we cannot deny him: his amazing capacity for
observation which helps conceal his defects as a creator.
He has an unending interest in everything--nothing seems
dull and tiresome. He likes to consider himself a bold, original thinker, but his ideas are usually from his feeling.
Brooding pity penetrates all life. Dreiser is especially acute

in his perception of man's capacity for suffering. Sometimes
he is simple, and then he is greatest.

1654 WHITAKER, Eleanor M. "A Descriptive Analysis of Theodore
Dreiser's Non-Fiction Work." MA thesis, University of Mary-
land, 1966.

1655 WHITE, Morton G., and Lucia White. "Disappointment in New
York: Frank Norris and Theodore Dreiser," in The Intellectual Versus the City. Cambridge, Mass.: Harvard University Press, 1962. Pp. 117-138.
Dreiser is called a naturalist because of his materialism
and determinism, or because he treated sex, violence, and
poverty with more candor than appears in the writings of
Howells. However, both groups came to share one feeling
in common: "disappointment with the city of New York."
Dreiser's quarrel with New York in the nineties was that of
a city-lover who had no alternative ideal of social existence
but rather a personal grievance against New York.

1656 WHITE, Ray Lewis, ed. Sherwood Anderson's Memoirs: A
Critical Edition. Chapel Hill: University of North Carolina
Press, 1942. Revised critical edition, 1969. Dreiser, pp.
451-459 et passim. See under Anderson, Sherwood (1942).

1657 WHITE, William. "Dreiser on Hardy, Henley, and Whitman:
An Unpublished Letter." English Language Notes, 6 (December, 1968), 122-124.

1658 _____. "A Dreiser Checklist in the Press." Dreiser Newsletter, 1 (Fall, 1970), 19-20.
Announces the publication of Theodore Dreiser: A Checklist, by Hugh C. Atkinson. Says it will not be definitive,
but will serve a much-needed use.

1659 WHITE, William Allen. "Splitting Fiction Three Ways." New
Republic, 30 (April 12, 1922), Spring Literary Supplement,
22, 24, 26. Reprinted in White, Twelve American Novelists:
The Novel of Tomorrow and the Scope of Fiction. Indianapolis: Bobbs-Merrill, 1922. Pp. 123-133.
Says with reference to Dreiser: "There are those who feel
that Dreiser's world is afflicted with misanthropy and worms.
As between a world of 'Simply to Thy Cross I Cling' done in
gaudy colors and a world painted from the mud of a pig pen,
many an average man or woman shrinks from choice. There
is no more art in Sister Carrie than in Pollyanna. It is
largely a question of the world in which the authors move,
of the philosophy of life which inspires the writer. Most
of us trek along on the middle plane out of the heights where
Pollyanna walks in trailing clouds of glory, and above the
depths where Sister Carrie sloshes in the mud and muck."

1660 WHITEHEAD, James Farnum, III. "Character and Style in
      Dreiser's An American Tragedy." Ph.D. diss., University
      of Virginia, 1970. DA, 31 (1971), 5433-5434A.
        Rejects the assumption that Dreiser creates great char-
      acters in his novel but cannot write. He says: "If Drei-
      ser's work is a 'moving human document,' it cannot be a
      'colossal botch' as work of art." Undertakes to explain how
      Dreiser creates character and how his style expresses char-
      acter and certain aspects of the novel's "vision."

1661 WILDER, Alma A. "An American Tragedy: The Transformation
      of Fact into Fiction." MA thesis, University of North Caro-
      lina, 1971.

1662 WILKERSON, James C. "The Altruistic Thought of Theodore
      Dreiser in Seven Representative Novels." MA thesis, Uni-
      versity of Florida, 1952.

1663 WILKINSON, Robert E. "A Study of Theodore Dreiser's The
      Financier." Ph.D. diss., University of Pennsylvania, 1965.
      DA, 26 (1966), 3356.
        This dissertation is divided into three parts: the com-
      position of The Financier, a comparison of the two versions,
      and the reception of the two versions. A detailed analysis
      is made of the lives of Yerkes and Cowperwood, illustrating
      how Dreiser blended real life and fiction.

1664 WILLARD, Daniel. "I Am Only a Railroad Man." Liberty, 8
      (November 14, 1931), 30-33.

1665 WILLEN, Gerald. "Dreiser's Moral Seriousness: A Study of
      the Novels." Ph.D. diss., University of Minnesota, 1955.
      Published in part in the following article.

1666 _____. "Dreiser's Moral Seriousness." University of Kan-
      sas City Review, 23 (Spring, 1957), 181-187. Reprinted in
      Lydenberg (1971), pp. 96-103.
        Dreiser's novels take place in a society that is itself con-
      stantly passing judgment on its members. It is a society
      in conflict with itself over the values it actually lives by and
      those it thinks it lives by. From it Dreiser isolates a number
      of representative individuals, sets them in motion, and ren-
      ders their lives in terms of the difficulties they encounter
      with the problems arising from the moral ambiguities that
      envelop their activities. By dwelling so insistently on moral
      questions, by endowing his characters with wills of their
      own, and by confronting them with real choices, Dreiser
      enables the reader to pass moral judgment on the characters
      themselves as well as on the society in which they live.

1667 WILLIAMS, Blanche C. "Twelve Men." New York Times Review of Books, May 11, 1919. P. 276.
Letter to editor.

1668 WILLIAMS, Philip. "The Chapter Titles of Sister Carrie." American Literature, 36 (November, 1964), 359-365.
The manuscripts show that the chapter titles were a very late step in the author's struggle to bring his book to publication. The intriguing chapter titles summarize the plot, and also tell a story about the writer in relation to his monumental work. Some signs that the titles were added as a device to strengthen the appeal of the story, perhaps as a last-ditch attempt to assure the acceptance of the book whose fate was by no means assured at the beginning. Continues by listing the chapter titles and discussing them from a poetic and imagery point of view.

1669 WILSON, Christopher P. "Sister Carrie Again." American Literature, 53 (May, 1982), 287-290.
Reviews the various stories, and sometimes myths, surrounding the 1900 publication of Sister Carrie. Concludes with the belief that Doubleday was not so much interested in defeating Dreiser's publication, as it was interested in bringing the "new author" in under a new light.

1670 WILSON, Edmund. "Equity for Americans." New Republic, 70 (March, 30, 1932), 185-186.
Review of Tragic America, which he calls a significant book that marks a definite new departure in the American intellectual world. Is the first American writer to come out flatly for Communism for America, and has tried to take the curse off the word by calling it "equity."

1671 _____. "Theodore Dreiser's Quaker and Graham Greene's Priest." New Yorker, 22 (March 23, 1946), Pp. 88 et passim.
Review of The Bulwark, which he says is not one of Dreiser's most tedious books. Language is less oafish than in some other works, and the personal point of view, the rhythm carries off the fumbling, vague vocabulary.

1672 WILSON, Gil (Gilbert). "A Proposal for a Dreiser Mural." Dreiser Newsletter, 3 (Fall, 1972), 1-5.
Author is Terre Haute-born artist, friend and admirer of Dreiser. Describes what he would like to see in the way of a memorial to Dreiser, but is somewhat dismayed by what appears to be a lack of interest in the matter.

1673 WILSON, James Southall. "The Changing Novel." Virginia Quarterly Review, 10 (January, 1934), 42-52.
Remarks on the diversity of aim and method and form in the current novel, and points out that there is nothing in com-

mon in the works of all important American novelists today,
including Dreiser, who seems to relate to no one. Concludes
by pointing out, however, that periods of rigid enforcement
of moral regulation or artistic convention have rarely been
eras of high spiritual adventure or of fine imaginative creation.

1674 WILSON, Jennie M. "A Comparative Study of the Novels of
Frederick Philip Grove and Theodore Dreiser." MA thesis,
University of New Brunswick, 1962.

1675 WILSON, William E. The Wabash. New York: Rinehart, 1940.
Dreiser, pp. 312-314.
Points out that nearly all writers from Indiana have one
quality in common: a certain mellow optimism. Dreiser is
the exception, his background being poverty ridden and devoid of all material comforts. Dreiser left Indiana before he
began to write. Yet, whenever he recalls his native Hoosier
background or revisits it, he grows as nostalgic and sentimental as all the others. It was Dreiser who wrote the words
for the famous nostalgic song composed by his brother, Paul
Dresser:
"O the moonlight's fair tonight along the Wabash,
From the fields there comes the breath of new-mown hay;
Thro' the sycamores the candlelights are gleaming,
On the banks of the Wabash far away."

1676 _____. "The Titan and the Gentleman." Antioch Review,
23 (Spring, 1973), 25-34.

1677 _____. Indiana: A History. Bloomington: Indiana University Press, 1966. Dreiser, pp. 218-227.
What damaged Dreiser most in Sister Carrie was that he
violated the Genteel Tradition and wrote about poverty and
sex as if they really existed in America, as indeed he had
seen them exist in Indiana when he was a boy. In those
days it was expected of Hoosiers that they write uplifting
stories about just plain folks or romantic tales of never-
never lands, and Dreiser did neither. The point of this
book is that Indiana, like any other state, has been the home
of all kinds of men and women, and the only danger Indianans
should ever concern themselves about is the danger of ac-
cepting only one category and, in fear, rejecting all others.

1678 WINNER, Percy. "Dorothy Thompson Demands Dreiser Explain
Parallel." New York Evening Post, November 14, 1928. P.
6.

1679 WINSLOW, Cedric Reimers. "The Crisis of Liberalism in the
Novels of Theodore Dreiser, Frank Norris, and Jack London,"
3 vols. Ph.D. diss., New York University, 1977. DA, 38
(1977), 2132A.

This study examines a number of novels in relation to the crisis and re-evaluation of the American liberal tradition which occurred during the late nineteenth and early twentieth centuries. Each author presents in his novels a world in which classical liberalism still informs the official values of society but is no longer a viable description of the realities of modern America.

1680 WISEMAN, Thomas Lynn. "The Prose Styles in Theodore Dreiser's Novels." Ph.D. diss., Tulane, 1979. DA, 40 (1979), 1474A-1475A.

Reviews the argument that Dreiser is a great novelist who writes "bad prose." This dissertation undertakes to examine the general configurations of Dreiser's style and the verbal features contributing to the "power" many readers have felt from his novels. Concludes that Dreiser's greatest strength as a novelist is in his representation in indirect discourse of the inner life of his characters. Dreiser has the ability to create a masterful portrait of the interplay between the physical universe and the mind of man.

1681 WITEMEYER, Hugh. "Gaslight and Magic Lamp in Sister Carrie." PMLA, 86 (March, 1971), 236-240.

Examines the imagery of the theater in Dreiser's novel, and shows how the theater is associated with the treasure-cave that opens to Aladdin and with the rich citadel that knights conquer in works of romance. The stage helps to characterize the mental processes of Dreiser's American dreams. It also helps to illuminate the ironic discrepancy between such dreams and unaccommodating realities.

1682 _____. "Sister Carrie: Plus ça change...." PMLA, 87 (May, 1972), 514.

Response to article by Mr. Rupin W. Desai (PMLA, March 1972) in which he objects to Witemeyer's assertion that Carrie does not change once she moves to New York. Witemeyer argues, once more, that she may not be quite the same: she is a few years older, perhaps more practical, but she has not outgrown the sadly immature psychology that characterizes Dreiser's American dreamers.

1683 WITHAM, W. Tasker. Panorama of American Literature. New York: Stephen Daye, 1947. "The Rise of Realism: Theodore Dreiser," pp. 219-223.

For faithful and accurate presentation of men and women whom the world calls "sinners" as well as the ambitions and desires which motivate them, he is unsurpassed. The unhappy circumstances of his own early life made him peculiarly well qualified for his work. There is a certain strength in his very heaviness. At any rate, much can be forgiven in the author of one of the most important novels of our century, An American Tragedy.

1684 _____. The Adolescent in the American Novel, 1920-1960.
New York: Ungar, 1964. Dreiser, pp. 261-263.
During the twenties naturalistic writers took a rather
broad view of their characters' lives, covering a number
of years superficially, instead of analyzing a few days thoroughly, showing that in the long run man is likely to be defeated by nature, by society, or by individual human enemies, and that his defeat or triumph is governed by chance
and by physical strength rather than by virtue or by divine
assistance. Cites An American Tragedy which covers Clyde
Griffiths from the age of 12 to his death at 23.

1685 WOLFE, Don M. "Theodore Dreiser and the Human Enigma,"
in The Image of Man in America. Dallas: Southern Metho-
dist University Press, 1957. Reprinted New York: Crowell,
1970. Pp. 317-337.
No one has attempted a more prolonged or rigorous examination of the nature of man than Dreiser. In the nonfiction
and short stories, Dreiser renews and continues his search
for the permanent and transient forces that shape the actions
of men. He rejected the concept of a world benignly planned
and was eager to uncover the deep springs of human motives.
Dreiser continued his search for certainty about man's nature
in vain until the end of his life.

1686 WOLLSTEIN, R. H. "You Know Mr. Dreiser: The American
Tragedian Turns His Freudian Eyes on Music." Musical
America, 49 (February 25, 1929), 35-37, 55-56.

1687 WOLSTENHOLME, Susan. "Brother Theodore: Hell on Women,"
in American Novelists Revisited: Essays in Feminist Criticism. Boston: G. K. Hall, 1982. Pp. 243-264.
Feminist readers of Dreiser must revise traditional notions
of Dreiser's place in the canon, but they also have a new
vantage point of seeing his work. This fiction at its best
arises not from hostility toward women or from great phallic
strength but from a powerful struggle perceptible within
the female psychical values, a struggle perceptible within
the fiction rather than in the outside literary world, a struggle that Dreiser at his best confronted honestly and humanely.
What is remarkable for the feminist reader of Dreiser is that
he so honestly dealt with his own primal rage and rarely reduced either men or women to the simple level of "victim"
or "villain."

1688 WOOD, Bobbye Nelson. "A Prototypical Pattern in Dreiser's
Fiction." Ph.D. diss., North Texas State University, 1974.
DA, 35 (1975), 7929A.
Examines a narrative pattern which Dreiser followed from
1911 through 1915. The pattern is always triangular in con-
struction and always contains the same three figures: a vin-

dictive parent, outraged by an outsider's violation of personal
and societal values; an enchanted offspring; and a disruptive
outsider who threatens established order.

1689 WOODRESS, James. American Fiction, 1900-1950. Detroit:
Gale Research, 1974. Dreiser, pp. 81-86. Bibliographical.

1690 WOODWARD, William E. The Gift of Life: An Autobiography.
New York: Dutton, 1947. Dreiser, pp. 232-234 et passim.
Author recollects a typical incident involving Dreiser:
"One day, six or seven months after I had employed Helen
Richardson, I dictated a letter to a friend of mine on the
Pacific coast. Just a friendly chat, and I mentioned some
of the books that I had been reading. I had just read The
"Genius." The real name of the character was Ralph Tilton,
who had been advertising manager of the Butterick publications. Dreiser's book was a fictional life of Tilton, who did
have many qualities of genius, besides being a drinker of
immense capacity. He was reputed to be an illegitimate son
of Henry Ward Beecher, but I do not know if that story is
true."

1691 WOOLLCOTT, Alexander. "Hand of the Potter: A Review."
New York Times Review of Books, October 26, 1919. P.
598.
Subject matter is hideous, but in addition to this the
play is not suitable to the stage. As in all of his novels,
Dreiser has written far too much exposition, description,
and whatever verbiage that would not be tolerated in the
theatre. Possibly could be pruned into shape for acting.

1692 _____. "An American Tragedy." New York World, October
25, 1926. Reprinted in Woollcott, Going to Pieces (New York:
Putnam's, 1928); also reprinted in The American Theater
As Seen by Its Critics, 1752-1934 (New York: W. W. Nor-
ton, 1934); reprinted and edited by Montrose J. Moses and
John Mason Brown, (New York: Cooper Squre, 1967. Pp.
247-249). Reprinted in Hennessey, J., ed. The Portable
Alexander Woollcott (1946). See under Hennessey, J., ed.

1693 WRIGHT, Austin McGiffert. The American Short Story in the
Twenties. Chicago: University of Chicago Press, 1961.
Dreiser, pp. 70-72 et passim.
More commonly the character in search of love is impeded
by inner problems and makes only a half-hearted effort to
find it. This is the pattern anticipated by the earlier Dreiser stories. Sometimes a character may make a tentative,
timorous, perhaps almost involuntary advance or appeal to
a potential lover. Cites stories from Free and Other Stories:
"Nigger Jeff," "The Lost Phoebe," "The Second Choice,"
"Married," etc.

1694 WYCHERLEY, H. Allen. "Mechanism and Vitalism in Dreiser's
      Non-Fiction." Texas Studies in Language and Literature,
      11 (1969), 1039-1049.
          Only rarely are his many and ponderous volumes of auto-
      biography and travel the objects of comment. Two reasons
      for this neglect are immediately apparent: one is that Drei-
      ser's novels are vastly more important than his writing in
      other genres; another is that his nonfiction is voluminous,
      of negligible interest, and with two or three exceptions,
      tedious in the extreme. ·Nevertheless, the nonfiction casts
      considerable light upon the central paradox in Dreiser's think-
      ing: his shifting back and forth between the two poles of
      mechanism and vitalism.

1695 YAMAMOTO, Shuji. "Religion of Dreiser: Its Four Aspects."
      Kyusha American Literature, 10 (1967), 70-74. In Japanese;
      abstract in English.

1696 YAMAZAKI, Masako. "Dreiser's Usage of Movement in Sister
      Carrie." The Toyo Review (Japan), 8 (1976), 73-85.

1697 YBARRA, T. R. "Swinnerton Calls Our Authors Virile." New
      York Times, December 15, 1926. P. 5. See Swinnerton,
      Frank.

1698 YEWDALE, Merton Stark. "Is Dreiser's The 'Genius' Immoral?"
      New York Sun, February 24, 1918. Section 6, p. 10.

1699 _____. "All Values Go Down Before Dreiser." Chicago
      Herald and Examiner, May 4, 1918. Fine Arts Supplement,
      p. 1.

1700 _____, ed. with Foreword. The "Genius." New York:
      Boni and Liveright, 1923.

1701 ZASURSKY, Yasen N., ed. with Foreword and Commentary
      in Russian. Essays and Articles by Theodore Dreiser. Mos-
      cow: Foreign Languages Publications House, 1951.
          Reprints seven chapters from Tragic America; six chapters
      from America Is Worth Saving. Also prints five articles by
      Dreiser: "This Is Churchill's Democracy," "War and Amer-
      ica," "The Russian Advance," "The Meaning of the U.S.S.R.
      in the World Today," and "Dreiser's Letter to William Z.
      Foster."

1702 _____. Theodore Dreiser: On the 100th Anniversary of
      His Birth. Literary Study, No. 8, Moscow: Znanie, 1971.

1703 _____. "Theodore Dreiser's An American Tragedy," in
     Twentieth-Century American Literature: A Soviet View,
     translated by Ronald Vroon. Moscow: Progress Publishers,
     1976. Pp. 223-240.
          The title of the novel, its composition, the landscape de-
     scribed, the authorial digressions and the logical development
     of the characters and their psychology together reveal so-
     ciety's responsibility for Clyde's tragedy. In this sense it
     became the banner of critical realism in twentieth-century
     American literature.

1704 ZEHENTMAYR, Aurelia. "Treatment of the American Business-
     man in the Novels of Theodore Dreiser." MA thesis, North
     Texas State University, 1965.

1705 ZIFF, Larzer. "A Decade's Delay: Theodore Dreiser," in
     The American 1890's: Life and Times of a Lost Generation.
     New York: Viking, 1966. Pp. 334-348.
          The whole that results from Dreiser's remarkably detailed
     manner is a world in which nothing stands between the in-
     dividual and the whirl of life. Dreiser looks and looks,
     wrings his hands, and looks again, but for all his details
     does not see families, friendships, or other forms of com-
     munity which act as protective screens between the individual
     and the onslaught of his environment. To look at matters
     conventionally and to say that such protections exist is, for
     Dreiser, to look at a wilderness and say it is a botanical
     garden.

1706 _____, ed. with Afterword. The "Genius." New York:
     New American Library, 1967.

1707 _____, ed. with Introduction. The Financier. New York:
     New American Library, 1967.

1708 ZLOTNICK, Joan. Portrait of an American City: The Novel-
     ists' New York. Port Washington, N.Y.: Kennikat Press,
     1982. Dreiser, pp. 61-67.
          Calls Sister Carrie the best known example set in New York
     City during the 1890's: "is the prototype of the modern city
     novel, dealing as it does with the dream of success in the
     big city, which entices the newcomer with its dazzling array
     of riches and pleasures; the high cost of this success; and
     the ultimate heartlessness and coldness of the great metrop-
     olis."
          Also discusses The "Genius": traces the career of Eugene
     Witla who at first finds fame and later finds defeat in New
     York. By the end of the book Eugene appears, like so many
     of Dreiser's characters, to have lost all--marriage, mistress,
     and career--in the alluring but ultimately treacherous city
     where materialism is shown to erode talent as surely as it
     corrupts values.

INDEX OF CO-AUTHORS, EDITORS, TRANSLATORS, AND ILLUSTRATORS

358, 359, 375, 389, 397, 422, 449, 508, 527, 541, 554, 604,
706, 707, 714, 718, 727, 732, 736, 741, 767, 801, 834, 883,
887, 891, 929, 1004, 1010, 1056, 1172, 1234, 1391, 1423, 1457,
1496, 1573

Darwin, Charles (includes Darwinism, evolution) 529, 755, 799, 854,
    961, 1079, 1214, 1436
Dawn (by Dreiser) 8, 90, 689, 715, 1063a, 1201, 1208, 1289, 1547
Death (of Dreiser) 22, 23, 231, 463, 1033, 1451
Debs, Eugene V. 304
Dell, Floyd 356
Determinism (see also Naturalism) 140, 300, 376, 606, 763, 881,
    1569, 1639
Dos Passos, John 972, 973, 1562
Dostoevsky, Feodor 752, 753, 1203
Dreiser Newsletter 394, 1357
Dreiser (novels, listed alphabetically)
    An American Tragedy 31, 36, 41, 60, 71, 75, 78, 103, 127, 128,
        133, 134, 142, 151, 156, 167, 168, 170, 178, 189, 191, 215,
        216, 221, 223, 253, 264, 265, 276, 289, 291, 316, 336, 347,
        371, 396, 410, 415, 420, 425, 426, 453, 456, 460, 471, 482,
        493, 502, 504, 510, 519, 528, 531, 534, 535, 547, 548, 551,
        565, 573, 628, 632, 654, 665, 671, 692, 703, 705, 712, 723,
        750, 767, 768, 769, 771, 772, 795, 806, 844, 850, 852, 865,
        876, 878, 879, 884, 908, 925, 926, 927, 931, 943, 957, 966,
        977, 990b, 990f, 991, 1015, 1027, 1035, 1061, 1066, 1073, 1092,
        1105, 1121, 1136, 1145, 1188, 1189, 1190, 1193, 1199, 1205,
        1215, 1222, 1244, 1252, 1262, 1264, 1272, 1288, 1313, 1318,
        1327, 1334, 1337, 1338, 1349, 1370, 1375, 1381, 1387, 1392,
        1393, 1403, 1424, 1465, 1482, 1489, 1500, 1508, 1519, 1546,
        1549, 1579, 1592, 1616, 1617, 1618, 1619, 1631, 1639, 1648,
        1652, 1660, 1661, 1683, 1684, 1692, 1703
    The Bulwark 24, 25, 86, 183, 217, 275, 316, 465, 500, 519, 536,
        537, 640, 738, 748, 778, 802, 815, 1026, 1034, 1111, 1167,
        1292, 1309, 1312, 1350, 1371, 1442, 1474, 1475, 1480, 1554,
        1574, 1576, 1639, 1671
    The "Genius" 57, 87, 98, 161, 179, 270, 353, 414, 421, 453, 598,
        654, 762, 830, 867, 895, 905, 923, 924, 995, 1019, 1043, 1177,
        1178, 1249, 1268, 1299, 1315, 1690, 1698, 1700, 1706, 1708
    Jennie Gerhardt 245, 332, 334, 346, 349, 624, 694, 794, 795, 847,
        909, 988, 1009, 1039, 1176, 1277, 1308, 1341, 1385, 1404, 1422,
        1433, 1509, 1615
    Sister Carrie 1, 53, 56, 57, 67, 77, 97, 107, 123, 132, 138, 139,
        160, 163, 164, 169, 173, 177, 193, 194, 195, 196, 200, 203,
        230, 238, 239, 240, 258, 263, 272, 273, 288, 305, 308, 310,
        314, 315, 334, 337, 362, 378, 388, 427, 457, 459, 472, 530,
        560, 566, 610, 620, 631, 634, 647, 648, 651, 654, 658, 659,
        671, 672, 679, 709, 742, 747, 754, 756, 779, 780, 787, 795,
        811, 813, 814, 876, 877, 913, 954, 965, 970, 985, 986, 988,
        990c, 996, 998, 1025, 1049, 1069, 1072, 1078, 1082, 1085, 1090,

Italian (includes Italy, etc.)   82, 964, 1197, 1211, 1396

Japanese (includes Japan, etc.)   663, 757, 1146, 1385, 1386, 1647
Jews (includes Jewish, etc.)   693, 960, 1330, 1345, 1401, 1416, 1571, 1626

Language and speech (see also Style)   116, 806
Legal affairs (includes law, lawyers, etc.)   155, 156, 335, 416, 905
Letters (of Dreiser; single items and collections)   257, 262, 321, 382, 387, 393, 445, 468, 515, 538, 585, 611, 650, 749, 803, 1633, 1657
Lewis, Sinclair   15, 218, 228, 454, 506, 657, 678, 793, 980, 1402, 1562, 1575
Liveright, Horace   283, 293, 599
London, Jack   197, 745, 1679

MacCullagh, Joseph B.   287
Magazines (magazine writing and editing by Dreiser; articles in magazines, etc.)   154, 661, 670, 724, 784, 832, 993, 1091, 1133, 1232, 1239, 1260, 1283, 1284, 1305, 1525, 1585
Manuscripts (collections of manuscripts by Dreiser)   26, 58, 380, 384, 411, 1642, 1644
Matthiessen, F. O. (bibliography of Dreiser by; also includes references to reviews of this biography)   63, 125, 143, 505, 756
Mencken, H. L.   79, 168, 173, 419, 470, 479, 496, 497, 498, 499, 515, 614, 673, 690, 853, 873, 1006, 1036, 1165, 1351, 1454, 1495, 1503, 1524, 1614, 1632
Money (as a theme in novels; includes wealth, affluence, economics, finance; see also novels in Dreiser's Trilogy)   81, 330, 990e, 1084, 1134, 1162, 1210, 1463, 1498, 1545, 1562, 1608, 1640, 1704
Morality   107, 746, 791, 1175, 1362, 1502, 1665, 1666
Movies (includes plays based on novels)   27, 28, 37, 40, 103, 109, 151, 291, 436, 548, 557, 712, 809, 865, 937, 1148, 1220, 1479, 1631

Naturalism (see also Realism)   35, 55, 89, 122, 126, 160, 165, 167, 171, 175, 222, 230, 259, 300, 313, 317, 318, 338, 339, 361, 376, 405, 458, 486, 516, 547, 582, 659, 680, 695, 731, 754, 757, 770, 795, 814, 837, 903, 904, 915, 919, 921, 968, 1016, 1032, 1068, 1076, 1079, 1083, 1106, 1107, 1132, 1136, 1188, 1196, 1203, 1214, 1225, 1233, 1235, 1274, 1295, 1343, 1415, 1429, 1464, 1500, 1505, 1510, 1534, 1540, 1541, 1542, 1548, 1591, 1596, 1597, 1600, 1601, 1602
Newspapers (work on newspapers by Dreiser; also includes articles by Dreiser)   142, 148, 152, 157, 323, 494, 506, 513, 660, 677, 724, 725, 740, 896, 946, 990j, 1067, 1198, 1283, 1294, 1409

Sinclair, Upton 628
Social themes and issues (see also Communism, Politics) 12, 13, 21,
    45, 121, 122, 149, 205, 228, 247, 248, 254, 319, 343, 372, 373,
    377, 392, 437, 462, 476, 492, 532, 533, 556, 605, 633, 716,
    755, 775, 792, 860, 879, 885, 897, 898, 902, 949, 982, 999, 1028,
    1068, 1109, 1110, 1113, 1122, 1162, 1163, 1211, 1221, 1222,
    1259, 1291, 1319, 1326, 1359, 1459, 1473, 1512, 1575, 1679
Spanish-American 276
Spencer, Herbert 827
Sterling, George 650
Stevens, George 27, 103
Strikes (labor strikes used in novels) 163, 164, 556, 636, 875
Style (use of stylistic devices in fiction) 3, 47, 51, 69, 94, 105,
    112, 158, 202, 271, 289, 502, 525, 530, 563, 618, 637, 646,
    708, 733, 759, 777, 789, 816, 859, 888, 892, 930, 939, 942,
    975, 990h, 1012, 1013, 1050, 1065, 1074, 1097, 1099, 1135,
    1139, 1152, 1168, 1194, 1218, 1219, 1243, 1257, 1311, 1389,
    1394, 1475, 1478, 1483, 1612, 1615, 1659, 1660, 1661, 1680,
    1688
Success (a magazine edited by Dreiser) 100, 785, 786
Sweden (Swedish, etc.) 65

Thoreau, Henry David 623, 625
Tolstoy, Leo 195
Tragic America (by Dreiser) 13, 277, 340, 743, 744, 866, 1290,
    1291, 1328, 1332, 1499, 1545, 1567, 1670, 1701
Transcendentalism 93, 357
Twelve Men (by Dreiser) 106, 188, 214, 241, 701, 819, 935, 1053,
    1075, 1098, 1128, 1251, 1265, 1266, 1278, 1397, 1598, 1667

Walker, Jimmy (Beau James) 522
Western (American West, etc.) 62
Wharton, Edith 627, 835, 990e, 1210, 1259, 1261, 1473, 1628
Whitman, Walt 829, 1209
Williams, Tennessee 64
Women (characters in Dreiser) 89, 99, 111, 199, 228, 260, 322, 337,
    342, 345, 433, 630, 664, 688, 697, 1081, 1103, 1147, 1275,
    1384, 1533, 1594, 1620, 1628, 1629, 1687
Woolf, Virginia 1098
Woolman, John (includes Quakers) 536, 1130, 1336
Wright, Richard 533, 665
Wyler, William 28, 868

Yerkes, Charles T. (see also Trilogy and Cowperwood) 578

Zola, Emile (see also Naturalism) 160, 547, 808, 1271